Reach and Fall

zeke petrie

trimarkpress

PUBLISHED BY TRIMARK PRESS, INC., DEERFIELD BEACH, FLORIDA.

LIBRARY OF CONGRESS CATALOGING-IN-PUBLICATION DATA

REACH AND FALL BY ZEKE PETRIE
COVER PHOTO BY MAGNUS WENNMAN
P. CM.
ISBN: 978-1-943401-70-3
LIBRARY OF CONGRESS CONTROL NUMBER: 2020905004
D-20
10 9 8 7 6 5 4 3 2 1
FIRST EDITION
PRINTED AND BOUND IN THE UNITED STATES OF AMERICA

A PUBLICATION OF TRIMARK PRESS, INC.
1525 NW 3RD STREET, SUITE 10
DEERFIELD BEACH, FL. 33442
800-889-0693
WWW.TRIMARKPRESS.COM

SPECIAL DEDICATIONS

Thank you Marty Babbington and Mike Keister for helping this book to see the printing press.

Barberton Public Library

It was here in the spring of 1991 that I was afforded the opportunity to do research about the country of Haiti. It's my hope that *Reach and Fall* will find its way onto the shelf in this building. Youngsters in generations to come will be able to read about a kid just like them that grew up in Barberton with big dreams. Inspiring future leaders to be fearless and to imagine a bigger world where they can do extraordinary things is the legacy I'd like to leave on my hometown.

Coach Marvin Beal

Coach Beal, who I affectionately called "Legend" was a teacher of mine at Highland Middle School. I didn't get to know him as a man, however, until my son Moses played middle school basketball. Coach Beal was the timekeeper at Mo's games. It was there we began to talk. That led to texting and emailing. On one occasion he said to me, "You're not gonna believe where I was the last time you emailed me."

I said, "Where the hell were ya?"

"Labadee, Haiti, on a cruise."

I responded, "Get the hell outta here," as he began to grin from ear to ear. Mr. Beal was the nicest, funniest, and most genuine human being you could ever come across. He was a standout athlete, and a very successful teacher and coach for thirty-five years in the Barberton school system. He was inducted into several Hall of Fames. He was a Hall of Fame Human.

The last time I saw him was at Acme in Norton, Ohio. I introduced him to my stepdaughter, Daina. He pulled me to the side and said, "Hey, it's been forever since I last heard from you. Where you been? No texts, no emails, nothing. You haven't even stopped down to see me at any of the games."

Mr. Beal, usually in a jovial mood, was way more serious on this day. I felt bad. I apologized. I said, "I'm going to come see you soon. I want to talk to you about my book I'm working on. I'd like you to give me a quote or two for this project." He smiled and agreed.

That day never came. Before we had the chance to do it he died on May 22, 2018, two days shy of his 72 birthday.

Seize the day. Legends are forever! Love you Coach Beal!

Mrs. Esther Ryan

One day at school in December of 1990 I received a package with a Pennsylvania Avenue address on it. It was a letter from President George Bush. I took it from the postman and rushed it down to Nurse Ryan's office. I presented it to her. When she finally realized what it was she became embarrassed to open it. She humbly laid the package down to the side of her desk. Shamelessly I persisted, "Mrs. Ryan please, open it." Receiving mail from the White House was not an everyday occurrence. I hurriedly picked it up, handed it back, and begged her to open it. She reluctantly agreed, opened it, and then gave it to me so I could read it to her. I was so proud. It was a great pleasure for me reading it to her.

I then ran over to Assistant Principal Miss Waxman's office to inform her that Mrs. Ryan had just received the 1,000 Points of Light Award from the President of the United States.

Later that day a local news crew came to the high school to do a story about this major happening. A picture of Mrs. Ryan was taken while she sat at her office desk surrounded by me, Dan Braswell, Debi Baker, and another student who was volunteering in Nurse Ryan's office. I was interviewed and told the reporter that I loved Mrs. Ryan like my next breath. It as a great thrill. She had such a tremendous influence on my young life.

When I graduated she gave me a photo of herself as a keepsake. She wrote on the back that I was one of her favorite people. I still have that photo twenty-eight and a half years later. Throughout the years she would check in with my mom to see how I was doing.

On May 9, 2019, Mrs. Ryan died at the age of 91. I'll always have her close to my heart.

Legends are forever! I love you Mrs. Ryan!

Phillip Wearne of Brighton, England

I met Phillip at the Walls International Guest House located in Delmas 19 in Haiti. It was the fall of 2010 when I happened upon this freelance journalist, TV producer, and author. I heard someone from across the room say, "Zeke of Haiti." Phillip had caught a glimpse of the Neg Mawon with Zeke of Haiti tatted on my upper left arm. I walked over to him and after making acquaintance I said, "You know Lawrence of Arabia my was my childhood hero, hence ZOH."

Lawrence was more Arab than the Arabs. Because of this I desired to be more Haitian than the Haitians. In that instant I would begin to have one of the most exciting and fascinating conversations of my lifetime.

Phillip told me about a man he once interviewed that knew Lawrence intimately. I must have asked him a hundred questions that morning. I had never felt so alive and so close to T.E. Lawrence in my thirty-seven years of existence than I did on that day. It was incredible. Philip gave me his Haiti Support Group business card – he was the vice chair – and he wrote his personal email account on it. He said, "Zeke of Haiti, we must get together soon."

Unfortunately our paths never crossed again. Phillip died of cardiac arrest at age 60 on March 14, 2018. Legends are forever Phillip!

Hugh Thompson & the My Lai Massacre victims in the Quang Ngai province of Vietnam

Here, on March 16, 1968 a company of American soldiers brutally raped, mutilated, and killed 504 innocent Vietnamese. Among the victims were 182 women – seventeen of them pregnant – and a 173 children, including fifty-six infants. The rest were old men. This massacre carried out by U.S. soldiers of Charlie Company only ended after Warrant Officer Hugh Thompson, an Army helicopter pilot on a reconnaissance mission, landed his aircraft between the American soldiers and helpless retreating villagers. Hugh threatened to open fire on U.S. troops if they continued their attacks. Thompson and his crew flew dozens of survivors to receive medical care.

Hugh Thompson would years later tell *60 Minutes* that he was ostracized and received death threats upon his return from Vietnam.

In 1998, thirty years later, Thompson, his crew chief Glenn Andreotta, and his gunner Lawrence Colburn were awarded the Soldier's Medal, (Andreotta posthumously), the United States Army's highest award for bravery not involving direct contact with the enemy.

Thompson's leadership provided the example for future generations to do the right thing no matter what the cost. Even if that means facing and turning your rifle against your own friends, family, and teammates. No excuses. What we do in this life echoes in eternity! Hugh died in January of 2006 at the age of 62.

Thank you Hugh! Your legend will live on forever!

Joe Delaney

It was November of 1983 when I came upon a Sports Illustrated article titled "Sometimes The Good Die Young." I immediately thought to myself that I must be destined to die young, because I was good. I was really intrigued to read this article about a young black man named Joe Delaney. Joe played football for the Kansas City Chiefs. It was on the afternoon of June 29, 1983, that Joe came across three boys who were thrashing and screaming in a water hole at Chenault Park in Monroe, Louisiana. There were many people in the vicinity, but it was only Joe that responded to the cries for help by rushing into the water to try and save the three boys.

One of the boys was able to fight his way back to the shallow area. The other two didn't make it, and neither did Joe. Delaney didn't know how to swim.

I sat there thinking "No, Joe! No! Why would you jump in if you didn't know how to swim?"

At that point in my young life I still had a healthy fear of the water. I didn't know how to swim either. I cried reading this article that was so eloquently written by the late legendary sportswriter and novelist Frank Deford.

The fact that Joe was a black man made it even more painful to me. The courageous twenty-four-year-old NFL football player lost his life without hesitation trying to save these youngsters while others stood on the sidelines and watched. This one act of bravery left a huge mark on my heart. Thank you Joe Delaney.

You're a hero for all of mankind to aspire to be like.

Your legend is forever!

The Late Great Brian Pierce
and his best friend Don Malarcik

I worked security on the weekends at Cascade Plaza in downtown Akron from the summer of 2002 to the summer of 2010. It was early on during this eight-year stretch that I met both Pierce and Malarcik. I'd see them coming and going during the weekends and I would go out of my way to make conversation with them. My instincts had me feeling that these guys had the qualities and characteristics of the late Bobby Fischer and the late Steve Prefontaine. The way they walked, their swagger, their toughness, their heart, and their contempt for mediocrity had me gravitating towards them. Malarcik once asked me to go running with him and the other guys he often ran with. Truth be told, I was a little intimidated that I might not be able to keep up with Don, so I never took him up on his offer. Pierce ended up inviting me on multiple occasions to go along with him to Happy Valley to watch his beloved Nittany Lions play football. My dad's parents were huge Penn State fans. They loved Joe Paterno. And although I really wanted to go with him, I never took Brian up on his invitations. Besides, I only worked weekends and I had bills to pay. So that was my excuse. I failed to seize the day with the generous offers from these same guys whose brains I was constantly trying to pick in an attempt to steal knowledge.

Here I was, working a lowly security guard job at the building in which they did business, but that never kept them from humbly sharing their time and experiences with me. When being in the presence of greatness, I always tried to grasp on and never let go. I was searching to take in all the wisdom that they had to give.

On one occasion right at the guard desk in the lobby of the plaza, I had a most intimate conversation with Malarcik. The convo was so deep and so intense that we were both moved to great emotion. I envied both Brian and Don for the nature of their friendship/relationship. I don't know that I have ever quietly loved and respected two guys more than Pierce an Malarcik.

The last time I saw Pierce in person was March of 2010. I ran into him in downtown Akron at the courthouse as I was finalizing my dissolution of marriage from my ex-wife Aslyne. Brian saw me and said "Hey, how's it going? What are you doing down here?"

I looked him right in the eyes and just froze. I was ashamed and embarrassed. I couldn't admit to him that I was losing my beautiful wife. He knew Aslyne because she had worked as a day matron in the National City Center back in 2002-2003.

Everyone in that building that knew Aslyne loved her. I could not share this devastating personal defeat to him. So, I lied and told him that there was an issue with my wife's immigration paperwork which somehow affected our certificate of marriage, and that's why we were there on that day. I introduced Brian to my two-and-a-half year old son Spartacus. He loved the name.

As the years passed I'd do my best to keep up with Brian and Don's professional careers. Often one or the other was headlining in the *Akron Beacon Journal* for their excellence at being what they were, the best criminal defense lawyers in the great state of Ohio. Pierce was the best trial lawyer this side of the Mississippi. Several years ago I gave my sister a telephone number. "If anything ever happens to me call this number," I said. "Malarcik and Pierce, call them ASAP."

It's not everyday you're afforded the luxury or have the privilege to rub shoulders with the Brian Pierces and Don Malarciks of the world. I'm very fortunate that I was graced with that chance.

Brian Pierce died of a brain aneurysm on October 25, 2019. His funeral/life celebration was held at the John S. Knight Center on November 3. The very same room where Andre Travis and I once addressed a large audience on October 21 of 2013 was now the site of the venue where Pierce's legendary life was celebrated. Held on a fall Sunday when NFL football reigns with the American public, the turnout for Pierce's memorial service was very impressive. It was standing room only. He was only fifty-one years old. Brian's wife Lisa, his daughters Mackenzie and Peyton, and son Colin were awe-inspiring on this first Sunday in November. They showed up and delivered goosebump and tear jerking resounding tributes to him. BP would have been so proud of all of them.

Troy Thornton, one of Brian's old buddies from Penn State also gave an incredible speech about his relationship with Pierce. It was fitting of

Brian's legacy to receive such a beautiful tribute that spoke not only of his greatness as a human being, but also of his flaws. This funeral was executed much like that of my late father's. People kept it real concerning Pierce's entire character just as we did with my Pops.

My personal favorite, however, was Malarcik's description of some of the more intimate times that he and Pierce shared, including both of them throwing down in a fist fight on a glass elevator in Atlantic City in 2008. I appreciated that more than anything because I have always fought with those closest to me at one point or another throughout the years.

I once got into a fist fight with my brother Ben and our childhood friend Jason Hance over a pickup game of basketball. On another occasion my good friend Donny Pavlik, toting the title of vice president at National City Bank, came into the Plaza on a late Saturday night looking to take my head off over a few shit talking texts that he took personally. He nearly put my cell phone through my chest cavity. We were locked up like Ric Flair and Dusty Rhodes tussling and struggling to gain footing on the recently waxed Plaza lobby floor. Donny was bigger and stronger and had the advantage at one point. He would ultimately let go after tearing my security uniform up pretty good. How we were going to explain that to anybody was the real issue, especially since it was all caught on security cameras. Brian had Don Malarcik, and I had Donny Pavlik.

Maroon 5's song *Memories* played as a picture slide presentation was displayed before Pierce's memorial service commenced. My wife and I were already in tears. It was arguably the greatest funeral I've ever witnessed.

Thank you Brian Pierce and Don Malarcik for being two of the most genuine and real individuals that I've ever known, and for your contributions to my life story. I'll never forget you guys. You both are true legends.

Legends are forever!

TABLE OF CONTENTS

FOREWORD

Zeke Petrie is a mythical figure, someone a journalist hears about but rarely meets. As fate would have it one hot sticky Haiti day in November of 2010, I met Zeke. Immediately, I hired him as my fixer for a return trip to the island set for January 2011. I'd been traveling to and telling the story of Haiti since 1987.

I knew the country fairly well. Not speaking Creole put me at a disadvantage, however. I've had many Haitian guides, but Zeke seemed an interesting guide to the tough streets of Port-au-Prince and to Vodou ceremonies in the countryside. Being a white guy from the Midwest (as Zeke is), in the ghetto where everyone is desperate for money, and no one trusts anyone, is a risky and dangerous endeavor. It takes a special personality to navigate Haiti, but an extraordinary one to navigate the slums.

And that was Zeke.

Twenty-eight and a half years ago, into the long and bloodied story of Haiti walked eighteen-year-old Zeke Petrie. Not an academic, a journalist, a social worker, a doctor, or a missionary. Zeke seemed passionately angry, and naive, an American who, in time, takes on the mantle of both local curiousity and pawn in a country that is incredibly confusing to the outside world and obtuse to even many Haitians. On its face, Zeke's story might seem like a hero's tale, but it isn't that simple. Zeke seems full of contradictions. He's angry about racial injustice and has empathy for the helpless, the sick, and the children of the ghetto. He is generous to a fault, but also strangely enamored of authoritarian leaders, gang members, military strongmen, and bygone dictators – and this is what eventually ended his sojourn in Haiti.

One might put Zeke's story in historical perspective as he does, seeing himself as a Lawrence of Arabia of Haiti, though Kurtz from Joseph Conrad's Heart of Darkness might be more appropriate. A combination of the two is more likely. Unlike Kurtz or Lawrence of Arabia, Zeke was a person almost without ideology, a direction, a historical education, and very little knowledge of how politics work. He was a person out of place, and out of time. At eighteen years old, having never read Conrad or Lawrence of Arabia, in time he came to resemble these characters all on his own.

After seeing The Serpent and the Rainbow, a chance meeting with a Haitian in an elevator in Chicago, and coming across a photo in a magazine of a Haitian child lying on a cardboard box in Cite Soleil, Zeke simply decided he wanted to go to Haiti and become, in his own words, more Haitian than a Haitian.

Zeke arrived in Haiti in August of 1991. After an initial trip to Jeremie, he got his first taste of Cite Soleil just a few weeks after a military coup against President Aristide. Cite Soleil is a violent, insular slum originally built by Papa Doc Duvalier. It's by far the poorest slum in Port-au-Prince and in the Western Hemisphere; a world completely alien to Zeke. But Zeke reveled in it. He learned Haitian Creole from the people, and his Creole was perfect street. His street cred became impeccable, and even though he stood out with his body covered in a white man's talisman of tattoos, he truly became a white native, and the Haitian people really liked him. Zeke is the guy who gets it, who talks to everyone, who lives with them. He's not just visiting and then spending his nights in fancy hotels eating and drinking a year's average Haitian earnings in one night.

I could take Zeke places he didn't go and vice-versa, and he could make things happen, explaining to surprised people what we were doing, charming the hostility out of everyone. Zeke was the liaison between gangs, hospitals, doctors, teachers, politicians, Haitian police, United Nations troops, missionaries, and NGOs. It was astonishing. As a sometime conflict photojournalist, I've seen the worst of humanity: unspeakable violence, suffering, disasters, desperation, and death. I went into the war zones then came away from them. Zeke chose to immerse himself during his time spent in Haiti and live amongst Haitians in social conflict zones, the slums – which most people in their right mind would never do – and thrived.

But, much like a tragic Greek hero, Zeke is flawed, and his flaws were his downfall, not only in Haiti, but throughout his life. His good deeds and desire to do "good" were tainted with plain human nature.

As a photojournalist who has covered Haiti for the last thirty years from a political and cultural perspective, I am certain that Zeke is an important story, not for the obvious reasons of white privilege or for that matter the misguided altruism of a sheltered Midwesterner, but for his contradictions. What his experience illustrates is the complexities of navigating the complicated conditions of a post-colonial country, a country run by horribly corrupt and violent leaders, and abused, invaded, and pillaged by the former slave holding colonial powers up until present times.

Zeke has had several years to ponder his legacy. Bad judgment, Haitian prison, three marriages, four children, addictions, vices, transgressions, combined with a multitude of health problems, have left him chastened and humbled. Though instead of riding off into the Midwestern sunset with his tail between his legs, he's writing his fascinatingly unique story, unapologetically spilling his guts for all to see. It's an important story for every American to read. American heroes are usually of a different sort: macho, gun toting, big mouthed, arrogant white men. And although Zeke could sometimes be painted by those who do not know him with these brushes, it's far from the truth. If anything he's the exception to that rule. Certainly containing some of those traits, he's the poster child for the American white man who's been thrown off his exalted throne. He's learned what suffering is, helped where he could, took his bruises, both emotional and physical, swam in the gutter, lived with people who have no hope, no money, no place to live, no education and is now the man a white American male should be. A man at peace with who he is, gracious, kindhearted, and long suffering.

The journey he sets out on with an African American male who has cerebral palsy is nothing short of extraordinary.

Reach and Fall, an incredible, heart-palpitating odyssey, is a riveting account of Zeke's life.

Les Stone

PART ONE
MY EARLY YEARS

My dad, Jeffrey Petrie, often retold the story of Secretariat winning the Triple Crown as he bounced me, at the age of 3 months, gently on his knee amidst the rumbling of galloping horses echoing through the television set.

"Come on, Secretariat! Give it all you've got!" The horse's chestnut coat glistened in the sun, muscles rippling as he turned each corner of the track at the Belmont Stakes. He had taken an incredible lead on the other horses. There was no way he could continue at this pace without collapsing, yet his lead continued to widen. He rounded the last stretch, clouds of dust trailing behind him. My dad couldn't sit any longer. He jumped up, grabbed me with one arm, and threw the other arm up in the air. "Go, go, go!!!" he hollered.

As Secretariat bounded across the finish line, he shouted and cheered as if he were right in those stands with the crowd. His eyes got misty. This was the most incredible race he'd ever seen in his life. Secretariat won that race by an astounding 31 lengths ahead of the second place horse, Twice a Prince. He looked down at me, his bright-eyed baby boy, and said, "Son, don't you ever forget this moment. I sure as hell won't."

My dad and I watched some incredible historic sports moments together with me sitting on his lap — Muhammad Ali's victory over George Foreman and Hank Aaron beating Babe Ruth's home run record, to name a couple. I was raised on the idea that with enough persistence and fight, you could overcome just about any obstacle.

I was born in Barberton, Ohio, as Jason William Petrie on March 5, 1973 to Bonnie Jean Fulcher Petrie and Jeffrey Lee Petrie. I was the second child of four, with an older brother, Jon; younger brother, Ben, and the youngest, my sister, Jennie. My dad worked nights at Babcock & Wilcox on Trident submarine nuclear missile tubes and attended classes at Akron University during the day, studying history and psychology, so he was gone a lot. My mom did her best to raise us kids and keep up on housework.

JULY 1978

I remember the midday sun was beginning to make things uncomfortably hot in our white, single-story house on 5th Street in Barberton, Ohio. It was the summer before I started kindergarten. Ben & Jon were playing with their toys, and Mom was hurrying to get the laundry and dishes done before Jennie woke up from her nap. My attention was fixed on the front yard. I was clad in ankle high socks and a pair of Aquaman Underoos, and I was practicing flexing my scrawny muscles by the front window. It was almost noon. He would be here soon.

A sturdy framed black man in a pressed pale blue button-up shirt approached the front steps. Slung over his shoulder was a tanned leather bag out of which peeked a jumble of white envelopes. My anticipation of the mailman's daily visit rivaled a kid on Christmas Eve waiting up for Santa. Before he could even knock on the door, I had already pulled open the screen door with my little hands and grinned up at the dark figure that shadowed the entryway!

"Hi Mr. Ricks."

"Well hey there, little fella! Look at those big muscles." I was mesmerized by Mr. Ricks' shiny black cap and shoes that made him look like a superhero. As a Navy veteran, Mr. Ricks took his uniform seriously. He was polished from head to toe. He reached into his pocket and pulled out a piece of candy.

"You better ask your mama if you can have it," he said to me, now kneeling at eye level. I mischievously nodded in agreement, a twinkle in my blue-green eyes, but didn't plan on telling my mom or my siblings about the treat. This wouldn't be the last time I'd smile while lying to Mr. Ricks.

4

Sometimes I would reach out and touch Mr. Ricks' smooth, ebony skin, starkly contrasting with my own pale complexion, or stare into his big brown eyes and wonder why his hair was so different from my own disheveled sandy blond locks. Living in a white middle class neighborhood, Mr. Ricks was the only black person I had ever experienced thus far, so my curiosity and fascination were piqued. Unbeknownst to my 5-year old self, I would one day be living in the first black nation to be founded after a successful slave revolt, a country that would both capture and torment my heart.

I adored Mr. Ricks. He made me feel like a million bucks, and with Dad working nights and going to school, I could never capture his attention fully the way I could with Mr. Ricks. When my dad was home, he could typically be found going through a pack of Camels and drinking beer while watching a ballgame. He'd started smoking when he was 14, and his time in the military, serving in Okinawa, led to more dependence on the habit. When the TV announcers interviewed the ball players after the game, I remember how disappointed my dad was when the athlete stumbled over his words and struggled to give responses.

"How can they play ball so well, yet not have a lick of smarts?" he would say, disgusted and shaking his head. "Listen, Jason, you have to focus on training your brain before you worry about training your body, and whatever you do, be great at it." I have always remembered his words, even from that young age.

There is one episode I remember very clearly. Our family had just finished dinner. My mouth was stained red, almost clown-like, from the spaghetti sauce. I parked myself on the woven rug in front of our television set to watch Super Friends. As the caped heroes flew across the screen, I watched eagerly, wishing so badly to join their league. Suddenly my arms began to itch. It began to distract me from the cartoon. When I rolled up my sleeve I noticed big, itchy, red splotches and there were more on my belly. It scared me, and the itching worsened.

"Mom!" I began to cry. "I'm so itchy! Make it stop!"

"Oh Jason, sweetheart." My mom's eyes filled with concern. She grabbed my hand, and we hurriedly walked the handful of blocks to The Barberton Citizens Hospital. We lived so close, and besides, my mom didn't drive.

5

The waiting room in the ER was bustling. The sounds of wailing children and the flurry of people moving in and out made me nervous about what was going to happen to me, but at least Mom was there. She ran her fingers through my hair as I laid my head in her lap. She was right next to me, so everything was going to be OK. Mom glanced up at the clock in the waiting room on a wall on the far end of the room. She let out a deep sigh, hoping we'd be in and out of there soon. Dad would have to leave for work soon, and she had to get back to take care of my siblings.

"Jason Petrie?" a nurse called out. Without a second of hesitation, my mom grabbed my little hand and hurried me back to the assessment area.

"Whew! Those are quite the hives, buddy," the doctor announced. He turned to my mom. "Let's get some Benadryl into him and keep him here for a while for observation."

My mom began to fidget, looking at the time again.

The night wore on as the medications began to kick in. I stared at the ceiling from my gurney as they wheeled me down the long, white corridor to my room. The nurses' white uniforms blurred with the bright lights and ceiling tiles flew by as my eyes got heavy, and I drifted off into a deep sleep.

"Don't worry, Mrs. Petrie. We'll take good care of him, and we'll see you in the morning," the nurse reassured, but I didn't hear. I was already dreaming.

When I began to come to again after my several-hour Benadryl induced snooze, I was completely disoriented. Even the smell was unfamiliar. I opened my eyes in the pitch black room. The only light came from a monitor on the wall. I blinked and rubbed my eyes, reaching for the edge of the bed. This was not my bed. Where were Ben & Jon? I sat straight up. Something was very wrong.

"Mom?" No response. "MOM!" I burst into tears. Finally a nurse entered the room. "Where's my mom?!" I cried desperately.

"Shh, sweetie. She went home. She'll be back in the morning. Now close your eyes and go back to sleep." She closed the door behind her as she left.

I began sobbing again, "Where's my mom?! I want to go home!" I kept wailing until the nurse returned again, this time with a stern look on her face.

"Hey, kid. You need to settle down and go back to sleep right now. I already told you your mom will be back in the morning. You're going to be in big trouble if you don't settle down." She slammed the door behind her this time.

I realized I needed to take matters into my own hands. I knew the way back home. It was only a few blocks. I could be brave and walk home in the dark. My stocking feet were slippery on the cold, tile floor. I wiped the tears away with my shirt sleeve and took a long deep breath, reassuring myself that I could do this. I headed into the dark hallway towards the light of the nurse's station. I felt so small, cold, and all alone. I could only think of one thing...home. That's where Mom was. I marched into the lighted area with determination. The nurse caught my eye. Oh no! She saw me! She motioned to two other nurses, one that I remember being male.

"Hey, get that kid!" Before I could make my great escape, two sets of strong arms held my scrawny ones.

"Let me goooo! I just want to go home! MOM!" I screamed as they hauled me back to my room. I could hardly see through the stream of tears and snot that were blurring my vision. The three white faces showed no emotion as they placed me in a restraint. I couldn't move my arms or legs no matter how hard I flailed. I eventually cried myself back to sleep, my tears of fearfulness turned into tears of anger at my mom. I don't understand. How could she have left me here all alone?

"Jason?" The familiar voice called my name again as I blinked my eyes open.

"Mom?!"

"I'm right here, sweetie."

The relief washed over me. "Mom!"

The tears began to flow again as I held her tightly so she wouldn't leave me again, the smell of her blouse reassuring me. I was so happy to see her, yet in the same moment, I felt so betrayed. I didn't care what other responsibilities she may have had that took her away that night. How could she have left me there? Could I ever trust her again?

No matter how tough I was on the outside, I would be unable to sleep anywhere other than home for years to come after that traumatic night in the hospital.

7

In my younger years, I could often be found lying around on the living room floor watching TV. Our television set was large and sat on the floor. Back then we probably had about six stations that came in via antenna – a few stations in black and white and a few in color. If you wanted to change channels, you had to get up and manually turn a knob, and when you'd turn it to change the channel, there'd be nothing but the buzzing white and grey static on the screen for several turns until you came to a station we received. It was a painful and laborious task as a young child trying to find my favorite cartoons and programs.

I loved to watch shows like *Super Friends, The Brady Bunch, The Little Rascals, Lost in Space, The Lone Ranger,* and *The Three Stooges.* One day, while turning the knob on the set, I stumbled upon the loud cracking of a whip and a young black man crying out in agony. I was immediately fixated on the program, my hand frozen in place on the TV knob. I was appalled at what I was witnessing, playing out on our TV set in full color. I couldn't comprehend in the slightest why the white man was beating the young black man. Watching it upset me, but I couldn't look away. My thoughts turned to Mr. Ricks. I was sick to my stomach. I remember hearing the black man saying, "My name is Kunta, Kunta Kinte."

Years later I'd remember vividly seeing those horrific scenes from the movie, *Roots*, starring LeVar Burton. I walked away from the TV, angry, with a burning hatred for the white man that was beating Kunta Kinte. I wanted to see him pay for his actions. What 5-year-old thinks like that?! In that moment I did, and I wanted him to pay dearly. From then on, my perception of white people was forever altered.

As the leaves began to turn colors and fall on the dried up, sun-bleached lawns in Barberton, I began kindergarten in Mrs. Railsback's class at Oakdale Elementary. The school wasn't far – only about a half mile away – so every morning I walked there with my big brother Jon, who was in second grade, and Jon's buddy, David, a neighbor who was also in his class. Jon led the way, and I hurried to keep up with the older boys. Jon led us to school on a different route almost every day in an attempt to avoid a group of bullies, but it didn't matter whether we turned up Cassell or Lake or any of the other streets off of 5th Street. The bullies seemed to find us each morning.

"Oh nooo. Here they come!" Jon warned.

I looked up from the sidewalk with wide eyes. I had been looking at the ground as I walked, taking care to not to step on a crack – I didn't want to break mama's back. A group of boys a couple of years older than us approached, jeering as they towered over Jon, David, and me.

"Hey kid. Nice backpack. Whatcha got in there? Hand it over, punk!" the kid leading the pack snarled.

"Leave me alone!" Jon pleaded, attempting to maneuver around the older boys.

We were only a few blocks from school. How did they keep finding us every day? Jon thought. But today was like every other day, and the bullies were at it again. One of them ripped Jon's backpack off of him while two others pushed David to the ground and took his backpack as well. One of the bigger boys dumped their bags out, taking their lunch money and strewing papers and books all over the sidewalk.

"Knock it off, you jerks!" David screamed, his face turning red with anger.

"There's nothing you can do about it, you little sissies!" the leader of the group taunted. I cowered, scared, my stomach in knots. *One day, I'm gonna make these jerks pay.*

I hated going to school. How could these kids that look just like us be so mean? What did we ever do to them? My mind wandered back to Mr. Ricks and his daily mail deliveries. I thought of him every time the clock struck noon. I hurried home after school let out every day in hopes to see him. By the time I'd arrive, however, he would already be gone.

At least Mr. Ricks knows I'm a superhero. He knows I'm tough. The sticks & stones speech from Mom didn't make things any better.

Unless the bullies were distracted with throwing a football around, they'd hassle us boys every morning. I was sick of it.

JULY 1979

In the summer of '79, our family moved from the east side of Barberton to the north end of town, to a house on Lloyd Street. With four growing kids, we'd outgrown the house on 5th. I loved that our new house had a second story. It also had a caged dog run in the back yard from the previous owners. They had even built in a sort of trap door in the inside of the house that led you under the house and into the backyard. This was also for the dogs, but it was a kid's dream house, and my siblings, other kids who lived nearby, and I could often be seen going out to the back yard through this trap door. As cool as our house was, the real highlight of moving to Lloyd St. was being in a different school zone. That fall, I'd start first grade at Memorial Elementary School. I hated Oakdale, and the bullying only worsened throughout my kindergarten year, so I was ready for change. This was a new beginning in so many ways – a fresh start.

In first grade, in Mrs. Whitman's class, Jamie Montgomery became my best friend. Some would say we could have even passed as brothers. We were both athletic and could run fast. When Jamie played soccer he'd make sharp cuts like the professional soccer players. I took note and replicated his moves during tag at recess and later on when I played football. Jamie was the first person I felt like I could relate to. We'd get in trouble in class for talking too much, and we spent hours upon hours at each other's homes after school.

One day, Jamie invited me over to stay the night. This was the first time I'd been invited to spend the night at a friend's house. I was thrilled. We watched TV, played some board games, and then camped out on the living room floor for the night. In the middle of the night, I woke up and realized I wasn't home. Anxiety washed over me as I relived that night in the hospital the year before.

I sat straight up and whispered, "Jamie!" Jamie was sleeping deeply, drool on his pillow. "Jamie! Tell your mom I want to go home right now."

When I finally woke Jamie up and he agreed to go talk to his mom, she told him that I just needed to go back to bed, and they'd walk me home first thing in the morning. Well, I wasn't happy with that answer and marched into her bedroom to talk to her myself. At this point I was visibly upset, my bottom lip quivering. "Mrs. Montgomery? I need to go home right now."

Mrs. Montgomery was quite cross, but got up and called my home several times until my mom picked up the line. We lived close enough that they walked me back home...in the middle of the night. I was slightly embarrassed, but my anxiety was too much to bear. I was just thankful to be home.

A few nights later, Mom was tucking us boys in bed. Jon, being the oldest, had his own bed over by the window, and Ben and I shared a bunk bed against the wall closest to the door. As the only girl, Jennie lucked out and got her own bedroom. My mom had a routine of going bed to bed, scratching our backs, tucking us in, and kissing our foreheads. Since Ben was on the top bunk, she decided to start there. I fumed, feeling like she should have started with me first. I tensed up and rolled to face the wall. My mom came down to my bed. "Sweetheart. Give mama a kiss goodnight."

My gaze was frozen on the wall. "I don't want to."

"OK. Well, I love you," she said as she started away from my bed towards Jon.

I quickly sat up in bed and stared my mom square in the eyes. "I don't love you, and I never did!"

Mom must have felt daggers piercing her heart. Her eyes welled up. She leaned over and kissed Jon. When she stood up, she kneeled down again at my bunk, thinking I'd apologize, but I was still seething. She said nothing more and left the room, her head down.

My mom had endured four C-sections, endless piles of laundry, and many a sleepless night on account of us. There wasn't a thing she wouldn't do to show that she loved us, and she loved us fiercely. But I could tell that this hurt her to her core. Surely cleaning up vomit in the middle of the night and dealing with temper tantrums paled in comparison to this. It took the wind out of her sails, and yet little did she know that this was only the beginning of the heartache and grief I would cause her.

Jon & Ben said nothing. Jon was too afraid of me when I was mad, and Ben was too little to really understand what just happened. But deep down inside, I was still hurting over feeling abandoned that night at the hospital during what was, to that point, the most traumatizing night of my life. I resented my mother for leaving me when I needed her most and I wanted her to hurt like I was hurting.

After my dad heard about what happened, my backside was temporarily hurting more than my little heart.

First grade came and went. There was no more bullying, so school was at least tolerable.

Mrs. Senser was my second-grade teacher. She was a heavyset, Jewish woman with big, round, brown eyes and short jet black hair. She was fairly strict, but when she did smile, it was a mile wide. At the end of the school year, Mrs. Senser got the attention of the class and said that she had an important announcement to make. She rapped her wooden, yellow #2 pencil on her desk.

"Ahem! The school district boundaries are being realigned over the summer, so some of you will be attending Portage Elementary, and for those of you that will be staying here at Memorial, we'll also be receiving kids from the projects. I hope you all have a great summer, and I look forward to seeing some of your familiar faces in the fall!"

Groans resonated throughout the classroom. "We're getting a bunch of black kids?" "My mom and dad are not going to be happy about this." "I hope I get transferred to Portage. I'm going to request it!" I distinctly remember some of the kids saying, "Ewwwww! We don't want black kids in our school!"

Decker School, which was down by the Norton Homes government housing, was going to be closing. All the kids from that area, mostly black and low-income whites, would be coming to Memorial, whereas many of the current Memorial students would be heading off to Portage Elementary, based on the way the new divisions fell.

The projects were just down the hill, a half-mile from where we lived, and since we were only a block from the school, I knew I'd be staying at Memorial. I was thrilled about it. I welcomed the chance to have black kids in the seats next to me. This transition would be one of the most profound things that would happen to me in my young life. I kept thinking about how much I missed Mr. Ricks. It had been a couple of years since I'd seen him, but even though that was light years away in my mind, I remembered him fondly like it was yesterday.

As I listened to the other kids whine and complain about having to share their desks and chairs with black kids, I relished in the opportunity to be close with them. Some of the kids heading off to Portage proudly proclaimed that they were glad they were leaving so they didn't have to be around the blacks, almost beating their chests with contentment. I, on the other hand, was glad they were coming to our school, and I didn't understand why most of my classmates were up in arms about it. After all, I had only experienced kindness from the one and only black man I knew, whereas the trauma and bullying I'd experienced was all from white people. White kids made my first few years of school a miserable experience, but now I was beginning to feel that things could only get better for me going forward. If I'd had my way back then, I would have shipped all the white kids out and all the black kids in.

I kept my thoughts to myself but was inwardly excited to meet more people that looked like Mr. Ricks. The anticipation of meeting black kids my age for the first time had excited me beyond belief. That summer couldn't pass by quickly enough. For the first time, I was genuinely eager for school to start that fall.

SUMMER OF 1981

My dad took Jon, Ben, and me to the much anticipated blockbuster hit, *Raiders of the Lost Ark*, at The West Theater in Barberton. When we got there, Dad took us straight to the concessions. We got popcorn, candy, and soft drinks, and hurried into the theater to find our seats. By the time we found seats, the movie was about to begin. My dad would recount to people years later that "those boys were so transfixed on the movie screen, especially Jason, that they never even touched their snacks or drinks." It was the first and only time my dad would recall the Petries letting refreshments like that go to waste. When the movie ended, we scrambled to salvage the room-temp popcorn and watered down soft drinks.

The tenacity and never-say-die spirit of Indiana Jones' character played by Harrison Ford is what drew me in. The action, adventure, danger, but most of all the heroic nature of Indiana Jones had me leaving the theatre that night saying to my pops, "When I get older I'm gonna be Indiana Jones." I was eight years old.

I recall another great film my father introduced me to: *Lawrence of Arabia*. In one of the opening scenes of that legendary film, the great Peter O'Toole, who played the character of T.E. Lawrence, lit a match and then

13

extinguished the flame with his bare fingers. He never flinched or said a word. A Brit in uniform next to him was watching intently and then tried to do the same. He yelled, "Ouch! That bloody hurts! How did you do that, Lawrence? What is the trick?"

Lawrence replied,"Sure it hurts. The trick is not minding that it hurts."

His response resonated deeply within me. Decades later, I would keep reminding myself, "The trick is not minding that it hurts!"

My dream as a young boy was to be Indiana Jones, Lawrence of Arabia, and Robin Hood all in one. Third grade and beyond would continue to lay the foundation for that dream to be realized. My father was influential in introducing me to cinema as a youngster, and it had an explosive impact on my young psyche.

Watching movies like *The Raiders of the Lost Ark, Houdini, The Fighting Sullivans, The Pride of The Yankees, Beau Geste, Spartacus*, and of course, *Lawrence of Arabia*, would bring to life a great imagination to my young developing heart, mind, and spirit. At an early age, I truly believed that I could do anything. Watching these films began stirring that strong belief within me. They fostered in me the idea that people needed me, and that somehow, some way, I would have a tremendous impact on the world one day.

My father's hero was Ted Williams, the greatest hitter that ever lived. He would often recount to my brothers and me how Ted was the greatest at everything he did in life. Not only was he the greatest hitter in the history of baseball, but he was also the greatest fighter pilot flying as John Glenn's wingman in the Korean War, and the greatest fly fisherman, according to my father. My dad set the bar high for us boys, using Ted as an example.

My father was a perfectionist. He, too, was great at everything he did. He excelled in mathematics, teaching, public speaking, and working on the Trident Submarine nuclear missile tubes. He played in local chess tournaments and came home with trophies he'd won. He played the cornet in the Barberton High School Marching Band, landing a full-page ad for King instruments featuring his photo one time after playing in The Orange Bowl in Miami. As if that wasn't enough, he also faithfully served his country in Okinawa for eighteen months with the Army. He was great at everything.

14

As a youngster he received Ted Williams' autograph on his ball cap up at the old Municipal Stadium in Cleveland; it brought to life the idea that he, too, could do anything. My dad was right-handed, but Ted was left-handed, and because my dad was obsessed with Ted's excellence, he taught himself how to bat left-handed. To me, this was just another example my dad showed me that no limitations existed, except for the limitations that I put on myself. I believed I was a superhero, and no one could tell me any differently.

I loved my third-grade teacher that year, Mrs. Winter. There were two black kids in my class, Emanuel "Manny" Hampton and Tammy Peterson. In the other third-grade class, there was a black kid named Kevin Howes. These three were my first black friends my age. Of the three of them, I would become closest with Kevin, but they all brought a welcome change in the culture at Memorial School. Prior to third grade, I had never seen black kids at Memorial. Manny, Tammy, and Kevin looked different, acted different, and even smelled different. I was intrigued by them and drawn to them more than any of the other kids in class.

That year, Kevin and Manny performed a breakdance routine at our school talent show. They had a big boom box playing music and were dancing in a way that many of the students had never seen or heard before. All of us kids were sitting in the school gymnasium in complete amazement. I remember feeling so proud. I wanted to be just like them in that moment. I began to experience great emotions on the inside, like I wanted to be black. Being black to me meant resilience, courage, toughness, defiance, and the ability to show up with all the confidence in the world at the drop of a dime when it mattered most.

Manny Hampton was a quiet guy. He never had a bad word to say about anyone. He was a bigger kid, but a gentle giant in my eyes. He was into comics and drawing, and he always had a pencil in his left hand, bringing things to life on paper. I remember he had a distinctive scar on his face. I enjoyed his company.

Tammy was a sassy girl with big brown eyes. She carried herself with a much different demeanor than the white girls I was used to. She had a strong personality, and expressed her opinions with great passion and energy. Tammy was taller than most of the girls in our class, and it seemed

15

like the other girls in class were intimidated by her. She had a temper if you crossed her.

Tammy often questioned Mrs. Winter's authority in class, almost looking to debate with her. She often posed the question, "Well why is it that way?" Mrs. Winter usually had no response other than to ask Tammy to sit down and be quiet. Tammy would ultimately sit down, but not quietly. It was the first time I remember seeing a student stand up for themselves against such an authority.

Although I wouldn't realize it at the time, I was learning a great deal from Tammy about questioning authority. Many years down the road I'd find myself in a very vulnerable position where I, too, was questioning authority. The power of one is above all things the power to believe in yourself. I witnessed this in Tammy up close and personal.

In school they seated us in alphabetical order by the first letter of our last names. It was my destiny to sit next to Tammy. It was a Peterson-Petrie thing. I had a front row seat to watching how one strong black girl conducted herself in the face of the oppressor. I loved Mrs. Winter, but for Tammy and millions of other African Americans, especially in the era we grew up in, any white faces who held positions of authority were the oppressor.

> *Never go down. Never go away quietly.*
> *Even in the face of oppression, stay vocal,*
> *committed, focused, and remain fearless even*
> *in your scariest moments.*
> *Thank you, Tammy Peterson, for what*
> *you taught me so well.*

Kevin Howes probably had the biggest impact on me and my developing personality as an eight and nine-year-old kid. Although Kevin wasn't in my class, I saw him at recess, before school, and after school ended each day. He was a short, stocky, athletic kid. Kevin loved sports and so did I. He also liked to talk a lot of trash, and so did I. Kevin and I were both shorter kids, but what we lacked in physical stature, we made up for in heart, toughness, courage, and never-say-die attitudes. We talked a big game regardless of the venue. Whether it was the mental challenge of playing board games, like checkers or Connect Four, or the physical challenge of playing football or basketball, we were both very vocal about speaking into existence what we wanted the end result to be.

I'll never forget the first time I invited Kevin over to my house after school. I remember parading him around my neighborhood, into my house, and in front of my family and friends. It was as if I had found my black counterpart. I remember him sitting on my sister's bed, just feeling so proud that my black friend Kevin was in my home. It was surreal. Kevin was the first black person to ever step foot in my mother's home.

I often get asked how I ended up where I did in life. That story begins with Mr. Leon Ricks, Manny Hampton, Tammy Peterson, and Kevin Howes.

School suddenly became more tolerable. I had found solace and a connection with Kevin that was different from previous friendships. I began to take things I wanted in life. One Friday afternoon, Mrs. Winter told our class that she had a bunny that needed a new home. "If you want the bunny, you'll need to bring me a letter from your mom or dad saying it's OK. The first student to bring me their permission letter can have the bunny."

I wanted that bunny, so I wasted no time. Right after school got out I ran home and told my mom about the bunny. Mom seemed unfazed by the simple request but knew she would have to run this by my dad first. He ran a tight ship at the Petrie household, and this would definitely need his stamp of approval. To everyone's surprise, including my mom, Dad thought having a bunny was a great idea, so he wrote and signed the permission letter.

The weekend went by so slowly. Monday couldn't get there soon enough. I tucked the letter in my backpack and checked on it several times each day to make sure it was still there; my OCD was in full force even in third grade. Monday morning, I woke up with a start, hurriedly shoveling spoonfuls of Captain Crunch cereal in my mouth before running out the door.

"Jason! Don't forget your coat!" my mom called after me.

"I'm fine, Mom." I yelled back without even glancing back.

When I got to the school parking lot, I waited for Mrs. Winter to pull in. Her rust red Cadillac pulled into the lot. She put it into park and stepped out. She was always so put together, her snow white hair tucked perfectly into a high bun, and her clothing pressed. She smelled good too – fresh and fruity. I was right at her door.

"Well you're here awfully early, Jason!" she chimed.

"I got the letter from my dad...for the bunny! Did I get you my letter first?" I inquired, wide eyed.

Glancing around the empty parking lot, save for a few other teachers' cars, she smiled down at me. "As a matter of fact, you are the first one!"

I was ecstatic. I sauntered into school with Mrs. Winter, pride radiating from my chest. I was first. I'd won. And the prize for winning? A cute white bunny with a black stripe in the middle of its back we named Bugs.

Bugs was a wonderful addition to the Petrie family.

Bugs wasn't the only addition to our family that year. We were attending Community Church of Portage Lakes at the time, and one Sunday, they announced that a group of students from China would be attending Akron University for an exchange program. Hosting International Travelers Friendly Family Program was looking for host families to help the students with lodging, activities, socializing, and an introduction to American culture. My parents decided that we Petries should sign up to host.

Over the next couple of years different Chinese students came in and out of our house, about five or so in total, but one would stand out amongst them all and become an honorary Petrie. Tian Ru Fang was a polymer chemist from the People's Republic of China. Our family affectionately called him Lu. He left his wife and two young sons back home in order to further his studies in the states. He was a family man, and the Petries loved him.

He was housed in an apartment in Akron, Ohio, not too far from the university with some of the other Chinese exchange students, but quite often he would come stay with our family. He became one of our own, and was even included in our family portraits. We learned so much from Lu. He had an aura of greatness about him: his look, his walk, his smell, and most of all, the way he carried himself. He was larger than life.

18

One day I asked my parents if I could stay the night at Lu's house. I had mentioned to Lu that I wanted to see where he lived. My curiosity had me wanting to know everything about this man, as I had only ever seen Chinese people before on television or in the movies. I wanted to take advantage of this opportunity to get to know someone from a country that only seemed to exist in my imagination. What are these people really like? How do they live? What do they eat? My parents were surprised by my request, remembering all too well the last time I had attempted to stay the night at Jamie's house. They obliged, and said I could go, but they sent my brother Jon along with me just in case.

The day finally came for me to spend the night at Lu's place. The neighborhood where he was staying looked much different from where I lived. It was dark and gloomy in a run-down part of town. I remember going up a small flight of stairs on the outside of his apartment building, and then going up another set of stairs once we were inside. It had a different feel and smell to it right from the start.

Lu had an injured blackbird in his house that he was nursing back to health. He would take it out to care for it with his bare hands, which intrigued me. He also had a few exotic looking plants in his dwelling space that caught my eye. That evening, sitting there in the quietness of his living room, I watched him practice Tai Chi. I was mesmerized. He started off in a sitting position, with his legs crossed and hands folded together, almost as if in prayer, but he was actually meditating. He breathed in deeply and exhaled slowly. He told me afterwards that he was visualizing. Then he rose to his feet and began to move in a way that made him resemble Bruce Lee. I sat and watched as he moved slowly and fluidly, each movement made with intention. It was incredible.

When he finished, I bombarded him with questions. "What were you doing?"

"Clearing my mind and finding peace and stability," he responded.

"Do you believe in God?" I inquired.

He looked straight at me, closed his eyes, and shook his head. "No, no I don't."

It must have pained him to tell me his truth, because surely he knew that this young little American was expecting him to say, "Yes indeed."

19

"So, Lu, where do you believe we go when we die?"

He began to explain reincarnation to me, emphasizing the role of karma. "If you were good during your lifetime here on earth, then you will return again as someone or something good, but if you were bad, then you would have already decided your own destiny and fate."

I was perplexed. "So, do bad people go to hell?"

"Bad people die and never come back at all," he replied.

John Lennon's "Instant karma's gonna' get you" began to play in my head. That was the only other time I'd heard the word karma. I still didn't have a good understanding of what it or reincarnation was all about, but I hung on Lu's every word. He was completely fascinating to me.

His house had an unusual aroma to it. A traditional Chinese dish was being prepared for my brother and me. When we sat down to eat, we were each given a bowl of a rich tasting, brothy, vegetable soup with something that resembled chicken in it. That night, Lu taught us how to eat with chopsticks. I sat and watched in awe as he used them to eat his soup. It was a sight to behold. Jon and I struggled with our set of chopsticks, but enjoyed trying something new. Mostly we just enjoyed watching Lu use his pair with finesse. When he had finished fishing out most of the contents of his soup with his chopsticks, Lu brought the bowl up to his lips and loudly slurped up the rest of his broth. I shot a glance over at Jon, and we both smirked. We both knew that Mom would have scolded us if we did that at home. Although I wasn't a big fan of the food served to us that night, I smiled and told Lu that I loved it. I was old enough to have manners; my mama taught me well. On that occasion I decided it was OK to lie because I didn't want to hurt Lu's feelings, and besides, it wasn't my first time telling a white lie. I already had a track record with Mr. Ricks whenever he brought me candy, and I agreed to ask my mom before eating it.

The evening wore on, and it was almost time to turn in for the night. My brother and I slept on a pull-out sofa bed. It was no surprise that I didn't do much sleeping that night, as I suffered from homesickness whenever I wasn't in my own bed. On this occasion, however, I was quite comfortable, and my mind was occupied with this new world I had found myself in with the Chinese – so much so that I didn't mind being away at all. I remember hearing Lu playing music from his homeland on an old record player. It made me feel relaxed, and I listened to it intently throughout the night.

Off and on, I'd hear the blackbird moving in the wide-mouthed jar Lu had put him in. It had no lid, but the bird didn't fly out of it, as its wing was damaged. Seeing the way Lu cared for and nurtured this little bird was a great example to me of compassion that I took careful note of.

When morning came we headed over to Akron University where there were many other Chinese exchange students playing ping pong. We watched Lu play for a short while until my father came to pick us up. It was a transformational twenty-four hours. I wondered if I'd been teleported to another world for the night.

Not long after my overnight at Lu's, he came to Memorial Elementary School as a guest speaker for the day. He visited with all of the classes and spoke in a general assembly in the gymnasium for our entire student body. On this particular day, it was Valentine's Day, and in my third-grade class, Tammy Peterson and I were chosen by our teacher to be crowned king and queen of our class. Each of us had to bring in a baby picture for the competition, and Mrs. Winter picked the king and queen based on who she thought were the cutest. The baby picture I brought in had me with a little ball cap on backwards, holding a baseball bat. I couldn't have been prouder that Lu was there to crown us. It was a very telling moment in time, almost prophetic. Who knew that three decades later I would have been married three different times to three different black women? In hindsight, it's clear to see that nothing in life ever happens by coincidence. Tammy and I were meant to be crowned together, and Lu was certainly meant to come into our lives.

One day in fourth grade, while out on the playground, I was kicking a soccer ball around with some of my classmates when Steve Thomas approached us. Steve was a bigger kid, a couple of years older than my buddies and I. He was popular in school, especially with the ladies, and he was athletic as well.

He came over and swiped the ball away from us, without even batting an eye, and punted it over to the other side of the field, where he began to kick it around by himself. It was as if he thought he had some sort of unspoken authority over us younger kids. My buddies looked down at the ground and shrugged their shoulders, conceding in a sense that this was

21

merely a survival of the fittest situation and that there was nothing any of us could do about it. Deciding it was a lost cause, they moved on and went to play on the slide and monkey bars instead. I, however, wasn't going to let this one slide. He wasn't going to get away with this; not on my watch.

I was no stranger to being bullied, beginning with my days at Oakdale, and I hated them. But instead of just letting it go like my friends had, I put my head down with determination and started towards Steve. It was my ball, no question about it, and I would do everything in my power to get it back.

In the Oakdale days, I was too young to think I could have done something about injustices, but now that I had Manny, Tammy, and Kevin as friends, I felt tougher and bolder. Their friendships made an already confident kid feel invincible. This strengthened resilience I now felt swelling up inside me gave me the boldness to take on this bully, despite our age or size difference.

I sized Thomas up as I watched him kicking the ball – my ball – around by himself. I knew one thing: I was faster than him, by a long shot. I knew that if I could just get my hands on the ball, he would never be able to catch me. I watched him and waited patiently, until the moment was just right. I noticed the ball had gotten away from him, just enough for me to move in quickly and pounce on it.

"This is my ball, not yours!" I shouted as I zoomed away with the ball. I felt like the roadrunner with a cloud of dust behind me. Steve looked surprised that I would challenge him. I glanced over my shoulder and saw him charging at me.

"You'll never catch me, you big bully!" I sneered. It wasn't long before he grew tired of chasing me and gave up. He was defeated, and I'd gotten my ball back. I won the battle. As the whistle blew and recess ended, we lined up to go back into the school. I saw Steve a few lines over glaring at me.

"Hey kid, I'm gonna get you!"

And get me he did the very next morning. I remember it being chilly that day. I was hanging out on the playground before school started, daydreaming and looking off into the distance. And then out of nowhere, "Boom!" An explosion went off in my right ear. Steve had snuck up behind me and fired a football at me at point blank range. The fact that it was cold that morning made the stinging all the worse. It hit me so violently that it knocked me off my feet, and I blacked out for a second as I hit the ground.

When I became aware of my surroundings again, I sat up holding my throbbing ear. Steve and his friends were laughing and jeering at me.

"I told you that I'd get you, you motherfucker!" He turned to the kids standing around me. "This little fucker stole my ball yesterday!"

It took everything inside me to fight back the tears. I stood up and took off towards the school. The tears were now flowing. I could feel my heartbeat in my ear, and it was ringing. I bolted into the office to tell Miss Spalding, the principal, what Steve had just done to me. She listened to my case and then motioned me to sit in a chair in her office until Steve was summoned. He marched in and explained that this was all my fault because I'd stolen his ball at recess and was cussing at him.

"That's a lie!" I protested. "He was the one cussing at me!"

While Miss Spalding made her decision, we were told to sit for several minutes until she returned. We were sitting directly across from each other, but neither of us said a word. I refused to even look him in the eyes. I still had tears streaming down my cheeks and my ear was on fire, red as a beet. Miss Spalding came back into her office with her verdict. She decided that we both merited a paddling – three swats each.

Back in those days, principals and teachers were allowed to discipline students as they saw fit. Steve didn't look the least bit upset, but I was terrified. I had never been disciplined in school before and I was afraid of what my dad would do when he found out. I thought, *I'm really gonna' get it when I get home!*

Steve went first. She brought him into the next room over, and the door closed behind him. I could hear the thunder of the paddle striking his ass. He emerged from the room with no emotion and went back to class. I was up next. I was used to my dad's belt when I'd get in trouble at home, but Miss Spalding was a girl, so I wondered how bad it could really be? She bent me over and...CRACK! A stinging sensation surged throughout my entire body. CRACK!...CRACK! Now the tears were really flowing, and it wasn't just my ear that was hurting.

The whole thing was ridiculous. Steve took what was mine, hit me in the head with a ball, lied to the principal about what really happened, and then I got paddled for it. I learned a valuable lesson that day: standing up to bullies and fighting for what's right often requires paying a heavy price. And boy, would I find that to be true in years to come!

Steve Thomas died in a car accident about six years later.

That year in fourth grade, I had my first black school teacher. Her name was Mrs. Walker. She was the Michelle Obama of her time, long before the world would even know who Michelle Obama was. She was built much the same as the former first lady, and I found her to be attractive and classy. She was nicely polished, often wearing bold, statement jewelry, and every hair on her head seemed to be in place. She wore a light, floral perfume that I really liked. But beyond her outward appearance, she had a command to her classroom that I wasn't accustomed to with my previous teachers. I was intrigued by her, and I liked her right from the get go.

It was during that school year that she introduced black history to our class. None of my other teachers had ever covered black history before. I remember Mrs. Walker passionately teaching us about Martin Luther King Jr. We learned about his inspiring life and listened to his "I Have A Dream" speech on an old record player that we had in the class. The thunderous voice of Dr. King sent shivers down my spine as if my entire body was on fire. I had never gotten chills from any kind of school activity ever before. We learned the lyrics to the song, "We Shall Overcome," and sang it together. Hearing the lyrics to that powerful song produced more chills. Mrs. Walker taught us about Dr. King's ultimate sacrifice when he lost his life fighting for the rights of millions of disenfranchised African Americans. I was filled with overwhelming emotions that made me feel so proud and alive. My appreciation for the struggle of black people became elevated.

My dad was an avid reader, so we had tons of books at our house. He always encouraged us kids to read. One day I stumbled across a set of books about World War ll and The Holocaust in a closet upstairs. The graphic pictures portraying the death and destruction that occurred was definitely not intended for the eyes of a young child, but my parents didn't know I had found them. Hundreds of naked, white corpses stacked on top of each other were in each and every book I opened. I almost felt as if I had just watched a movie. Maybe they were just sleeping. Surely this wasn't real. They were just lifeless pictures in a book, right?

I became obsessed with going back to that closet and pouring over those pictures day after day. Each time I went back to view them, I hoped for a different outcome – something other than the mass graves and the piles of dead bodies in the giant shower rooms where the Jews had been gassed. I was hoping to see some sign of life, but there was none.

I realized that what Mrs. Walker introduced to me as a young student was another sort of holocaust that had taken place in my own country. We talked about slavery in her classroom, and she was quite candid about it. She talked about the injustices that blacks had brutally suffered over so many centuries in the western world.

It made the story of Martin Luther King Jr. even more heart wrenching and electric. "We shall overcome, we shall overcome, we shall overcome someday, oh deep in my heart, I do believe, we shall overcome some day…" Tears welled up in my eyes as I sang those words. Mrs. Walker came over and put her arm around my shoulder, rubbing it gently to console me. She said nothing, but in that moment we connected deeply. I'll always be thankful for the things I learned in Mrs. Walker's class that year.

Fourth grade was full of challenges, obstacles, and hardships. Swimming lessons were a mandatory part of the Barberton schools' fourth-grade curriculum in the 1980s. Every year the fourth-grade classes from each elementary school in Barberton visited the Barberton Natatorium two times a week for about a month to learn how to swim. I clearly remember that first day of lessons.

My bare feet hit the cool, wet cement with each step, and the overpowering smell of chlorine left me feeling lightheaded. I approached the edge of the pool with my classmates, the shouts of other kids and an occasional whistle from an instructor echoing throughout the building. I wasn't sure what to expect as I didn't know how to swim. My stomach knotted up as we awaited instructions. Despite my lack of experience, I didn't think I was afraid of the water. A stocky woman with a shiny black swim cap on her head came up to our group.

"I need to know how many of you already know how to swim, so raise your hand if you can."

Several of my classmates' hands began going up in the air around me. Not wanting to be left out or look dumb, I raised my hand too.

"Those of you that raised your hand, I want you to come with me over to the deep end. The rest of you that can't swim, stay right here," she said, motioning towards the shallow section.

There was no way I was going to let my pride be trampled on. It was evident early on that the kids who could swim were seen as having a higher valor. I began imagining myself as Indiana Jones. My mind flashed back to the scene in the *Raiders of the Lost Ark* where the Germans had boarded a ship on the open sea looking for Indy, to no avail. Shortly afterwards, as the black men on the ship were still trying to find Indy, one of them spotted him, with great excitement, coming out of the ocean water and onto the submarine that the Germans were in.

That scene, and the never-say-die spirit of Indiana Jones resounded inside of me. *I'll show this swim instructor what I'm made of.* Just then she called for all the swimmers to get in the deep section of the water with her. I snapped out of my Indiana Jones dreamland and quickly followed all the kids into the deep end, but as I climbed in, I found myself hanging on to the side of the pool for dear life.

When it was my turn to go with the instructor under the water and down to the bottom of the nine-foot-deep pool, I latched on, and down we went. When we came up, I was coughing and choking down water. I hurriedly attempted to gather my composure, knowing that I was in big trouble.

"Now I need to see you do that by yourself," she said, looking at me suspiciously.

On the verge of tears, I finally admitted to her that I couldn't swim. The embarrassment of admitting it hurt more than anything. She chastised me verbally for lying about being a swimmer, and then sent me over to join the non-swimmer group of kids. My pride was bruised, and I felt defeated mentally. For the next several weeks, every time the class was about to board the bus to go to swim lessons, I'd try to find my way out of it, somehow. Whether it was purposely leaving my swim trunks at home, or faking being sick, I wanted nothing to do with swimming.

Later that school year, I was out playing football on the playground with some of my classmates. I caught the ball and made a quick cut, turning my ankle. *SNAP*! I fell to the ground in excruciating pain, holding my ankle. I was unable to walk so a couple of kids helped me back into the school. At the hospital, the x-rays showed it wasn't fractured, but badly sprained, and I ended up in a splint for four weeks. I had to use crutches until I could finally bear weight on it again.

As if that wasn't enough for a 10-year-old to deal with, that spring led to more difficult times. I went through a spell of several weeks where I was perpetually tired and sleeping all the time. My parents found my behavior odd as I was a really active kid – always full of energy, so they decided to bring me in to the doctor. The blood work revealed that mono was the cause of my fatigue. Because of the risk of spleen rupture, I wasn't allowed to participate in any contact sports. I felt isolated from my friends and what I enjoyed doing the most – being active. It was all I knew: running, riding bikes, playing sports – that was the only language I spoke or understood. I was miserable.

Mono is commonly referred to as the "kissing disease," as the virus is often contracted by kissing or sharing a drink with someone who has mono. So of course, kids at school started teasing me about it. That was about the same time that kids started teasing me about having a big nose and big lips, although I remember this teasing happening as far back as second grade. After mentioning it to my parents, my father would affectionately joke that I did, indeed, have the features of a black man. He'd say, "Well, we did have a black mailman while living over on 5th Street," and he'd laugh. Of course, I had no idea what that meant as a kid, but I look back on that now and chuckle. My father told me not to worry about what the other kids were saying. He told me that I would have to start being mentally tough and not minding what other kids said or did. I didn't so much mind the teasing about looking black. What I did mind was the derogatory tone that was always used.

My father grew up in an era that was even more racially tense than my own childhood. My parents met in September of 1964, during the heart of the civil rights movement, at the Little Creek Amphibious Base in Norfolk, Virginia. My father was in the United States Army, but was sent to the Navy School of Music located there. Any member of the U.S. military that played in the band was required to attend. My mother also worked on the base in personal services and vending. My dad went in one day to get a locker key made, and my mom ended up being the one who helped him with that. He got his key and left, but he returned the next day and told my mom that the key didn't work, which was a lie. It was just an excuse so he could come back and see her again. Four months later, in January of 1965, they got married, and only two weeks after tying the knot, my father was sent to Okinawa for 18 months.

Before my father left, though, he caused quite a stir with my mom's side of the family. My dad had several black friends that he wanted to invite to the wedding, but as my mom's parents were from the south, they strongly objected to his wishes. Being the rebel that he was, he fought tooth and nail with his soon-to-be in-laws over it, and ended up getting his way, but not without leaving a bad taste in the mouths of my mother's side of the family. Every summer, our family would make the annual trek back to Norfolk to visit my mom's family, and I remember feeling the tension between them growing up.

My dad loved the underdog, the disenfranchised, the ones that questioned authority, the ones that never should have made it but did because of their resilience, persistence, and toughness. I distinctly remember my dad retelling the story of Tommie Smith and John Carlos, each with a raised black gloved fist in the air in a "Black Power" salute during the playing of the National Anthem at the 1968 Mexico City Olympics. He would talk about this moment with great pride and respect, knowing the boldness it took for these two men to stand up on the medal podium while the world watched them protest the mistreatment of blacks in the United States and the slow progress of the civil rights movement.

My dad was a "stick it to the man" kind of guy and a rebel yeller, and that part of his DNA was evident in me at an early age. My father studied every religion; he was a seeker of truth. He read every book that he could get his hands on, and he introduced my brothers and me to J.D. Salinger's *The Catcher in the Rye*, the first literary masterpiece I'd read where the author didn't edit out any curse words. My dad recounted to us Boston Red Sox Ted Williams' defiant actions towards the press, who Williams didn't care for. "One time while rounding third base and heading for home, Ted spit in the direction of the press box!" my dad would say with a twinkle in his eye. He would tell us about Bobby Fischer's defiantly brash greatness being displayed on the world stage of chess against the Russians. He would talk to us about Pistol Pete Maravich and his trademark floppy grey socks, and how his game spoke of great showmanship that blended confidence and charisma. There was Dave Wottle's 800-meter run at the 1972 Munich Olympics where he came from way behind to claim the victory. Steve Prefontaine, an all time great middle and long-distance runner, would run all of his races hard from start to finish. Despite the critique he received from his famous trainer, Bill Bowerman, for his style, Steve would always say, "To give any less than your best is to sacrifice the gift." My dad talked about these moments of greatness regularly as I grew up; to me, these men were an example to be followed.

Everything my father introduced me to had great meaning: examples of defiance, rebellion, never quit attitudes, toughness, courage, and of people who lived out the idea that whatever you do, do it with passion, go hard, and do it with all your heart. It would lay a foundation of belief inside of me that anything was possible. It was OK to be different and to question authority so long as you were true to yourself. But Dad hated liars and phonies, and he made it very clear that he'd never tolerate that in any of us.

My father's aim for us to always strive for perfection, however, would lead to what I'd come to know years later as Obsessive Compulsive Disorder (OCD). For me, everything had to be perfect. This became apparent in school from an early age. My penmanship, even as a young man, was excellent. I loved writing in cursive, and even more, I loved the compliments I'd receive about how beautiful my handwriting was. Every word – every letter – had to be perfect. If I ever made a mistake on paper, I would never use an eraser. Using an eraser would dirty the appearance of the paper I was working on, which was not acceptable to me. Usually I'd write with no issues, but occasionally if I made a mistake – God forbid – I'd rip up the paper and start over. If I made another mistake soon afterwards, I would quickly grow frustrated with myself to the point of tears. The OCD was a thorn in my side.

This obsessiveness with perfection was my latest vice. Those days were trying for me between the bullies, the homesickness when I'd be invited to stay the night with friends, my fear of the water, and now the OCD. I would have to fight to overcome these issues.

FIFTH GRADE

Going into my fifth-grade school year, I had a big chip on my shoulder. I felt that I was a really good athlete and wanted to be recognized for that. I was the fastest runner in my grade every year, and that gave me tremendous self-confidence. My father's love for baseball had him steering both me and my brother Jon in that direction. So, during the spring of my second-grade year, I tried out for the Minor B Indians and made the team. My dad was really proud, but my enthusiasm for the sport wouldn't last long.

The practices were held on brutally cold northeast Ohio spring evenings. Hitting that hard ball on those frigid nights, or even catching the ball, made my hands sting. The better players on the team were the nine-year-olds who already had a year of experience under their belts. I was only eight. It was a miserable rookie experience for me, watching the dandelions grow out in right field.

Later that summer, I signed up to play "pee wee football" for the Memorial Warhawks. At the very first practice I got the snot kicked out of me. I was done. I didn't want anything to do with organized football at that point. I took the walk of shame with my head lowered to tell my dad I had quit the football team after only one practice. Needless to say, my pops was very disappointed. He just looked at me and shook his head. My grandpa, John, my dad's dad, didn't want me playing football anyway. He said it was too dangerous. That made my decision to quit much easier for my dad to swallow. I was relieved to be off the hook. The following year I didn't return to playing baseball either. I still liked playing baseball and football, but more when it was played on my terms in pickup games with my buddies. I wouldn't play any organized city team sports again until my sixth-grade year when I returned to playing baseball with a bang.

Between third and sixth grade, however, I played for the Community Church of Portage Lakes kids' softball team. I was a star on that squad, and I loved it. I felt like this was more on my terms – just how I had envisioned it. My brother, Jon, who wasn't much of an athlete, played too. This way, my dad could involve both of us together in sports. It worked for us, and we had lots of fun playing. Besides standing out on the softball field and being the fastest kid in my grade, I could also show off my athleticism in gym class at school and back home in my neighborhood with all my friends. Excelling in anything sports-related, and making sure everyone noticed, was what mattered most to me.

During that fifth-grade year, a group of us boys in the neighborhood had branded ourselves as "The Hoodsmen." We thought of our neighborhood as the north end of Barberton kingdom! We were the kings of it, and in our minds, its rightful owners. Parkview to Yale Street, and Norton Avenue to Morgan Street was our jurisdiction and the territory we defended. "The Hoodsmen" consisted of myself, my brother Ben, Frank Jennings, Tim Widner, Rich Getz, Travis Olds, Dave and Mike Koncz, Mike and Paul Brabson, Jay Belkey and Glenn Bixler. We were a dirty dozen, if you will. The twelve of us spent the majority of our time playing sports, riding bikes, playing flashlight tag at night and seeing what mischief we could get into.

We beat all the other neighborhoods in the vicinity playing pickup football, basketball, and baseball. We talked a lot of shit, caused a raucous wherever we showed up, and did our darndest to piss people off. It didn't matter whether it was neighbors that we didn't like, or bullies from other neighborhoods, we would go out of our way to let people know that we were the ones in charge of this hood. We stole a lot of candy and baseball and football trading cards from the local convenience store, Lawson's. We would often walk into Lawson's with only fifty cents to our name, yet walk out with a bag full of stuff. We broke into neighborhood churches, homes, and our elementary school at Memorial. We often climbed up on top of Memorial School, pretending to be carrying out secret Navy Seal missions at night. We would act stuff out as we witnessed it on TV and in the movies. We would sometimes get our hands on porno magazines and then run off to a local area called the sandbanks, that was hidden

31

and isolated, to peruse the scandalous pages. People called the Barberton Police on us several times.

It was with this group of kids that I ended up viewing my first dead body. I'll never forget that cold March morning in 1982 as we headed out for school. The coroner was wheeling someone's body, zipped in a black bag, on a gurney out of a house on Harvard Avenue that sat behind us. There were cop cars with lights on, an ambulance, and lots of yellow tape surrounding the house. We slowed our pace to take it all in. Our neighbor, Mark Headley, was charged with aggravated murder of his female companion, of only a few months, Sandy Burger. He had beaten her to death. It was experiences like this that made the bond between us neighborhood kids stronger.

Several years later, in 1987, we heard news that a rapist in Barberton was on the loose. We "Hoodsmen" were constantly on the lookout for our neighborhood. Gary Chastman, the accused, would finally be apprehended in Colby, Kansas, convicted, and sent away for life. He was only seventeen. Until Gary was locked up, we felt responsible for the welfare of our community. We loved our neighborhood, and to this day we all still check in with each other to see how things are going in the area. During these formative years, that fighting underdog spirit – the "me against the world" mentality – was born. It was with this particular group of peers that my athleticism and leadership skills really started to emerge.

One day my dad told me that he wanted to speak with me "in his room upstairs." Anytime "upstairs" and "in his room" were used in the same sentence it usually meant I was about to get his belt on my ass for disciplinary reasons. So of course, I was immediately concerned as to why my father wanted me upstairs in his room. He didn't seem angry or anything. I slowly walked upstairs behind him, nervous for what was about to happen. He sat me down on the bed and looked me square in the eyes.

"Jason, I know a father isn't supposed to say something like this to any of his kids . . ." his voice trailed off as he glanced at the floor. "You're my favorite though. I love you the most out of all your siblings. I've always favored you. Of course, I love your brothers and sister too, but you have something special. You're a leader, and your brothers and sister follow you. Your friends follow you. You're a great student and athlete, and one day you're going to do great things, and people will continue to follow you. Because of who you are, I expect more from you than your siblings. You will have more pressure on you to excel and to succeed. You will carry a bigger burden than the others, and that comes with great responsibility, but a responsibility I know you're more than capable of handling." He paused for a moment before saying, "Never speak a word of this to your siblings."

I nodded in agreement with his request. He hugged and kissed me. I'll never forget that heart to heart discussion we had that day – man to man. I remember it as though it happened yesterday. I can still hear him saying those words to me. My father's words gave birth to a new strength within me. From that day forward, nothing could faze me.

It felt like I had just been knighted Sir Jason, as though I was a modern-day Alexander the Great. My father often spoke of Alexander's exploits, and legend has it that Julius Caesar came across the statue of Alexander the Great in his travels on assignment to be the junior governor of what is modern day Portugal. It was brought to Caesar's attention that he was the same age as Alexander when he died, age twenty-five. Caesar burst into tears at that revelation. At that age, Alexander had conquered everything from the Adriatic Sea to the Indus River, but in contrast, Caesar had only managed to get himself elected to the equivalent of a municipal court judge and was on his way to be some other guy's lieutenant. I always felt the need to impress my pops after that. His approval meant everything, and I didn't want to disappoint him.

Mr. Rudy was my gym teacher while I was at Memorial School. He was short, stocky and arrogant, and could always be found wearing a pair of tight fitting athletic shorts. I really liked him. During my fifth-grade year Mr. Rudy had a competition in each of his gym classes that included three events: push-ups, sit-ups, and a fifty-yard dash. It was a challenge to see who could do the most push-ups and sit-ups in a minute's time and who could run the fastest fifty-yard dash. I not only won all of three of these events amongst all of us fifth graders, but I even topped the record for all of the sixth-grade classes as well. Of course, that didn't go over too well with the sixth graders, knowing that a fifth grader had beat them all.

The next morning before school started, I arrived to the front entrance and found a few of the popular athletic sixth graders standing outside waiting for me. There were two guys named Mike and another guy named Joe with them. One of the Mikes sneered at me, "There's no way in hell that you're better than us 'Pee-on-a-Tree'!" he said, purposely slaughtering my last name, Petrie. "You big cheater! We all know you're not as good as us. You're not getting past us unless you admit that you cheated!"

Just then, Mr. Rudy appeared around the corner. He confirmed to the bitter sixth-grade bullies that I had, in fact, beat them in each and every event before proceeding into the school building. This made them even more cross with me. The jeering continued. "You big cheater, nigger lips . . . nigger nose!" They continued hurling insults at me until the first bell rang and we went our separate ways to class. From that day on, those three would continue to call me "Pee-on-a-Tree." But the derogatory way they described my features really got to me. I found myself staring at my nose and lips in the mirror when I got home that afternoon. Kids had teased me about having a big nose and lips before, but no one had ever referred to them using "nigger." Kevin, Manny, and Tammy had these same features too. Why was it so bad to have a wider nose or fuller lips? Why was being black or being called a nigger so negative? What had people like my black friends done to be mocked like this? My young mind spun with confusion and dismay. I tried to brush it off by focusing on the fact that I had indeed beat all the fifth and sixth graders in the gym class competition . . . without cheating. In my mind, I had proven, to not only myself, but to all the kids at Memorial Elementary School, that I was, in fact, the best athlete at the school by a long shot.

At the end of my fifth-grade year, the city of Barberton held a race at the high school football stadium for the fastest kids from each grade from each of the schools. All of the elementary schools in Barberton participated: Memorial, Portage, Oakdale, Woodford, Johnson, and Santrock. I represented my fifth-grade class from Memorial, and I'd be running against the five fastest fifth graders in the city. This was my moment to shine. I'd have the chance to prove, once again, that I was the best.

I noticed that there were a couple of black kids that I was going to be racing against. I was pumped about being in the same arena with black kids my age with the limelight on us. I always felt that the white kids my age were not on my level athletically, so to have the opportunity to see where I would stand against black kids was a thrill. It was the first time in my life I remember feeling nervous and excited to the point that I had butterflies in the pit of my stomach.

We lined up in the thick grass at one of the goal lines of the football field, the 50-yard line being our finish line. I was wearing my favorite pair of white high tops, with the laces tucked into the sides. I was too cool to tie them. The stands were packed with people waiting for the big race to begin. The gun went off, and I took off flying down the field. Usually, when I was racing other kids, I was so fast that I wouldn't see anyone else in my periphery before crossing the finish line. On this occasion, however, I was neck and neck with a taller, light-skinned, black kid the entire race. He kept my pace, stride for stride. As I closed in on the last ten yards, he was still right next to me. At the last second, he burst ahead with a hard lean forward as we both crossed the finish line, breathless and panting. Time stopped for a moment. Could I have just lost? No, please God, no!

Moments later, the announcer declared over the loudspeaker, "The winner of the fifth-grade race is Tron Jenkins!" The black kid who just defeated me started jumping up and down, elated to have beaten me. He was yelling as he continued jumping around and pumping his fists in the air as if it was a touchdown dance. I could hear people around me talking about how Tron had won. *Who is Tron?* I had never heard such a name before. I felt sick to my stomach. This was supposed to be my race, my victory, my first-place ribbon. I walked slowly towards the sidelines, my eyes looking downward at the field.

The damn grass slowed me down, I just know it. The fact that my shoelaces weren't tied probably didn't help either, but I was too angry to notice at that time. I walked away without shaking hands with or congratulating this black kid named Tron. I glared at him from a short distance away, watching him still carrying on and rejoicing over his victory. I was crushed. Defeated. I couldn't bear that thought of having to look at myself in the mirror and admit to myself that I wasn't the fastest fifth-grader in Barberton. What a brutal reality check. Being the best was my identity, and what gave me great self-worth. I was probably the sorest loser to ever come out of Barberton. For the first time, I'd found a black person that I didn't like, and his name was Tron Jenkins. This wouldn't be the last time I'd be compete with him.

My parents decided to send me and my older brother, Jon, off to summer church camp for a week after my fifth-grade year. The church our family attended at that time was called Community Church of Portage Lakes and had ties with Stony Glen Camp. An entire week away from home? I think everyone, including myself, believed that the homesickness I'd suffered since childhood had run its course and would no longer be an issue. I was much older now, more confident, and more mature. After all, I'd passed the test already when I'd stayed overnight at Lu's house. Surely, I'd be fine. As an insurance policy, however, I had asked a good friend of mine from school, Benji "Ben" Nutter, to go along with me. Ben's mother thought it a great idea and sent him along for the week. I was relieved that Ben would be coming with me. My brother Jon was two years older than me, so he would mostly be with the older kids. The plan seemed golden. I'd do just fine with Ben by my side, I mused.

Before I knew it, the time had come for us boys to head off to camp. After getting us all situated at the registration table, my parents loaded back up into our station wagon and pulled away down the gravel road, a trail of dust kicking up behind the car. I watched until the dust settled, and immediately began second guessing my decision. The camp counselors began calling out names, and assigning campers to their cabins. Ben got called into one of the lines, and shortly afterwards, my name was called, but to a different line. My heart sank. I realized we'd be in different cabins. Our master plan had been thwarted, and I was extremely upset. Without Ben as my "overnight insurance policy," I feared the worst.

My lodging for the week was a large A-frame style cabin. I was already familiar with it because my whole family had stayed in that same cabin once before during a church function. This time, however, I had absolutely no family or friends for my peace of mind. That first night I felt really uneasy about going to sleep in my bunk. I was assigned to a top bunk. I climbed up the creaky, wooden ladder and crawled into my sleeping bag. I tossed and turned, staying awake as long as I possibly could before I finally gave in and fell asleep. I awoke sometime in the night and immediately flashed back to that traumatic night at the hospital. I sat up in bed and looked around in the darkness of the room. Everyone was fast asleep besides me. Panic set in. I needed to get the heck out of there and go home. I climbed down from my bunk in the pitch-black room, and scurried off to the bathroom, trying to avoid the other campers' bags strewn across the cabin floor. I flipped on the bathroom light and saw my reflection in the smudged mirror, tears streaming down my flushed cheeks. I sobbed quietly, not wanting anyone to know I was crying like a baby. Although inwardly, I felt like the same five-year-old kid from that scary night six years earlier, now that I was eleven I knew I needed to act tougher about this on the outside.

Here I am now, over three decades later, and I can still remember how I felt like it happened yesterday. I spent the entire rest of that night in the bathroom sobbing. That was one of the longest and most miserable nights of my life.

The sun couldn't come up fast enough. At the crack of dawn, I went straight to my counselor and told him that I needed to go home. I was completely exhausted from being up most of the night, and I imagine my eyes were bloodshot. Surely, he would take pity on me and accommodate my simple request. He looked down at my slight frame and smiled reassuringly, "It's OK buddy, everything is OK, you'll be fine. You've only been here one day. We're gonna do a lot of fun things this week, and you're gonna have a blast. Keep your chin up, kid."

I glared at him, unamused. Clearly he didn't understand or have any earthly clue who he was dealing with. I kept my composure, but cursed him out under my breath as I turned and walked away. In a matter of less than twenty-four hours this entire church summer camp deal had gone south.

Throughout my elementary years, I heard curse words at school, on TV, and on occasion, coming out of my father's mouth. I found myself cursing as well, mostly with the neighborhood gang I ran around with. On one occasion in my pre-teen years I remember cursing out my older brother Jon right outside the side door of our house. I had no idea at the time that my dad was home and heard every filthy word that came out of my mouth. I was dropping "mother effing" this and "mother effing" that. I thought I was so cool and tough. Cussing made me feel like I was older than I actually was, and I loved it. After hearing what would have put a sailor to shame, my dad came outside, grabbed me by my hair, dragged me up the stairs, and beat my ass with his belt. I only momentarily regretted what I had said to my brother. I really only felt bad because I was caught. I meant what I'd said.

I had a healthy fear of my father, and this camp counselor wasn't him, so I didn't see him being in any position of authority over me. I glanced back at him, still stunned by his lack of empathy and failure to cooperate with my demands. I could feel my face turning a shade of red as I continued mumbling curses at him under my breath. *Look motherfucker, I want to get the hell outta here, so stop being a little shit face and let me go home.* I kept trying to convince myself to really let him have it out loud, but my conscience held me back. Even though I didn't fear him, I still feared my pops and what he would do if I actually cursed out this camp counselor, considering what had happened when he caught me cursing last time.

I sucked it up, breathing out a huge sigh of frustration, and went to breakfast, kicking up bark chips as I went. I realized I had asked my friend, Ben, to come with me to this camp, so I couldn't just leave him behind, could I? The breakfast was horrible, and my frustration at not being listened to made me lose my appetite. I poked at the dry scrambled eggs with my fork, taking a few nibbles before taking my plate to the dirty dish bins. A night of barely sleeping, and now a rumbling stomach from hardly touching my breakfast, was a bad combo. I went outside before the activities began and saw Ben across the way. He was with the other campers he was bunking with for the week. He was bright eyed and seemed to be having fun – perhaps the time of his life. He saw me, too, and flashed a smile in my direction as he waved. I didn't know how I was going to break the news to him that I wanted out. That second day of camp dragged on miserably.

During archery practice on my first full day of camp, I slipped away from my group and ran off into the woods. Stony Glen had plenty of woods for a kid to get lost in. I spent the majority of that afternoon hiding in the woods, planning my great escape. As the sun began dropping down below the tree line, I made my way back over to where the A-frame cabin was located. By the time I showed back up at camp, everyone was getting ready to head over to the dining hall for dinner. No one seemed to notice my absence that day. I begrudgingly went along with my cabin group. Even though I had barely eaten anything for two days, I still had zero desire to be part of anything camp related, food or otherwise. All I could focus on was how badly I wanted to get out of there and go home. The sun dipped below the horizon, and I dreaded the thought of another long night ahead. That evening all the campers were sitting around the fire, and I finally had a chance to sit with Ben. I confided in him that I wanted to leave. Ben furrowed his brow in confusion, not understanding why. At that point I no longer cared what anyone, including Ben, thought about my wanting to go home. No one understood the misery I was going through.

The campfire time broke up and everyone started heading back to their cabins. That night, I couldn't fall asleep at all. I was up all night. It was just like that movie, *Groundhog Day*. I spent the majority of that night in the bathroom with the lights on, crying my eyes out. I didn't want to be in the dark. By the next morning, all of my emotions were at a heightened level – the lack of sleep and food making me feel raw. With dark circles now formed under my weary eyes, I went straight to my counselor as soon as he woke up. "Listen, I need to go home right this minute," I demanded.

I was now speaking to him as though I was in charge. I was speaking to him with an extremely disrespectful tone. Yesterday's friendly face was nowhere to be found. He scowled at me as he hurriedly whisked me over to the camp's headquarters, not wanting this confrontation to continue with the other kids watching. After my counselor had a few words with the director, Mr. Ben Walker, behind closed doors, he headed back to join the other campers, leaving me alone with him. Mr. Walker, who later went on to run The Haven of Rest Ministries in the Akron area, knew my parents from church. I breathed a quick sigh of relief, thinking that he was my golden ticket to the phone call to my parents I needed. Finally! Mr. Walker would handle this and get me the hell out of here.

Boy, was I wrong. Mr. Walker looked at me with the same disappointed face I'd seen on my father many times before. He spoke to me firmly. "Young man, you're going to go back to your cabin mates, apologize to them and your counselor, and then you're going to start getting along and participating like everyone else." My heart sank as I realized this plan had backfired on me.

"But you don't understand," I pleaded with him, tears beginning to well up in my already sleep-deprived eyes. "I need to get out of here and get back home right now. Please!"

Mr. Walker stood up from his chair, clearly not interested in entertaining my plan. "Mr. Petrie," his voice becoming sterner, "you're going back to camp right now, ya hear?"

I lowered my head in defeat, not sure what my next move would be. I feared Mr. Walker in a respectful way, but I wasn't buying any of his grandiose ideas, that things would work out if I just went back to camp. I submitted to his authority . . . for the time being.

My attempts to escape had all been futile. I wasn't sleeping, or eating, and I felt more like a prisoner than a camper. I didn't know how much more of this I could take before reaching my breaking point. It was in that moment of desperation that a new survival instinct/leadership skill was born in me. I approached two of the kids my age that were staying in my cabin. I knew them from my home church: Larry and Scott. I sat them down during a break right before lunch. I let them both know just how much I hated Stony Glen Camp, and I decided to convince them why they should hate it, too.

"Just think, we come here to this stupid camp, they make us do these stupid activities all day that are boring, and the food tastes terrible! I mean, we could be home right now doing what we wanted – watching TV, riding our bikes, and having fun. Come on, follow me, let's get outta here!" They glanced at each other, nodding their heads in agreement, and off we went, sneaking off onto a trail that led into the forest.

After walking through the woods for a very long time we found ourselves completely lost. We had no idea where we were. I could see that Larry and Scott were visibly upset. We continued on for a while longer until we finally stumbled upon a main road that ran through the camp. Of course, we were so turned around that we couldn't determine which direction led towards the road, away from the camp. Since I was leading the resistance, I took a good look both ways before heading in the direction I was sure would get us out of camp. As we walked down the gravel road, we realized too late that we were actually heading back towards camp. We'd been spotted by a counselor!

"Aha! There you three are! Get over here!" My heart sank. We defectors all got led back to Mr. Walker's office.

Me versus Mr. Walker, Round Two! Ding! Ding!

When Mr. Walker heard what was going on now, he was enraged. He took Larry and Scott into his office, crying and sniffling while they gave their side of the story. To this day, I still don't know what they told Mr. Walker. They exited the office, still in tears, neither one of them looking at me as they headed out the door and back to camp. I sat there, nervously anticipating my sentence. Mr. Walker came out of his office, his face beet red, and pushed up his sleeves as he approached me. He seemed to have grown a foot since I'd last seen him. He grabbed a metal folding chair and slammed it open in front of me backwards. He sat down, straddling the chair and folded his arms over the back of it, staring so deeply into my eyes I almost felt like he could see my soul.

He blitzed me so intensely with his words, I could feel the spit from his mouth hitting me in the face like a mist as he barked at me. Although he never actually cursed at me, he may as well have. I had never seen a Christian man, besides my father, react so angrily about anything in my life. He lectured me about what a young Christian man should look and act like and went on to tell me about how much I had failed in that aspect. "I'm calling your parents to get you out of here right now!" A spark of hope lit up inside of me.

Checkmate, motherfucker!

Of course, I kept those colorful words to myself, but I was beaming from the inside with satisfaction. I'd won round two. "All I wanted was to go home; that's all I wanted. I didn't do anything wrong! You should have just let me go home when I first asked you."

Mr. Walker retorted, "Oh you're gonna go home alright, and you're never coming back here ever again!" It was as if I was hearing Martin Luther King Jr.'s voice cry out, "Free at last, free at last. Thank God almighty we are free at last!" I was overjoyed.

It wasn't Mr. Walker's fault. He was a good man just doing his job. He didn't know what he was up against, so in my heart I forgave him.

I got word that my mom was coming to pick me up. She had recently obtained her driver's license. I was so relieved my dad would not be accompanying her. I remember seeing Ben in passing as I was preparing to leave camp. "Well, I'm going home." He looked at me, both perplexed and disappointed, as he said goodbye to me. I no longer cared what anyone thought about it, even Ben. I didn't even care what my parents would think about all of this. All that mattered was that I was going home! My wish was finally granted. As trying as this camp experience was, it was going through these mental and physical challenges that would develop new character traits within me. I developed a confidence in my own abilities that proved that I was capable of speaking to, convincing, and leading my peers.

Not long after returning home from Stony Glen Camp, I returned to that infamous Barberton Natatorium where a year and a half earlier I had suffered such great defeat. I headed down there with my brother Ben and some neighborhood friends one hot summer afternoon to cool off in the pool. The roof of the natatorium was retractable, and during the summer months they'd remove it to let the sunshine in. It made it feel like you were at the beach. They sold popcorn, candy, and soda there. To us kids, it was paradise.

I didn't have any pressing desire to get in the water that day, although the hot, humid weather made me reconsider. My only other real experience in the water up to that point was the shallow waters close to shore of the Chesapeake Bay, and at my Aunt Vicki's pool in Norfolk, Virginia, where we'd visit every summer. She had a four-foot, above-ground pool that you could stand up in comfortably. We loved it because it provided some much welcomed relief from the summer weather. Her pool was an oasis of sorts.

On this particular day at the natatorium I found myself sitting in the two-foot shallow section of the pool all alone. I borrowed one of my friend's goggles so that I could look under the water. I submerged my head and began looking around. One of my friends nudged me and said, "Dude, you should check out that hot girl over there under the water!" Of course, out of curiosity, I obliged. It was a whole new world I was discovering under the water's surface, and it began to ease my discomfort about being in the water. It was entertaining as well. The goggles were tinted black; it was like wearing underwater sunglasses. I felt really cool wearing them.

I happened to have a quarter in change left over from the spending money I had taken along with me, so I got out of the pool to retrieve it from my pants pocket. I turned it over a few times in my fingers before dropping it into the shallow water. The sun reflected off of the shiny coin, making it look like sunken pirate treasure. I waited for the coin to reach the pool floor before retrieving it with my head submerged. I kept scooting back further and further into the three-foot and then the four-foot deep section of the pool each time I went underneath the water to get it. The more comfortable I became with each dive, the braver I felt.

At that point, I was mimicking what I had seen in the movies of people swimming and what I had observed other kids doing in the pool. I boldly let the quarter drop in the nine-foot section. I dove down, kicking off the wall for momentum, spreading my arms and sweeping them behind me like I'd watched others do. I felt like everything was going in slow motion. *Oh my gosh! I'm doing it! I'm swimming!* I leaped up out of the water, yelling to my brother and our friends, "Did you see that?! I can swim!!" I cried out. "I can swim! Did you see me?!"

Discovering how to swim on my own was one of the prouder moments of my life. I wasn't taught to swim, and I didn't learn how to swim. I found out how to swim on my own – just myself, the borrowed goggles, and the shiny quarter. I would go on one day to teach not only my own kids but other people's kids how to swim by using the "goggles and quarter" method. For kids, it all starts with first being comfortable underneath the water. Everything else falls into place soon afterwards. Being able to swim would not only save my own life one day, but it would also have me competing in races with elite triathletes.

SIXTH GRADE

Larry Soyars, our next-door neighbor who lived in an upstairs apartment on Lloyd Street in Barberton, became my dad's best friend, and an honorary member of our family. Larry was from New Philadelphia, Ohio. He was a few years older than my dad, but they shared the same birthday – October 27. Larry graduated in 1958, and by 1959 he was serving in the Marine Corps. "Force Recon 2nd Marine Division!" he'd always say to me. He was an expert marksman with a rifle.

Larry would recount to me how he had once been a mere hundred meters away from Russian soldiers during the Cuban missile crisis in October, 1962. "You gotta be a dog, J. You gotta be tough, J," he'd always remind me. Then he'd rise to his feet, marching in place, and break into the Marine Corps First Call Reveille. His voice sounded like thunder bolts striking land, and the electrical force would cause me to jump to my feet. I'd salute him while I marched through the living room and around the dining room table. Not since the days of my father and I marching around the dining room table while "Script Ohio," the legendary marching band song of the Ohio State Buckeyes played, had I been so excited.

Larry would always get us Petrie kids fired up. We would affectionately call him "Mad Dog" Larry Soyars. Larry's Marine Corp tattoo, "USMC" with a paratrooper coming down over mountains on his upper right arm, was the first tattoo that I'd ever seen up close and personal. Larry was usually wearing shirts with sleeves, so on occasion I'd say, "Uncle Larry, can I see your tattoo?" He'd always oblige and show me proudly. "Semper Fi, J!"

Larry was a two-time member of the all USMC football team. After leaving the Marine Corps in 1963, Larry attended Western Kentucky University. He played linebacker next to Dale Lindsey, who went on to play pro football for the Cleveland Browns. Legendary offensive line coach for the Washington Redskins, Joe Bugel, was a graduate assistant on that Western Kentucky Hilltopper's team Larry played for. He always reminded me of that because I was a big Washington Redskins football fan as a kid. Larry eventually suffered a right knee injury while playing college football. It was a devastating injury because he had hurt that same knee while playing football for the Marine Corps. Lindsey had once told Larry, "I'll see you in the pros if you're healthy enough." For Larry, that would be the end of his football career. In the spring of 1966, Weeb Ewbank of the New York Jets invited Larry to a free agent camp. Unfortunately, he couldn't pass the physical test. It was just the beginning of a lifelong struggle and dark times ahead.

Larry's father, who everybody called "Big Tex," was a burly six foot seven inch man weighing in at 280 pounds. When Larry was young, his father was abusive, both physically and verbally, to both him and his older brother, Paul. Tex was a drunk and would beat Larry until he reached the age of sixteen, when Larry finally started fighting him back. That long history of abuse began to rear its ugly head when he was a junior in high school. He came in late for a football practice one afternoon and got into it with an assistant coach. The coach pushed Larry into a locker in front of all his teammates, and he reacted by punching the coach square in the face. After a short and violent scuffle, they had to be separated. The head coach looked at Larry and said, "Go home, Daddy Wrap," which was one of Larry's nicknames. As Larry recounted this story to us kids, he would proudly say, "J, I still started in the game that Friday night." He was just that good. It would have done the entire team a disservice to bench him for a game.

In 1967, Larry married Lois Henderson, a single mom of three children. Back in those days, not many men would take on such a burden. He treated Lois's kids like his own. Larry and Lois went on to have their own son, Michael, in the fall of 1968.

From 1965 until 1972, Larry worked at B.F. Goodrich, a tire company. He got promoted to the role of district sales person for Ohio, West Virginia, Kentucky, and parts of Pennsylvania. In 1972 he was making good money and even earned himself the luxury of driving a company car. Larry was the man! Then one day, in the fall of 1973, his glowing career went straight to hell when out of the blue Larry suffered a nervous breakdown while at his office. His boss found him on the floor in a state of panic, crying, screaming and flailing about. At six foot two, weighing 260 pounds, it took several men to restrain him. From there he was sent to the VA Hospital in Brecksville, Ohio. Larry spent the next four years of his life at that horrible place, undergoing twenty-five shock treatments throughout the duration of his stay.

Larry was so well liked by everyone at his job – especially his boss – that they continued to pay Larry's salary for a year after his breakdown, helping Lois and the kids stay afloat during that really tough stretch. Larry's boss visited him regularly at the VA hospital. In the fall of 1977, he was released from the psych ward, and he was never quite the same afterwards. He moved into a rooming house on his own and began

45

receiving a government check each month for his mental illness. Despite his financial difficulties, he faithfully paid child support for his son. Larry and Lois were no longer together because he suffered from paranoid schizophrenia and agoraphobia: the fear of certain places and situations where the person feels that their environment is unsafe with no easy escape route. As a result, Larry suffered from anxiety, helplessness, and embarrassment, taking meds for the rest of his life in order to function.

In the early 1980s Larry moved in next door. My dad hit it off with Larry right away, and before long my parents had made an arrangement with him to come over and eat dinner with our family every night, which he did for several years. On occasion, even though he lived next door, he'd even spend the night, which is saying a lot for an agoraphobic. He would stay over late into the evenings, watching TV shows, movies and sporting events with us. He would sometimes even babysit us kids when my parents weren't home. I distinctly remember that Larry was with us on the night Doug Flutie threw the "hail Mary" touchdown that beat Ohio born Bernie Kosar's Miami Hurricanes in 1984. He watched the Celtics and Lakers wage war in the NBA finals with us. We would be cheering for Boston and chanting, "Beat LA!" with Larry. Our house would be literally shaking.

Larry's son, Michael, played and starred for the state powerhouse, Barberton Magics, basketball team in the mid-1980s, led by legendary coach, Jack Greynolds. My father was a history major receiving his degree from Akron University in 1976. He would substitute teach for Greynolds from time to time. Due to Larry's mental illness, however, he never once got a chance to watch his own son play a game in high school; yet he was ever present in our lives. We Petrie kids didn't know any differently; we never looked at Larry as being ill. Larry would always talk about how you "gotta be tough" and how "you can't be a chicken heart. There's nothing to be scared of J," he would say. Then out of nowhere, he'd start up with the Marine Call cadence again. I'd always salute him whenever he'd chant like that. I spent some of my most memorable childhood moments with Larry. He taught me toughness, perseverance and resilience. It wasn't until almost three decades later that I'd realize how impactful Larry had been in my life.

When I was seventeen years old, I remember a Marine recruiter coming to our high school to give a presentation, hoping to gain some young recruits. I was interested, so I went up to him and said, "I am a Type 1 diabetic. Do you guys take diabetics?"

His eyes scanned me up and down, "No, I'm sorry. We don't."

"That's OK," I quickly retorted, "cuz I was raised by a Marine Recon paratrooper. You don't want any of this. You'd need three Marines to equal one of me. I'd rather be a Navy Seal anyways!"

The recruiter smirked arrogantly at me with daggers in his eyes. I stared back at him coldly, my arms crossed in front of me, challenging his reaction to my response. He had no idea he was looking into the soul of a "Mad Dog" Larry Soyars protégé. Larry, more than anything or anyone, showed me how to suffer and yet keep fighting the good fight. His stamp on my legacy was sealed a long time ago.

Larry Gregory Soyars died on May 22, 2002, of cirrhosis of the liver due to the chronic effects of all the medications he'd been on for so long. On his deathbed he told his son Mike that the only thing he regretted in his life was not getting one last chance to punch his father right in his teeth, "that son of a bitch." Prior to his passing, Larry had requested that my father, Jeff, play taps at his funeral. I still regret not getting up to speak at his funeral and sharing with everyone the impact he had on my life. It wouldn't be until many years down the road that I would get the opportunity to rectify that. Thank you, Larry!

My sixth-grade year was spent at Highland Middle School, which I wasn't too pleased about. The majority of my closest friends including Manny, Kevin, and Ben got assigned to the other middle school across town called U.L. Light. I had finally gotten somewhat comfortable in school by the fifth grade and now I felt like I was starting all over again from scratch at a new school.

The sixth graders were called "ankle biters" by the older students at Highland. We weren't respected by anyone, and being the youngest grade in this new school, we went straight to the bottom of the barrel once again. And to top it all off, I was on my own as my closest friends were at the other middle school. I rode the bus to school every morning with my brother Jon and some neighborhood kids. I was miserable. I would find myself staring out the bus window, wondering what Kevin and Manny were up to across town. I missed them sorely. Fall and winter seemed to drag on without my closest buddies around.

That year I began to notice that I had to squint to see what was written on the chalkboard from the back of the classroom. I was embarrassed that I had to wear glasses as a result, but being able to see a lot better was incredible. My relationship with my "specs" was bittersweet. As much as I loved being able to see clearly, I was extremely self-conscious about wearing glasses and worried what other kids would say about it. I'd heard all the "four eyes" and "squints" jokes that other kids with glasses had to endure.

In gym class that year, I ran my first timed mile at 6:07, and I wasn't even running my hardest. I felt distance running could be an option for me, where normally I was just a sprinter. That spring, I also returned to playing organized team sports as a twelve-year-old for the Major Athletics, a Barberton Little League baseball team. It would be perhaps the very first time that I'd dealt with politics and favoritism in sports as a youth. I was a speedster; I had a great glove in the outfield, tracking down fly balls that were hit almost anywhere. All my teammates knew the best outfielder played center field, but even though we all knew I was the better fit for that position, the coach's son was the center fielder to start the season. That's the position I wanted.

As the season progressed, my skill sets in the outfield were highlighted repeatedly as I made one incredible play after another. I made diving catches look effortless. The coach finally had no choice but to start his best outfielder, yours truly, in center field.

Later in the season we had a showdown with the league's best team, The Major Orioles. Their team was oozing with talent. I found myself once again in the same arena facing off with none other than Tron Jenkins. Here we were, a year after that monumental fifth grade 50-yard dash where I embarrassingly lost to Tron.

I sat in the dugout talking to our catcher, Tony Gotto. Gotto talked as much trash as I did, so we were always yapping about something. I turned towards Gotto and said, "They better hope I don't get on base, 'cuz if I do, I'm gonna' steal second and take Tron's teeth right out of his face." I could taste revenge. My dad would often talk about the overly aggressive

Ty Cobb slide with me, and I was primed to set it into motion with my own dusty cleats.

I sped onto first base with a base hit over the outstretched arms of Jenkins at shortstop. I was gearing up to steal second and everyone in the joint could tell. Jim Six was playing second base for the Orioles. He was a really good ball player, cocky, and was mouthy just like Gotto and me. Both Tron and Six were anticipating that I'd make my run to steal the base on the next pitch. The pitcher wound up and threw a ball to the batter. I took off towards second, screaming profanities and kicking up a cloud of dust behind me like a bull running towards a matador. Tron and Six both ran over to cover the bag and take the throw from the catcher, Nick Karabatsos. As I approached the bag I slid in as high and as hard as I could with my cleats pointing upward. It would have made Ty Cobb proud.

I had every desire to bodily harm these guys. Dirt flew up in the air into the faces of both Six and Jenkins as I rose up onto the bag, the three of us in one big cluster coming together. The ball was overthrown and skipped into shallow center field, so Paul Howe, the Orioles center fielder, ran in to back up the throw. Seeing Paul, and knowing both him and his father, Chuck, who was one of the Orioles' coaches, were church folks, made me stand down. I had intended to cause a bigger raucous. The umpire ran over to proclaim me safe and also to chastise me for what he'd just heard coming out of my mouth. I was lucky he didn't throw me out of the game right then and there.

Tron glared at me, then turned towards Six, saying, "Man, this 'nigga' is crazy!" I chuckled inwardly, having just heard that coming from the mouth of a black kid. You're damn right I'm crazy! For me, this was the moment that I had officially arrived on the scene in Barberton team sports. The chip on my shoulder was growing bigger by the day.

SEVENTH GRADE

Going into my seventh-grade year, my older brother, Jon, was off to high school, so I'd be going to Highland by myself. I always had one or more of my siblings at whatever school I was attending up until this point, so I was really on my own now. During this particular school year, my gym teacher, Mr. LaRoche, made a huge impact on my ever-growing self-confidence. The guys that used to call me "Pee-on-a-tree" were all eighth graders now. The days back at Memorial flashed through my memory again like deja vu.

One day while sitting in music class, Mr. LaRoche walked in flanked by the school's football coach, Mr. Passarelli. LaRoche was a bigger man that wore thick, pop bottle glasses. LaRoche used his finger to scan the room until he stopped, pointing right at me.

"There he is," he motioned to Passarelli. "That's him right there."

Passarelli nodded as he looked at me, "OK, yeah. I know Jason."

"You definitely want him on your football team, coach. He's a hell of an athlete," LaRoche said confidently. My gym teacher had seen my talent firsthand in gym class, whether we were playing football, basketball, running, jumping, or competing in a variety of different sports. I excelled at everything I tried, athletically, and LaRoche saw me as a talented, athletic kid with great potential. What he and Passarelli didn't know, however, was that there were a few eighth graders that would have been more than happy for me to play football that season. They were all looking to exact punishment for what had gone down a couple of years back at Memorial. We boys had a way of proving ourselves and taking care of disputes out on the playing field.

Of course, all those eighth-grade guys on the football team were bigger and stronger than me and were regularly lifting weights. I was no match for them, so I didn't want any part of it. Needless to say, I didn't play that year. LaRoche timed everything in his gym classes: the mile run, the 50-yard dash, the shuttle run, and so on. He always had a pencil or pen tucked behind his ear and a small note pad in his pocket to keep stats and times. As a former high school football coach, he always had a shiny whistle around his neck and had us kids running drills like we were on his team. He once timed me in the shuttle run and told me later that week that mine was the fastest shuttle run he'd ever recorded in all his years as a gym teacher. LaRoche encouraged me time and time again not to waste my God-given abilities.

That same year, I tried out for the Highland Scots basketball team, although I had never played organized basketball before. A couple of the same eighth graders that didn't like me from the football team were also playing on the basketball team. I'd always believed that the greatest athletes play basketball. My speed, agility, athleticism, and overall aggression put me in a great position to excel, regardless of my lack of experience playing the sport. The bigger and stronger eighth graders couldn't hit me on the basketball court the way they wanted to hit me on the football field, so I was good to go.

After tryouts, I waited anxiously for the list to come out to know if I'd made the cut. We only had one team for the middle school, as sixth graders couldn't play, and they combined the seventh and eighth grade into one team. The time came, and the list of who made the team was hung in the boy's locker room. I pushed my way to the front to scan the list for my name. I saw name after name of eighth graders. I knew I would surely make the team, along with a handful of skilled seventh graders . . . and then I saw my name, Jason Petrie. It felt like it was written in lights, I was so excited. However, my excitement was quickly tempered by the notion that I was not likely going to be given a lot of time on the court, considering that I was the inferior as a seventh-grader. The eighth graders that had played the previous year were going to see the most minutes on the floor. The few of us lucky seventh graders that made the cut would rotate dressing for games. The times I did get the opportunity to wear a uniform, my chances of actually getting in the game were slim to none. I despised sitting on the bench, whether I was dressed in uniform or not, and I didn't care much for my older eighth grade teammates either.

One afternoon we traveled to Perkins Middle School in Akron for a game. The Perkins team was all black. It was the first time that I saw a middle schooler dunk a ball. My mind was blown. I dressed in uniform for that game knowing that I'd never even sniff the floor. Who was I kidding?! With that in mind, and because the Perkins team was all black, I rooted for Perkins to destroy my team quietly on the inside, and turns out, that's exactly what happened. I reveled in the disappointment of our eighth graders after the game. To me, they were all still inferior bullies who deserved to get bullied themselves. They got what they had coming for them, I thought: a beat down on the basketball floor by black athletes.

51

I loved it!

That year ended with me thinking to myself that I would come back the next year and be the best basketball player in the school. During my time at Highland, I was fairly inactive socially, so school was pretty miserable. I was a bright kid, so my grades remained high, but I derived most of my self-worth from how I performed athletically. I anticipated being the big man on campus as an eighth grader. Things could only go up from there, I hoped.

That spring of 1986, I was drafted to play for the Tigers, a Senior League team which was the highest level of Little League Baseball in Barberton for thirteen- to fifteen-year-olds. Coach Ray Haynes told me that he drafted me because of one specific play he had seen me make as a 12-year-old the year before. "It was a diving catch you made, fully extended in center field." Coach Haynes recalled. "You're the best defensive center fielder in our league and we wanted you." Of course, that added to my self-confidence.

My mom's parents came to watch me play that spring all the way from Norfolk, Virginia. My granddaddy, William "Bill" Fulcher, was a World War ll Navy veteran, and he loved baseball. I got my middle name, William, from my Grandpa Bill. Surely he was proud, watching me put on a show for him out on the field.

The game I played when granddaddy was in town was against the Orioles. Ironically, the Major League Orioles baseball team was his favorite team. He loved Cal Ripken Jr. True to their namesake, the Orioles in the Barberton Senior League were one of the better teams. In that game, I got a base hit single off of pitcher, Mark Hill. I threw Eric Hanlin out at second base from the outfield as he tried to stretch a single into a double. He was one of the league's best hitters at the time. Later that game, I robbed Mike Lattea of a home run, making a tremendous defensive play as I tracked down a fly ball and crashed into the wall with my glove extended over the fence in right center field. These guys were the Orioles' version of "The Big Three," like LeBron James, Dwayne Wade, and Chris Bosh were for the Miami Heat. They were All-Star players in the league. I remember my granddaddy saying to me after the game that what he had just witnessed was well worth the trip to Ohio. I beamed up at him with pride. At the end of the season I was selected as the starting center fielder for the Barberton

Senior League 13-year-old All Star team. I was continuing to forge an identity through playing sports.

EIGHTH GRADE

In mid-July of 1986 I showed up at Highland Middle School to walk on for the football team. Not since the one day of practice I survived with the Memorial Warhawks when I was in elementary school had I ever tried to play organized football again. I continued to play backyard football with my neighborhood friends throughout the years, and despite the lack of any formal practices, I felt that I was elite in comparison to the other eighth graders at Highland. It was in sports, once again, where I found much of my self-worth based on how good I was at the sports that I participated in. Looking back, I think my OCD definitely played a role in this. If I wasn't the best at what I was doing, it wasn't good enough.

I already had the chance to play both organized baseball and basketball, so now only football was left unexplored. At the first practice, Coach Cornell quickly recognized that I was the best athlete he had at his disposal. He put me at the tailback position right away and I started learning the terminology in the football playbook. The first couple of weeks were non-contact practices where we wore only shorts and helmets. Even without all of our gear on, it was so blazingly hot out there. I knew the first day of contact and hitting would soon arrive, and it was a day I wasn't looking forward to at all. The memories of getting the snot kicked out of me the last time I'd played contact football were still fresh in my mind. The last thing I wanted to do was to relive that day.

I was lined up against Jody Smith on the first day where we practiced hitting with pads. Jody was a little bit shorter than me, but he was solid, stocky, and the hardest hitter on our team. I had seen the way professional football players hit on TV, so I made my best effort to try mimicking that as I braced myself to hit Jody. When our pads collided it felt like I'd hit a wall. He continued hitting me several times, and my cleats scraped up the grass as I slid backwards with each impact. I was getting bludgeoned by him. I spent that entire practice getting hit hard by several other kids that were bigger than me. I began second guessing my decision to give football another shot.

The next couple practices were more of the same. Then one day, out of nowhere, in my mind, I felt myself snap out on that football field. I decided that enough was enough, and I wasn't going to take any more punishment! I wanted to be the aggressor - the one that everyone was afraid to get hit by. It was a hot day in August, the day I started unleashing holy hell on my teammates. Jody came up to me in the locker room after practice that day saying, "That's the way to hit, Petrie, fuck yeah, man!" I swelled with pride. I was getting noticed by one of the best players.

I started hitting with so much tenacity that Coach Sobnosky moved me from the defensive backfield, where I had started, to the defensive line. None of the offensive lineman could block me. I was so explosive off the ball that they had a hard time keeping me out of the backfield. On offense, I started off as the tailback. Our first scrimmage game was against Copley Middle School, and I ran the ball 40 yards to the right side the first time I touched it. I scored from about four yards out later that same drive. This did my ego good. I had now taken another sport by the horns.

As the season progressed, I ended up splitting time at the tailback position with another really talented athlete named Dan Cogar. We split the carries each game until he got moved to quarterback later in the year. It worked out well for both of us since we were expending so much energy on the defensive side, so it kept us fresh. In every sport I played, I took the most pride in my defensive play. Defense was about energy and effort, and I had plenty of it.

I also remember the night we played at Kent Roosevelt Middle School. The first play of the game, my number was called to carry the ball sweep right. I took the handoff, got the edge, and headed up the open field for what I thought was a sure touchdown. But just when I thought I was about to score, I saw a blur out of my left periphery. Demetrius Wright was coming for me, and I could hear him snarling like a lion on a hunt as he gained on me. He slammed into me like a train wreck, violently, which nearly tore my jersey right off of me. I hit the turf and got the wind knocked out of me. I wasn't down for more than a second before Demetrius yanked me up off of the ground by my jersey. My head was spinning. I stood there in a daze as the rest of the Kent players rushed over to him, barking and howling as they congratulated him for that impressive play. They danced around me like a pack of hungry wolves. I found myself encompassed in a circle of Kent players. They had the home field advantage, and the raucous Kent crowd was echoing the team's excitement over that brutal play with their screams of affirmation. I pointed to our sideline, then hobbled over to the bench, still trying to catch my breath. I checked myself out of the game offensively. Coach Cornell sent Cogar in for me. He had wanted the starting tailback position, so I let him take the brunt of the punishment for the rest of the game. Jason Hance, our quarterback at the time, was in tears, yelling at the offensive lineman to block somebody. We lost that game to Kent. It was my first – but not last – run-in with Demetrius Wright.

Most of our games played out the same way, and we ended up with a losing season. We didn't have enough good athletes at Highland to compete with the other middle schools.

As the season was winding down into the last couple of weeks, I began to struggle with doing even simple, basic plays like taking a hand-off from the quarterback or catching an easy screen pass. I felt shaky, somewhat dizzy, and my hands were always trembling. It was quite bizarre, but I tried to ignore it and chalked it up to the colder weather as we were well into October.

Our final game of the year was a week away, and we were going to play our rivals on the other side of town, the U.L. Light Lancers, in the city championship game. U.L. Light was loaded with talent in comparison to our Highland Scots team. My arch nemesis, Tron Jenkins, was a star wide receiver for them. Kevin and Manny both played for the Lancers as well. However, the most prominent player for U.L. Light was a linebacker by the name of John Squires. John was team captain for the undefeated Lancers and wore Dick Butkus's number 51. He was bigger than both Jody and Demetrius, so I eyed him up and down nervously. I had a pit in my stomach that whole week leading up to the big game. I even missed a practice because my insides were such a wreck from my nerves being so worked up in anticipation.

On the first play of that game, in front of a packed Barberton High School football stadium, my number was called. "I-wing left -36-whamon 2," the quarterback yelled. Cogar was quarterback that game, and I was lined up a few yards behind him. Across the line I caught a glimpse of Squires. There he was, number 51, wide-eyed and snarling. The ball was snapped. I took the pitch and tried to hit the edge hard to the left. Regardless of the play call, I was always trying to get to the edge. I was faster than everyone else, so I felt that if I could get to the sidelines, I could get up the field where I wanted to be. Number 51 was hot on my trail. I got about three yards up the field and then *KABOOM*! Squires ran right through me into the sidelines. He hit me like Washington Redskins free safety Sean Taylor hit Buffalo Bills punter Brian Moorman in the 2006 NFL Pro Bowl. I was covered in the little black cinder rocks that made up the Barberton track that encompassed the football field. I even had them in my teeth. All I could hear was the yelling and screaming of the other Lancers players as I lay there spitting the rocks from the track out of my mouth. Squires towered over me, staring at my curled-up mass on the ground, as if to let me know he had more where that came from. I had never been hit so hard in my life.

Squires took my will with him that day. I played the rest of that game concussed, but after that collision, I no longer had any desire to play football ever again. My football career was ended with that hit. If anyone was ever born to play in the NFL, it was John Squires. He was the only guy I'd ever met that could take my will and make me submit. This encounter with Squires was so impactful, that I've thought about it at least once a month for more than three decades.

Tragically, not even a year later, Squires was in a swimming accident and ended up paralyzed from the waist down. He lost the use of both of his legs. Lesser individuals would have never recovered from such a significant injury like this, especially as a young teen, but Squires had great willpower and determination and was a great athlete. Prior to the injury, he had played football and wrestled. He was captain of the wrestling team his eighth-grade year going undefeated and winning every match by pin in the first period. He most likely would have gone on to receive a full ride scholarship to play D-1 college football or for wrestling. To this day, he is arguably the greatest athlete that I have ever shared the same space with. To have all of that taken away from him was devastating. Twenty-nine years later, I would have another encounter with him, but this time would be much different. Instead of taking my will and making me submit, he'd send electricity through my entire body and soul and give me the will to fight on.

As my eighth-grade year continued, I turned my focus to my real passion, the game of basketball. This year I was hell bent on being a holy terror on the basketball court. Even though I was short in stature, I was a force to be reckoned with. I could run, jump, and was lightning fast. I was aggressive on the court, especially on the defensive end of the floor.

Coach Yonker named me and Chris Smith the captains of the team. Routinely, during the morning announcements at school, they'd give the results of the football, basketball, and volleyball games the night before. They would list the names of student athletes who scored the highest number of points and note if the game was a win or loss. But it wasn't until I showed up on the scene, however, that they'd start talking about great defensive efforts. I was all over the court, getting steals and diving on the floor for loose balls. I made playing defense cool.

"Jason Petrie gave a tremendous defensive effort at last night's game with eight steals and caused havoc all over the court!" The announcement echoed through our classroom as I smiled proudly. I always looked forward to those accolades.

While all the other kids wore high top basketball shoes, I wore low cut, gray Nike running shoes. My teammates jokingly called my shoes "Air Petries." Other kids were worried about looking cool, but I was trying to find any subtle way I could to be different and stand out. I was the highest scorer at a game one night at Nordonia with twenty-two points. The next morning, Mr. Passarelli, our art teacher and former Highland football coach, exclaimed after hearing the morning announcements, "Wow Jason Petrie! Twenty-two points? You're the Dennis Hopson of Highland Middle School!" Hopson was an Ohio State star basketball player in those days, so I beamed when he mentioned me in the same breath with him.

Although we weren't a very successful team as far as wins and losses, I was growing ever so confident in my skills on the court. Basketball was officially my game. At Highland, regardless of the sport, I felt as though I was playing alongside predominately inferior athletic talent. The time came where once again, just like the city championship against the U.L. Light football team, we would now meet their basketball team for the annual citywide bragging rights. It was a big event each year in Barberton.

I hated U.L. Light, yet at the same time I wanted to play alongside those guys because Kevin Howes played for them. I tried hard to shoulder my team's load, but we just didn't have enough talent. U.L. Light beat us badly, led by my personal rival, Tron Jenkins. During the game I suffered a deep cut on the back of my left hand. Jason Ondrus, a guard for the Lancers, had tried swiping down at the ball in an attempt to make a steal. Incidentally his finger nail caught me pretty good. As I jogged over to the sidelines leaving a trail of blood on the court, it was Terry Presto, the Lancers Head Coach who bandaged me up. It would have been nice to have you playing on our side, he said. It was one of the high tributes ever paid to me. Presto is a Barberton legend.

At the end of the season, Coach Yonker awarded me the 1987 Highland Scots basketball MVP trophy. I still have that trophy sitting on my mantle at home. It was such an honor.

My middle school years were not a very pleasant time for me as I was still trying to find my footing in life and fit in socially. I did, however, have the good fortune of having a few really good teachers and coaches that impacted me greatly: Coach Rick Yonker, Coach Jim Passarelli, the late Coach Marvin Beal, the late Mr. Tom LaRoche, the late Mr. Larry Bidlingmyer, and the late Mr. Gene Shuman. I'm forever grateful for the impact they had on me.

PART TWO
HIGH SCHOOL AND THE BIRTH OF
ZEKE OF HAITI

NINTH GRADE

I began high school in the fall of 1987 and finally reconnected with Kevin, Manny, and all of my old Memorial classmates that had gone to U.L. Light, but by that time, everyone had changed and things were never quite the same. My locker at school was right next to Jimmy Ripley and Donnie Chambers. Ripley and Chambers took over half of my locker space, telling me they needed more room for all of their stuff. I didn't have much say in the matter as they were popular juniors and I was just a freshman. They were both black athletes, and since I was partial to blacks, I obliged. Besides, Ripley was on the basketball team and I was already trying to connect with him, hoping that would give me an advantage.

September faded into October, and it was time for basketball conditioning and tryouts. The first few weeks I was working and playing so hard, trying to find my way into the legendary Barberton basketball program, that I went home feeling ill every night after practice was over. I had abdominal pain, dizzy spells, chills and vomiting. I tried ignoring it just like I had ignored the shakes I'd gotten during the past football season. I sucked it up and kept going.

Every summer, when my family spent a couple of weeks in Norfolk, Virginia with my mom's side of the family, my brother, Ben, and I walked to Crossroads Elementary School. It was just down the road from my grandparents' house. The school had indoor and outdoor courts and we played on both. The kids we played against in Norfolk were all black. They were ferocious athletes and extremely talented ball players. They talked a lot of trash, and of course, the games were played on their courts, so it could be intimidating for a couple of white kids who were not from the area. But Ben and I didn't blink. In fact we thrived on playing against such highly skilled players. It made us play a better game. We would battle as hard as we could against these kids in pick-up games of street ball, but we usually lost. However, these summer days spent playing against those tough kids in Norfolk made me the player I was, going into high school.

The coaches made their cuts, and as expected, I made the freshman team. I was selected as a starter and named one of the team captains. I soon had my second run-in with Demetrius Wright from Kent Roosevelt, same opponent, different sport. Playing against Demetrius brought me back to the days playing with those kids from Norfolk. Playing against them had unknowingly readied me to play against the Demetrius Wrights of the world. We went hard out on the basketball court, and just like down in Norfolk, the opposing team came out on top. Kent beat us. I was becoming accustomed to defeat, yet it didn't discourage me. Playing against the challenge Wright put up just made me hungry to improve my game. I lived for the competition.

As my freshman year progressed, however, I began a battle with an unknown opponent. I continued finding myself feeling ill on a regular basis. I kept chalking it up to how hard I played every night at practices and games, but it was more than just that. The fatigue began to overwhelm me. I constantly had the shakes, was thirsty, and had to urinate often. I first noticed these symptoms back in the fall of 1986 during football practice, but sixteen months later, they didn't go away. In fact, my symptoms got harder and harder to ignore.

One night during a game at Ravenna, I stole the ball and dribbled down the floor to make an easy, wide open, uncontested layup. I couldn't get the ball up to the rim and missed it badly. I just couldn't find the energy to make my body do what I needed it to do. I felt like I was wading in cement. I collapsed onto our bench on the sideline. I couldn't muster up the energy to keep playing. Coach Niskanen thought I was having some sort of attitude problem and dismissed it as that. He had no idea, nor did anyone else, that I was suffering tremendously and had been for the past several months.

My mom took me to the doctor to be evaluated. They drew some blood and told us they'd be in touch when the results were in. I remember it was

62

Donnie Chambers' mother, Katie, who drew my blood for the testing I had done. On the morning of February 5, 1988, I was in gym class. I noticed a student come in from the other side of the building and hand off a note to my gym teacher, who was also the JV basketball coach, Mr. Daily. For whatever reason, my eyes were locked on him. It was as if I knew that note was for me.

"Mr. Petrie!" Coach Daily loudly called out. "You're outta here. They want you in the office."

I had a sinking feeling in my stomach. *Crap. What did I do now?* My instincts told me something was wrong immediately.

The results of my blood work were in, and my mom called the school to have them send me home as it was serious. I went home and was greeted with the bad news by my mother. I had diabetes. I had no clue what it was, had never heard of it, and immediately thought I was going to die. I was numb from the news. I went upstairs to the bedroom I shared with my brothers and grabbed my small pocket Gideon New Testament Bible sitting in my dresser drawer that my dad had given to me. His father had given him that Bible on November 10, 1953, when he was ten years old. I started to read and pray. I was so scared. The last time I touched this Bible I had just been through a period of self-inflicted trauma when I was six years old. One afternoon in the early spring of 1979 I was outside playing with my brother Ben. I coerced my younger brother into throwing rocks with me from our next door neighbor Mrs. Bochi's gravel driveway out on to 5th Street, which was very busy traffic-wise. We were both immersed in this juvenile activity and having so much fun. Before long there was a section of street covered in gravel outside of our home. From there we headed back in between our garage and Mrs. Bochi's garage. Ben looked on as I began to smash out already cracked garage windows with some larger rocks. Hearing and seeing the glass shatter was a rush. I got carried away with it and accidentally cut myself on the base of my right thumb – a scar that is visible to this very day. I was bleeding profusely. At the same time this happened, a Barberton Police car was pulling into our driveway.

I immediately left Ben behind and jumped over the fence that encased our backyard. I took cover inside of our big blue spruce tree where my imaginary fort sat. I was scared, bleeding, and contemplating what to do next. After a few moments passed, with my heart pounding, I bolted for the back door. I slipped quietly into the house and scurried quickly to my bedroom I shared with my brothers, leaving a trail of blood behind. My mom was occupied in the front of the house with Ben and the police officer. As I hid in my room I heard Mom calling my name. I leaped up and ran to the living room. Before my mom could say another word, I went right in on my little brother and how he had caused the cut on my right thumb. I exclaimed that it was Ben's idea to throw the rocks and break the glass. Ben was only four years of age. Mom looked at me in disbelief. I continued stuttering through my words blaming Ben. My mother and the police officer were not buying my official account I gave to them on what had just transpired. The officer had originally been called to 5th Street to check in on its new makeover. There were rocks everywhere.

The officer left. Mom cleaned and bandaged my wound. All that was left now was to wait until the next day when I would finally see my dad and have to answer for what had happened. The next morning, Dad beat my ass with his belt.

In the days after this incident, I ended up on the living room floor watching the movie *Jesus of Nazareth*. Mom and Dad were both present. The scene where Jesus was flogged and crucified broke me. I fought back tears. I did not want my parents to see me crying. Pride already showing in my six year old self. The following day I found myself in a discussion with my mom about why Jesus was killed in that manner. Why was he treated so badly? What did he do wrong? This conversation led us into my parents' bedroom. I sat on their bed, engaging Mom with questions normal six year olds probably don't ask. It was then and there my mom led me in what Christians know as The Sinners Prayer. The gateway to salvation through Jesus Christ. Mom prayed, and I repeated after her verbatim. My conscience had me looking for redemption for my sin against my brother Ben. I longed to feel redeemed. Mom assured me that I was now going to heaven because of the prayer.

Can a six year old really understand something of that magnitude? I don't know! All I know is on that day, I did. A few weeks later, on May 9, 1979, my dad presented me with this Gideon New Testament Bible that I was now currently holding while praying for Jesus to deliver me from this

64

affliction called diabetes. My parents knew more than I did concerning the disease I was suffering from, but there were questions I was asking that they simply couldn't answer. The doctor told us Type 1 diabetes, the kind I was diagnosed with, is hereditary, but my parents didn't know of anyone on either side of our family that was diabetic. I was the only one. This one event – this diagnosis, more than any other event in my life – altered the course of who I became.

Akron Children's Hospital became my place of residence for the next eight days. I was admitted there until my symptoms and outpatient treatment plan could be established. It was there that I learned what diabetes was: an endocrine disorder that affected my blood sugar, and how I needed to manage it. I felt like a human pin cushion with all the finger pricks, blood draws, and IVs. It was the beginning of a new era for me. I learned how to inject myself with insulin and so did my parents. My mom was the only one in my family who ever gave me an injection, and I only let her do that once – that was enough for me. I didn't even bother giving my dad the opportunity to do it. I was an OCD control freak and the diabetes would make that condition even worse. By this time in my life, as a freshman in high school, I was now nine years removed from that fateful night at the Barberton Citizens Hospital, and I was fine with staying away from home.

My basketball teammates, spearheaded by Jason Ondrus and AJ Hite, sent me a letter with well wishes to the hospital. Jason's older brother, Mike, who was a nurse, came to visit me while I was there. He helped explain to me, in terms I understood, what I was now facing. He gifted me a practice jersey from former Akron Zips basketball star, Joe Jakubick. Jakubick had led all Division 1 college basketball players in scoring in 1984 – a local legend. I was thrilled to receive it.

I watched a lot of TV while I was admitted, so I was in my hospital bed watching the 1988 NBA All Star game when a few of my teammates came to visit me. The TV announcer was calling Isiah Thomas, who was my favorite player, "Zeke." The guys tagged me with the nickname "Zeke" on that day, and it stuck. That hospital room was where the name Zeke was birthed.

Later that same night, I was in my room watching the news when the tragic story aired of Kevin Humble and Lance Hackim, star athletes at our rival high school, Cuyahoga Falls, who were killed in a horrible car accident six days prior. I was hit with the sober reality of how quickly one's fortune could change in a matter of a heartbeat. They were killed when their car went off a cliff and down into a ravine while coming home from a Cleveland Cavaliers basketball game at the old Richfield Coliseum. Two other young men were paralyzed in that same crash. The last I had seen Lance was a year or two earlier at a Jack Greynolds summer basketball camp in Barberton. Lance was a year ahead of me, and his younger brother Landon was a year behind me.

The Hackim brothers were really talented basketball players. I remember back to that basketball camp getting matched up against Landon in a one-on-one tournament where the first one to three baskets was victorious. I won the coin toss and got the ball out first. Before I knew it, the score was Landon 2, me 1, and he had the ball for game point. I slapped the floor while in an aggressive defensive stance, bucked up hard, and blocked him. Then I scored, stopped him again, and scored again. I came from behind and won! It was probably the most thrilling victory I'd ever experienced.

Landon quickly ran over to his brother, Lance, who had been intently watching his younger brother playing against me, and I heard him telling Lance, "The only reason he won was because he got the ball out first."

I rushed over to Lance, who I'd never spoken to before. "Yes, I did get the ball out first, but Landon was up 2-1 on me and had possession of the ball to win the game twice."

"Well good job! Way to play, man!" Lance responded, extending his hand to shake mine. The act of being so gracious on behalf of his brother, even in the face of defeat, left an imprint on me. I've never forgotten that gesture after all these years.

Both the Hackim brothers and Humble had the world at their fingertips. Lance Hackim and Kevin Humble would have surely been D-1 athletes had the wreck not taken their young lives. Landon went on to play Division 1 college basketball for Miami of Ohio and became one of the RedHawks all-time leading scorers.

In the blink of an eye, Kevin and Lance's lives were gone, and here I was, lying in a hospital bed with a disease that killed the great Jackie

Robinson. I was beginning to realize that in this game of life, everything could change in an instant and nothing was guaranteed. The hospital staff informed me that diabetes was the leading cause of blindness, kidney failure, heart disease, and impotence.

"What is impotence?" I wondered aloud. After they explained it to me, I kind of smirked, thinking that certainly impotence wouldn't affect me – not anytime soon, at least.

SUMMER OF 1988, PRE-10TH GRADE

One summer afternoon after playing ball with my friends I ended up at Frank Jennings' house. Frank was like a big brother to me. On this day, both Jason Ondrus and Kevin Howes were with us. Although I couldn't tell you whose idea it was, the subject of watching a porno flick was broached. As a young man, my only other experience with pornography was looking at dirty magazines that my friends and I got our hands on. We'd run off to the sandbanks on the outskirts of the neighborhood to look at them. Or while down at Dave and Mike Koncz's house where, on occasion, we'd watch dirty movies when their parents weren't home.

It was broad daylight, and the four of us hot-blooded young men were watching men have intercourse with women. We witnessed anything and everything you can imagine in this porno movie. Men treating women like objects and speaking to them in a vulgar manner that diminished who they were is what impacted me. I thought, Oh wow, this is cool, this is what it's all about. I wondered when I'd get the chance to participate in such activities.

The four of us sitting there trying to act composed must have been a sight to see. Each one of us was positioned a certain way, attempting to cover up the evidence of our arousal. A pillow over Jason's lap, a blanket covering Frank's thighs, Kevin's one leg perched up on a chair at a certain angle, and me in the very back of the room sitting on my rear, bent over with my arms across my knees, acting as if watching something like this was business as usual. After about an hour of this I couldn't get out of there fast enough. I abruptly said, "Hey guys, I have to go," and I hurried home.

67

I was only a few doors down. Frank also lived on Lloyd Street.

I remember at this point having pain in my stomach and testicles. A pain I didn't recall ever experiencing before. Not in this particular manner, anyway. This was much different, and much more intense. I was thinking, *My God, what did I just do on the jog back over here from Frank's place?* After a while the pain would subside. Later that evening, I found myself thinking about the porno film I had watched earlier. It moved me to arousal again. In that moment I went to the only place that I knew I'd be able to find a remedy for my current dilemma.

My brother Jon had a box underneath his bed full of dirty magazines. I went and quickly retrieved one. I really hadn't been in to girls all that much, and it wasn't as if I even desired to have a girlfriend at all. My basketball was my girlfriend. I slept with my ball. Wherever I went, my ball went, including school. I just wanted to have a pretty girl to do things with – the things that I had viewed in dirty magazines and movies. Was I asking too much? After several minutes looking at one of Jon's magazines I couldn't take it anymore. I was about to explode.

I had a raging erection that started to hurt and ache. It was very sensitive to the touch. I was about to enter in to my own garden of Eden with forbidden fruit. In the moments that followed I'd experience my first real orgasm. I really had no idea what was happening. I started mimicking the movements and actions that I had watched the guys in the porno doing. I was kind of holding myself and half rubbing and half pulling on my hard penis. At this point I was as stiff as a two-by-four. I had a clear liquid coming out of the tip of my penis that I was unfamiliar with. I didn't really remember sex education at Highland Middle School covering this sort of thing. My mind was racing with filthy thoughts. It was all heading to a climax. I remember vividly the moment of eruption to this very day. The sensation was so great and so intense, but it wasn't something that I could say I enjoyed. The ejaculation part of it was stopped and started a few times over because what I was feeling was so overwhelming. It really was. The orgasm wasn't a clean one by any means. I was, in fact, a little terrified of what I just saw come out of me. I would have to clean this white stuff up off the floor swiftly. I thought, *Nobody can know about this. I will never speak of this.*

For a young Christian boy who was trying to live right in the eyes of God and please Him only, this new addictive practice was torment for me. This one act would soon turn into multiple acts, repeated again and again daily and weekly for years to come. I was a diabetic with OCD tendencies and now I'd have to deal with whether or not masturbation was right or wrong? The Bible says to think on and do whatever is pure. What I was thinking and doing before and during masturbating was not pure, so certainly it was wrong and sinful. This would now become the thorn in my flesh, and it would haunt me throughout my teen years and into my young adult life.

I remember years later having a deep conversation full of great substance with my father about the subject of masturbating. My dad told me it was a great question that he himself wanted to ask God. My dad said God made men a certain way, with certain desires. It was God's Will and by His design that He made us this way, in fact. But then God says you can't do this, and you can't do that. You can't touch this and you can't touch that. My pops would say, "What kind of sick joke is that?" But my dad would then always remind me that God does what He wants, when He wants, and who are we to question Him? Yet the both of us would always be full of questions for Him. To no end we would be in search for answers. It's just how Petrie men were.

10TH GRADE

Going into the 10th grade, I was finally at a point in my life where I felt I knew what I wanted: to play varsity basketball for the Barberton Magics High school team, and be great at it.

Going back a year in time as I was preparing to enter my freshman year, the Barberton High School soccer coach, Mr. Bob Chalmers, called my mom's house. I answered the phone. Coach Chalmers asked me to come out for the soccer team. I was taken aback by the request because I had never had a rapport with Coach Chalmers before that day, and frankly, I thought soccer was for sissies. I was kind of embarrassed. I thought maybe he didn't understand with whom he was speaking. I politely told him no.

69

He insisted on telling me all the advantages the game of soccer had to offer me. He asked me again to think about it. I told him that I just didn't want to play soccer. A couple days later he called again. I told him no again. Coach Chalmers didn't take no for an answer. He went on to tell me that I had everything it took to be a great soccer player.

There was only one problem, I didn't want to play. I didn't know whether to feel annoyed or flattered.

That same fall Mr. Passarelli, the art teacher from Highland Middle School who was now coaching the freshman football team, asked if I was coming out to play for his football team. I wanted no part of it and said no. Passarelli didn't seem to take my answer very well. He seemed angry, as though my decision not to play was a personal shun/slight towards him. I did not know how to explain to him that John Squires was responsible and to go speak with him about it. I liked Passarelli and I hated the fact that I was disappointing him in any way. I'd end up purposely avoiding him at all costs going forward.

U.S. Gold Medalist and Barberton track and field coach Glenn Jeep Davis would ask me to come run for his track team. I conveniently had the built-in excuse that I couldn't run track because it interferes with basketball open gyms. Marvin Beal was the Barberton baseball coach, and he asked me to come out for the baseball team. He said I'm not going to beg you, I am not going to ask you twice. I had the same built in excuse for him, too.

The spring of my ninth grade year I'd disappoint yet another coach of mine, Ray Haynes. I'd start off my final year with the Senior Tigers in the Barberton Baseball Senior League only to quit halfway through because I wanted to focus on basketball. I broke coach Ray Haynes' heart. His wife was diabetic so he had a certain level of compassion for me. He had even said, "OK J, you don't even have to come to practices, just show up for the games." As appealing as that was, I just didn't want to play anymore. Although I had made the 15-year-old Barberton Senior League All Star team the year before as a 14-year-old, I was now solely focused on playing basketball only.

What sold me out more than anything else was the performance of Isiah Thomas in game six of the 1988 NBA Finals. Isiah badly injured his ankle, yet continued to play and fight through it on the biggest stage versus the L.A. Lakers. I hated the Lakers. I was moved to tears that night as I watched him play on one foot and score forty-three points in the L.A. Forum. It was the most inspiring thing I'd ever seen. That night I went all in for the game of basketball and I would never look back.

If that Zeke could do it, so could this Zeke. I'd have a really good 10th grade basketball season starting for the junior varsity team. I was named a captain. Coach Daily turned me loose. He rewarded me with the ability to shoot it wherever I was on the floor because I was a decent shooter, and because of the all-out effort I gave on each possession during practices and games. I played much harder than everyone else including the upperclassmen. I really enjoyed that season because I had fun playing alongside Kevin Howes, Jason Hance, and Tim Robertson. One of Tim's older brothers, Alvin, played in the NBA for the San Antonio Spurs. He was a four-time NBA All Star.

On one occasion, Tim had complimented me on my physical ability. Although he didn't know it, it meant a lot to me personally. Tim and I caused a lot of havoc for the other teams' guards that we played during this season. Defensively, we really got after it. Towards the end of the season I was asked to come to the varsity practices as the varsity team prepared for the state tournament. Jimmy Ripley was the senior point guard and the one I'd be matched up with in practice. From drills to scrimmaging he was my draw. He was bigger and stronger but that didn't keep me from going at him.

One night at practice Ripley and I were on the floor, battling for a loose ball. His fingernail ripped off into the palm of my left hand which is still visible to this day. My hand was a bloody mess. It was that sort of crazed insane type of intensity that won the coaches over. They would let me know that I would, in fact, be dressing varsity for the tournament game against Medina. Back in those days, little five-foot seven-inch, 155-pound white kids didn't just dress varsity. It was a big deal and I was well aware of the honor and privilege. I worked for it. I was right where I belonged.

The night arrived that I'd wear a Barberton varsity basketball jersey for the very first time. The layup line was electric at Copley High School where this tournament game was played. Music was blaring. I was getting right up by the rim for every layup I made. I was jacked up and ready to go. My chances of actually getting into the game were slim, but I was juiced nonetheless.

In the fourth quarter as the game came to an end, with us losing handily at this point, the coach said, "Petrie you're in." There was about a minute left to play in the game. My heart was pounding. I got in the game and I was going hard up and down the floor. There was a foul called and thank God for that. I was out of breath. The adrenaline and excitement of the moment was overwhelming me. Free throws were awarded to the other team. The second free throw was missed and in an attempt to get the rebound, the elbow of a kid from Medina smashed into my right thumb. It felt like I had been shot in my hand. I was in so much pain. As the clock expired I hurried off the floor and into the locker room to be seen by the trainer, Mr. Culbertson. He kind of wiggled my thumb a couple times and said it looked OK.

"You should be fine," he said, "just put some ice on it." I left the arena that night in terrible pain. For the next month I lived with being very uncomfortable every day with that same pain. Finally I couldn't take it anymore. My mom took me to the doctors. The verdict: my thumb was broken. I'd wear a cast for the next five weeks.

During that time I'd fill my syringes and give myself insulin with my left hand. I'd wipe my ass with my left hand. I played a lot of basketball on my own using only my left hand. I was now masturbating with my left hand. My dad consistently told me that Petries never do anything halfway. It's either all or nothing, he'd say. He told me in confidence that his grandfather Petrie had hung himself. He was German. He had been a supporter of Adolf Hitler. After finding out what Hitler had done to the Jewish people he was so overwhelmed with guilt that he took his own life. He was all in, or all out. For a Petrie, there's no in between.

I often wonder if my great-grandfather knew that the U.S. Federal Reserve had once supported Hitler's regime. Would he have seen things differently and maybe not have taken his own life?

Now in my mid-teens I was showing those same signs of the Petrie bloodline. We were Germans, and the Germans were some tough sons of bitches, my dad would say, always quick to remind me that Adolf Hitler was not German and wasn't a true representation of the German people.

In the spring of 1989 I finally had my cast removed and I was able to start playing full go again and I really started to excel. During spring and summer open gyms, former players from the Barberton basketball program would often show up to play. In an instant at an open gym one night I'd be hurt again.

Former Magics star player Dougie Walker went after a loose ball on the floor at the same time I did. We both dove in head first. Walker's head went right into my rib cage. I suffered badly bruised ribs and was on the shelf again for another few weeks. By the time I returned to play again I was introduced to new players that were brothers, one that would be a senior, and one a sophomore in the upcoming school year. They would be joining the basketball program. I wasn't very thrilled about that. Jason Ondrus and I were all set to be the guards that received most of the playing time for the coming year. We were both homegrown Barberton kids. The two new brothers were not from here. They had transferred in from another city. Their father held a high position in society and had a close relationship with the current Barberton basketball coaches. I would get to experience first-hand what local politics looked and tasted like. Going into the next school year I'd be a junior. By this time in my young life, and probably even much earlier, my grades really started to decline. After the diabetes diagnosis I'd often use the diabetes to my advantage. If I didn't feel like going to school, if I had a test that I hadn't prepared for, if I was due to give a report where I was required to stand up in front of the class, I wanted no part of it and I'd use the diabetes as my way out of a situation that I didn't want to be in. It came in very handy. I always had that card in my back pocket to play.

Overall, my attitude concerning my grades fell off. I went from being an honor roll student as an eighth grader at Highland to just a mediocre, run-of-the-mill, "average Joe" student by the 11th grade. That not bothering me was the biggest issue. It was a real shame that I let this happen because I was so bright intellectually. My grades were always good enough that I remained eligible to play sports, and that's all that mattered to me.

11TH GRADE

It was in October of 1989 that I'd have my first surgery, so I was now missing more time away from basketball. I needed all my wisdom teeth removed. I was very concerned about being put to sleep. My blood sugar dropping, going into a coma and dying was terrifying. It was all I could think about. I remember walking the people responsible for my surgery through the do's and don'ts of how to handle putting me to sleep because I was a diabetic. I was precise. I wanted them to confirm to me that they understood and were competent. It was my OCD in full force as I tried to make sure I was in total control. I was given an injection and told to start counting back from ten. I don't remember reaching seven and I was knocked out.

When I finally came to I had no idea where I was. I was on Queer Street. I was very groggy. I found myself in a very dark recovery room, all alone. I tried desperately to sit up and drag myself out of the bed. I started vomiting violently. My sugar was really high. I looked in bad shape. My face was quite swollen.

Later that night in bed at home a significant happening took place. The earth shook in San Francisco. I remember laying in bed for hours, fixated on the TV set, watching the aftermath of the earthquake. That was the first time, other than the Space Shuttle Challenger exploding, that I remember ever remaining glued to the television over a news event. I was in bed, in pain, and watching people across the country going through pain of their own.

Earthquake, pain, and San Francisco. These three words many years down the road would take on a whole new meaning. Wow, what a life!

Basketball began in late November and I was playing on the varsity team. I started off on the wrong foot right away. I requested to wear number 55. My granddaddy Bill, my mom's father, had died on May 5, 1988. May was the fifth month and he passed on the fifth day. The coaches would refuse my request, which was hurtful to me. They said the larger numbers were for the bigger players. That bothered me greatly. My attitude changed drastically after that.

One night at Ravenna, early in the season, the younger of the two brothers who transferred to play at Barberton was inserted into the game before both Jason Ondrus and myself. The older brother, a senior, had already taken the starting point guard position from Ondrus. This was especially devastating for him because he played a lot of varsity ball the year before. Ondrus and I were both juniors. The younger brother, who was a sophomore and who was afforded this great opportunity for political reasons in my eyes, would now be the death nail for Ondrus. He would quit the team that night. I rode home with him and he was so upset. I was angry for him.

Next we played home versus Stow. I got into that game and did some damage. I was on the floor causing havoc for Stow's guards. I brought the crowd to their feet after a couple of helter skelter defensive plays that ended up turning into points for us. I was a crowd favorite because of the way I competed. I played with a different fire than everyone else. In the end we lost a tough one. Things looked up though, or so I thought. Kent Roosevelt was up next. Demetrius Wright was another rival of mine in my mind, and moments like this were what I got up for. It's why I played.

I checked into the game off the bench early on and I was wired. First time I got the ball, I dribble-drived to the right elbow going by Demetrius and shot a double clutch jumper over Klytus Williams, who was from Africa. Williams could jump out of the gym. He had closed out on me and forced me into the double clutching of the ball. I missed the shot and the coach pulled me out of the game right away. I didn't see the floor again the rest of that game. Needless to say, I was pissed.

Springfield was up next and this is where the ultimate blasphemous treason was committed in my eyes. I was demoted to the junior varsity for that game. For what reason, I don't know. Maybe bad body language? I was furious.

I went out for warm ups late, walked through them, then went over and sat at the far end of our team's bench several minutes before the game was to start. The coach called me over to be a captain at the pre-game, mid-court meeting with the other teams' captains and referees, but I refused. I said my sugar was low and I needed some orange juice. I motioned over to one of the other guys on the team to go in my place. I didn't even look at the JV team's players as my teammates. I viewed them as inferior to me. I was a varsity player.

The game started and I was roughing Springfield JV players up, being extra physical with them, and talking all kinds of trash out there. The game seemed pathetically easy to me. I would make a play and as I was running back down to the other end of the court, I'd look up at the Barberton varsity players and coaches in the stands, and I wanted to spit in their direction. They were all kind of dead to me at that point.

I ended up dressing for the varsity game later that night. At one point in the second half the coach called my number. As I ran by the coaches on the bench to check in, the head coach yelled out, "You better play hard, or it will be the last time you ever play."

In all the great history of the Barberton basketball program, I was the last kid that any coach would ever have to talk to in this manner. I played harder than anyone who ever played in the program, especially all my current teammates both in practices and games. I went into the game and played like a buzz saw. A few steals, a couple layups, and several floor burns. I played possessed.

My picture ended up in the *Barberton Herald*. It showed me going after a steal during that Springfield game. My displeasure with everyone in the basketball program was now very apparent. A couple of games later versus Canton Timken, the team was supposed to wear shirts and ties to the game in unison. Some games we wore shirts and ties and some games we wore team sweat outfits.

On this particular night, however, I wasn't in the mood to wear a tie. I wore my sweat outfit instead. I was really just pushing back in my own way.

I headed towards the locker room to get dressed and the head coach said, "Petrie, get the hell outta here. Go home, you're not playing tonight."

He was very angry that I didn't comply with the team dress code. I turned around and left without saying another word.

The final blow came when my former teammate from Highland, Chad Jenson, tried to take his own life. Chad was never really happy playing basketball. He was so tall and everyone just expected him to play. I think he always felt pressure to play because of other people's expectations. He was always quiet, distant, and very unhappy. He had tried to make it playing in the Barberton basketball program but it just never worked out for him. It was evident he didn't want to be there. I, for one, always enjoyed his company, though. He was different, just like me.

When the news came in that Chad had tried to kill himself and was admitted to Akron Children's hospital, I immediately headed to the coaches' office. I told them that our next game versus Tallmadge should be called off or suspended. I said we should be more concerned with Chad's well-being than playing a game. They looked at me with disbelief. I had gone in that office with great conviction. I had no plans myself of dressing for that game regardless of what anyone else did or didn't do. That next game at Tallmadge I sat by myself on the bus. I talked to nobody.

When we got there I sat in the locker room all alone for the entire three to four hours that we were there, for both the JV and varsity games. I know in my heart of hearts it wasn't just for Chad that I was showing defiance, I had a beef with the entire program. I was now at a point of total disconnection. The two new brothers, who for political reasons ended up on the squad, negatively affected team chemistry in my estimation. My childhood friend, Jason Ondrus, left the team. I had been demoted to JV for the Springfield game. I was pulled prematurely from the Kent game. I had been sent home for a team dress code violation. And then the surprise transfer of one of my old rivals from elementary and middle school, Tron Jenkins. He came back to the Barberton school system during that basketball season after a two-year absence where he had been attending school and playing basketball for St. Vincent St. Mary. He showed up and immediately took a starting position on the team.

Chad's unfortunate situation was put in the forefront of my agenda to make a bigger point. I went into school the next day after the Tallmadge game, and as fate would have it, I ran into the head varsity assistant coach in the hallway.

I said, "Coach, me and my parents have talked about it, and we feel like it's in my best interest to stop playing basketball and work on getting my diabetes under better control and focus on restoring my grades in school to a higher average."

All that was made up off the top of my head in that moment. It was very spontaneous. I didn't plan it in any shape or form. That conversation with my parents never really took place. I had taken my destiny into my own hands. To feel as though I was always in control of my own destiny and fate through hard work was paramount to my mental well-being. In that situation, I no longer felt that way, so I cut the nose off to spite the face.

That need to be in control of what I deemed to be important was everything, and it would become a detriment to me later down the road. I would suffocate not only myself, but I'd damn all those close to me because of it.

And now basketball, my identity – everything that I loved and lived for – was gone. My parents, especially my father, were really disappointed when they found out that I actually left the team. My dad came clean to me in that moment and told me that he had recently gone down to speak to the coaches about me and how hard I worked after being demoted to junior varsity for that Springfield game. My dad was very proud, and he didn't beg anyone for anything. I was his favorite child and he went to bat for me. To this day I still think about how devastating that must have been for my pops. He knew what a big deal playing Barberton basketball was. In years past he'd substitute teach for legendary Barberton basketball coach Jack Greynolds. He just wanted me to play.

In Petrie fashion I'd always say I wasn't cut, and I wasn't kicked off the team. I left and did it on my own terms just like Frank Sinatra. "My Way!"

On May 12 of this year we lost one of our own. Travis Olds died in is home during a house fire from smoke inhalation. The rest of his family, his parents and two younger brothers, luckily were able to escape the inferno on Harvard Avenue. My brothers Jon and Ben, childhood friend Tim Widner, who was a cousin of Travis, and I served as pallbearers during his funeral at the First Church of Christ on the corner of Harvard and Summit in Barberton.

This was a somber time for all of us in our neighborhood. It was a reality check that life was not fair. Travis was the youngest Hoodsmen, but pound for pound, might have been the toughest. The kid was all heart. He had to be tough because we put him through all kinds of physical and verbal abuse. But just like anything, he was ours to do that to. God forbid anyone else do it. I can pick on my little brother, but you better not.

RIP Travis Ethan Olds.

————————

POST 11TH GRADE, PRE-12TH GRADE SUMMER OF 1990

June of 1990 I was at home sitting in front of the television watching Isiah Thomas put on a show in game one of the NBA Finals versus the Portland Trail Blazers. I looked over at my mom and said I wanted to go spend a month in Norfolk. The rest of the family would be going down at some point in July so I figured a one-way plane ticket would do and I'd just ride back home with the family. I had my heart and mind set on playing basketball again somewhere my senior year of high school. Going to Norfolk would get me ready for that. My granddad had passed, but my grandmother, Jean, and great-grandmother, Nannie, were still there. Nannie was born on September 11th, 1895. She was ninety-four years old and I always enjoyed sitting and talking with her. I'd ask her a lot of questions about what it was like growing up in the early 1900s. I remember talking with her about the Titanic sinking. My conversations with her were mesmerizing and fascinating. I was enthralled with her every word.

While spending time there I got up late mornings and headed out to Northside Park. I took some crackers, fruit, and drinks with me and walked the mile to get there. I spent hours on those courts getting myself better. If I was all alone I worked on my individual skills. If there were other guys there I ran games. On the court it was a predominantly black crowd, which I much preferred. I always looked at white players as inferior athletes in the game of basketball so I relished the opportunity to play against the more elite black players.

I spent about six weeks in Virginia honing my game. By the time August rolled around I was asking my dad to make a phone call to Cuyahoga Falls head basketball coach Henry Cobb. I wanted to play basketball again so bad that I was prepared to do anything to make that happen, including playing for a rival team of Barberton. I had played on a summer league team the year before that Cobb coached. He loved my toughness on the defensive end. It was during that summer a guy named Bill Curley, who had played point guard for the Falls, came up to me after one of the summer league games and told me that I was the toughest guard defensively that he had ever played against in his life. Another guy named Jim Ballard, who played for the Falls the year before, and who was on my summer league team the previous year, started calling me Sweet Pea. He treated me with great affection as his teammate. I really liked the guys from the Falls and I always wanted to play alongside Landon Hackim anyway. I was now ready to make the transfer.

A couple days later I was at Crisman Park in Barberton playing basketball. On this particular afternoon I was getting ready to leave, after playing several games, but decided to hang around for one more game. It would be the last one I'd ever play during my high school years. I was dribbling hard down the court for a layup and out of nowhere a kid named Matt Szlanfucht came from an angle and crashed into me hard. My right ankle, the same one I had hurt in fourth grade, rolled again. I knew instantly it was all over for me. The pain was excruciating.

Jason Hance, my best friend throughout my high school years, carried me off the court and placed me into another friend's car to transport me to Barberton Citizens Hospital. I suffered a third degree sprain and was told I'd be in a cast for about four to six weeks. I was devastated. Before my father could even make the call to Coach Cobb it was a mute point. My senior year of high school was going to start out with me using crutches. I thought I was really fucked.

About a week later I made one of the worst decisions of my life. I decided that I was going to be like my hero, Isiah Thomas. In my mind, I went back in time to the NBA Finals in June of 1988 when Isiah fought through his badly sprained ankle and scored forty-three points on one leg. It was truly the most inspiring thing I'd ever witnessed. I cried, watching him battle hurt that night. Tears were streaming down my face. So now I was in that same position. Basketball was my identity. Isiah was my hero. My nickname was Zeke because of him. I can't overstate enough just how much Isiah Lord Thomas lll influenced my young life.

I had one of my close friends, Tim Widner, retrieve for me a saw from his grandpa's tool set and help me saw the cast off. I thought it was the brave warrior thing to do, not knowing just how much that decision would plague me with pain for the rest of my life. We got the cast removed but I was still hobbling around badly in pain. I tried to put on my basketball shoes, tie them up tight, and go play.

My good God, I don't know what I was thinking I could barely put weight on it. I was overwhelmed with emotions. I was sobbing. The realization that my basketball playing days were really over was traumatizing to me. Basketball was my identity in my mind. I had this grade three ankle sprain that I had a cast on for. After one week of wearing it I cut it off. How was I gonna hide this from my parents? I re-wrapped the ankle in an ace bandage and continued using the crutches.

12TH GRADE

Getting around the high school on crutches was miserable. The first semester I was signed up to take drivers ed class, which was way over in the Industrial Arts Building, across the street from the high school. It was quite a haul to make it all the way over there using crutches. At that point I was using an aircast. After a couple of days of doing that commute between buildings I decided to drop the drivers ed class. I thought I'd just take it next semester instead, no big deal. I wouldn't receive a driver's license until sixteen years later.

After dropping drivers ed I picked up a study hall period in its place. It was during this transition that I'd come across a new student at Barberton high that I'd never seen before. He was much different from the normal average Joe student in the way he walked and talked. He carried himself with a maturity I hadn't yet experienced among my peers. His name was Rick Kramer. Meeting him would be life transforming.

It's very important to note and I can't stress this enough: when my basketball dreams were shattered, I did not know what direction I was going in anymore. I had no back-up plan. I had some friends in high school but I didn't run with any certain crowd. I loathed the clicks and popular kids that hung out together. I was always the first one to stick up for kids who seemed out of place. I did not enjoy my high school years whatsoever

81

outside of playing ball. Basketball made it tolerable for me.

I was somewhat socially challenged in the fact that I never once went to a dance in high school. I didn't date. My basketball was my girlfriend. I'd end up spending my senior prom passing out gospel tracks with none other than Rick Kramer himself, which brings me full circle. Rick possessed great manners, he had a charismatic personality, great wit, and he was very much already honed on political correctness for such a young student. And to top it all off, he was a born again Christian. I had spent my previous seventeen years in turmoil on the inside. What was right, what was wrong? The telling of white lies, the masturbating while thinking of things impure, feelings of hostility towards white people. I'd beat myself up over any sin or personal hangup. I tried so hard not to sin, and when I'd fall flat on my face during what seemed like a daily experience, I often grew frustrated to the point of giving up.

Rick was the first person to show me what it was like to live unashamed of the gospel of Christ. He came into my life at the right time. I needed him, and he breathed new life into me, he really did! We would be there for each other as we both tried to hold ourselves accountable to the standard set in God's word.

In the meantime, my family was in between attending two different churches, Manchester Trinity Chapel and Norton Grace Brethren. Both these churches would have a tremendous impact on my life via two experiences they provided me. Grace Brethren in Norton would be sending a group of young people to visit Moody Bible Institute in Chicago. I signed up right away. I was very familiar with Moody because of the radio station WCRF in Northeast, Ohio. Back in those days, WCRF had lots of Moody programming. They had some interesting Christian programming for young people, although it was not very popular with me and my siblings.

Every afternoon when we got home from school, sometime around the four o'clock hour, my dad would make us listen to Moody radio on WCRF, and we religiously took part in these family devotions every day. We hated it, and we much preferred to be outside running around with our friends. But my dad ran a dictatorship in our house. What he said you didn't question, even though he raised us to question everything. It was the ultimate do as I say, not as I do. My dad drank beer, he smoked cigarettes, he cursed, he had women, yet with all that said, he made us learn about Almighty God, the trinity, the father, son, and Holy Ghost. We were required to memorize and recite Bible verses by heart. Looking back, I believe this was where my young mind was trained for this kind of thinking. If I was doing good over here, and not doing so good over this way, it wasn't so bad, because my good outweighed my bad. It was my religious check and balance.

God bless my father, for he meant well, and it really was the hammering of these things into my spiritual consciousness that gave to me great compassion for the poor, and placed me on a St. Francis of Assisi type of addiction. I remember eating cereal and watching TV on a Saturday morning and seeing one of those "Feed the Children" paid programs, usually showing poor, naked, and malnourished kids with extended bellies and flies all over them while they were eating a bowl of soup or rice and beans. It would immediately take my appetite away and make me angry. I'd either turn the station or get up and walk away, I was so turned off and disgusted by it. This led me to the Bible, verse James 1:27: "Religion that is pure and undefiled before God the Father is this; to visit orphans and widows in their affliction." That would become my battle cry and mantra going forward. It was ultimately what sent me to Moody Bible Institute in Chicago as I was desperately trying to find my new identity. This was now my WHY!

I must point out, however, that I somehow missed the rest of that verse in James 1:27. It ends: "And to keep oneself unstained by the world." I conveniently missed that part. Maybe I didn't want to see it. In any event, this was my new calling. This was what I preached. And if I was going to help the poor, orphans, and widows, you'd better be on board too. For this was right and true religion in my eyes!

James 1:27 was my go-to card. This is what led me to Moody. And on one particular day of fate, my destiny was revealed to me in the form of a young black man in an elevator from a foreign land.

I had just come from downstairs at Moody College where I had run into a poor black mother of two small children. She asked me for money. She had been out begging in the streets all morning long.

I said, "Do you know where the Cabrini projects are?" She said she did.

I said, "I'll give you $5 if you lead me there."

So I went to get $5 from the dorm room I was staying in. Each one of us were assigned to a dorm room where a current Moody student would kind of act as a chaperone on our behalf. I proudly said to the young man that I was rooming with that I was on my way back downstairs to give a poor black lady with kids some money.

He quickly said, "Oh no, don't do that. People like that are always out there panhandling."

He was very negative in his tone about it. Upon seeing his reaction I stopped short of mentioning to him that I was on my to visit the legendary Cabrini Green Projects with her, too. I was really turned off by his negativity and judgment concerning the poor. I thought, "We are Christians, we help people, right?" I couldn't get out of there fast enough.

Youth Pastor Roger Scarbro had given us an itinerary we were all supposed to be following each day but that was no longer my focus or in my interest. I was now breaking the rules of engagement, but I didn't really give a damn!

As I headed into the elevator to go back downstairs, a young black man hurried in behind me, asking me in his thick accent to hold door, please. He seemed very nervous, disheveled, and out of place. His hands were full of books and school materials. As we exited the small confines of the elevator the young man tripped and fell, dumping his books all over the floor. I reached down to help him pick up his belongings. He was very fidgety. He said, "Oh thank you sir, thank you very much," in his foreign accent.

I said, "No problem you're welcome, my pleasure. Where are you from?"

His eyes widened. "Me, I'm from Haiti." He had a thick Creole accent. Time stood still. Everything slowed down and I was stopped in my tracks in that moment.

I get goosebumps recounting this story. I often wonder where this man is today. What became of him? It was this meeting that would change the course of the history of my life and lead me on to my destiny.

I remembered seeing the movie *The Serpent and the Rainbow* about a year earlier. It was about Haiti but it didn't really mean anything to me at

84

that time. I specifically remember what I thought to be a tiger, but turned out to be a Jaguar, in a jungle scene in the beginning of that film. That was my introduction to Haiti.

The young man went his way and I went mine.

This meeting of fate in Chicago was the second round introduction and not a coincidence in my mind. I believed it to be from God Himself. Since that day in Chicago in October of 1990, Haiti has been the central focus of my entire adult life.

As I made my way out of the building, right outside the door sat the young woman with her two kids. I walked with her and the kids to the Cabrini Green Projects. Cabrini Green was legendary. I had to see it for myself. I didn't happen upon one white face while I was there. The place was huge. It was something right out of the movies. Black people at every turn. I remember seeing boys and girls playing, jumping rope, loud music blasting. As I walked around that entire project area it seemed as though hundreds of eyes were piercing through my soul. I had heard nothing but negativity concerning this place. It was a violent area. I wasn't scared, however. I was excited. I felt alive.

Years later, in February of 2000, an African American girl named Erica that I worked with told me that, in a dream, God showed her that black people look at me and see themselves. "You're just in a white body, that's all. When you walk in a room of black people you make them feel comfortable and put them at ease right away. You have a spirit and a presence that resonates with us."

I could see that and feel that, years before, as I walked around Cabrini Green with the young mother and her kids, coming across one black face after another. I never felt any hostility. Quite the contrary. People were looking at me and through me with what seemed like nothing but love and respect, almost as if they all had seen my life story up to date, and had prior knowledge that my journey started out with a black man.

I was greeted with smiles from black women and children, and "What's up?" and "What's happening?" from black males. It was really incredible. The dangerous Cabrini Green Projects on the Near North Side of Chicago, and I couldn't have felt more at home. I was more concerned that the white people back at Moody would give me grief if they found out what I was doing or where I actually was. I had been transported into a different world.

Cabrini had the feel of a prison. It was surreal. After a while I said to the young woman, "I have to be getting back." She started to walk with me a block or so, and then I told her she was free to go on her way. I'd be OK, I'd find my way back. Cabrini wasn't really that far from Moody anyway. I gave her and her children hugs and thanked her. I remember saying that I wished I could do more for her, but I just didn't have that much money. She assured me the $5 I had given her was a blessing.

On my way back to Moody I placed a phone call home to my parents on one of the old public street phones in the city. I felt larger than life. I felt grown and independent. I wanted to let my parents share in that part of my journey. I was in Chicago on my own.

I often long to return to those days of what seemed like innocence in my younger years. I just wanted to set out and change the world.

That fall of 1990 into the winter of 1991 I really started to grow in my spiritual walk with a lot of assistance from my newfound friend, Rick Kramer. We each held the other accountable. I'd never experienced such a friendship before.

We went to see the legendary contemporary Christian music artist Steven Curtis Chapman in concert that winter in the Akron/Canton area. Chapman's hit single, "For the Sake of the Call," would become my battle cry. Steven took the stage that night, the lights came on, and all you heard was choral voices in the background singing loudly, "We will abandon it all, For the Sake of the Call, no other reason at all, For the Sake of the Call, Holy, Devoted, to live and to die For the Sake of the Call."

And then one light came on in the middle of the stage where Steven appeared. He started to sing the lyrics. It was thunderous. The building shook. I had tears coming down my face.

In that moment I knew that I was going to Haiti. God was speaking to me. What a privilege it was I felt. My body was on fire. I was chosen by the Almighty God of Heaven and Earth. If He is for me, nobody in the universe can stand against me.

I left that night with a feeling that, to this day, I can't even explain to do it justice. These feelings and emotions would give me a relentless courage that has never left me in this life. I would ultimately become the modern-day disciple Peter. I would be the first one to defend Jesus with a sword of passion, yet be the first to deny him with ego driven pride and selfish actions. I'd break His heart while breaking one Old Testament commandment after another in the years ahead. I've broken nine of the ten to date.

In February 1991 came the Ohio State High School basketball playoffs. In the Regional Semifinals Barberton played and beat Cuyahoga Falls. It was particularly tough for me to sit by and watch because I would have been playing for one of those two teams. To this very day I always say that I was the missing piece for both the Barberton and Cuyahoga Falls state title hopes, respectively. Had I been playing for Barberton, the Magics team would have possessed a guard that was capable of causing St. Joe's All State point guard Tony Miller a lot of grief.

Barberton would lose to St. Joe's in the Regional Final. The Falls team lacked a guard to play alongside and compliment Landon Hackim in their backcourt. I would have been a perfect fit for them.

I remember watching those games passionately and rooting against my own school. I was rooting against the same guys I had once gone to battle with. I was thrilled when they lost in that regional final. I was home beating my chest. Those guys didn't have a chance in hell to win without me, I said. It was sort of the vindication I was looking for. A feeling that truly has never left me.

This was where things got really blurry.

The spiritual transformation that I was going through would kind of soften those hard feelings I had against the Barberton basketball program's coaches and players. But not entirely. I was very selfish and angry that my basketball life had prematurely ended the way it did. I blamed the coaches. I was supposed to be a big part of winning a state championship for Barberton. I felt as though the coaches robbed all of us hometown Barberton kids of that moment by making some selfish politically driven moves of their own, particularly by bringing in the two brothers who weren't from here. That move ultimately cost them me and Jason Ondrus. Nick Karabatsos would end up transferring to another school. In my heart and in my mind I was convinced that the three of us absent from the team cost Barberton a state title in 1991. Nobody could tell me any different.

I often wonder if I'm the only one who still takes it this hard. I wasn't even part of the team in '91. This would set precedent for how the rest of my life would play out. On the inside, I was always at war, with a dark spiritual battle playing out in my heart, mind, and soul. As I've been writing this book, these battles have not ceased. I'm still very much haunted by past demons.

You often hear of someone giving an incredible testimony. Everyone applauds them for a great story of transformation. Then everyone goes home. What usually goes unmentioned is that the fight never ends after returning home. The persecution from the enemy only intensifies. Each human being, no matter how good or clean, is always one bad decision or one momentary slip up away from downfall. Pride, ego, greed, and selfishness play a big role in a young man's life. Pray without ceasing, the Bible says. It's for good reason it says that. Here I was coming into my own, truly starting to find myself as a young man, but I got caught back up in my feelings about the Barberton basketball situation that seemed to continue to haunt me. I would look on my former coaches and teammates with great contempt for years to come. And for what? I didn't have girlfriends in school, I had basketball. I didn't want to let go but I had to. I had to let go and let God!

Events to come in the spring of 1991 would soon put it all to rest and send me onward to my destiny!

I was now really starting to feel God speaking to me in the form of dreams and other things concerning Haiti. I remember one time waking up with low blood sugar in the middle of the night. I went downstairs to get some orange juice and cereal. I turned on the TV at 2:30 a.m. and there was a news story about Haiti. On another occasion I came across a magazine with a picture of a child lying on a cardboard box. The caption read "Cite Soleil." I said, "That's where I want to go." At every turn Haiti seemed to be front and center.

88

I started going to the Barberton Public Library with Rick every day after school, not so much to study, but to look at as many books about Haiti as I could get my hands on. I went through every book the library had with Haiti in its title. I specifically remember reading one book that mentioned a foreigner living in Port-au-Prince as a shadowy figure. Unbeknownst to me, twenty-one years later, that shadowy figure would manifest in me.

While making the daily afternoon trek to the library I noticed two very beautiful young girls that were always sitting together at the same table occupied with their school work. They were students at the private girls' school, Our Lady of the Elms in Akron. Ana Usero was the older one. She was an exchange student from Spain. Alysia Muffet, her friend, was a freshman who lived in Barberton. Alysia's family was playing host to Ana. I was really taken aback by Alysia. She was really cute and I was smitten by her.

During my high school years I never once went to a dance. I'd end up spending my senior prom passing out gospel tracks to other students with Rick. I had one girlfriend, Eleanor Hess, who was a senior while I was a junior. I met her the spring of my junior year. She was a volunteer working in Nurse Ryan's office. I faked low blood sugar one day just to have an opportunity to be close to her. It worked, and before you knew it, Eleanor and I were a happening, at least I thought so. Only problem was that she was taken by a guy that was already out of school. He was driving and had a job. I couldn't compete with that.

After a couple months I told Eleanor that she had to make a decision. I gave her an ultimatum. I said with great conviction, "It's either him or me." Certainly she'd pick me, I thought. I was an athlete, I was better looking. I was gold. She had been with him before me, and he was her first love, so she chose him. I was devastated and heart broken. But I'd get over it!

My inexperience with girls, mostly due to my real love, the game of basketball, put me in a situation where I didn't really know how to present myself to Alysia. If there was such thing as love at first sight I was crushing hard.

My time getting to know Alysia would be short-lived, however. I would be graduating soon and my life was on a collision course with destiny. Besides, I didn't have the courage to tell Alysia how I felt about her. She would be the one female that, from time to time for the rest of my adult life, I would think about and ponder, what if?

One day while at the library in the month of May I saw a flier about a man named Dr. Stuart Merriam who was a World War ll veteran and had started a Christian mission in Papua New Guinea. He was scheduled to speak at the Barberton Evangelical Friends Church. He was to be accompanied by four natives of that country. The five of them were on the flier: this white man flanked by four dark-skin blacks from New Guinea. The natives were all dressed in garb from their homeland.

I was transfixed on this photo. They were visiting the Friends Church, right next to U.L. Light Middle School, on a Friday night. I got there early and took a seat towards the front on the left-hand side. I remember thinking to myself, "Where are all the people?" The turnout was low, but I didn't mind. I preferred it that way. I was so excited.

Suddenly the building started to shake. A loud noise and pounding of drums erupted inside the church. These four natives to the eastern half of the island of New Guinea came running in, chanting war cries in their native tongue. It was incredible. My heart was pounding. That was the most enthralling thing I'd ever witnessed.

The world wasn't aware that people even existed on the island before World War ll. The natives were described as savage cannibals. Warrior killers.

They all raced up to the front by the pulpit and assumed their war positions.

I was completely locked in. Then Dr. Merriam appeared and introduced the four horsemen that he had brought with him all the way from Papua New Guinea. There was Patrick Osborn, Kege Yasinamo, Mack Yasinamo, and Jason Pake. Patrick and Kege were older. Mack was my age, and Jason was only six, but he carried himself in a much older and mature fashion. Dr. Merriam explained what we had just witnessed, the meaning of it all. He would go on to speak for about the next twenty minutes or so but I didn't hear a thing he said. My eyes were zoned in on the four natives. I watched their every move.

Before I left that night I took one of the pamphlets they were passing out. My eyes lit up immediately. I saw that they were coming to Manchester

90

Trinity Chapel the following week. I went home and told my parents all about it. I begged them to call the pastor of Trinity Chapel and volunteer us as a host family. In a matter of forty-eight hours we got word that we would be playing host family to the two young boys, Mack and Jason. I was never so thrilled in all my life. My dreams and visions of going to Haiti were now coming alive through this team that had come all the way to Barberton from halfway across the world.

The day came for their arrival. We went out to the church to pick the boys up. I was so proud to take them home with us. My mom had prepared her legendary sloppy joes recipe for dinner that evening. Mack and Jason loved it. After dinner I took them out on a long walk around my neighborhood. As the sun started to set we ended up at the Memorial School playground, just sitting and talking. I was leaning on every accented word that came from both Mack and Jason's lips. My brother Jon brought his telescope down to the school field so that we could look up into the solar system and see the planets, moon, and stars. Mack and Jason had never seen anything like it. It was such great fun to watch them experience things like this for the very first time and see their reactions.

Seeing Jason interact with everyone was a real treat. He was so full of life and asked many questions. He wanted to know about everything. He was experiencing a new world. Much younger than Mack, he had more of a carefree, unashamed approach to everything, which made it a very special experience. My God, I thought, was this heaven? I had to pinch myself. As we laid in bed my conversation with Mack went late into the night.

Sunday came and we all went to church together. We even took my friends Rick, Tim, and Frank. Dr. Merriam and the guys put on the same show for us at church as they did the week before in Barberton. And just like that they were gone. Onto the next church, and the next state. I wanted that weekend to last forever. It went by so incredibly fast. They'd stay on in my heart and in my mind.

Graduation day, as I started to make my climb up a small flight of stairs to cross the stage at E.J. Thomas Hall in Akron, Ohio, to receive my diploma, I was met by Mr. Dague. He was congratulating every student and quickly asking each one of us what our plans were for the future. What was next?

I looked at him with great pride and said, "I'm going to Haiti."

His eyes got big and round like saucers. "REALLY?" he said in great astonishment.

I said, "Yes sir!"

He said, "Wow, that's very interesting, good luck!"

Of course at that point I still had no idea how I was actually getting to Haiti. All I knew was that I was going.

POST-GRADUATION, SUMMER OF 1991

I picked up a job as a busser/dishwasher at one of the chicken houses on the west side that Barberton is nationally famous for. July would quickly roll around. I was now a month removed from graduation.

One night my dad said, "What are you now planning to do with your life going forward?"

Without batting an eye, I said "Dad, I've told you before, I'm going to Haiti."

My dad flew into a tantrum. He was so pissed off. He said, "What in the hell are you talking about, going to Haiti? With what? With who? How? Where? When?"

He was cursing in between all those questions. "Get the hell outta here," he said.

I knew my dad believed in God, and I knew he was born again, so how could he not understand? I think with most people of faith, just like in my dad's case, people say that they believe, but most don't really believe. It's usually more lip service than anything else. It's protocol as far as Christian speech is concerned.

My dad went to bed furious that night. I had gone upstairs after being berated by him, feeling a tremendous burden to somehow prove to my father that this was God's doing and not mine. I sat on my bed, opened up the same little Gideon New Testament Bible I got from my dad twelve years earlier, and I turned the radio on to a Christian station called WHLO on AM radio. Within moments there was a commercial talking about the country of Haiti.

I literally started to tear up. God was talking to me. I needed to somehow, someway, get my dad to hear this same message from God.

The very next morning God delivered His message loud and clear.

We awoke to see my father on the living room floor, having a heart attack. My dad was a drinker and a smoker. But he was also a runner.

Years earlier, when I was in grade school, I took him out to run with me at Crisman Park. He couldn't make it to the park and back without stopping that first time out. He stuck with it, though, and ended up becoming a distance runner. He soon ran his first 5K, and eventually ran up to a half-marathon distance. On this particular morning he had just come in from a run. He always ran in the early morning hours. Tim Widner who had spent the night with us, upon hearing my mom's initial cries that my pops was having a heart attack, came running down the steps and right out the front door in a panic. My dad had always been like a father to Tim so he was very emotional and terrified to see my dad in that state on the floor. He loved my father.

I came running down behind him. I was yelling and cursing, "Fuck, what the fuck? Did you call 911?" I screamed at my mother.

"Yes," she said.

I could barely look at my father, who was coughing and choking and rolling around on the floor. Time slowed down in those horrifying several minutes. I went out onto the front porch to clear away the chairs to make room for the medical personnel that would be arriving. I wanted to make sure they had clear passage and easy accessibility. I was cursing them for their tardiness and when the paramedics arrived I reprimanded them for taking so long. They started to work on my father, who was sprawled on the floor. One of the paramedics said to the other that it didn't look good. My dad would recount later to us he remembered hearing that.

They hurried my pops out the door on the gurney and into the ambulance and I was overcome with great despair. Had I caused this? Was my dad's cardiac arrest from the stress I put him through? That was a low point for me.

93

My father would pull through, all thanks to the God of Abraham, Isaac, and Jacob. I was very grateful. The message from God was sent however. And in the coming days God would reveal His will.

What was coming on the horizon would be extraordinary.

My mom had made a trip to the bank a few weeks later, but this wasn't any old trip to the bank. She returned home with a look on her face like she had seen a ghost. I remember it vividly. She looked at me almost as though she'd been transported into a different dimension. She wasn't really looking at me but through me into my soul. She was very pale.

She said to me, "You're not gonna believe this. I just came from the bank where I spoke to my friend Janet that works there as a teller."

Janet said to my mother, "So what is Jason planning on doing now that he's out of school?"

My mom said, "Oh he's got some crazy idea that he's gonna go to Haiti. Can you believe that? He's been driving his father mad with this crazy talk."

Those words weren't yet dry coming off my mother's lips and the pen dropped from Janet's hand. A man, Janet said, had left moments before who was looking for someone to go to Haiti for him.

Complete silence fell over the both of them. It was this one improbable moment frozen in time that would literally set forth into motion events that would alter the course of history in the lives of hundreds and thousands of people in the days, weeks, and years to come.

My mom was well aware of the grief that everyone had given me since October of 1990 when I had announced, upon returning home from my trip to Chicago, that I was going to Haiti after high school. I had been ridiculed by friends and family alike who would say things like, "It's just a crazy idea. Something is wrong with you."

It was during these days in the summer of '91 that my family and friends would be afforded the chance to see real faith playing itself out right in front of their eyes. I never let anyone discourage me. I trusted God and Him alone. Everyone in my life at that time would never look at me the same way ever again.

Telephone numbers were now exchanged via Janet at the bank. A phone call was placed. The man who had made his way into the bank on that fateful day was eighty-year-old Reverend George Hawthorn, from Scotland. George was a Methodist preacher. He had been involved in Haiti since about 1974. He had founded the Haiti Gospel Mission in Jeremie, Haiti.

After speaking with George over the phone we set up a day and time to meet. George came to pick me up since I was not currently driving and didn't have a car. He came to my house, introduced himself to my parents, and we headed out. He asked me if I was OK with going to Bob Evans to eat. I was like, sure, I didn't care where we went. All I was interested in was when I was going to Haiti.

At Bob Evans he asked me what I'd like to eat. I said, "I'll have a Diet Coke." I wasn't the slightest bit hungry or in the mood to eat. The only appetite I had was for Haiti.

George looked at me like, are you kidding me? "This is Bob Evans, I'm buying, you don't want anything?" I think he may have been embarrassed to be sitting there eating by himself.

He ordered for himself and asked me again what I'd like. With quick wit I said my sugar was high, which was why I couldn't eat. That seemed to put him at ease.

The conversation started and it seemed very clear to me early on that George was every bit of his eighty years of age as far as his mental state was concerned. He wasn't as sharp with his speech, and he was very redundant.

He said, "So you want to go to Haiti?"

I said yes sir, and quickly gave him a brief rundown on the past nine to ten months of my life. That was done in a matter of fact way to let the reverend know that I was called and chosen by God Himself to go to Haiti. I thought it important for me to make that very clear to him.

He said, "Have you ever given a sermon? Can you preach?"

I said, "No I haven't," but I assured him that if, in fact, that was a requirement I'd be more than willing and able to do so. Truth be told I wanted absolutely no part of doing any preaching whatsoever. In my own mind I already had visions of being a great leader of men, and it looked nothing like preaching in a church.

George then cut to the chase and got right down to the heart of what he wanted from me. He told me as matter-of-factly as he could, "I need you to take over running an orphanage and a church for me. I have a Haitian lady named Yvrose that is currently running it for me but I am very displeased with her and I need someone to step in and take the helm."

He then told me how his wife, Madalyn, had died several years earlier and that he had recently remarried a lady from The Philippines. His new wife's name was Fe. She was half the reverend's age, at thirty-nine and pushing forty. He went on to add that Yvrose was not fond of his decision to remarry. Yvrose knew George's late wife and didn't think he should be getting remarried. She looked on Fe with great contempt. Yvrose had recently been on a trip from Haiti to the United States where she had come to Barberton to visit with George. The visit didn't go very well as Yvrose and Fe had an exchange of words which put George in a difficult position. He wouldn't go against his beautiful 39-year-old bride from The Philippines and side with Yvrose, who was roughly the same age as Fe.

I listened. Then the meeting took a turn into an entirely different direction. A man that George referred to as Brother Berkley walked in and seated himself at the table with us. He kind of had an aura of arrogance about him but it didn't really bother me. This Brother Berkley then started to give me his resume with credentials a mile long. He was involved in financial support of George's mission in Haiti. Berkley then said something that shocked me to my core. I'll never forget it. I can still hear him in his arrogant, white-privileged voice, almost as if he was a plantation owner of slaves from hundreds of years ago.

He said, "Don't be messing with any of them girls down there."

I said, "Excuse me?"

"There are a lot of young women down there," he said. "So make sure you ain't getting involved with any of them."

At this point in my life I hadn't really ever had a serious girlfriend. Girls were the last thing on my mind. I wasn't even thinking about being in a relationship of any sorts with Haitian girls. It really had never crossed my mind. Then he said arguably the most astonishing thing that I'd ever hear in my entire life. He said there was an American down there named Bob that visited Jeremie from time to time, and that he was always messing with the Haitian girls. He said, "I guess the longer you're there, the better looking they get. I just don't understand it," and he shook his head in disgust.

I nearly fell out of my seat. I was in a state of disbelief. How could this Christian man who served God speak in such a manner? He was a blatant racist! I moved quickly to respond.

"I'm focused on doing what God has sent me to do," I said. I knew that he would understand that kind of Christian lingo. All the while Berkley talked, George was literally scarfing down the food on his plate with no regard for human life.

It's tough for me to recount this in great detail this many years removed. I can still see and hear the both of them sitting at that table. It was the most bizarre meeting I could have ever imagined. It couldn't end fast enough.

But if tolerating Reverend Hawthorn and Brother Berkley were what it cost to go to Haiti, I would gladly do it. Haiti was my focus. Besides, I just needed to get there. God would certainly lead me upon my arrival to the country. *Fuck these guys*, I thought.

The very next day George called me on the phone to ask me things he evidently forgot to cover in our meeting. He was definitely going senile in my opinion. He asked if I had my driver's license. I responded that, no, I didn't yet have my license. He said, "Well, can you see about getting it before you go? I have a truck down there that I'd like you to drive."

I had, on two previous occasions, driven my dad's old blue station wagon so I knew I could drive. I said to him that I would become a resident of Haiti and get my license down there.

He then said, "Do you have a passport?" I said no, I don't. Back then protocol didn't require American citizens to even have a passport to travel to Haiti. I found that information out through making a few phone calls. Whatever it took, I needed to get to Haiti and get there fast. Getting a driver's license and a passport would just slow down the process of getting there and I was not going to let those things deter me or slow me down at this point.

"I'll be damned," I said to myself.

A ticket was purchased. I'd be leaving on Tuesday, August 27, 1991. Now all that was left to do was wait. The birth of Zeke of Haiti was imminent.

Photo by Guerly Photo, Jérémie

PART THREE
SEARCHING FOR MY 'WHY?'

The night of August 26th, 1991 . . . the hour had finally arrived.

For the last ten months I had been preparing myself for this moment. With everyone in my family off to bed, I had some quiet time alone to reflect on this long journey that only I had believed in. The anticipation of tomorrow's historic happenings was incredible. I couldn't sleep at all nor did I want to. My juices were flowing. Since I wasn't going to bed I grabbed a cassette and put it into the old VCR we had. On this particular cassette was the 1989 war film *Glory*. I hadn't yet seen it so I was intrigued. The movie depicts the events of Colonel Robert Gould Shaw, played by Matthew Broderick, leading the first all African-American regiment, the 54th Massachusetts Volunteer Infantry during the Civil War. Colonel Shaw puts together a strong and proud unit of black soldiers while fighting prejudices from both his own Union Army and the Confederates. The character that really brought the film to life for me was Trip, an escaped slave played by Denzel Washington.

As the movie ended I remembered the dumping of dead black soldiers into a mass grave where Colonel Shaw ended up laying side by side with Trip. Shaw had Trip flogged by whip earlier in the film for punishment after trying to escape. At one point in the film Trip told Shaw that he wouldn't carry his flag, and that they were all in a real fucked-up situation. Trip said, "We are all covered in dirt, "ain't none of us clean." In the film's final battle at Fort Wagner, Shaw leads the attack on the fort and is gunned down by a hail of bullets. Upon seeing this, Trip is moved with great passion by Shaw's example of bravery, runs to grab the flag, the one he had said he would not carry, and turns to urge all the other black soldiers to "Come

On!" He then is gunned down.

The film was intoxicatingly right for the eve of my first trip to Haiti. "Give 'em Hell 54" vibrated inside of me. I was inspired by the courage and sacrifice of both Shaw and Trip. It was on this night that I truly started to believe in destiny. I believed that the Hand of God was resting on my shoulder. It's a feeling to this day that I still can't explain. I had chills running throughout my core. I didn't know how, but I did believe that God was going to use me to do great things!

At about 4:30 a.m. I was getting ready to leave with my dad to head up to the Cleveland Hopkins International Airport. My mom appeared from her bedroom. Tears were flowing down her face. She did not want me to go. Only a mother can know such emotions I think. She told me she loved me and to be very careful. I assured her that I'd be OK and told her not to worry and I'd call her the first chance I got.

"I love you," I said.

Although it was my father that I took after, my mother was the one I really looked up to. She was the heart and soul of the Petrie family. Alas, me and my pops were off. The drive to Cleveland was pretty quiet. My dad was really proud of me. This moment was for him just as much as it was for me. Together we both believed in a higher calling.

I stepped out of the car and got my luggage situated. My dad came over to me and we embraced. He said, "I love you son."

"I love you too, dad."

And just like that the umbilical cord was cut from both my parents. It was my time to fly, and I was gone with the wind.

AUGUST 27, 1991 – THE JOURNEY TO HAITI BEGINS

I said a prayer, boarded my plane, and was off to Raleigh Durham, North Carolina. From there I'd fly to Miami. While at the gate in Miami waiting to board the flight to Port-au-Prince I was noticing a lot of nicely dressed people. I, on the other hand, was in shorts and a t-shirt. I was about to go to the world's first black republic, often referred to as the black Sparta. It felt like I was going to the Africa of the Western Hemisphere. I had only ever seen Haiti in the news, from books I had read at the library, from the movie *The Serpent and the Rainbow*, and from a photo in a magazine where a small naked child laid on a cardboard box in the slum of Cite Soleil. In my mind I had my own visions of what Haiti looked like, and it wasn't a picture of people in suits and ties. I had no idea what to fully expect. All I knew was that I was young and full of energy, and that God had sent me here.

"We are beginning our descent into Port-au-Prince, Haiti. Please fasten your seatbelts, return your seats to their full and upright position, and stow away your tray tables. The flight attendants will make their final rounds to collect any items you wish to discard."

The pilot's announcement shook me from my gaze down on the barren, mountainous terrain. The sparkly, crystal blue sea was so inviting. The landing gear groaned as it lowered in preparation for landing. Beside me a Haitian woman did the sign of the cross and then raised her hands slightly as she prayed aloud in Creole. I peered out the window again to see hundreds of rusty tin shack roofs reflecting the midday sun. Cite Soleil.

Boom! We hit the tarmac and taxied to the area where we would disembark the plane. A round of applause went up for the pilot mixed in with some heartfelt Hallelujahs for Bondye – God. More signs of the cross. Two sets of stairs were wheeled to the side of the plane. Before the plane fully stopped, it seemed to me that all the Haitians on the plane had already gathered their bags and were standing in the aisle. The fast pace of Haiti started on the airstrip. I slung my backpack over my shoulder, and then was bumped and nudged to the exit by passengers in a hurry to make their way off this bird. The hot, humid air hit me in the face as if I'd opened an oven. There was a funk in the air that smelled like a combination of sewage, sweat, and burning garbage.

"Wow!" I exclaimed, although no one seemed to hear me.

I thought of the men in suits on the plane with me and was so thankful I chose shorts and a t-shirt instead. From the top of the stairs, I looked out to my left. The horizon was painted with mountains beyond mountains, the airport on my right. A chill went down my spine despite the heat. It was sort of an out-of-body experience that was surreal. I had dreamt about this moment. My sense of purpose was strong as I descended the stairs.

Several Haitian policemen awaited the incoming passengers at the bottom of the stairs. Their crisp, pale blue shirts, navy slacks, and dark blue caps almost reminded me of Mr. Ricks, except their stern faces hidden behind black sunglasses, and their oozie submachine guns that were locked and loaded, made me think more of the Tonton Macoutes I'd read about.

Haitian military soldiers dressed in both olive green and khaki uniforms were also flanked on both sides. They wore helmets and held M-16 machine guns. I straightened my posture a little as I walked by them, following the other passengers as we proceeded to walk out onto the tarmac and into the airport where immigration was.

I had seen this movie before but now I was an actor playing in this theatre. It was awe inspiring. I had read about the Duvalier Dynasty of Papa Doc and Baby Doc with their legions of strong armed Tonton Macoutes. I was a kid from Barberton, Ohio, that had big dreams and big visions. I had the audacity to believe that God sent me here to play on this big stage. While I looked around for where I was supposed to go next, people hurriedly cut in front of me.

My mind darted to Yvrose. *Will she know what I look like? How much does she know about why I'm really here?*

I wiped away a bead of sweat that already formed on my brow. I was used to the stifling Midwest summers, but coming out of that nice air-conditioned airplane, my body was still trying to adjust to the sweltering tropics.

I pulled out the green immigration form as I approached the counter. "Bonswa," the official behind the desk bellowed, "Passport and immigration forms please" and he reached for them with his large, ebony hand. I said I didn't have a passport, but I did have an Ohio State ID and my birth certificate. I handed them over. The official reviewed them, he stamped the back of my birth certificate and signed it, "Welcome to Haiti." I heard music as I rounded the corner past the immigration counter – nylon stringed guitars, banjos, goat skin drums, and maracas keeping a lively rhythm I'd never heard before, yet made me feel right at home. A group of men dressed in red shirts cheerfully greeted the arriving passengers with true Haitian hospitality. An older man with leathery skin and a handful of teeth belted out the lyrics in a deep, raspy voice. Twoubadou music first hit Haiti's shores in the early twentieth century. The music migrated from Cuba via Haitian sugar cane field workers coming back home. It has an easy going island vibe fused with Latin flair. The songs tend to be about hard peasant life, lovers, or both, and are sung with great spirit. I stood there a moment soaking in the culture, a twinkle in my eye, before continuing on. I felt that I was right where I was supposed to be. I felt at home.

As I headed out of the airport entrance Yvrose was standing right there waiting for me amid a deep sea of black faces. A scene from biblical times it was. In that moment the Bible was about to finally feel real to me. Everything I was taught in Sunday school at church growing up would come to life.

I walked through a maze of humanity. The Haiti heat increased among all those bodies.

The first face I locked in on was a dark-skinned black man with very big lips. He only had one leg and was using crutches. His name was Johnny. He had his hands outstretched and asked me for money in broken choppy English.

I walked along with Yvrose, luggage in tow. There must have been a thousand hands reaching and grabbing in my direction.

"Blan, Blan, banm yon bagay blan."
"White man, white man, give me something, white man."

I was perspiring like never before. A very slim, dark-skinned man wearing black shades and a top hat quickly approached us. He grabbed my luggage and threw it into the trunk of his vehicle. I had offered him my assistance with the luggage but he hastily declined my help almost as if he was annoyed that I'd even suggest helping him. This guy was a professional and that was made evident. Yvrose sat up front and I took my place in the back.

We drove through an incredible sea of black bodies. Palms of hands extended in the direction of our car. We were in an old-school, black crown Victoria that was kept in pristine condition, especially on the inside. I was drenched in sweat. The air conditioning was relieving. The tropical heat could be devastating in comparison to where I was from in Ohio.

105

Our driver, who resembled an old Tonton Macoute, was shewing away in disgust anyone that approached the car asking for handouts. There was so much congestion with traffic that it was stop and start for what seemed like forever. I never imagined Haiti having so many cars.

We finally arrived at Madam Carrier's house in Delmas. I only knew this particular information because George had written it on a piece of paper for me. Upon arriving I was shown to the room I would be sleeping in. I was told that they would call me for dinner after a while.

After everything I had been through up to that moment just to get to Haiti, I wasn't going to just sit in some private guest house bedroom in silence waiting for dinner to be served. My dreams and visions had me showing up, mounting a horse, and riding into the mountains. This house in Delmas looked nothing like my dreams. I got up, found Yvrose in another room in the house, and said to her, "I'm gonna go out for a walk."

She was hesitant to agree but I insisted I'd be fine. Although to this day I don't remember what part of Delmas I was in, I do remember that Madam Carrier's house was real close to the main Delmas strip that ran from Petionville all the way to downtown Port-au-Prince. I headed out and quickly arrived on that busy strip. I took a right and started walking downward. It was bustling with traffic and people everywhere. That's a scene I can still see in my mind. It was far more intense than Cabrini Green in Chicago. It seemed like there were a thousand eyes fixated on me (that soon would become like a drug). There were black people for miles, coming and going.

I was pretending to walk as though I had some intended destination, but all I really wanted to do was officially announce to the Haitian people that I was here. I moved along ever so confidently. It was my feeling out process. I walked for probably about a mile or so, then I turned around and headed back up from where I came from. Much of Delmas has the same look to it so I had remembered some landmarks to make sure I made it back OK. That two miles was my official introduction to Haiti. That may have been the only time in all my years in Haiti while out in public view of the masses that I was never approached or asked for anything.

When I returned to the house both Madam Carrier and Yvrose seemed a little upset with me for being gone so long. They were worried. I felt a

106

little embarrassed and assured them that I was alright. What I would find out in years to come was that in most cases, when whites come to Haiti for whatever reason, they are very sheltered by whoever is playing host to them, whether it be Haitian or American. I wouldn't be subjected to any of that sort of nonsense, however. I was different, I was the exception. God had sent me here.

Yvrose informed me during dinner that the next morning we would be flying out to Jeremie. In my room that night I pulled out a tape recorder I had brought with me to log voice entries for a journal I decided to keep. Lawrence of Arabia kept one, and so, inspired by him, I would also. After recording for several minutes the happenings of the last twenty-four hours, I made the mistake of playing it back and listening to it. I thought it sounded stupid. I said right there and then never again. My journal keeping days were already over. That decision would arguably be the biggest mistake I'd ever make in those early days in Haiti. I'd do anything to get that back all these years later, along with so many intimate details I'll never be able to recount.

The next morning couldn't get here quick enough. I felt as though there would be something waiting for me in Jeremie, and I needed to get there to see for myself. It was a miserably long night at Madam Carriers. It was very hot. The mosquitoes must have known they had a rookie in town because they ate me alive. There was no electricity that night so the fan in my room was of no use, which would more often than not be the case during my years in Haiti. It was paramount that I'd have to get used to being uncomfortable.

Morning came and we were off to the airport. We would fly to Jeremie on a Mission Aviation Flight. It was a smaller plane that fit about eight people. The pilot asked me if I would like to sit up front with him and wear a headset. He didn't have to ask me twice. This was some Indiana Jones type stuff that I was looking forward to.

During the forty-five-minute flight to Jeremie I chatted with the pilot and he pointed out some things about the landscape. As we started our descent I got a quick scare. Coming down the view looked like something out of a Vietnam war movie. We got closer and closer to the ground and I saw no runway whatsoever. I looked over at the pilot and he was so involved and intense with the controls. It was windy. I was bracing myself. We started coming down, almost touching the tops of the palm trees.

Then, out of nowhere, a dirt landing strip appeared. There was about sixty seconds that passed where I was really concerned, although I wasn't going to let the pilot see that. I was now feet on the ground in the Haitian countryside. Certainly God would have something waiting for me. In the back of my mind I was remembering why George had chosen to send me. It seemed like such an overwhelming task for an 18-year-old to actually take upon himself in a foreign land. I never really ever looked at it as George sending me however. It was God who sent me in my mind. And for me personally, the orphanage and church business wasn't as sexy as my dreams of being a great leader. I wanted and expected something far more grandiose.

The dark Beige Mitsubishi truck that George had talked with me about driving was sitting underneath a tree at this primitive airport in a place they called Nimewo 2 in Jeremie. We got in and headed towards town. It was a few miles of dirt road and countryside living all the way back into the city of Jeremie. Naked and barefoot kids ran amuck around small thatched huts on both sides of the road. Biblical times came to life here. There were goats and sheep scattered about. I saw cows, a man riding a horse, and an uncooperative donkey that was reluctantly crossing the road right in front of us. The donkey sent a back kick right into the grill of the Mitsubishi truck. It sounded like a bomb going off.

Yvrose quickly stopped the car and jumped out to verbally scold the donkey's owner. The man was very discouraged with the ass he was trying so hard to dictate direction to. Yvrose was giving to the man what Haitians refer to as presyon – basically applying heat or pressure verbally with the knowledge that you have no real intention on taking any action against said person. It's really fascinating theatre in Haiti on a daily basis, watching confrontations brought about by daily life struggles.

As we got closer and closer to town my head was on a swivel. I was taking it all in. From time to time Yvrose stopped and made small talk to the locals and handed out petty change, another gesture often shown to the poor in Haiti by those that have. We made a quick stop at a boutique that Yvrose had downtown. We finally arrived in Caracolie where the

108

orphanage was located. The entrance was blocked by a big metal gate that was locked from the inside. Yvrose beeped the horn several times and moments later a very abnormally small black man with a hunchback named Celi-Pierre pushed open the gate. We entered and went all the way to the back. I got out of the truck and was greeted by scores of young, smiling black faces. At that time there were roughly twenty-six kids living in the orphanage. Approximately twenty-one girls of all ages and five boys ages ten and under. The boys were housed in a room out back where the pig pens were kept. Yvrose had a full stock of some pretty big pigs. On occasion, they would kill one to eat, or sell them for money.

Celi-Pierre was responsible for overseeing the boys. The girls were all kept in the main house. They were supervised by a house mother named Maritane. Maritane had two boys of her own. She would become like my Haitian mother. Maritane would constantly ask how I was doing. She'd often ask me if I wanted or needed anything to eat and drink. She would go overboard trying to appease me and make sure that I was always comfortable. I really appreciated her for that. We shared great affection towards each other.

It was very recognizable to me early on that Yvrose had and played favorites. One of the boys named Alphonse, who was nine years old, was a favorite of Yvrose and he was allowed to come in to the main house. He often would be spared sleeping out back and let in the main house to sleep. Alphonse was often forced to endure the ire of the other boys because of the privileges he was given. But in Haiti nothing is free. Nothing is ever as it appears to be. That would come at a cost.

Alphonse had to report the goings on in the back to Yvrose, sometimes pitting him against Celi-Pierre's word on occasion. He would end up spending a lot of time at my side and would become instrumental in my learning of Creole. I made it clear to everyone early on that Alphonse was my guy. Don't fuck with him.

A 4-year-old girl named Jezila was another favorite. Yvrose treated Jezila like her own since she didn't and couldn't have any kids of her own. Jezila could get away with antagonizing the other kids and whether she was right or wrong, you didn't cross her because Yvrose always sided with her.

Then there was a young teenage girl named Maria. Maria spoke some English, much to my surprise. She seemed to have a bittersweet relationship with Yvrose. Almost contemptuous as I saw it. Maria had spent some time in Cincinnati, Ohio, at the home of an African American they called Brother William. From what I was told she went abroad to have an operation on her lower extremity. She had some issue going on with one of her legs that needed to be addressed. They were able to secure a visa for her to receive treatment. The only problem was that Maria had the opportunity to taste the good life in the United States. It was only for a little while, however. Soon she was sent back to the all-too-familiar drudgery she knew as Haiti. We gravitated towards each other because of the English language. She made my transition from English to Creole smoother, at least in the beginning. She would become a slight hindrance at the same time.

My hunger to learn Creole was lessened somewhat because I constantly had Maria to bail me out. During the first forty-eight hours in Jeremie I tried to absorb all that I could. I was forcing myself to commit to believing that this current situation I found myself in was exactly where God wanted me, and I needed to be a good servant and except the fact that holiness is in right action and courage on behalf of those who cannot defend themselves, and goodness.

What God desires is this, I continued to remind myself.

Although George had told me he wanted Yvrose out, she was all I knew at that point. She spoke English and treated me kindly. I was forced to embrace her. I really had no other choice. I was given a room in the very front of the orphanage right next to Yvrose's room. The first night I spent in that room I was greeted by a humongous tarantula in the shower. My initial reaction was *FUCKKKKKKK*. My bedroom had an adjoining bathroom with a shower.

As unsettling as that was it would only get worse.

The electricity was spotty and often non-existent. I fell asleep as often would be the case with a fan blowing on me only to wake up two hours later in a puddle of sweat while being eaten alive by mosquitoes. And I'll never forget that ungodly sound of something big moving about in the pitch darkness of my room. I had no idea what it was but it sounded incredibly loud. It literally sounded like another human being moving around in the room with wings. I started to hear a buzzing sound, much like that of a bumblebee. Going into Haiti I was not aware that there were massive flying cockroaches. Night is when they are a terror. It ended up flying right into the side of my head and had me leaping from my bed in panic. These things usually inhabit the latrines and they reek of a stench that is indescribable. I would often wake up in the mornings during my time in Haiti exhausted. I spent long, dreaded nights of no electricity in the heat, terrorized by mosquitoes and flying cockroaches. It was something I'd learn to endure because I thought this was just part of what you go through when you're called by God. It was a right of passage. Many missionaries would come to Haiti throughout the years feeling called by God. That calling often times didn't last very long because of such inconveniences.

George once mentioned to me that one couple he sent to Haiti for him quickly returned back to the states because they were scared to death to drive in the mountains where the wheel of the vehicle was often times just inches away from a 2,000 foot cliff drop.

On the morning of my second day in Jeremie I headed out with Yvrose to the boutique she had downtown. I'd come to find out later that often times what was donated or sent to the kids in the orphanage by Americans abroad would be placed in her boutique and sold for profit. The boutique had its advantages in my case, however, because it got me from out of the orphanage during the day, which I preferred, and helped me in quickly learning the Haitian gourde and its value or non-value in comparison to the American dollar.

I would have my very first taste of coffee one day while working the boutique. It was a rainy, much cooler, day. Yvrose offered me some coffee. I replied that I'd never had coffee in my life. She poured me some scalding hot black coffee with sugar. I've been drinking coffee ever since.

On this particular day I was introduced to an American missionary couple. At first I was very excited to meet them. That fervor wouldn't last long. The couple was driving a very nice SUV Jeep. The home they were staying in was quite nice compared to that of your average Haitian home. Most notably, they lived isolated from the people and had a big generator to boot. I was very shocked and turned off by this discovery. I thought that this couldn't be what Steven Curtis Chapman was talking about in his song, *For The Sake of The Call*. Missionaries were supposed to become one with the people they were serving.

As I looked closer I noticed a young Haitian girl that seemed unkempt in the home, who was going about and performing house chores. I saw another woman outside of the house washing clothes by hand. I was perplexed. It was all quite bizarre to me.

What blew me away more than anything was the manner in which the white man spoke to these Haitians at his house. Even though I couldn't understand the Creole that was spoken between them, his tone and body language were anything but friendly. When I finally asked him who these people were and what they were doing here, his response to me was a matter of factly "they were hired help."

I recalled this episode years later when I visited the Visa Lodge hotel/ restaurant in Port-au-Prince. I had stopped through to say hello to the brothers that owned it – Jean Michel and Dimitri Carvonis. I was having a drink and chatting with some locals when a white couple came in with a very young black Haitian child to have dinner. I first assumed they were adoptive parents but when I heard them speak Creole I thought that they must be involved in missions of some sort. After sitting for a while waiting to be served the couple grew impatient. The man went out of his way with demonstrative hand gestures and raised his voice in disgust over the slow service. In a matter of moments their waiter appeared, looking disheveled. The white man began to speak down to and berate this poor Haitian waiter. He was reprimanding the waiter for being slow and incompetent. He talked to this man like he was less than human. It was jaw dropping to witness.

I bring this up because far too often this would be the narrative in describing the conditions of the modern day mission field in the country of Haiti. Missionaries in Haiti were there to be served and not to do the serving. This, of course, was devastating for me as a young man who believed in God and who was trying to do right by Him. I felt as though I had been duped by Christians. Was it at all possible that being a missionary was like this everywhere and not just in Haiti? It was more of that same negative sentiment I had towards whites in my younger days as a kid. The

112

whites to me were far more egregious than blacks could ever be.

If all that wasn't depressing enough to my young spirit, soon there were more disheartening scenes to witness. In my first two weeks in Jeremie I went to the prison downtown a couple of times to feed the prisoners who lived in a God-awful predicament inside those walls. It was like being in a dungeon. I would go from cell to cell, passing out bread. Yvrose would also take care of the guards at the prison with gestures of food handouts and small monies exchanged. Then there were a few occasions where poor mothers would come with their children in hand wanting to give them away.

Yvrose and Celi-Pierre would move hastily to shoo away children that looked ill and sickly, yet would quickly embrace and entertain the idea of taking in the kids that looked more healthy and attractive. I watched all this with a heightened sense of urgency. To try and better understand the Haitian people I would often just sit in silence and observe them from afar as they interacted with exaggerated body language and emotional, very loud, and unreserved speech.

It can be very lonely when you're in a foreign land and you can't understand what people are saying. Not just lonely but frustrating and very irritating. Often I'd hear everyone laughing and glancing in my direction and wonder, geez, are they laughing at me? I hated that feeling. I was already annoyed that nobody could say my name Jason correctly. They would always call me Jackson. One day I said just call me Zeke. That was easy for everyone and they loved it. I was never called Jason again in Haiti until May of 2012.

The only cure to make the loneliness birds go away was to learn the language so that I was no longer dependent on others like Yvrose and Maria to speak for me, or to leave it in their hands to give me proper translation. How could I know that they were always telling me the truth? I would be told in years to come that I speak better Creole than many Haitians. That was said to me often because of how bright I was, and not necessarily because I spoke better Creole than natives of the island.

The most fatal mistake over the decades in Haiti, and I'm sure in every other country around the globe, revolves round leaving it up to others to speak for you, because your fate often lies with those who bathe in ignorance. Studying the every move of Haitians would become a full time job for me. I was so obsessed and invested emotionally in this endeavor. I remember one time sitting outside of the orphanage in silence, watching a group of Haitians fight and argue. I was moved to tears. I so badly wanted to engage them in dialogue, but couldn't.

This has got to change, I said to myself. And change it would!

On days that I didn't go downtown to the boutique I could be found back at the orphanage trying to get to know the kids better. Getting to know names and personalities was a full-time job. I played a lot of soccer with the boys in the hot sun. Most of them wouldn't last long in that blazing heat. They would always ask me, "Do you not feel the sun blan? Is it not hot for you too?"

With the younger girls I would play jump rope, rock-paper-scissors, and hot hands. They loved that kind of playful intimacy. They'd want to touch my hair and my skin. A young girl named Rositha would often pinch me and say, "Eske li fe mal?" ("Does it hurt?") She was curious to know if I felt the same pains that she did. They were all very much intrigued when a blan was accessible to them. They were always full of questions.

The older girls were mostly stand-offish and usually didn't give me the time of day. A couple of them were very flirtatious and outgoing, however. On one particular afternoon I asked Alphonse and Maria to walk with me into the back hills of Caracolie. We scaled the orphanage back wall and turned left. That would take us there.

Up in that area people lived in the stone age. Thatched huts went on for days with butt ass naked kids running everywhere. All you could hear from the mouths of the children was, "Blan, blan, gad yon blan." ("White man, white man, look at the white man.")

Up in this area you were more likely to cross people who were really a part of the old school Haitian folklore culture of practicing Vodou. Haitians that served the spirit world were easy to find in this vicinity. In this area I came across many of the same women that came to Yvrose's church to get free rice handouts. Up here they'd be found dancing to the beat of the Vodou drums. Nothing in Haiti is ever as it appears. Late at night you could hear the Vodou drums blasting away with music and chanting well into the early morning hours. Ironically enough, I actually enjoyed hearing this at night. I was embracing the culture. Most Christians go to places like Haiti to save the people from their sins. I went to embrace them for said sins. I really enjoyed hanging out with these people. They were much more engaging than the Christian community in Haiti.

Yvrose would have Church, a Bible study, a youth group, and choir practice almost every night of the week. It was overkill. I often noticed the kids dreading that they had to go so often, and then try hard not to fall asleep while being there. Pretending to be emotionally invested was very important under Yvrose's watchful eye.

George had given Yvrose the blueprint to how Christians did things in the States, and she took it, ran with it, and exaggerated the shit out of it. Again, George's biggest blunder was not learning any Creole and being totally reliant on Yvrose to translate for him. It's very important to note that although not all Haitians practice Vodou, you bet your goddamn bottom dollar they all believe in it. The ones that have the most beautiful smiles and nicest personalities are usually the ones embedded the deepest within the Vodou religion. It was a manipulative balance of different worlds and cultures that to this day has kept Yvrose at the helm of the Haiti Gospel Mission in Jeremie.

When Yvrose found out that I was mingling with the peasants, she wasn't very pleased, and discouraged me from participating in such activities. See, for Yvrose, the more I understood the language, the people, and the culture, the worse it was for her. Keeping me ignorant and dependent on her was everything.

One evening I slipped out back with Alphonse and up into those hills. A man possessed came running into my direction. He went flying by me and scaled right up into a tree effortlessly. He remained perched up in the tree barking and howling like a wild dog. I was transfixed on him. It was the first time I'd ever see anything like it with my own eyes. Vodou was fascinating to me. Years later I find myself in a peristyle in Petionville with hundreds of Haitians crammed into this small space. Drums were pounding, music was blasting, people were in a crazed frenzy. The entire place was vibrating and the ground was shaking and moving underneath

115

my feet. I was soaking it all in as I closed my eyes, wondering what Napoleon Bonaparte's troops must have felt as they heard the Haitian war drums beating and the ground underneath them literally start to tremble on the approach of the Haitian rebel fighters. They must have been terrified.

A tear slowly rolled down my face while I thought about these things. I was so passionate about this place called Haiti. This fact I would start to ponder early and often, and very deeply and profoundly: If the Haitian people used Vodou to smash human slavery around the globe and overcame their white slave captors who were said Catholic Christians that were keeping them enslaved, then how could anyone have the audacity to say they were wrong or bad for that? I'd often ask myself, "Why are white missionaries in Haiti again? We all pray to the same God in Heaven, don't we?"

I would eventually go deeper into the abyss to understand Vodou in more specifics. I wanted to know everything and understand it completely.

Within three to four weeks in Jeremie I just didn't feel right. I felt confined. I didn't feel free. What George wanted and what I wanted did not look the same. I wasn't a real big fan of Yvrose by that time, but I didn't dislike her enough to really have the desire to unseat her from power at this mission. And I was way too green anyway. I felt in my heart that I needed to get back to the States to sit down with Pastor George and have a heart to heart discussion. It couldn't be done over the phone.

I informed Yvrose that I had decided to return to the States to work some things out but didn't get in to any detail with her. She seemed very surprised. Certainly she knew that George would be grilling me with questions about her.

Two things of note would happen in my final few days in Jeremie on this trip. Yvrose and I took the kids on a beach outing to a remote little stretch of sand called Anse d'Azur. It was an isolated strip located down a mountainside not too far from the Jeremie airport in Nimewo 2. We parked the truck off to the side of the dirt road and hiked down the side of a cliff to get to this beautiful body of crystal clear blue water. What appeared to be somewhat similar to a German U-boat, but not confirmed, was sunken right off the coast and visible from the beach. I had remembered seeing it from the air when coming into Jeremie on the plane. The head of it was

116

just barely sticking out of the water, depending on the tide. The kids told me not to swim too far out because this particular body of water was filled with *anpil dyab*, meaning it was infested with many devils and evil spirits.

The kids told me, "Dyab sa yo ap manjew wi, Zeke." ("The devils in that water will eat you.")

Of course I scoffed at that notion. I told them that was nonsense and couldn't be true. I said, "I'm gonna show you guys it's not true," much to their chagrin. They believed what they believed and I couldn't tell them any different. They looked at me as though I had a death wish for even entertaining the idea of testing these evil spirits. You could hear some of the kids saying, "Oh Bondye, oh Bondye." ("Oh God, oh God!")

Without hesitation they ran over to tell Yvrose of my intentions to prove to them that their theory concerning these devils was absolute nonsense. Yvrose hurried over to me and suggested that I don't go too far out. I smiled and told her that I was just going to swim out to the submarine and stand on top of it so the kids could witness for themselves that there was nothing to fear. I had expected her to smile and agree but she just looked at me with a blank stare as though I was a madman.

I motioned to all the kids to watch me as I started swimming out. I got to the submarine, stood on top of it, and waved to everyone. After spending a few moments exploring I swam out a little bit further. When I finally decided to swim back in I had an overwhelming feeling that I was stuck in cement. I tried with great effort to swim hard but I couldn't make any progress. The water was a little choppy and it was pretty windy that day. I continued to struggle. The harder I tried to swim back, the father away from shore I went. I could see everyone on the beach in the distance running around playing and having a good time. I tried to call out to them but nothing came out of my mouth. I was so consumed with just trying to stay afloat at this point I had nothing in my voice box to even utter a peep. Besides, Yvrose and the kids didn't swim. They had told me, they had warned me, and I didn't listen.

The only thing I had going for me was I had the good fortune of being a very good athlete, though at that point I was not in very good condition. As I recount this story I still don't really know how I got back to shore other than on God's favor. I'd love to take credit and say that I was such a beast and that I beat the ocean on that day in a one-on-one duel. That wasn't true. At one point I was straight begging for God to spare me from being swept out to sea. I was whimpering off the coast of Haiti like a little bitch.

And just like that I felt my body become loose in the water. Almost as though I had been washed into a current that pushed me back into shore. I had stopped swimming and was just surviving when this happened. I was gassed with nothing left in the tank. When I finally washed up onto the beach all the kids mobbed me. They were smiling and cheering and laughing. They had no idea where I had just come from, and that just moments earlier I was on the brink. After seeing and feeling the hero's welcome from the kids, I was not about to tell any of them about my plight in the water that they claimed was filled with bad spirits. I laid sprawled out on that sand, looking up to the sky, quietly thanking God.

The kids helped me up and as I came to an upright position, feeling my feet on solid ground, I proudly proclaimed to everyone, "You see guys, there's no such thing as devils and evil spirits in that water." The kids were like, "Wow, that's so cool."

I was such a fucking liar that day. My pride is what mattered most. I'd soon learn though. My God, would I soon learn. This would be the first of my nine lives used up.

In the days before I was to return to Port-au-Prince and then head back to Ohio a couple of things happened that would really throw a monkey wrench into events going forward.

Maria came knocking on my door one evening fighting back tears. She said that she wanted nothing more than to get out of the orphanage and get back to the United States. She told me she didn't like Yvrose. She said that Yvrose wasn't who she appeared to be.

"My matant is not a good person," she proclaimed. (The kids were made to address Yvrose as *matant*, meaning "aunt.") "She lies. She's a dyab." I was taken aback by that proclamation. Maria said, "Please tell Brother William for me. I know he will come for me."

She gave me his address and telephone number in confidence. I assured her that I would do all I could to help her. Two days before I was to leave a white missionary couple, Rosemary and Jay, came by the orphanage. I was scheduled to go out on the same flight as Jay.

The day was here for me to leave. The kids were all very saddened that I was going home. Most of the kids, even the older girls who didn't usually pay me any attention or give me the time of day, all piled in to the back of the truck to take me to the airport. I stood in the truck's bed all the way to the airport, wearing my Sunday's best. I even wore a tie for the occasion. Pastor George had made sure I took a tie along with me to wear for church. This trip to the airport, however, was the only time I wore it.

It was during this fateful trip that one of the teenage girls named Leonne started to show me great affection. She stood next to me in the back of the truck and we were locked arm in arm as we rode out. I had so many outstretched arms and hands grabbing on to me I couldn't decipher who was who. But Leonne was very aggressive and clung tightly to me. Riding on roads in Haiti in the back of a truck is fair reason to hold on tight to anything, or anyone, for that matter. It can often be very dangerous. Leonne holding on to me for dear life was very surprising because I hadn't had much interaction with her my entire time there. She was a very quiet girl. She had beautiful dark black skin. Interestingly, Leonne was a blood cousin to Maria.

There were two other sisters named Gertha and Rositha that were also cousins to both Leonne and Maria. They had told me that they were not originally from Jeremie. They said, "We are from a place far away from here called Monn Kabrit," or Goat Mountain. Of course that revelation left me asking them, "Well, if it's so far away, how in the world did y'all end up here in Jeremie?"

I'd find out soon enough that this was just how the orphanage business in Haiti worked. Kind of like a recruitment of sorts. Monn Kabrit was a very poor mountain village overlooking Croix-des-Bouquets. There was no accessibility to water in Monn Kabrit other than when it rained. The only other way to get water was to take a long truck ride down to Croix-des-Bouquets to retrieve it in buckets, and then make the long trek back up the mountain in a truck once again. A life not easy for those people. This intimate knowledge left me scratching my head in wonder. If there

119

were so many children already in great need in Jeremie, why go all the way across the country looking to take children in? And all four of them had at least one living parent. They weren't true orphans.

That would end up being a familiar theme going forward. The majority of those kids in that orphanage and in orphanages around the country would have at least one living parent.

George would have some explaining to do, I thought to myself. Or was it possible that he didn't even know of these affairs himself?

These matters would be addressed on a later day. I was now leaving Jeremie. In my short time there my affection for Maria grew. Little Alphonse was attached to my hip and I loved him. And with the love and emotions that Leonne was now showering on me I couldn't help but feel drawn to her. It felt great. Receiving affection from a girl was not something I had a lot of experience with.

We took a group picture at the airport right before I boarded the small MAF flight with Jay. I made sure to hug and kiss everyone before I boarded the plane. When I went to hug Leonne goodbye she refused to let go. She broke down in tears. She was carrying a doo rag to cover her face while riding in the back of the truck for protection from breathing the dust, as many Haitians often do. I asked her if I could have it. She agreed and gave it to me. By that point the pilot was motioning to go. As the plane took to the sky I grabbed the doo rag and held it to my nose to smell it. It had the scent of Leonne from just moments ago. I continued to hold it close and breathed it in deeply. I wasn't a few minutes in the air and I was already feeling sick for leaving. That doo rag would not part from my side until I once again returned to Jeremie, Haiti.

Yvrose stayed behind in Jeremie with Rosemary. Jay and I were picked up at the airport in the capital by some of his associates and we were taken to a Christian guest house called the Villa Ormiso. I didn't know anything about Port-au-Prince or the surrounding areas back in those early days but the Villa Ormiso was somewhere in or around Carrefour area. I remember it had a pool. It was fairly cheap. I stayed the night and flew out the next day.

I wasn't very comfortable while there. I was pretty lonely. I didn't talk to anyone. I couldn't stop thinking about this young girl Leonne and the lovely gestures she made towards me.

As I prepared to leave the next morning I would make a huge gaff. If 18-year-olds make stupid mistakes this would definitely be one of them. I decided to send my tape recorder back to Maria via Jay. Inside, where the tapes were placed to play, I folded up a very small note to Maria which read something like this:

> *Maria, don't worry about Yvrose. Don't let her bother you. Don't listen to her or pay her any attention.*
>
> > *I love you,*
> > *Zeke.*

It was something very innocent yet very ignorant and naive. I wrapped the electric cord around the recorder nice and tight. The small note wasn't even visible. Since I knew Jay was going back to Jeremie the next day I said, "Hey, can you give this to Maria for me?" Maybe the dumbest thing I could have ever done. Trusting the American that I did not know in the slightest was an error of epic proportions. In my own innocence, I sent the recorder so that Maria and the rest of the girls could listen to music cassette tapes. I sent the note to not give Yvrose so much credence. I wanted to keep her spirits up. I mean, I already knew that George wanted Yvrose gone anyway.

It was an egregious mistake in judgment on my part. Jay would end up delivering the package but not to Maria. It ended up in the hands of Yvrose instead. By the time that transaction took place, however, I was already stateside.

Haiti was all I could think about for almost a year's time dating back to October of 1990. In a matter of thirty days since first landing on Haitian soil I was already back home. But not for long.

From the moment I departed Haitian airspace I started to experience a real uneasiness in my emotional state. I felt an overwhelming despair. It made me hurt. My body actually became ill.

I got home really late on the night of September 26 and went right upstairs and laid down in my bed. The empty quietness in that moment killed me. I turned over, buried my head into the pillow, and wailed violently. Those muffled wailing sounds were strong enough to reverberate all the way back to Haiti. The only consolation I had was the scent of Leonne's doo rag that never left my side. For whatever reason, I was feeling that I should have never left Haiti. I should have stayed.

I'd spent that night dreaming the most vivid dreams. The next day was more of those same emotions followed by more intense dreams. I didn't want to get out of the bed or leave the house. I sunk into a deep state of depression I'd never before experienced.

My third night home on September 28 I had a very bad nightmare about Haiti. A nightmare that rivaled the one Bill Pullman's character had in the movie *The Serpent and the Rainbow*. It was terrifying. My mom woke me on the morning of September 29. She called upstairs to say there was gunfire in Haiti.

I said *what?*

"It's been all over the news this morning," she said. "There's been a military coup."

I raced downstairs and froze in front of the television and watched the events unfold on CNN. I quickly tried to call Yvrose at the orphanage in Jeremie. I couldn't get through. All communications had been cut off. This event would really be what thrust my life in the direction that it would ultimately take.

I talked to George over the phone that day and he told me not to plan on going back down to Haiti any time soon. He said it was way too dangerous. Of course that was the last thing I wanted to hear. The biggest reason for me coming home was to meet up with him and sit down to have a transparent discussion about how we were going to move forward. There was so much for us to talk about. This particular phone call, however, would be the last one I'd ever have with Pastor George. I would never see him or speak with him again. I was about to take matters into my own hands.

I moved quickly to get my passport. For the next few weeks I returned to work at the Barberton chicken house, where I had worked right after graduation. To save money I purchased a one-way Greyhound bus ticket from Akron, Ohio, to Miami, Florida. Going forward I made up my mind that everything was going to happen on my terms. After securing my passport I was gone. I sort of kept my parents in the dark about everything.

They were not aware of George telling me not to go back. I kept that information from them purposely.

After the thirty-three or so hour bus trip to Miami, I was able to get a ride to Miami International Airport from an African American male's father, who was a minister. I had met the young man on the bus trip down. I got to the airport in the wee hours of October 27, my dad's birthday. I remember asking some of the first people I came across at the airport if they knew who won the Braves vs. Twins World Series game six the night before. It's funny how some things never leave you regardless of where you find yourself in life. Sports was part of the fabric I was cut from and that would never go away. That morning I purchased a one-way ticket back to Haiti via Haiti Trans Air. It was a much cheaper flight than American Airlines. I remember boarding the plane and noticing that one of the wings seemed to be heavily duct taped together. It resembled something right out of the Flintstones. I was not bothered. It made no difference to me. All that concerned me was getting back to Haiti. The flight was nearly empty. So empty, in fact, that the flight attendants were offering two and three meals to passengers. I didn't mind that at all because I was starving.

Haiti was much different this time around. There would be nobody waiting for me at the airport. Nobody knew I was coming. When I got through customs and retrieved my luggage I took that same walk I had taken just two months earlier out the airport exit doors. Only this time it was a barren place. After the coup it became like a ghost town, and there were strict street curfews. It was fairly easy getting a Haitian taxi at the airport. I flagged down the first one I came across. This guy had the look and demeanor of another old school Tonton Macoute. I said, "Sir, can you please take me to the Villa Ormiso Hotel?" I told him that I had American dollars that I needed to change. I also asked if he could drive me through Cite Soleil. He said that he wasn't sure where the Villa Ormiso was but that we would find it.

He drove to a location directly in front of the National Palace and a man with a wad of Haitian cash quickly approached the vehicle. I got my dollars changed. He then turned around and looked back at me and dipped his sunglasses to get a better look at me. He said, "Are you sure you really want to go to Cite Simone?" In his choppy English he informed me that it would cost me $10 extra. I agreed and off we went to Cite Soleil.

All my research at the Barberton Public Library concerning Haiti was now coming into play. For Cite Soleil was originally Cite Simone named after President Francois Duvalier's wife, Simone. As we approached the Western Hemisphere's largest slum, the driver said, "Here we are, blan. We mustn't stay long," he made clear in his tone.

We drove around for a short time and I was spellbound by what I was witnessing. Poverty unimaginable. Residents of Cite Soleil had been devastated by the coup just weeks earlier. Naked children ran everywhere. Many with extended bellies and reddish colored hair. The driver then exclaimed, "Enough of this, blan. Let's go."

After making several stops and asking different people about the exact location of Villa Ormiso we finally came upon it. I was still very green and very unsure concerning my whereabouts in Port-au-Prince at that point. Everything sort of looked the same to me. Everything kind of looked like real poverty.

Arriving at the Ormiso I was very surprised to see the two familiar faces of Rosemary and Jay. They seemed astonished to see me and asked immediately what I was doing there. Why did I return to Haiti under such dire circumstances? I didn't really care for their tone. I came to find out they had been held up in that hotel since the days after the military coup. I suspected right away that something wasn't right. I wasn't happy at all with how they received me.

When they found out my intentions to go back to Jeremie by bus, they moved hastily to discourage me. Rosemary, in an attempt to frighten me, said there were communist rebels in the mountains I would travel through to get to Jeremie. She had no idea who she was speaking with. Rhetoric of that nature only encouraged and hardened my stance and conviction on what I was going to do.

After being shown to my room I ran into two African Americans from San Francisco named Reggie and John. They were very encouraging. A Godsend, really. I shared a little bit about me and what my plans were. They both embraced me with open arms and offered any assistance or help I might need. Reggie gave me a booklet with Creole and English vocabulary words and phrases that could be of great use. I was so grateful that they took time and interest in me. In those days traveling to Haiti, I always believed that God would make a way. Meeting these guys was surely no coincidence.

I avoided dinner that night so I wouldn't have to speak with the American couple that now seemed to frown on my presence. I didn't want any part of being around them. They were the second missionary couple that I had met in Haiti, and I was discouraged by both of them. I started thinking to myself that surely Jay must have opened up my tape recorder and found the note I left for Maria. It would have been easy for him to take that out of context. They seemed so hostile towards me now. I didn't understand.

The next morning both John and Reggie were busy. Reggie had a Haitian friend that he entrusted me with for the day. I went downtown with this guy to purchase my bus ticket to Jeremie for the next morning. He had some other errands to run so I tagged along with him. During one stretch we did a lot of walking in the downtown district on Grand Rue.

This is where I'd see my first dead body.

The man I was following literally walked right over what appeared to be a really thin woman laying underneath a white sheet right on a street corner in public view. There were flies all over the sheet. I was so close behind the man and my head was on a swivel everywhere, taking in all the sights and sounds. When we came across the body he skipped right over it and then I leaped up over the body right behind him. I was very startled. I couldn't believe what I just saw. He continued a brisk pace and never lost a beat. I was trying to get his attention and then I grabbed his arm and said, "Didn't you see the woman back there? Are you gonna help her?"

"She's dead blan," he said. "Nothing you can do for her."

That was my first real culture shock. Death seemed like no big deal in Haiti. It was business as usual.

Later that night at the Ormiso, Reggie told me that he'd drive me to the bus station early the next morning. Getting around Port-au-Prince would have been so much more difficult without these guys helping me out. Both Reggie and John were sent by God, I swear it. Early the next morning John presented me with a Bible. He prayed with me and then Reggie took me downtown to the bus station. Before getting out of the car Reggie said a prayer with me and then he was gone. Now it just got real. For the very first time I was officially on my own in the country of Haiti.

The bus ride to Jeremie was incredibly beautiful and very brutal at the same time.

Port-au-Prince to Les Cayes is approximately one hundred and twenty miles and takes about four hours. That part of the trip wasn't too bad. Les Cayes to Jeremie is approximately sixty miles and takes around five hours. That particular part of the trip is a very arduous one, through harsh mountainous terrain and could be absolutely miserable. From start to finish traffic can be congested and the bus can break down, or the tires go flat. That can make the entire trip last anywhere from ten to twelve hours, depending on God's good humor. The bus only makes a few stops along the way, the main stop being Les Cayes, where people would find a place to use the bathroom and find food to eat that was conveniently being sold right there on the roadside. At any other time along the route you were put in a position to hold it until you got to the next stop. Most stops would consist of passengers getting off at their destinations.

There are times along the road in the mountains that the tires of the bus are just literally inches away from a cliff which drops two thousand-plus feet down. You'd hear the Haitians inside the bus singing and praying to Jesus loudly throughout that duration. On this, my first trip, I tried to get the spot up front with the driver but it had already been taken. I was forced to sit in the sardine can that made up the main section of the bus where they jammed as many human beings as possible.

When I said that I wanted to be more Haitian than the Haitians someone was listening and I was getting that opportunity early and often. If, for example, there was seating for three people, they would make sure that, at the very least, six were placed in that spot, doubling the profit. Passenger comfort and safety was of no consideration or consequence.

I was seated up front on the passenger side next to a woman and her 3-year-old son. She was forced to hold her son, who was probably riding for free, on her lap. That was the price she'd have to pay. After sitting there for a while, watching her labor with him, I finally decided to offer my assistance. One thing I'd learn the hard way in Haiti, the second you show any pity to a Haitian, that's when you get eaten alive. Trial by fire it would

126

be. I ended up holding that little fella on my lap for what seemed like forever.

At a brief stop made in the mountains for passengers to get off, I got off the bus with this boy to use the bathroom. As we were getting ready to get back on the bus my wallet fell out of this little boy's shirt. Somehow along the way the wallet I had in my pocket ended up in this little boy's possession. I was speechless. It was kind of funny, but not really. All the money I had plus important telephone numbers and contact information were in that wallet. I was very fortunate to make that discovery by default before it was too late.

By the time I got into Jeremie it was early evening. I took a motorcycle to the orphanage, expecting a hero's welcome. When I got there the place was abandoned. Nobody was there. I stood bewildered for a few moments. Then out of nowhere a young man named Berto appeared. He informed me that Yvrose had fled into the mountains with all the kids sometime after the military coup weeks earlier. He went inside with me and got me situated. He told me to stay put and that he'd be back shortly. When he returned, much to my surprise, he was dressed in full military garb. He was wearing his olive green uniform with shiny black boots with an M-16 in hand.

"Let's go Zeke, come with me," he said. Yvrose had put him in charge of the place while she was absent.

I proceeded to walk all the way across town with him. He told me that he was in charge of my personal care, wellbeing, and safety for now. I couldn't have felt prouder to have my own personal military guard/escort. My God, did that make me feel engaged. Later that night I sat in the empty quietness of the orphanage, talking with Berto well into the early morning hours. He wasn't much older than me. He spoke some English, which was very helpful. I bombarded him with questions about the Haitian military and asked what sparked the coup. I remember asking him specifically what would he do personally if the U.S. military invaded his homeland.

This question would prove to be prophetic being that three years later this is what would happen. Berto responded that if this occurred, he'd go to work. I smiled. He smiled back. I liked his moxie right away. He was just like me or I like him.

127

I spent the majority of the next day hanging out at the orphanage by myself. Berto had sent word to Yvrose via motorcycle messenger that the white man named Zeke had returned and was waiting at the orphanage. Man, did word travel fast in Haiti. By late afternoon Yvrose had already shown up.

"Zeke, what are you doing here?" she said. "Did you not hear the news in your country about the overthrow of Haitian president Aristide?"

My only response was I had to come back. Interestingly enough, many of Yvrose's kids from the orphanage once performed for President Aristide on a previous visit to Jeremie. They played instrumentals in a makeshift band that would often play at the church and for funerals. Another side hustle to bring in money on occasion. The instruments had been donated from abroad.

Yvrose, like many other Haitians, usually played great politics themselves. It's something that's learned over the years. You learn to say "Viv" or "Long Live" about whoever is in power at the time, and you say it with conviction. "Long live Duvalier," "Long live Aristide," and now it was, "Long Live FAD'H," the Haitian military. Yvrose was now moving quickly to dissociate herself from Aristide's Lavalas party.

She said to me, "OK, let's go. It's getting late and we have a couple hours' drive into the mountains to get to our destination tonight."

Yvrose had made the decision to flee into an area that she was originally from called Tozya. It was a smaller village tucked away deep in the heartland of the Grand Anse region. There is a river that runs through it called "rivier glas," meaning ice river. The water in that river is ice cold. For about the next two months this would be where I called home.

It was during this stretch that I'd really start to feel like a Haitian. Lawrence of Arabia had become more Arab than the Arabs, and my goal was to do likewise in Haiti. I'd become more Haitian than the Haitians. During the drive through the mountains that evening Yvrose asked me if I loved Maria.

I said yes, of course, "but I love all the kids. I love you too."

She then said, "Would you like to marry Maria?"

I said, "Oh no, no, not at all."

That would be the last we spoke of it. What I had going for me was that

128

Yvrose and George were feuding. I learned and leaned on playing politics and playing it well so I'd be able to navigate this stretch of my life in Haiti as it related to George and Yvrose.

We arrived in Tozya late that night. As we got close Yvrose started honking the horn and all the kids came running to greet us. I was mobbed upon stepping out of the truck. It was very dark and difficult to see. The only illumination was from the lights of the truck. But just like a Jedi using the force I would be able to distinguish who was who in the darkness. I could hear Leonne's voice. I recognized her smell and her touch. She hugged me and I held her tightly. It was a blissful few seconds in the Haitian night for me. Maria had grown somewhat shy towards me by that time and understandably so. But soon everyone would get past the misunderstanding and know that the white man named Zeke was there for a heavenly purpose, and that he loved everyone, and didn't plan on getting married to anyone anytime soon.

Yvrose placed me in the house of a man named Gino. Gino had a wife and several children, two of whom I grew very fond of. His oldest daughter, Guerda, was 12. Guerda was responsible for all the tough duties like going to the river multiple times a day to retrieve water in buckets which she would carry back on her head the three quarters of a mile. She handled all the cooking and cleaning. I was moved by how harshly she was treated by Gino. I would go out of my way to give her special attention. I would sometimes give her small change, food, or treats. Whatever I had I'd share it with her. Every morning I ate peanut butter and bread and made sure she got some of it.

The youngest of Gino's kids was an infant/toddler they called Ti Mamoune or Little Mamoune. Her little helpless, broken down body was always propped up in a small wooden chair in a little thatched hut they used as a kitchen space. Ti Mamoune was mentally and physically disabled. She had tiny legs that were of no use to her. Surely she must of been the victim of cerebral palsy. She would always rock back and forth with a glaze over her brown eyes as she looked off into the distance with a smile on her face. I often sat in this little hut she was confined to, talking and singing to her as Guerda was busy about her work. I would start making the trek to the river at five a.m. with Guerda to help her carry the water. I'd also go to the river to bathe and often I would drink the river water. I'd go far upstream, where the water was very cold and tasted good. Living in that type of environment could be harsh for anyone, let alone a diabetic.

Alphonse was staying in my room with me. He was always by my side. There was an outhouse to use as a bathroom a short distance from the house. On one occasion after midnight I had a bad case of diarrhea. I'd awakened to bad stomach pains. I shook Alphonse awake and said Alphonse, "I have to kaka." ("I have to shit.") Haitian kids were all scared to death of the midnight hour. According to Haitian folklore that is when all the "lougawou" – werewolfs – roam freely, wreaking havoc on whoever dared to cross their path. I assured him that we would be fine. With only the moonlight to guide us we set out to the shit house. I took a match and a candle to illuminate where I was about to sit and shit and thank God I did.

The stench coming from the hole I was about to perch myself up on was enough to make you sick. It wasn't just the smell of human feces. Roaches swarmed everywhere. I went through ply after ply of toilet paper with no regard for what I was really doing in my haste to get the hell out of there. I remember Alphonse calling out to me, "Zeke, eskew vanse fini?" ("Are you almost done?") I fucking loved that kid. He was a ride or die for me.

One night my sugar went low in the middle of the night and I woke up a little discombobulated. Alphonse quickly retrieved two unripe grapefruits from underneath the bed we slept on. I ripped through those grapefruits with my bare hands till they bled and sucked out all the sour juice. That sour juice, although it tasted terrible, sustained me through the rest of the night until dawn when I could get some more to eat and drink. It was during these days that I'd be thrust into seeing life for how fragile it really was and still is.

I was walking back from the river one morning with Alphonse when we heard cries of "Amwey, amwey!" meaning "Help, help!" The wailing got louder as we approached. As we got closer people filled with great emotion were leaving a house. Without any shame I politely asked if I could enter the home to see what was going on. The people of the home obliged. Alphonse refused to enter so I told him to wait outside for me. "Do not leave," I reminded him. With his head down he mumbled something and half-heartedly nodded. He wanted no part of hanging around for whatever

130

it was that was going on.

I walked into the house and went to the room where all the commotion was taking place. In this back room lay a man who had just minutes earlier passed into the next life. As I stood over him, staring at his lifeless body, I started to pray:

"God, You are the same God today as You were during the time of Abraham, Isaac, and Jacob. Please hear my prayer and breathe life back into this man. Please I beg you God!"

I really believed God would hear my prayer and act upon it. I expected the man to get up and walk, but, nothing. As a young man full of great pride, I don't know if I wanted to see that man get up and walk to show those people that we were present in God's real power, or more for my own self-righteousness to be magnified. I walked away, feeling great sadness, and being very disappointed.

It was during this same time I was introduced to a white American male that lived in the vicinity. He supposedly had a mission there. He lived in a meager thatched hut. This white man brought me to see a young boy suffering from TB that had his entire neck wrapped in gauze. The man unwrapped the gauze, and I can't even describe what I saw next: a gaping hole in this young boy's neck from infection. I could literally see inside of his neck. It was gruesome. This young boy would die just days later.

I stopped by to see the white man in passing a few days after the fact when he informed me about the fate of this young child. We walked over to the house where the boy was living. We went into the home and there two bodies on the ground were covered in sheets. That's when the white man informed me that tuberculosis was responsible for wiping out the entire family that lived in this hut. This little boy and his mother would be the last ones to succumb to it. The entire family was decimated and killed by a treatable disease. That was hard to stomach for me. I couldn't digest that at all. To make that situation even more distasteful, the locals hurled insults at the white American and accused him of being a masisi, a homosexual in Creole.

As the years passed by I learned one thing for certain. If you were a white man in Haiti, living alone under the auspices of doing mission work, you'd be branded a masisi by default. Papa Doc had once exiled from the country several Catholic priests for such accusations against them and their alleged relationships with young boys/men. As I look back, that particular white man did have some curious things about him that raised eyebrows. He lived in a hut way out in the bush with a couple of young Haitian boys. The boys were very quiet and didn't talk much. Red flags were raised around this white man for sure. I was only eighteen and still yet very ignorant about all things Haiti. I was learning on the fly.

An event that would shake me to my core even more was about to take place.

One morning as I headed out to walk to the river I ran into a young Haitian man who spoke some English. He called out to me, "Yo man blan?" ("What's up my man?")

"Yo, what's up my nigga?"

I was very surprised to hear English like this coming from Haitian lips. We spoke for a few minutes and from what I gathered he had once been in the States and was a possible deportee. I found him to be very interesting and engaging. I said it was nice to meet him and hoped to see him soon. He smiled and agreed.

In the early afternoon on my way back from the river this story took a-turn, right in the same area of homes where the Haitian man had died. I heard a lot of yelling and screaming and headed over to see what was happening. Much to my surprise the same young man that I was speaking with earlier that morning was tied up and pleading his cause to the locals. He had been accused of stealing from people's gardens and also stealing somebody's horse. They had this guy hogtied, thrown onto the ground and beaten like an animal right in front of me. He was flailing and crying out on the dirt floor inside this home we were standing in. I can still hear his screams, howls, and shrieks from the thuds of a thick wooden stick that was used on his bare back and legs.

After the beating he begged for his life. He looked directly at me and said, "Please blan, save me."

I said to him, "Why did you steal?"

"I'm poor, I don't have anything. I did it to survive blan," he told me. "I don't have anybody. I'm on my own here in this country."

I then tried to offer to pay for this man's debt. I petitioned on his behalf

132

for them to spare his life. I was quickly rebuffed. One of the locals patted me on the shoulder and in broken English said, "Blan, this is not your problem. This is not your fight. This man is a criminal by nature. It's not the first time he's done this. Let us take care of this vòle (thief)."

A man approached on horseback. They tied this young man that had just been brutally beaten to the back of the horse. He was made to walk like this all the way to Pestel to where he was to be tried for his crimes. A few days later I was told of his fate. He had been beaten and dragged from behind the horse and had his legs cut off. He died a terrible death.

In countries like Haiti, if you steal you are literally taking life-giving resources from others. The penalty is often found in vigilante justice, which usually results in death as it did for this guy. I lost sleep over that. The fragility of life in Haiti would prove to have an earth-shattering impact on my psyche.

In the days following these traumatic events I fell gravely ill. For the next couple of days I was bedridden. I could not physically get up out of the bed other than to give my insulin. That was a very laborious task. I remember at one point just lying on the bed while looking at the tin roof and smiling like a fool. As uncomfortable as I was with hot and cold temperatures, chills, and pain throughout my entire body, I couldn't help but think to myself, what other 18-year-old American in the world currently finds himself to be so privileged, to get to experience such living? I counted it as joy, just like the word of God said to do.

Leonne, Guerda, and Alphonse took care of me around the clock. I wasn't getting any better, however, so Yvrose finally decided to take me to be looked at. Alphonse, little Jezila who never left her side, and Leonne came with us. On November 25 we went to a place somewhere in Haiti's southern mountains called Bonn Fin. A hospital there, Hospital Lumiere, was constructed through the work of an Apostolic Christian mission.

Upon entering, we walked around and had a look in some of the rooms. We saw a tiny little girl with reddish yellow hair who was nothing but skin and bones. She had tubes in her nose and her little head was just kind of helplessly bobbing back and forth. I brushed flies away from her face as I looked upon her with so much pity. I totally had forgotten that I was even ill in that moment. My God, that made me so fucking sad.

133

I was seen by an American doctor a few minutes later. They drew some blood from me. When the doctor found out that I was diabetic his concern heightened. He was asking me all kinds of questions doctors normally ask. How are your sugars? How much insulin do you take, how often? How are you refrigerating your insulin?

"Your sugar is very high and you're currently suffering from malaria, which will cause your sugars to sky rocket," he said.

"I never check my sugar, I quit doing that a long time ago," I said. I told him that I mix two bottles of insulin, a short acting one and a long acting one. I told him that every day is different so the amounts of insulin I give varies from day to day. And no, my insulin wasn't refrigerated at all.

This particular doctor might have been having a bad day, I don't know, but he unleashed a verbal assault against me, one that I'd never before experienced.

"Your blatant negligence is staggering," he said. "Do you think this is some kind of game? Do you really think it's a joke? You can and will die out here."

I don't recall giving him a rebuttal. I was stunned at his demeanor and disposition. I was in such a weakened condition already and I think that was the reason a normally combative young man like myself stood down in that instance. I was given a medication called chloroquine which in and of itself is a poison that kills the malaria virus. We went to Les Cayes from there, where I was able to make a collect call to my family in the United States. It was late November by this time and I had totally forgotten that I promised my mom back in October that I'd call her when I arrived in Jeremie. A month had passed and they had no communication from me. I was, for whatever reason, oblivious to it all. I was just trying to get through daily life in Haiti at that time. Very selfish of me.

I was told that shortly after I left for Haiti, Pastor George called my house looking for me. My mom told him that I went back to Haiti. George flew off the handle and said, "I told that boy, do not go back down there right now." He was enraged that I went against his wishes. In his fit of anger he said to my mom, "If that boy gets shot and killed it's not my fault. I'm not responsible for anything that happens to him. If he ends up dead or in prison there is nothing I can do about it."

Of course, this upset my mom greatly. So when days passed and I never called to check in, my parents were frightened that something terrible happened. I had flown to Haiti on October 27. It was the week of Thanksgiving when I got around to making that call. After the conversation with George, my parents made calls to the Greyhound bus officials and the local police and detective Mike Ocepek of Barberton. Ocepek put in a missing persons report and contacted local authorities in Miami. Doing their own investigation, Miami authorities found out that I did board a Haiti Trans Air flight out of the Miami International Airport and that I had left the country. I had, in fact, illegally boarded the flight because in those days, it was not legal for someone like me to travel to Haiti on a one-way ticket. I had no official paperwork declaring me a resident of Haiti.

On each trip to Haiti, American citizens were given a ninety-day visa. So at the very least, my family was made aware that I did leave the country and that I was currently somewhere in Haiti. Their focus from that point was directed to the U.S. Embassy. A cable was sent to the embassy in Port-au-Prince asking for the whereabouts of Jason Petrie. Hospitals and prisons were checked to no avail. No news was good news in that case.

On the paper work you're required to fill out when entering Haiti, I had left the address for the orphanage in Jeremie, Haiti in Caracolie. Finally someone from Jeremie confirmed with the Embassy in the capital that the blan named Jason Petrie, a.k.a. Zeke, had been seen. Nobody knew where I was, but my family was told that there had, in fact, been a sighting of me in Jeremie. That information was able to put my parents somewhat at ease.

That night when the operator came across the phone and my mom heard the words, "Will you accept this international collect call from the country of Haiti, caller can you please state your name," and I said, "Jason," my mom said, "Yes, yes!" She was ecstatic to hear me on the other end of that line. I probably spent a good twenty minutes or so talking with the family. I remember my brother Ben telling me two things. He said that he and all the guys from the neighborhood had planned their own Haiti invasion to come find me, and that Magic Johnson had contracted the AIDS virus. I was stunned by this news. Back in those days in Haiti we were cut off from the happenings in the world other than a few stations on the radio. We were isolated in the Grand Anse region. No internet, no

135

computers, no cell phones. It was a different world we once lived in.

It was such a joyous occasion to talk with my family that night, sharing with them my life-changing experiences while standing inside of a little hot booth at a telecommunications center in Les Cayes, Haiti.

Traveling back through the mountains we encountered a small team of Americans that were holding a medical clinic in the region. Walking around and observing what was going on I came across a very long line of Haitians who were all waiting to get shots/vaccinations of some sorts. I mentioned to the lady running it that I was a diabetic and that I was well versed in filling syringes and giving injections. She quickly grabbed me up and said, "You're hired." She instructed me on what syringes to fill and who got which shots. Before I knew it I was sticking one person after another with injections in their asses. I hit one particular man in a bad spot. He bled profusely after I stuck him. I felt terrible watching him screech in pain. I wasn't aware that I didn't even have protective gloves on while doing this. I was so naive and oblivious to those precautions. I was just happy to be in the fight and to be doing something to help others. Wearing gloves to protect myself never crossed my mind.

Sometimes I miss those innocent ignorant moments as a young man of just living fearlessly and with reckless abandon, trying to help and assist the less fortunate. I was very proud of that experience. Being ill and at the same time helping those that were ill was a sign of great fortitude. It was special.

From there we went to Pestel. We ended up staying the night at a private residence right on the water. I was introduced to the legendary Madam Jacques. She baked her famous konparet (sweet bread) for me. It was incredibly delicious. I would soon be addicted to the konparet. From there we headed back to Tozya. In a few weeks we would be leaving to go back to Jeremie.

The last few weeks in Tozya I observed the Haitian ways of life, the demonstrative way that the Creole language was spoken with great body language, accent, the use of hands, and sounds made with the tongue and lips. It was Haitian theatre at its finest. If you don't speak the language, it can be very easy to misinterpret what is actually going on most of the time.

Haitians talk a lot of trash. *Yo djòle anpil.* And that was right up my alley because I did, too.

A guy that I had once gone to school with named Frank Imhoff would years later refer to me as the Gary Payton of Barberton High. Payton played in the NBA for the Seattle Supersonics and he was always yapping and talking a big game. I think for a lot of young men who are undersized, yet possess great talent and potential, part of the process of reminding people that they are formidable, especially in my case, is through unbridled communication. That became a permanent fixture in my character and who I was. In Haiti, it is very much the same situation for the disenfranchised masses. You have hundreds of thousands of underprivileged people with out-of-this-world potential in all walks of life that have no opportunities or chances to break through in this harsh environment they find themselves in. So the way in which they communicate and orally express themselves, using everything available to them, is deep rooted passion overflowing. I couldn't have fit into another culture any better than I fit right into the Haitian culture. There were, however, stark contrasts in my mental makeup compared to that of Haitians. This is where it became very evident that grinding poverty can affect one's entire mental and physical being.

I would see Haitian men getting their shoes shined almost every day. I thought to myself why? It was dusty and filthy outside. In a matter of moments the shoes they just paid to have shined would become dirty again. Yet they'd choose to pay the shoeshine guy the money regardless. In a place of such crushing poverty where money was hard to come by I thought it to be a frivolous waste of time and money. To the Haitian, however, looking pristine was all that mattered. The judgment they cast against one another for something as simple as dirty shoes was a direct result of the house negro versus field negro division caused by the white man during slavery. I would often notice Haitians bathing three or four times a day. I'd question the use of the water. To me it seemed like a waste, especially with clean water scarce in many places in Haiti. In a matter of minutes one would be hot and sweaty all over again.

In 1995 my father visited Haiti for ten days. He'd often recount to people how he was once so very impressed when he saw a man in Port-au-Prince bathe in what appeared to be filthy water in the downtown city streets. He said the poor man had nothing, but in his quest to be presentable he bathed nonetheless, even if the unclean water was all he had available to him. Being clean, looking clean, smelling clean is very important to Haitians. In Haiti if you don't appear tidy in public you'll suffer ridicule. On Sundays, the Haitians en masse will go all out to dress in their Sunday best, *pou fe moun we*, meaning, to make people see. Dressing up and looking their best is more a religion than the religion itself or the observation of the religion through ceremonies in religious establishments. Even more absurd is the fact that their once-slave captors who themselves were Catholic/Christians were somehow able to coerce Haitians into joining their religious establishments even after all the atrocities they committed against them. It was as though the Haitian people were taught to do things in a certain manner without ever questioning authority, and whoever got out of that line of thinking would be chastised.

I thought, wow, this was such a life of contradictions. This sacred land called Haiti with all its great history, the slave rebellion led by legendary figures Toussaint Louverture and Jean Jacques Dessalines, these great warriors couldn't have been of this same mindset, could they?

When the rains fall in Haiti the Haitian people usually scramble to find quick cover. Haitians believe strongly in the fact that rain water on the skin will make you ill. It would always bring a smile to my face to see kids profiting off the rains to take the chance to bathe outside in it, no big deal, innocent fun. Until an adult scolded them verbally about getting out from under the rain water. They would say, "Wap malad wi." ("You're going to be sick.") I would think about the slave rebellion in that instance and how the Haitian men surely must have spent days and weeks and months fighting in the rain. When did Haitians become so soft in their nature?

Years down the road in my desire to learn more about the Haitian way I would reach out to a man named Lynn Garrison. Lynn was a Royal Canadian Air Force fighter pilot. Years later he'd become a political adviser to Haitian General Raoul Cedras. I had placed a few different phone calls to him between 1998 and 2002. He was in South Florida during that time. He mentioned that Haitian President Aristide had put a hit out on his life and that was why he was no longer in Haiti. He would frequently get together with the Duvalierists in South Florida. In one conversation I had with Mr. Garrison, post 9/11, we happened to be discussing the events of 9/11 and what was currently going on in Afghanistan. Lynn said that Haitians were mere puppy dogs in comparison with Afghan fighters. Garrison had been a former mercenary in places like Nigeria, South East Asia, El Salvador and Honduras, to name a few. He was well traveled and knew his stuff. I'm very glad at the time I hadn't the full resume of Garrison at my disposal because it might have intimidated me to speak so freely with him. I had very candid discussions with him and I was still yet only in my 20s. And as much as I didn't want to believe, what Lynn said was true about lack of toughness in Haitians. He referred to them as puppy dogs. I knew he was spot on. That was very difficult for me to understand and to digest, especially concerning the brave and heroic nature of Haitian history. Coming full circle as a young man who was now living in this culture, soaking it all in, and wanting greatly to believe in the Haitian masses, it became tough for me. I found myself asking more questions. As much as I had in common with the Haitian people, my mindset was much more of an independent free thinker with the spirit of a revolutionary. The Haitians to me seemed as though they were still enslaved and in a mental captivity of sorts. That was hard for me to fathom. I can't overstate that enough.

Now we were going back to Jeremie and the orphanage life that I grew to detest. As December came to an end, and we were now entering the New Year of 1992, Yvrose became more and more abusive to the kids in a way I hadn't yet seen before. She started running the orphanage like a dictator. I was growing ever so discouraged and I wanted out. After pondering it over and over I decided that I'd go back to the States and try to solicit some support and go forward in Haiti on my own. I informed Yvrose of my plans. She seemed surprised. I think that we had both grown accustomed to being around one another, and that for the most part, we got along OK. She tolerated me, I tolerated her. It was just the Haitian way.

Before leaving, the white man named Bob who Brother Berkley once told me about, showed up at the orphanage to visit. He had come to Jeremie to see a girl that he was courting at the time named Marie-Lourdes. I think Bob was right around forty-two years of age at that time. Bob had been married previously to a wealthy Haitian woman from Petionville who he had two kids with. They were now divorced and he was much like a kid in a candy store with all the beautiful Haitian girls that were now available to him. He loved the attention. Bob entering the picture would ultimately play a huge impact in my life going forward. Having patience was something as a young man I lacked considerably. I had none whatsoever. Patience is a virtue but for me it was a nuisance.

JANUARY 1992

When the day came for me to leave in mid-January all the kids were very sad again. As I arrived at the airport I started having flashbacks and was flooded with emotions of how I felt the last time after leaving. As the pilot called for all passengers to board I froze. I couldn't get on the plane. I felt sick. I couldn't leave. I said to Yvrose, "I can't go."

Although she didn't show it in her emotions, she must have thought I was a damn fool. I don't know. We headed back to the orphanage and didn't speak a word on the way. When we arrived the kids were ecstatic that I decided not to leave. I was greeted with hugs and kisses as though it was the first time they had ever seen me. After a few more days I was struggling mightily with what I really wanted and what I needed to do. I needed to take action. I kept saying to myself, "There has to be more than just this. This isn't why I was sent to Haiti, to sit here and rot at this Jeremie orphanage."

I told Yvrose that after discussing this with God I had now decided to really leave this time around. She kind of laughed and said, "Are you crazy?"

I smiled and let her know that she was very generous in her remarks. I wouldn't have been so generous to myself. I got my new ticket to leave the very next day. Bob actually had a plane ticket from Jeremie to Port-au-Prince that he was no longer going to use. He offered it to me. The next day I'd be leaving without anyone knowing. It would be my new friend, Bob, who was twice my age, who would take me to the airport this time. Just like that, in late January of 1992, I was gone from Haiti yet again. And just like the time before, I was heartbroken. I really had no idea what was going to become of my time in Haiti, but I had to search for a new purpose looking ahead.

I returned to the States and I was miserable from the moment my plane touched down in Cleveland. It was now the heart of winter in Northeast Ohio and cold temps greeted me. I moved quickly to tell my parents that I wanted to try and raise some support for myself in Haiti. With that said, however, I didn't really have any structured and well-thought-out plans for what I wanted to accomplish. I was able to arrange a sit-down, face-to-face, meeting with the pastor of Community Church of Portage Lakes. That was my home church as a young kid and the church I was baptized in. I thought, no big deal, I'll give this guy my pitch, he will buy into it and I'll be back on my way. I gave to him my best presentation on how God had sent me to Haiti for a reason and because of that calling on my life, the church should add me to their monthly mission's budget. I left the meeting with the pastor feeling pretty good about my cause and my chances of gaining monthly financial support. Surely, they'd be on board, I thought. I mean, it was God's will for me to be in Haiti anyway. How else could anyone explain away how I ended up meeting George?

A short time later I received news that the church appreciated my heart for Haiti but at that time, their mission's budget was strapped and already stretched to its capacity. Therefore, they would not be able to support my cause. I took this as a personal slight. My church-going days were now officially coming to an end. In the meantime, I ended up finding work through a temporary agency.

A miserable, lonely, and cold month of February now headed into March. I felt lost. I started to drift farther and farther away from praying and reading the Bible. That part of my life was now nearly non-existent. By late March I had saved enough money to get another Greyhound bus ticket to Miami, and for a round trip ticket to Haiti from Miami. I told my parents I was leaving again and going back to the orphanage in Jeremie. I made this decision for no other reason than I felt that I could no longer live in the States. I was floundering around miserably with no cause, no rhyme or reason, and no "why?" Haiti was my why! My why that I didn't really exactly know the meaning of. I just knew it was mine, and nobody could tell me any different.

In late March I once again boarded the Greyhound bus out of Akron, Ohio. I got to Miami and this time I secured a round trip plane ticket. After arriving in Haiti, I got a cab to take me to Grand Rue in downtown Port-au-Prince. I had the driver drop me off at the exact location of the bus station where the buses departed for Jeremie. This was the very first time I was really on my own in the capital. Port-au-Prince was a much different monster than the provinces. In the countryside things were much more relaxed. In the capital things were helter skelter. I got along with my Creole well enough at this point to have a pretty good command of my situation. This was my first opportunity to see the city life in a different perspective.

I stayed that night in a little hole in the wall dump of a hotel on Grand Rue, and was offered some Dominican prostitutes for my entertainment. I declined the invitation, however, and tried to get some sleep. It was a miserable night but my adrenaline was running high so I wasn't all that annoyed. I was up and ready to go at the crack of daylight. For this trip to Jeremie I was not going to get stuck sitting on the inside of the bus. I requested a seat at the very top of the bus. The driver said to me, "No, blan, it's not good up there. You won't be comfortable up there and it's not safe." He didn't understand who he was speaking to.

I insisted and the driver finally agreed and granted me my wish. On top of the bus, where all the luggage was strapped down, I was literally fifteen feet in the air. I had to find a place somewhere to sit on top of all that stuff. Even in the early morning hours the traffic through Port-au-Prince was heavy, so we moved along slowly. But as we got out onto Route National 2 the bus picked up speed and soon I was holding on for dear life. The wind alone was enough to blow you off the top of the bus. Once the sun came up it got warm and it was easy to get baked up there. I was having the time of my life.

Into the mountains after leaving Les Cayes behind was where the trip became something straight out of the movies. The scenery was so incredible. The perspective from sitting in that elevated position was something I could never get from inside of the bus. The bus tilted from one side all the way to the other during some of the harrowing turns on those mountain passes. Up top I was holding on tight while being awed by

142

the exhilarating views. There was a ladder connected to the bus on the very back end. The guys responsible for the bags would scale up and down that ladder on multiple occasions throughout the trip. I would observe them holding on effortlessly, and of course, I felt the need and desire to do it, too. So I asked one of them if I could have a try at it. He looked at me like I was crazy. The guy said, "No, no, no, blan. It's no good." He said it was very dangerous in his broken English.

I said, "Pa gen pwoblem, M pa pè." ("No problem, I'm not afraid.")

After persisting he let me have a try as he shook his head in dismay. I wasn't a minute in to holding onto that ladder and my arms were already starting to burn. Then the bus started to climb a very steep part of the mountainous terrain. I was holding on so tightly it took my breath away. I couldn't speak or call out. I tried several times to reach up and pull myself back up onto the bus but I didn't have enough strength. The bus was continuing to grind on. The couple of guys that were on top were occupied with other things and they were not noticing or aware of my struggle. Those guys had made it look so easy. Rail thin and barefoot, they just skipped along the top of the bus. While standing on that back ladder they talked with passengers in the very back window seats while holding on with one hand. These very meager-looking, rice- and-bean eating Haitians were tough as nails and wiry strong. I was impressed.

When the bus finally evened out on level ground I grappled my way back to the top. I was exhausted. I couldn't lift or move my arms by then. One of the Haitian guys working on top of the bus looked over at me and smiled. He said, "Ou we li pa dous blan?" ("You see it wasn't sweet white man?") I had no response. This modern-day Indiana Jones was now licking his wounds and his hurt ego.

There was a place on the road during the journey to Jeremie where a mountainous overhang was so great that everyone on top of the bus had to laid down as to not be crushed or knocked off. It was one of the most strenuous undertakings that I'd ever gone through. That takes guts, man. As we were on the final straightaway entry into Jeremie the bus picked up speed. I made the fatal error of relaxing too quickly. As I was taking in all the sights and sounds, one of the guys on top of the bus began calling out at the top of his lungs, "Blan, blan, blan, regarde." ("White man, white man, white man, look.")

I glanced over at him while the wind was ripping through my hair and my ears and my eyes watered from the dust. He was gesturing to the top of his head and then pointed out in front of me and then back to his head again. As I turned to look out ahead of me my eyes grew big like saucers. I threw myself down as fast as I could and felt something smack right off the top of my head. We were going at a pretty high rate of speed and were perched up so high that the electrical wires were a very serious and dangerous issue. I was oblivious to it all as a rookie sitting on top. This man, in fact, saved my life. I was a few precious seconds away from being a victim of decapitation. Hence, the reason behind the bus driver not wanting me to sit on top from the very beginning.

I was so fortunate. That was now my second of nine lives used up in my young Haiti history. My love affair with this country would run deep and come at a great cost.

When I arrived back at the orphanage the kids were very excited to see me. Yvrose seemed indifferent. Much to my surprise, however, the room I once called my own was now being held up by Bob. Not only was Bob in my room, but he was now staying in that room with one of the older teenage girls named Marie-Mate. Bob had evidently started up a relationship with Marie-Mate right after I left back in January. His purpose coming back to Jeremie to find one girl had ended up with him finding a different girl altogether. I couldn't help but harken back to Brother Berkley's comments concerning Bob. He seemed pretty shameless about the entire affair. He was a well off, white male in his forties, who had shacked up with a teenage girl in this orphanage that George had founded back in the 1970s. Wow, times had certainly changed. I'm pretty sure that Bob peddled off some hush money to turn the other cheek.

When I questioned Yvrose about it she nonchalantly wrote it off as, "This is just who Bob is. He loves Haitian girls, especially the dark skin ones." I was a little embarrassed for the both of them. Interestingly enough Marie-Mate was yet another of Leonne's cousins, originally from Monn Kabrit.

I now took up in a different room inside the orphanage. Over the next few months I continued to learn the Haitian culture and the Creole

144

language. I grew even closer to Alphonse. I often sent him to the house of Madam Seneque to buy me the konparet bread that I loved so much. Although Alphonse was not a big fan of making the trek all the way downtown to purchase it, he loved eating his share of the bounty. The konparet tasted so good. During that period my relationship with Leonne started to grow, too. There weren't ever many private moments to be had, but on occasion when we were afforded the chance to be alone somewhere in a dark corner or crevice, we would embrace and sneak a kiss. It was relatively still very innocent.

I had the feeling that Bob was now in a position of authority. I yielded to him concerning any of the responsibilities I once had in the operations of overseeing the boutique, making sure the kids were up and ready for school, and that they made it to church promptly. I gave way to him concerning all those things. I spent my time doing whatever the hell I wanted to do. My relationship with Yvrose became pretty nonexistent by this point.

I had the good fortune of meeting two new friends in Jeremie. One was Enel, and the other was Phaubert. I was hanging out and getting to know both of them as much as I could. Enel spoke some English, which was very helpful in communicating. I spent my days running off to Anse d'Azur, swimming, running around Caracolie with Alphonse stealing mangoes from private properties with street kids, hanging with folks who participated in Vodou ceremonies, and just continuing to immerse myself in the culture. I felt free. Every once in a while I'd hang out with Bob but those instances were few and far between. I often sensed that Bob had a jealousy in his heart towards me. I was much younger, and I was more well-liked, not only by the kids at the orphanage but in the Caracolie community, where we stayed.

On two separate occasions I had to step in and save two of the kids from Yvrose beating them with a whip. One day I heard a lot of commotion out on the side of the orphanage. I peered out a window and saw one of the boys named John on his knees in the dirt pleading for mercy. He was in tears, begging Yvrose for a pardon. All he was wearing was a pair of torn up shorts. She whipped his bare back like an animal. She even whipped him on his head, hands, and feet. I hurried out of the house and stepped in

145

to make her stand down. I never did find out what John had done, but at that point I didn't really even care. I could not stomach watching in silence as a young kid was beaten in that manner.

A few days later, Yvrose chased another of Leonne's cousins, Gertha, over the back wall of the orphanage, and flogged her in full public view.

I had followed them both right over that back wall to step in and spare Gertha a grave beating. I stepped between them as Yvrose was in full swing of her whip. I took a couple of the lashes in Gertha's stead before she finally relinquished the beating. Gertha was holding onto me so tightly that her nails pierced my skin. I was now bleeding from Yvrose's whip and from Gertha's nails digging in so deep. She was screaming and was terrified. All of these things started to take their toll on my spirit. My energy for this type of living was slowly dying off. It was now late June and my ninety-day visa would be expiring. It was time for me to leave Haiti once again. This time around, it was easier to leave than on my previous trips. There was no hesitation.

Yet, after returning home, the loneliness birds soon overwhelmed me once again.

I spent the next three months living at home and working for a temporary agency that sent me to factory jobs. Throughout that time, I kept in contact over the phone with my friends Enel and Phaubert. When September rolled around I was planning another trip to Haiti. Before I left I went to see my Grandpa Petrie at the hospital. He had just fallen victim to a major stroke. I went alone to visit with him. I talked to him while he lay there unconscious. I made a promise to him that I would do some great things in this life. I told him that I would ask God's favor to restore his physical body and that I loved him very much. I flew back to Haiti the next day.

It had already been arranged for Enel's father, Erick, who lived in Martissant, to pick me up at the airport. I stayed at Erick's place with the rest of his family. The next day I took the bus again back to Jeremie. This time I had some good fortune and was able to sit up front with the driver. Arriving in Jeremie, I went straight to Phaubert's place. His father rented a place on Rue Brice Aine in downtown Jeremie. I insisted that we immediately go to see all the kids at Yvrose's orphanage. Phaubert reluctantly agreed.

I did not really have a full understanding back then that Yvrose was feared by many in Jeremie. There were always whispers of her being heavily involved in Vodou. She was said to be serving the Lwa, or spirit world, which was said to have given her great power. She was always kind of able to dictate her will on other Haitians because she had financial backing from abroad. Yvrose could afford to pay bribes to officials at her discretion for whatever her objective was.

Phaubert, knowing these things all too well, did not want Yvrose to be looking on him as the guy who was now influencing the white man named Zeke. When we got to the orphanage, Yvrose was not there, and neither was Bob. I was informed that Bob had left Marie-Mate, and that he returned with his most recent girlfriend, Marie-Lourdes. He was living somewhere with her in downtown Jeremie. I asked to see Leonne. When Leonne appeared in front of me she had her head down and seemed to be very sad. I asked her what was wrong. She kept her head lowered and would not look at me. I saw tears coming from her eyes.

I said again, "Leonne, what's wrong cherie?" (Cherie means "sweetheart.") That's when others in the room told me that Yvrose had beaten Leonne on a few occasions because of revelations made to her that Leonne and I had been in a relationship. I became furious. I offered to her the chance to leave with me. I said, "Come with me now, you can leave with me tonight and be free of all this madness." She looked at me with tears flowing and shook her head no. She couldn't go with me. I begged and pleaded with her for several minutes. As all this was happening I got a final glimpse of Alphonse. He was standing off by himself, watching, and you could see that he was emotionally distraught because of this. Alphonse loved both me and Leonne, but he knew that he had to show his allegiance to Yvrose or else. He remained silent. He and I both knew that this would probably be our final parting of ways and that our time together was over. Once I walked out those orphanage doors I would never come back through them again.

I tried giving Leonne one final embrace but she did not reciprocate. I gave her a quick kiss on the top of her head and said, "The day you finally decide to leave this dreaded place I will be here." I walked out the door without ever seeing or speaking to Yvrose. It was a painful and lonely walk from Caracolie all the way back downtown with Phaubert. We didn't speak a word to each other. I took a deep breath and thought, "Wow, this part of my Haiti life is now really over."

After returning to Phaubert's place I could sense he was not at ease with the current state of events. I assured him that everything would be OK, and that this was God's will. Man did it hurt, though. Where would I go from here?

Phaubert lived in an old, wooden-framed house with three of his brothers. Pierre Claudel was the oldest of the brothers and a fascinating person to me. He was serious minded and very much an intellectual. He would tell me that he'd never do as his father did to them, having several children with multiple women. He held that against his father, as I think a lot of young Haitian men do. Haiti has always been one of the most densely populated countries in the world. The entire country is the size of the state of Maryland with eleven million inhabitants. That could be somewhat avoided if measures were taken, a responsibility not often applied by people in the third world. In a country like Haiti, birth control has been more or less nonexistent. With so many Haitians observing Catholicism for their faith, it's basically a non-factor.

Pierre Claudel not only held great resentment towards his father, but he also had a strong dislike for how the government of the United States operated its foreign policies over the years. He started with the Kennedy assassination and continued right on into Vietnam. That led into a discussion about the first Gulf War and Saddam Hussein. Back in those days I was very cocky and pro American. We would have some intense debates in Crenglish, both Creole and English. I smile when reminiscing on those days. They were conversations that would be of great use to me. I learned from him and soaked it all in like a sponge.

Staying at Phaubert's would get me used to very long, hot nights of trying to sleep without electricity. Although the orphanage didn't always have electricity, we did have a generator that was often used. The heat down in the city was worse. The cockroaches, rats, and mosquitoes were terrible. The rats were often as big as cats. It was something that I had signed up for, and as miserable as it was, I had to, once again, trick myself

148

into not minding it. I had to get comfortable being uncomfortable. There was nothing else.

On the morning of September 17, I headed out on my own to run and swim at Anse d'Azur. Somewhere between nine and ten a.m. I began my run. The sun was already hot. I was about half way when my breathing started to become labored. Sweat was streaming into my eyes, which made them burn like fire. It got so bad and I was so warm that I could no longer breathe. I was gasping for air. I had never been overcome by such exhaustion in my entire life. I had never felt like that before.

I finally stopped dead in my tracks as I was sucking for oxygen. I was bent, over totally depleted. I was thinking to myself, "What in the fuck is wrong with me?" It was not a low blood sugar. I thought maybe this was what the Haitian heat can do to you. The sunshine down by the equator is no joke. I turned around and headed back to town. I was not right, something was wrong. My lungs and my insides were hurting me.

Later that night I went to the Teleco station in town to call back home and check in with my family to let them know I had made it to Jeremie and inquire about how Grandpa was doing.

My mom answered the phone and said, "Jason, your grandpa died today."

"Oh no," I said, "When did he pass?"

"He died this morning."

After taking a few moments to confirm the approximate time of his death, I found it was exactly at around the same time I had been out running that day. I quickly explained to my mom what had happened to me that morning. That made me really stop to ponder this life and how spirits can be connected no matter the distance between them. There are no oceans deep enough and no mountains high enough that could separate such a connection. I had felt my grandfather taking his last breaths that morning with the tightening of my chest, almost to the point of explosion. Wherever and whenever there is death, we are always reminded that there is life, and life goes on. It does not stop for anybody, ever!

The next day I ran into Bob down by the Teleco station. He was very surprised to see me as I was him. He quickly started in on Yvrose, calling her crazy. He said he was done with her. He evidently had a blow out with

149

her concerning his love affair with Marie-Mate, and he just up and left. From what Bob had conveyed to me, he had offered to Marie-Mate the same thing I did with Leonne. "Come with me," he said, and Marie-Mate said no. All these girls at the orphanage were scared to death of Yvrose, and for good reason. Even at my young age I understood that. Bob did not, however. Bob, with all his pride and arrogance, felt slighted. He went right back to his former girlfriend, Marie-Lourdes, like nothing had happened.

Living in a country like Haiti, where lines are very easily blurred, it's easy to start living a double life, especially if you have no moral values or discipline. Bob said, "Zeke, come with me, I'll show you where I am staying." Bob was now holed up right next to the cinema downtown, in a one-room shack that could only be accessed through a narrow corridor. There I would meet Marie-Lourdes for the first time and a neighbor of theirs named Masline. Just two months earlier Masline had given birth to a baby girl named Sabine. They were staying in a little shack across from Bob. Masline had a son named Jono who was about two years old.

From the first moment I laid eyes on Sabine I was in love. She was so beautiful. Her big brown eyes looked up at me and she would flail her little arms and legs with contentment while I held her. I would go back the very next day to see them and every day after that. Masline asked me if I would take Sabine with me. I responded that I would love to but that, most likely, it would not be possible. One morning, I was laying on this big bed in the house while talking to Masline. Sabine was sleeping on the bed, so I thought. Before I knew it Sabine had a handful of my hair and gave it a very strong tug, as if to say, "Pay me attention, white man. You're looking for a purpose, well here I am."

I promised Masline one thing, that I would start helping her with Sabine as much as I could afford to financially. I would be ever present in her life going forward, and she would call me "papa" from the time she began to speak.

One afternoon I was sitting out on the gallery of Phaubert's place, just people watching, when out of nowhere a beautiful young girl walked by. She was wearing a pair of sunglasses. She stopped right in front of me, tilted her shades down and exposed her eyes, and stared at me. I was a bit taken aback by a young girl having that kind of self-confidence, being that engaging, and oh, by the way, taking an interest in me. I was very impressed by her beauty. She was wearing a black shirt and white shorts. It's funny some of the things you never forget.

We exchanged names. She asked me who I was and was this where I lived? I said, "I am Zeke and this where I am currently staying but I am from the States."

She said, "My name is Johane."

Without trying to let her know that I was thrilled to meet her, I insisted on walking her back to wherever it was that she was going. She lived in an area called Borde up past the general hospital in Jeremie. When we arrived at her house she introduced me to some of her siblings and also her mother, Irmine. It was cool. I was happy to have a beautiful girl who took interest in me and to meet some new people. After spending a little while chatting I headed back to Phaubert's place.

On the way back I crossed paths with a woman they called Madam George. She was standing right out front of her residence with a really cute dog. I greeted her, she greeted me, and we made some small talk. She invited me to come have coffee with her sometime. I accepted and told her that I would return again. Unbeknownst to me I was speaking with the aunt of Haitian military General Raoul Cedras. Cedras hailed from Jeremie. After learning this I made sure to see her as often as I could. I spent a lot of the rest of that trip to Haiti playing basketball at a court by the library right up the hill from Phaubert's place. That would become a great joy for me, to play the game I loved so much growing up alongside Haitians.

Visiting with Madam George, my friend Enel, going to see Sabine, becoming closer with Johane, and going swimming at Anse d'Azur is what I spent the remainder of my time in Jeremie doing.

Before I left Haiti, Johane and I were officially a couple. She told me that she was only thirteen, which surprised me. She looked older. At that point, I didn't care because a relationship had already been established. More importantly, her mother knew that I was nineteen and she did not mind, so I did not mind either. In Haiti, things are much different than in the United States. You often see an older guy with a much younger girl. It took me a while to get comfortable with it, but soon I would not only be

151

comfortable with it, I'd be thriving in it and making up my own rules as I went along.

As mid-October approached I headed back to the capital on a bus once again. Enel's father, Erick, would be waiting for me. We went back to his place in Martissant and had dinner with the family. That night I had a discussion with a bunch of young men that were out in the street in front of Erick's place playing dominoes. They started questioning me on who I was going to vote for in the upcoming presidential election in the United States – George Bush or Bill Clinton?

They said, "Blan are you going to vote?"

I said, "Yes I am." They asked me to vote for Clinton for them. They hated Bush and believed him responsible for the military coup against Aristide a year earlier.

I smiled and said, "Sure I'll vote Clinton for you. I will give you guys a voice in the upcoming election." They all laughed and cheered and thought it was great.

When November rolled around, however, I went to my old elementary school at Memorial and punched the Republican card for George Bush. Why? I have no idea why. Growing up as a non-denominational Protestant Christian it was the thing to do, and I did it. That would be the first and last time that I'd ever vote for anything in my entire life. Voting is arguably the biggest scam that the powers that be have ever pulled off. It gives you a feeling of a false sense of security that your voice actually matters. At the local level, and even sometimes on the state level it might, but when it comes to the federal government of the United States, those presidents have already been hand-picked long before the year of the election. I would learn a lot more concerning these affairs much later in life, but for the time being, it felt irrelevant to me.

END OF 1992, BEGINNING OF 1993

From mid-October until late January I continued to work for a temporary service, which sent me out to do local factory work. That's how I made my money. In early February I returned to Haiti yet again. I couldn't stay away for long. I was homesick for Haiti and I needed her badly. Enel's father once again picked me up at the airport and then came another long bus trip to Jeremie. By this time I was a grizzled vet of that particular voyage so I was no longer annoyed by anything I encountered on that journey. I was always very excited to make that final entrance into Jeremie. I knew in a matter of moments I was going to share in some wonderful reunions. That was always one of the magical things about Haiti. Experiencing the emotional highs and lows of coming and going. Leaving was always a time of great despair. Arriving, however, was always euphoric. It was a drug, and I was an addict. I grew dependent on it.

After getting situated at Phaubert's place I went straight over to see Sabine. I would always bring toys, shoes, and clothes for the kids. Sabine was six and a half months by this time. I snatched her up and told Masline I would be back later. I took her with me to go see Johane. Johane was very excited to see me. I took a few pictures with her and the family. Her father was recently deceased. I had never met him. He had been living in a place called Abricot. Her mother, Irmine, was really super nice to me and we got along well. All her siblings liked me so everything just felt right.

After spending a couple of weeks in Jeremie that February I was going to go back to spend the remainder of my time in the capital. I wanted to get to know Port-au-Prince better. I did not like Port-au-Prince as I did Jeremie, but I was still searching for what my ultimate purpose in Haiti was. It was Tuesday, February 16, the day before my brother Ben's birthday, which is why I can remember this event so vividly. I wanted a new experience, so instead of taking the bus back to the capital I decided to take a boat. I had bought a ticket for the Neptune. The Neptune was a 150-foot boat with three decks. It made weekly trips to transport people, farm animals, charcoal, and other cargo from Jeremie to Port-au-Prince and back. The trip was about a 150 miles and usually was about twelve hours long. I boarded the boat one late afternoon as they were finishing loading everything on board. The Neptune's captain blew the horn to let all the townspeople know that it was about time for departure.

I went in and sat in an inside cabin for a while. Not long after I started to feel ill. The vessel was overflowing with people and livestock. It reeked of people's sweat and animal shit. I thought to myself, twelve hours of this?

I'd rather take the bus. The Neptune's Captain St. Clair, who I called Mr. Ben, was now blowing the boat's horn repeatedly, making his final calls. Hermann, father of my good friend Kattelene Fleury, worked on the boat, and he had introduced me to captain St. Clair the day before. I was all ready and excited for this trip, but being a diabetic and not feeling well, I started to have second thoughts. I was left sitting there on this boat amongst a sea of humanity in undescribable controlled chaos.

At the last possible second, as the Neptune's engine was starting to churn, the captain again sounded the horn. I leapt up from a cramped position inside of the boat. I couldn't breathe. I was pouring in sweat and now experiencing great stomach pain. I grabbed onto my bag, threw it over my back, and began pushing my way through a mass of people to try and make it off the boat before it left port. When I finally made my way down on the outside of the bottom deck I was yelling and cursing at people to "get the fuck outta my way." The steps leading up to the boat had already been drawn up. At that point I had made up my mind that there was no way in hell that I was going to Port-au-Prince on this night. I summed up the courage and leaped from the boat as it was starting to pull away from the wharf. I was cursing the entire time.

"Motherfuckers," I yelled out, "Fuck that! FUCK ALL OF YOU." I went right back to Phaubert's. When I entered his house his eyes lit up and he got the biggest smile on his face. He said, "Brother, you don't go?"

"Fuck that!" I said. Phaubert laughed hysterically. He said, "I thought you wanted to be Haitian, my man."

I said, "Fuck you!" We embraced, both of us laughing.

Thursday morning, February 18, 1993, you could hear a great, collective wail throughout the area. News started to slowly trickle in that the Neptune had sunk late Tuesday night into early Wednesday morning. The townspeople were in mourning on a level of Biblical proportions.

Exodus 11:6: "Then a loud wail will rise throughout the land of Egypt, a wail like no one has ever heard before or will ever hear again."

This was the case with the Neptune sinking off the coast of Haiti. You could hear the cries of the people for miles away. It was truly like being taken back into Bible times. Everybody was weeping! It was like one loud moan of great pain that echoed across Jeremie. In Haiti, it's always loud.

Wherever there is city life there is much noise. It's one of the things you get so used to that when you are removed from it, you miss it. People threw themselves to the ground in a convulsive state, crying out to God.

News of the Neptune sinking halfway through its voyage to Port-au-Prince late Tuesday night had the city of Jeremie in a state of shock. Rough seas and heavy rains in the pitch darkness had caused a panic among the passengers. Although there was no passenger list, it was believed that approximately 1,200 passengers were on board that night – 1,199 after I jumped off. As someone who saw with my own eyes the boat being loaded well beyond its capacity, I would say that there were closer to 2,000 people on board. In the black of night when the rains started to come down hard the Neptune started to pitch and roll. Panic ensued. Many of the passengers rushed to one side of the boat, many others rushed to the upper deck, one climbing over another. That sudden shift in weight caused the upper deck to collapse on hundreds of people below and the boat capsized, spilling people, cattle, and cargo into the ocean. It's estimated that the Neptune went down near the coastal town of Miragoane. As someone with first-hand knowledge of what the scene looked like just hours earlier in a calm sort of chaos, I can't imagine what it would have been like later that night during that frightened stampede of humans in the darkness of that vessel out on the open seas. It would have been absolutely terrifying. One lady died with all eight of her children. Nine hundred people drowned. One Haitian Red Cross official was quoted as saying he thought the death toll would reach 1,500 or even more. There were about three hundred passengers that survived, including the captain, who suffered heavy criticism from the public. The Neptune should have never carried more than seven hundred passengers. The boat had little to no safety equipment, and it had no emergency radio. Haiti's Navy at that time was nearly inoperative so the rescue response was very delayed. People were still being pulled out of the sea two days later by the U.S. Coast Guard. Survivors were found along a thirty-mile stretch from Miragoane to Petit Goave and Leogane. They even found people as far as the Bahamas.

People survived by floating on bags of charcoal, the carcasses of dead animals, and one woman was saved by holding on to a bucket. There were hundreds of dead bodies in that water. One of the U.S. Coast Guard cutters involved in the search and rescue operation had picked up so many bodies that they quit counting. Lt. Commander Larry Mizell of the U.S. Coast Guard said it was one of the worst maritime disasters in recent history.

News of the wreck didn't come to Jeremie until Thursday morning because of the total lack of communication between Port-au-Prince and the provinces. Jeremie was cut off and isolated from the world.

I was asked by my friend, Kattelene, to go out on a search and rescue speed boat with a few others to find her father, Hermann. Without hesitation, I agreed. Friday morning we gathered together to set off but due to the bad weather and very rough conditions of the sea we never made it out. Hermann's body was never found. I ended up speaking with my mom on the phone that night. I had told her what happened. She said they were watching the news and saw the story come across the screen. My mom had inclinations and instincts that only a mother could have. She had quietly wondered whether I could have been on that boat. I said to her, "You know me too well. I was on the Neptune at the time of its departure. I was not feeling well and I aborted literally last second." This was Haiti's Titanic. I am fortunate to live to tell about it. This was now my third of nine lives used up.

Generals Raoul Cedras and Philippe Biamby came to Jeremie to visit after this great national tragedy. I had a chance to meet them. That would not be the last time I'd shake hands and rub shoulders with Haitians of such high rank.

In early March I left Haiti again. I wouldn't return until September.

For the next six months I'd continue with a temp agency and more local factory work while staying at home. I'd call down to Haiti and speak with Phaubert and Enel to keep up with what was going on in country. An economic embargo had been put in place on the military regime since after the coup back in September of '91. It had been two years of embargo by this point and "average Joe" Haitians were being squeezed and drained of what little financial resources they had. Inflation was high. Meanwhile, the desired effects against those in power were pretty much non-existent. Because of the black market, the military junta led by General Cedras and the National Police led by Colonel Michel Francois flourished and tightened its grip on power. There were a lot of political killings in those days, but many innocent civilians were also killed.

A paramilitary group known as FRAP'H, Front for the Advancement and Progress of Haiti, led by Emmanuel "Toto" Constant, terrorized and decimated local peasant groups and grassroots organizations in attempts to smash the last remnants of the Lavalas movement altogether. I often followed the CBS Evening News nightly with Dan Rather to keep up with international news. I was always on the lookout for any news coming out of Haiti. As I was now leaving again for Haiti in September, I received news that Reverend George Hawthorn had died on September 9. I kind of met that news with an indifference of sorts. Yet, I always acknowledged him when explaining to people how I first ended up in Haiti.

Upon arriving to Haiti this time I stayed the night on Grand Rue, right in the heart of downtown Port-au-Prince, where Phaubert's Aunt Milly lived. Another bus trip to Jeremie was in order. After getting into Jeremie I headed straight to Phaubert's place, got situated and went to get Sabine to take her with me up to see Johane.

I was greeted by Johane with the somber news that her mother, Irmine, had fallen ill. She was bedridden at this point. During the few weeks that I spent in Jeremie on this trip I went to visit with Johane's mother on several occasions. Although I didn't know this at the time, I suspect Irmine must have known that she was dying.

On one afternoon I spoke to her privately about marrying Johane. We had tried to arrange a sort of quick last minute Acte d'Civil marriage but the days had grown too short and I lacked some documentation, which was required, and I was also strapped for cash. The timing was all bad. I tried to get this marriage expedited because of certain matters involving Irmine and her reasoning. Her husband was already deceased, and now she found herself on the brink of the next life after this one. Her youngest child, a daughter named Aslyne, was only nine years old.

I was very fond of Aslyne. She was very engaging and full of life. She would come sit on my lap, ask me a ton of questions, and shower me with affection. She had big brown eyes and the most beautiful smile. Anytime I arrived at the house to see Johane or Irmine, I first sought out Aslyne. I had a fondness for her that was palpitating. *One day this girl is going to be something special*, I thought. She was full of great potential.

This quick and easy courthouse marriage, however, was never realized.

During the time spent in Jeremie on this particular trip I had been informed that I was being sought after by a guy named Theodore. Theodore was a big, black, muscular gentle giant with a lazy eye. He was non-educated and very slow mentally. He often did odds and ends for Yvrose. Before I could go find him he found me. One morning he showed up on Phaubert's doorstep to tell me that he needed me to come to his place in Caracolie. He lived in a small, very meager one-bedroom hut. I obliged and went with him.

Inside his place there was a young boy sleeping on a cardboard box that was spread out on the dirt floor. Theodore woke the boy up and when he rolled over I noticed that it was John, the boy I once saved from a beating by Yvrose. John looked up at me and rose to his feet to embrace me. Theodore then started to explain that Yvrose had just recently kicked John out of the orphanage and that he had taken refuge at Theodore's place in the meantime. I looked at John and said, "Why did she kick you out?"

He started to whimper and said that Yvrose had sent for him to bring food from the orphanage to where she was, at the boutique downtown. At one point on the way downtown John tripped and fell, dumping the food all over the ground. John, in his frightened haste, attempted to put all the food back into the container without explaining to Yvrose what happened. Yvrose would end up accusing him of trying to poison her. He was kicked out to the streets immediately. Of course, this was according to John. I was never able to confirm it. I knew what Yvrose was capable of so I chose to believe him.

John was twelve years old. He was old enough to know right from wrong. At the same time he was also savvy enough to know how to survive. He was yet another one of the kids in this orphanage that was founded by George that hailed from another part of the country. He was born in Port-au-Prince.

Theodore said he could not care for and keep John. He asked if I could take responsibility for him. In the time I had spent at the orphanage I had barely ever spoken a word to him other than when I delivered him from a beating. I wasn't at all interested in him to be honest. Alphonse had been my guy. I really wasn't aware that John had even existed before this. Yet, I had a weakness – the one weakness in Haiti that you cannot afford to have, and that's pity. That damn verse again, James 1:27 rang loud and clear. It was as though my spirit could see years into the future, which was telling me to proceed with great caution.

I said to Theodore, "Let me check with Phaubert's father, and I will get back to you."

I went straight to Phaubert's dad's place that day to ask the man known as Boss Claude if he would be OK with me leaving John to stay with Phaubert and his brothers. Boss Claude's first intuition was to say hell no, but after pondering it for a while, he decided to meet my request with a "yes" with two conditions: that I send money when I can, and while John lived under the roof of a house he was paying for, he would be at Boss Claude's disposal to run errands, be a messenger boy, and a porter. I said, "Deal," without even consulting John. His opinion mattered not. He was fortunate to have a roof to sleep under and a plate of food every day.

I now headed back to Port-au-Prince to spend a few days in early October. I took a small plane out of Jeremie instead of enduring the beating of a long bus trip. I ended up sitting in the front with the pilot, and once again, having a chance to use the headset and converse with him. This pilot was a young blond-haired man with a cast on his hand. He spoke in a much different tone than that of the white Mission Aviation pilot I once flew with. As we talked during the 45-minute flight I told him how much I loved Jeremie and hated Port-au-Prince.

"Port-au-Prince has way too many people, too much trash, too much noise, it's filthy and it smells like shit," I told him. Without batting an eye this young pilot said, "Port-au-Prince has all the pretty girls, and lots and lots of parties. I love Port-au-Prince!" I'd never forget that discussion and the impression it made on me.

When I got back to the capital I returned to Phaubert's Aunt Milly's house on Grand Rue. I ended up sitting out on Grand Rue just watching and studying the people. Phaubert had family on Rue d'Centre which was smack dab in the middle of the city. I started to learn to navigate the downtown streets all the way up over to the National Palace. One day while out walking I was thirsty and stopped off at a corner bar. Even though I had no idea where I was, the Bar Normandie would now know of me.

I heard commotion next door. The place was teeming with men who had guns. These were men in plain clothes. I had never seen anyone other than military or police carrying guns in the public arena. I heard a man yell out, "Frappe!" and the crowd of men yell back, "Ouvè!" again and again. Toto Constant was in the building calling out to "Knock!" to which people responded, "Open!" His far-right, paramilitary group, FRAPH (Front for the Advancement and Progress of Haiti) had their headquarters right next to the Bar Normandie. I had a clear view of Constant with a radio in his hand, walking around, receiving all kinds of accolades from the men inside. Being very young and still very ignorant to the political underworld in Haiti, I had no idea that Toto was a CIA operative. The place was electric. The energy on the inside of that building was incredible.

In the days to come the men in that building would be the driving force that turned the U.S.S. Harlan County back around and not allowing it to enter Haiti's main port. Constant would later brag and say it was a showdown between him and President Clinton. He was a very engaging personality. I would learn this throughout the years, that on the news and in the media, some men were portrayed as villains. Yet if you were afforded the opportunity to sit with these villains and have a civil discussion, they became human, and not the monsters they were being reported as. It was quite fascinating. At the time, I had still only yet been involved in this theatre known as Haiti for two years. I was very eager to learn more and more about what and how things worked. I always wanted to be on the side of the poor masses. That was the most important thing to me.

I would leave Haiti in mid October of 1993 and not return again until March of 1995.

JANUARY 1994

The morning of January 7, 1994, my mom woke me and said I had an international collect call from Haiti. It was Johane's oldest brother, Hantz. With great sadness in his voice he told me that his mother, Irmine, had died. I could feel his grief and sorrow through the phone. I told him that I would do what I could for them and a day later I sent $350 via Western Union for the family to pay for Irmine's funeral.

Calling Haiti in those days during the embargo was not easy. It was very difficult to get an open line of communication through to Jeremie. On some occasions, I'd try over and over again without any luck. And when I was finally able to secure a line through it was very difficult to hear what was being said and often, it was delayed with an echo. Take into account that I was also speaking a foreign tongue not of my own, and sometimes as the voices on the other end cut in and out, it was incredibly challenging to understand what was being said. Those phone calls were very expensive to boot. My communication with Johane and her family would become all but non-existent. We would go weeks on end without ever speaking through no fault of our own. That would end up ultimately being the death nail of our relationship. Slowly, because of the lack of communication between us, we'd start to drift apart. We were already apart physically, and now emotionally and mentally as well.

A few days after the death of Irmine I started working a job at Middlebury Manor in Akron. It was a nursing home smack dab in the middle of a bad area. I was hired to work security. Working this job would end up having a huge impact on me in a variety of ways.

On February 12, 1994, I was taking a heavy bag of trash out to a Dumpster across the street, right before the end of my shift at seven a.m. It was really cold and icy outside and I did a split on the ice as I started to throw the bag in. I felt a sharp tearing sensation right through my groin and into my testicles and penis. It was awful. I was taking the bus to and from work back then and during that particular bus ride home I was in tremendous pain. When I got home and tried to pee it was burning me. I put off going to the doctor because I was old school. I would only go to the doctor if I was dying.

Dealing with this annoying discomfort and burning sensation started to become a lingering issue. Masturbation was no longer an enjoyable experience. At twenty-one years of age I did not want to get used to living like this. In the meantime, I continued working at Middlebury Manor while suffering quietly. It was an injury I was embarrassed about and I didn't want anybody to know what I was going through.

While working at Middlebury Manor I met a very cute, short, and dark-skinned woman from Sierra Leone in Africa named Margaret. Her accent was lovely and she had the biggest butt I had ever seen in my life. She was very different, and very beautiful in my eyes. I grew fond of her. Margaret would tell me of a Haitian friend of hers named Fadia who lived in Akron. Of course, this was very intriguing to me. I had to meet this girl from Haiti.

Margaret shared our contact info and it wasn't long before Fadia and I were talking and becoming friends. I then met Fadia's aunt and uncle, Gerrard and Gabrielle, who we called Gerry and Mòmòtte. They had been living in the U.S. for quite some time and had two adult sons, Pierre and Paul. They were an older, light-skinned couple hailing from Les Cayes and Camp Perrin in Haiti.

Gerry and Mòmòtte became like my Haitian parents. They were great mentors for me and taught me so much about Haiti and the Haitian people. We would often have passionate discussions and debates concerning their homeland. I soaked it all in like a sponge. Gerry had fled Haiti shortly after Francois Duvalier had come to power. I learned so many intimate details and characteristics of Haitians that I otherwise would have never known. Having them in my life was a tremendous advantage to me as I continued to explore the depths and substance of all things Haiti.

Through Gerry and Mòmòtte I met another Haitian couple, Wilner and Yvrose. Wilner and Yvrose had a daughter still in Haiti named Glory and two young sons, Whitney and Donald. They were a much younger couple than Gerry and Mòmòtte and I ended up having some really fascinating discussions with them about Haiti. On occasion, Fadia and I babysat Whitney and Donald when Wilner and Yvrose were both working. On one afternoon I had Whitney with me and we rode the bus from Akron to Barberton. We spent that afternoon running around Lake Anna. Whitney was terrorizing the ducks and the swans. One of the swans challenged Whitney and bit him. Whitney, without batting an eye, went after the swan at the edge of the water. I had to quickly pull him back from going in fully clothed. Whitney had stayed engaged almost as if he had come prepared for a battle.

It was a telling sign. Years down the road, Whitney Mercilus led the nation in sacks during his junior year at the University of Illinois and went on to be the first round pick of the Houston Texans in 2011. He is currently playing linebacker in the NFL for that organization.

By the time August rolled around I was still suffering from pain in my groin area. Between March and July I had already visited a couple of different doctors and one urologist who examined me with a long scope that went into the tip of my penis and he couldn't find anything conclusive. That was a very painful visit. I continued to search for more opinions, which led me all the way up to the Cleveland Clinic. A female doctor examined me and it was quite embarrassing. She put gloves on and examined my rectal cavity with her fingers. That was when I was diagnosed with a prostate infection, which caused me lots of grief not only in my groin area but into my stomach and down through my legs. It must have been a residual effect of the initial injury, and over time got worse. Going untreated for so long put me in a lot of pain. Living in that type of pain and discomfort became mentally taxing on my spirit. Knowing something was wrong and not being able to find out was brutal.

After finally getting a diagnosis I was relieved. I would get the right medication and slowly but surely get better. I didn't start feeling normal again until September – nearly seven months after my injury. This would not be the last time in my life that I'd suffer from great physical pain and not know why. I was going to get used to being comfortable with being uncomfortable, that's for damn sure.

On September 17, 1994, I was on edge monitoring the events in Haiti. President Clinton had dispatched former President Jimmy Carter, General Colin Powell, and Democratic Senator Sam Nunn to negotiate the return of President Aristide to power with Haitian Generals Cedras and Biamby. It wasn't really a negotiation. It was basically the U.S. officials telling the generals they had to leave now or face an American military invasion. As negotiations were stalling during these talks President Clinton finally ordered President Carter to leave immediately. The military invasion had been green lighted. U.S. troops were already airborne. In the waning moments President Carter finally got General Cedras to agree to stand down and to peacefully go into exile. It was Haitian theatre at its finest. The Haitian generals really had no intentions on standing their ground against the U.S. military might. Operation Uphold Democracy was under way on September 19, 1994.

Watching all of this take place from afar was very difficult for me personally. I became very sad and depressed, not only because I missed Haiti, but because of the weight of somehow missing my calling in life. The remedy called for in those times and during those long lonely nights was listening to Haitian Konpa music groups, Zin and Lakol. I'd fall asleep every night listening to those cassette tapes.

On October 15, 1994, President Jean Bertrand Aristide was restored to power by the United States government backed by the United Nations. I watched it all play out on CNN Live. It was truly a historic day and one that brought a new hope and new life to Haiti. I couldn't wait to get back someday soon.

In December of 1994 I picked up a job working at the Quaker Square Hotel in downtown Akron as a bellman. I was afforded the opportunity to meet people like Lonnie Anderson and Tony Randall. Tony was married to a very young girl at that time. I had nice conversations with him while seeing him to and from his room and carrying his bags during his stay. On the day he left he tipped me a particular five dollar bill that he called a lucky bill. He said to me, "Zeke, you are a very interesting young man. It has been a great pleasure speaking with you. Good luck in Haiti and with everything you do." Hearing words like that from a legend like Randall made me feel like a million bucks.

One afternoon I'd find myself in one of the hotel elevators with business and hotel tycoon Jay Nusbaum. Mr. Nusbaum told me to take my hands out of my pants pockets. That threw me for a loop. I just looked at him with a deep long stare of great contempt. I had no idea who he was at the time, however.

He then said to me, "I'm Mr. Nusbaum, I run this place. Take your hands out of your pockets, it looks unprofessional."

As we stepped out of the elevator I slowly but surely complied with his request. But I was not happy about it. It was tough for me to work at

164

this hotel and interact with so many wealthy people, especially after my time spent in Haiti. I had a healthy dislike for people with great wealth. I thought again back to Erroll Flynn in *The Adventures of Robin Hood*, taking from the rich to give to the poor. That is what I always wanted to do in my life.

MARCH OF 1995

In March of 1995 I would take some time off from my job at the hotel and take a trip back to Haiti. I was well liked at the hotel. I'd already put in my ninety-day probationary period so I appealed to Jay Nusbaum's son, Jeff, to let me take a few weeks off for a humanitarian trip to Haiti. I liked Jeff a lot. He was much different from his father. He was relatable. He wasn't always around but when he was I enjoyed conversing with him. My supervisors finally signed off on it and I was back in Haiti.

Phaubert greeted me at the airport. He brought Sabine with him on the bus from Jeremie to Port-au-Prince just days before. I was so thrilled to see them both once again. The next day we went to the smaller airport down the road from the main airport to get tickets to fly to Jeremie the following day. Then we headed back up the road on foot to the main airport. I was carrying Sabine when we came upon a mob beating a man to death. I quickly handed Sabine over to Phaubert and said to stay there.

I ran ahead to this gruesome scene of a man with his hands bound behind his back while he was being bludgeoned by a few different men that were holding big two-by-fours and stones. The man was a bloody mess and pleading for his life. I was scared and angry. Fight or flight, and I fought. Adrenaline was at an all-time high and without any reservations for my own safety, I got myself between the man who was getting the beating and the men beating him. I defended this man and fought off these attackers while suffering some blows on my body that were intended for the man that was bound.

It seemed like forever but in a matter of moments a couple of Haitian policemen showed up and took the man getting the beating into custody. As the police were attending to this man another man was brought to the scene. He, too, was a bloody mess and one of his eyes were swollen shut. One of the men who had been delivering street justice in Haiti then made me aware that the individual I was defending had robbed and beaten this man with six other guys. The man who had been robbed and beaten was so pathetically meager and graceful in his speech it angered me. He said that he didn't want to see harm come to the man who had just nearly killed him moments earlier. I became enraged at the man I had just been defending with my life. I ran over to where the police were holding him and smacked him as hard as I could in his head. I wanted to hand down a *Lawrence of Arabia* type judgment of my own. In the movie, Lawrence had once saved a man when the man had fallen asleep and fell off of his camel unbeknownst to everyone else while they crossed the desert. Lawrence risked his own life to go all the way back to get the man against the will of the other men and even after being advised not to because it would mean a death sentence for him in that harsh environment. At some point later, the same man Lawrence had saved in the desert ended up killing a man from another tribe in a dispute. To avoid conflict between the two tribes of Arabs, Lawrence executed the man himself. I would have definitely killed that man with my own hands on that day in March of 1995.

The entire time there were U.S. military troops standing nearby watching all this happen and doing nothing about it. They were standing behind a chained fence and barbed wire with razor sharp metal. I walked over within earshot of them and I started cursing them aloud. I cursed them and their mission. They cursed back at me and made threats. I called them "pussy ass cowards." I said, "Why are any of you here if you're just gonna stand by and do nothing while watching Haitians kill each other?" This was now life number four of nine used up for me.

Phaubert, Sabine, and I flew to Jeremie the next day. Back in Jeremie I had a surprise run-in with Leonne right up the hill from where Phaubert lived. Because I was no longer with Johane I had mentioned to her that I was still waiting for her. She now seemed more open to the idea. I assured her that I would stay patient in the meantime. After Leonne and I conversed for a few minutes I continued on up the hill to visit with Madam George, where I ran into a group of white American teenagers from Indiana. There was a young man amongst them named Dewitt. Dewitt's mom lived in

Indiana. His dad lived overseas. Dewitt told me that he had lived on the continent of Africa and also in Israel. He was already well traveled at a very young age. We hit it off right away. I would play chaperone to the group for the time they were in Jeremie.

I also met a young boy named Jean Michel that tagged along with this group of young white kids from the states. In Jeremie, Jean Michel is known by the nickname Ti Konplo. Ti Konplo in Creole translates into "little schemer/conspirator." He would become a legendary figure in Jeremie in the years to come. Ti Konplo told me that I was the first white man that he ever looked upon as a Haitian. He said, "Ayisyen ou ye Zeke." ("Zeke you are Haitian.")

A few years down the road I would end up speaking with Dewitt on an international phone call from London. He was attending Oxford at this point. He told me that he had written an essay about me for a class he had in which there were 2,000 students. He told me that his professor was very impressed with his presentation and this man named Zeke in Haiti. Little things like that encouraged me to keep on with the pursuit of finding my reason why in Haiti.

By the beginning of April I was back in the States and back working at the hotel for the next three months. Towards the later part of July I was fed up with the bellhop gig. I had made good money in tips at the job but I grew tired of seeing well-to-do people come and go who had lots of cash to throw away. I also grew annoyed with the way people in management talked to me and other employees. In my mind I was much more educated than these people. I was much more traveled and cultured, too. I thought they were very ignorant and disrespectful.

A black man working as a shoe-shine guy at the hotel during my tenure was a practicing Muslim. His name was John. John was pro-black and anti-white, make no mistake about it. But he knew how to play the game. He shined the white man's shoes just as nice, if not better, than that of his black counterparts. He would bullshit them and politic them and stroke their egos the entire time he serviced them, all the while smiling to their faces. Deep down he couldn't stand any of them. He'd refer to them as crackers to me privately. He said to me, "I like you Zeke, or at least I can tolerate you, but you still a cracker."

One day I said, "John, I'm busting up outta here. I'm gonna quit. I'm going back to Haiti. I'm gonna stick it to all of them here at the hotel, bro."

He got a big smile on his face and said, "Get the fuck outta here, you serious? What you fittin' on doin' Zeke?"

"Just you wait, you'll hear about it soon enough."

He said, "No shit Zeke," with his big shoe shine grin, "you gonna stick it to the man?"

I said, "You're goddamn right I am."

A couple of days later it was really busy at the hotel. There were several tour buses full of people coming to check in on this day. The amount of luggage was overwhelming. I couldn't keep up with it all. The lobby became so congested with luggage that they started to have me wheel it in the back out of sight, behind the front desk. My lunch break was looming and I felt my sugar starting to get low. My pager was blowing up with calls from the front desk about things they needed me to do.

I hurried by the front desk and said, "I'm going to lunch, my sugar is low, I'll see you later." As I headed up to the front entrance to walk out those front doors for the last time I saw John coming in to open up his booth where he worked shining shoes. I said, "See you around Johnny, I'm the fuck outta here. I'm going back to Haiti."

He said, "Get the hell outta here," with a big smile, laughing hysterically.

I said, "It's crazy busy in here, they're gonna be pissed when they see I don't return from lunch." I thanked him for the deep spiritual and political debates that we shared together. I learned a lot from him.

He said, "Zeke," as we shook hands for the last time, "I can't stand these peckerwood crackers man. You're the first cracker that I can honestly say that I have ever tolerated. I like you Zeke."

I said, "Thank you, brother John, it means a lot coming from someone like you." I glanced up at the clock and said, "Well brother, I got a bus to catch. Shits gonna hit the fan here in about a half hour or so when they see I don't return. Enjoy your front row seats to the show Johnny."

He laughed hard and yelled out, "Get the fuck outta here kid." I saluted him and took off running. On that day I stuck it hard to the man. In this case it was Mr. Jay Nusbaum. It felt good! A few years down the road I'd pass by the hotel looking for John. I was informed by someone at the hotel that John had died.

RIP John. I received some real hardcore life knowledge from you and I will forever be grateful.

I flew back to Haiti a few days later. Upon arriving Phaubert greeted me at the airport with some very surprising news. There had been a blow up – a mutiny – at Yvrose's orphanage days earlier. A few of the older teenage girls wanted out and they all left, including Leonne and three of her cousins, Gertha, Marie-Mate, and Maria. Phaubert informed me that they were now back up in Monn Kabrit where they were originally from.

I quickly sent for Leonne to come back down from Monn Kabrit to stay with me. We stayed at one of her cousin's places in Santo 22. She had another cousin in Santo 8 that we frequented also. John and Sabine had both come to the capital with Phaubert on this trip, too. I spent the next six weeks running between Monn Kabrit, Phaubert's Aunt Milly's place on Grand Rue, and Leonne's cousins' places in Santo 8 and 22. Up in Monn Kabrit, Leonne's family was split down the middle. Half were Christians, and half were Vodouisants. I spent my time politicking both sides and bouncing back and forth between them.

The road from Croix-des-Bouquets to Monn Kabrit was a very dangerous one because of the mountainous terrain and unpaved roads. There were always deadly accidents on that mountain. Often times you'd see dead bodies on the road between both places. It was a long desolate strip of road leading out of Croix-des-Bouquets, which made it a convenient place to dispose of bodies. On a couple of occasions I saw dogs eating what was left of human corpses.

I attended a Vodou ceremony in Carrefour with John and I was granted access to film it. It was a mesmerizing experience for me. I watched a man cut a turtle's head off and drink its blood. The drums being played were incredible. The ground was shaking underneath my feet. I watched as women were overtaken by spirits and were in a sort of trance while they flailed their bodies all over the place. I was becoming even more rooted in this place called Haiti and I couldn't get enough of it.

I would lose my virginity during this trip at the ripe old age of twenty-two. Leonne and I had sex on a piece of cardboard on a dirt floor in a one-room tin shack in Santo 22. You could hear the rats scuffle around in the dark room as Leonne and I became intimate for the first time. I had no idea what I was doing. It would take a couple cracks at it before I finally got the hang of it. I would finally seal the deal at her other cousin's place in Santo 8 about a week later. We were now officially a legit couple.

I spent my days ripping and racing all over Port-au-Prince. Riding on tap taps, hanging on with one hand on the very back of them. I was in and out of Cite Soleil, hanging with new friends and playing basketball. This big city Haiti life which I once despised was newer to me and I was loving it. It was action packed. The countryside had a slower pace but this city life was fast paced and hardcore. I embraced it.

I made acquaintance with a guy one evening who worked night shift security at the old Military General Headquarters across from the National Palace. He agreed to let me come in and walk around. I sat in the very room where 11 months earlier former President Carter had sat and negotiated terms with the Haitian generals. I went into an empty room that was once General Cedras's old office. I took a full tour of the building that night. Upstairs, in the far right corner, there was a bathroom that had a shower. The history behind that building fascinated me. I saw it as a great privilege to be given access to it. I wanted to experience it all.

My father decided to make a trip to Haiti and see for himself what this place was all about. He came at the end of August and stayed approximately ten days. Before he came, however, I fell ill. I was worn down physically and ended up with a fever. I was vomiting and had diarrhea. I suffered with these symptoms for several days before my father made it to Haiti.

When the day finally came for me to pick my father up from the airport I could barely stand up and walk. We were scheduled to take a boat to Jeremie but that was now out of the question. A couple of days into my dad's ten-day Haiti experience my health would take a turn for the worse. I had lost so much weight. I couldn't keep any food down. I had grown sickly thin.

Phaubert's cousin, Jojo, took me in a cab to the General Hospital. I couldn't walk, I was so weak. I left my dad behind with Phaubert, John, and Sabine to fend for himself. Jojo left me at the hospital and had to go off to work. I laid on the floor in the emergency room, barely conscious, for quite some time before I was tended to. Someone on a gurney in the room expired and they took the body off, quickly changed the sheet, and threw me up on it. Before I knew what was going on they were trying to stick a needle inside of my arm. I tried fighting them off for a quick second. I knew that hospital was HIV/AIDS-infested and I was terrified. I had no choice but to let them have their way with me. They put an IV in me immediately. They also drew some blood to run tests. I laid in misery, listening to the cries of human beings in agony all day long, half-awake in the stifling heat. They brought in a man whose arm was chopped off. There was blood all over the emergency room floor. I was having an out-of-body experience.

I was finally told that I was suffering from typhoid fever and they wanted to admit me. I said, "Oh, hell no." I ripped the IV from my arm, sending blood squirting everywhere. The person in charge chastised me and I cursed him. I said, "I'm fucking outta here, goddammit." The IV fluids that I was receiving all day long did wonders. Jojo had bought me some antibiotics. I drank as much as I could for the next few days and continued swallowing the antibiotics and by the end of my father's trip I started feeling much better.

On our second to last night in Haiti I gave my dad a tour of the old military headquarters. We took a bunch of photos there that night. I got the film developed after returning to the States, and found that not one picture came out on the entire roll. To me that spoke to the dark spiritual nature of not only that particular building, but the presidential palace as well. Human sacrifices are said to have taken place in these buildings to appease the dyab in the Vodou religion. And although that's left up to interpretation, I know what I know from first-hand experience and from what I learned from Gerry and Mòmòtte concerning Haiti.

My dad did enjoy the nightlife in Port-au-Prince. It caused him to reminisce about his time in Okinawa. He really enjoyed drinking the Prestige beer and trying to communicate with the locals. We went to Cite Soleil on our last day in Haiti. This was the day that would change the course of the direction of my dad's life forever. After witnessing what he saw there he said Haiti was definitely the most devastatingly poorest place he had ever seen in his life. After that day he would never step foot inside a church again.

My father had petitioned Gideons International before making the trip down to Haiti about getting twenty-five Haitian Creole bibles to distribute. They gave him the runaround before finally deciding to send them. He took that hard. How could they not treat such a request with great enthusiasm and expedite it immediately? He took the slow response as a slap in the face. After his trip to Haiti where he laid his eyes on so much human suffering he became angry and blamed Christians. I, for one, couldn't have agreed more. We left Haiti together the second week of September. My dad had spent his entire ten days there without taking one bowel movement. It wasn't that he didn't have to, because he did, but the sight of the outhouse was such a turnoff to him that he held it in. He barely ate the entire trip. He drank and smoked quite a bit, however. The stress on his almost 52-year-old body would soon take its toll.

We got home from Haiti on September 9th and my dad declared that he was done with Christians and going to church. He wrote them all off as hypocrites. On Monday, September 18, he suffered his second heart attack. Five weeks later on Monday, October 23, he suffered his third one. We had only been back from Haiti just over six weeks and my father had two heart attacks back to back.

There must have been some type of correlation between my father's shunning of the Lord God related to his health. My dad was a Frank Sinatra type of guy. He was going to do it his way or no way.

During that fall I picked up a job working security at JR Engineering in Barberton. I sent money back to Haiti for Leonne, John, and Sabine as much as I could. In the meantime, I went to the International Institute in Akron to see what I could do to bring Leonne to the states. I felt as though I owed her a great debt for what she had done for me years earlier when I fell ill with malaria in Tozya. I did love her. I was very comfortable with her. I thought she had suffered enough at the hands of Yvrose on account of me so I was focused on making this happen. I was also twenty-two and thought it was time to get married.

At the end of December I picked up another job at the YMCA in Akron at the Firestone branch. I moved into an apartment with my older brother, Jon, on Norton Ave by Cox Funeral Home, a couple of blocks from where I grew up on Lloyd Street.

JANUARY OF 1996

In late January I went back to Haiti for about a week to see about getting Leonne's passport, and that started by getting documents like her birth certificate in order. We would need these if she was going to get a visa. On the way up the mountain there was a brutal accident with scores killed when a truck careened out of control and went over the cliff. Bodies were everywhere. It was another example of the brutal reality that was Haiti. That sort of trauma can take its toll on the mind.

I stayed up in Monn Kabrit with the side of her family that was heavily involved in Vodou. One of her uncles named Sadyefè was a Hougan, a male priest in the Vodou religion. He had a peristyle that I'd often enter in to and visit. I was continually seeking and inquiring into how Vodou really worked. During the nights, Leonne and I had sex in her grandmother's house as the Vodou drums played outside our door early into the morning hours. It was intoxicating. Her grandmother Fotilia, who we called Aiya, was a Manbo, a female priestess in the Vodou religion. She was particularly feared in Monn Kabrit for being a dyab. I got along with her just fine.

On my last day in Monn Kabrit I stayed at Leonne's other grandmother's place. She was on the Christian side. Her name was Therez. I came out of her house really early one morning and I found myself paralyzed with fear as I stood face to face with a dragon-like creature that was monstrous in size. I couldn't move. I had only ever seen creatures like this in the zoo or in the movies. I stood still without breathing. It was staring right at me.

Some years later I would be home in the states watching Steve Irwin's *Crocodile Hunter* TV show and his wife, Terri, talked about this reptile called the Rhinoceros Iguana. She went on to say that these creatures are only found in Haiti and the Dominican Republic. I leaped up out of my seat, yelling that I once came face to face with one of those things. Haiti provided me the great fortune of such experiences.

In March I found out that Leonne was pregnant after all the fucking we had done. Both of our birthdays fell in March, mine on the fifth when I would turn twenty-three, and hers on the sixteenth, when she would turn

173

twenty. We are both Pisces. This was a fantastic birthday surprise for me. I was excited to be a dad.

Again, in those days communication was still hard to come by. When I spoke to Leonne again in April she informed me that she had lost the baby. I was heartbroken. It really bothered me. She, however, didn't seem the slightest bit annoyed. A Haitian man had once told me, "Zeke, Haitians are like flies. You smash one and kill it, and nobody cares." That was made evident to me by Leonne's reactions over the phone. I was very disheartened by it, but I had to move on.

Going into the summer of 1996 I was now working as a camp counselor with the kids at the Firestone branch of the Akron YMCA. It kept me busy and my mind occupied as I continued to recover mentally from Leonne losing the baby. In August I returned to Haiti to go with Leonne to the U.S. Consulate in downtown Port-au-Prince for her visa interview. I had handled all her paperwork through the International Institute's immigration attorney Pat Barger. Pat served as my lawyer and she was all business. I really liked her. After waiting in a long line all morning at the Consulate she finally got her interview and was granted a visa a day later. It was a K-1 fiancé visa which required us to be married within ninety days of her entry into the U.S. If we were not married within that time she would be considered an illegal alien.

One very interesting conversation took place with me, Leonne, and some of her extended family members at a home in Bon Repos the day before we left Haiti together. One of Leonne's female second cousins asked me why a white man like myself wanted to marry an ugly poor black girl like Leonne. She asked this very candidly with a great sense of conviction in Leonne's presence. I was taken aback. I was even more surprised that her words were not objected to by anyone present in the room. The girl asking me this did so with such sincerity and a longing to hear a truthful answer from me. In Haiti that class division, that color division, still runs ever so deep. This second cousin of Leonne's, Leonne herself, and Haitians by the hundreds of thousands, will often times view themselves as not worthy because of their class and color. Direct evidence of the mental chains that slavery produced and left behind for centuries yet still.

174

My response was a simple one. I said, "I love her. She's a beautiful black girl. I love her black skin."

Her rebuttal to me was that I lied, she's ugly. "Li pa bel. She's not beautiful. There are so many pretty light-skinned Haitian girls, why would you choose Leonne?"

I said "She's beautiful to me, she's a really tough girl. She's a fanm djanm, I like that a lot."

Intimacy like this with Haitians would help me to delve deeper into trying to understand the Haitian psyche.

Leonne and I returned home to the States. Summer camp with the Y kids was nearing an end. I took Leonne along with me for the remainder of those days working with the kids so she could get out and about a little bit. She was very quiet and reserved. She didn't make much of an attempt to talk to anyone. She was a good Christian girl though, a very good person. She was very obedient. She was well put together and I enjoyed having sex with her. That in my mind was the greatest benefit to being married. We were married in a courthouse wedding on October 30, 1996.

For the next year we lived quietly and humbly while sharing an apartment with my brother, Jon. Leonne cooked and cleaned and took care of the house. When she was finally able to get a work permit she got a job at the Sheraton Suites hotel in Cuyahoga Falls. She would take the bus every day to work because I still hadn't yet taken care of getting my license or a car.

I got a new job working at a factory in Barberton called Malco's, and for the next few years, bounced from job to job while still continuing to travel to Haiti. Leonne's steady income freed me up a little bit to afford me the financial freedom I never enjoyed before.

AUGUST OF 1997

In August of 1997 I went back to Haiti. At that time Sabine was back, living in Jeremie, and John was making due, living with some friends of his in Port-au-Prince. Leonne and I were supporting them from the States. I sent John in advance of my arrival to get Sabine so I could spend some time with her while in Port-au-Prince. I didn't have the time to go to Jeremie this trip and I did not want to put my body through the pounding of traveling by boat or bus.

On this trip to Haiti a fire would be rekindled with Johane. In August of 1994 Johane and I officially broke up over the phone. She had moved on and started seeing a guy named Jude long before this, however. A friend of mine in Jeremie had alerted me to their relationship. I berated her over the phone about it when she finally came clean. She then scolded me verbally, saying after her mom died, she never heard from me. I told her that it was not my fault. I would always try to call and could never get through. When Johane and her siblings lost their mom they went to stay with their grandmother in Lasous. Johane no longer had eyes watching over her and when Jude stepped into her life he convinced her that the white man named Zeke wasn't ever coming back to Haiti for her, and to forget him, and she did.

My last words to her that day on the phone, when she stood in a booth inside the Teleco station that I used to go to, were, "One day you will live to regret this decision." I promised her that.

As fate would have it I ran into her in a Delmas neighborhood where she was spending summer vacation at a cousin's house. She looked so beautiful and I desired her. I spent the night with her and we had unprotected sex. I think some of this infidelity was because of whispers I had once heard among some of Leonne's relatives that she might have purposely aborted the baby back in April of 1996. Now that she was pregnant, someone told her, I might not come back for her. Fearing that and being mentally fragile may have caused her to abort the baby. It even made me wonder whether she was pregnant by someone else? Could that be the reason she aborted the baby? Although I never could confirm these things, and Leonne denied them, it stuck through my heart like a thousand knives. It was painful. I was hurt.

I think I was now on a personal vendetta to repay those who had transgressed against me. It's always important to stress this fact. At this point in my life I was no longer reading God's word and my praying to Him was almost nonexistent, unless of course I needed or wanted something. So I fucked Johane with no hesitation. Johane would have been my wife had her mom not died.

That cleared my conscience of any wrong doing, until I got back home. Within twenty-four hours I was honest with Leonne and told her about my affair with this girl named Johane. I felt badly, yet part of me just desired to see her hurt just like me, and to see her authentic reaction. She was pretty emotionless. She shed a few tears for a brief moment. I held her and told her that I still loved her. I just really wanted to see some passion on her side. I demanded that. I don't know that I had any real intentions of ever going back with Johane because I felt she betrayed me. That still bothered me. Trusting her would be difficult. But she was very beautiful and a great love-making partner. I would keep that going as long as I could get it. Clearly, I was now walking a slippery slope.

Living in the States with Leonne and Jon became mundane. I was thinking to myself is this it? There had to be more to this life. I would slowly but surely start to drift apart from Leonne emotionally. She was always void of showing any emotions. She was not highly educated. She was just plain meager and simple. I was sometimes embarrassed to present her places in public because of her lack of communication skills.

As we shared an apartment with my brother, Leonne and I, for the most part, lived a tranquil lifestyle. But on a couple of occasions emotions ran high, with us arguing, which turned into physical confrontations. A few different times in Haiti I had witnessed men being physically abusive to women. I saw some fights between male and female companions in both Jeremie and Port-au-Prince. Domestic violence in Haiti was rampant back then. As I watched this type of violence play out over a period of time, it would become normal. It was no big deal, business as usual. Although I didn't realize it at the time, that type of stuff was seeping deep into my psyche. It was starting to become something I tolerated. What you tolerate you indeed encourage.

I continued on working local factory and security guard jobs. I was playing with house money. Jon paid half the rent and we paid half the rent. Leonne working full time at the hotel always provided us a steady income. That freed me up to work wherever and whenever I wanted. We continued making due in the meantime. We sent money back to Haiti for the kids I was supporting and for some of Leonne's family.

APRIL OF 1998

As the spring of 1998 rolled in I took advantage of Leonne's flexibility at work to continue to travel to Haiti. I was still searching for my why? For what reason did I end up going to Haiti in the first place?

In April I went ahead on my own, but my brother, Ben, soon followed in May. When Ben arrived in Haiti we flew to Jeremie together. I was really excited and thrilled that my younger brother was seizing the opportunity to see my world through different lenses and a new perspective. Ben was consumed by the sights and sounds of Haiti from the minute he touched down. It was a culture shock for him, but he embraced it and adjusted quickly. Ben had been a pretty good athlete himself growing up, and that would come into play on his inaugural trip to Haiti. Phaubert was part of a basketball team that he played for and helped coach in Jeremie called Pwa Nomal. The best team in Jeremie was a team called Tempo, which was financed and coached by Haitian Paul Altidor, who was from Jeremie, but now resided in Boston. Altidor's Tempo team had beaten Phaubert's Pwa Nomal team by some seventy points in a previous matchup between them. This was now the playoffs, so Phaubert asked me and my brother Ben to play for his team. Of course, we gladly agreed to play.

A couple of days before, Ben, Phaubert, and I went to see Paul and talk to him about the upcoming game. Paul's team had all the best equipment from the shoes, to the uniforms, and newer basketballs at their disposal. They also had all the best players. Their guys were big, fast, strong, and well coached by Altidor to boot.

Paul greeted us warmly with a big smile. He was very generous and agreed to let me and my brother play for Pwa Nomal, even though we hadn't played the entire season. I went in on Paul right away with the trash talk. I said, "Your Tempo team is in big trouble now that these two white boys from Ohio are in town."

Paul laughed and said confidently, "Oh yeah? We are gonna see."

Phaubert couldn't contain his excitement. He knew with the Petrie brothers on board that his team had a shot. The game was to be played at the basketball court in Jeremie by the Sténio Vincent Library up the hill from where Phaubert lived. Because of that we felt that we had a home court advantage of sorts. It was Jeremie's version of Rucker Park. They packed people in to watch the games. People filled to capacity the three decks of cement seats and it was standing room only all around the court.

At tip off it was still light outside. As the sun went down the light fixtures were turned on and we played under the lights. The place was electric that night. Loud music blared during the warm ups. Fans were already talking trash. This was one of the special moments I lived for. Phaubert started me with the first five and Ben was sixth man off the bench. I was pressuring Tempo's guards up and down the floor, something they were not accustomed to and they did not like it. I had about a dozen steals, which led to a lot of easy fast break points for us. I was talking all kinds of trash to these guys. Their big guys started to take it personally and really made the physicality of the game extreme. They pushed, shoved, and threw some vicious elbows, and set some teeth rattling screens. At one point I was even talking trash to the referee.

Ben played really well, hitting some big three-point shots for us to help keep it a tight game. Tempo was not used to playing in such a tightly contested game. They always blew their opponents out. That was until the kids from the great state of Ohio showed up. The Tempo team's confidence was exuded in the fact that coach Altidor wasn't at all even bothered by our request to play in such a big game and agreed with no hesitation or reservations. They allowed Pwa Nomal to bring in two free agents without any objections whatsoever. That was arguably the most fun I ever had in my life. I lived for competition of that nature. I was jacked up and talking shit to the folks in the crowd who were cheering for Tempo.

With four minutes to go in the game the score was Tempo 54, Pwa Nomal 50. Tempo was at the line shooting a free throw. The ref was giving Tempo every call imaginable in their favor. It started to become evident to me that he was trying his best to dictate the outcome and ensure that Tempo won. I started getting in his ear about the calls and then I slapped him on his ass, which led to a technical foul and them at the free throw line with us only trailing by four points.

As the free throw was about to be shot, in classic Haitian fashion,

179

the lights went out to an angry roar of everyone in attendance, and the game was over. Tempo was declared the winner. They were very fortunate because at that point they were hanging on for dear life. Phaubert never once took me out of the game. I played so hard. I had been diving after loose balls on the concrete. I left my guts on the floor that evening. When I went back to Phaubert's after the game I vomited profusely. All night long I vomited.

Although we had left the court that night very disappointed, everyone in attendance went home knowing that they witnessed two blan from Ohio putting on a gutsy show on an undermanned and undersized team against some Goliaths in comparison. I thanked coach Paul Altidor for allowing me and Ben to play. Fourteen years later, Paul Altidor became the Haitian Ambassador to the United States of America serving in that post from May of 2012 until February of 2019.

After Ben and I returned home from Haiti in May he invited me to attend a Promise Keepers event with him held at the old Pontiac Silverdome. Ben was heavily into church. He was attending the House of the Lord in Akron, which was pastored by Reverend Joey Johnson. Ben had met and become friends with an African American male named James while attending the House of the Lord. James was married but living a double life. He was a closet homosexual who was trying to fit into society and be accepted by the church community. He was still going through that painful process of trying to be someone he wasn't.

Ben told me that this event had a revival theme to it. I had never been to Detroit so I jumped at the opportunity. Besides, at that time, I was enjoying total autonomy in my comings and goings at the house with Leonne. She wasn't going to object or voice any displeasure in whatever I chose to do. Doing what I wanted when I wanted were the only things other than sex that made these married days tolerable. I hate even uttering those sentiments because Leonne was such a beautiful, kind spirit. She had just been through a rough upbringing in Haiti which produced her hard exterior.

James was also with us. After we checked into the hotel where we were going to spend the night, and James stepped out of the room, Ben hit me with the news that James was a homosexual. Until that point, I hadn't

180

realized just how homophobic I was. I lashed out at Ben immediately. "Get the fuck outta here! Are you fucking serious man?" I was now pissed at Ben for bringing me along. I saw this as a sort of premeditated action. My presence was what would put him at ease with James. He was just as homophobic as I was. "I get it, I understand, but fuck bro," I said. Ben said to just act normal. I was like, "OK, OK, but fuck you."

Ben and I slept in one bed, and James slept in the other one. That weekend went by without incident. As a matter of fact, surprisingly enough, I enjoyed the time there and James company. If you didn't previously know, you would have never guessed that James was gay. That made it a much easier transition for me personally.

James and I would exchange numbers and become friends. He was married and not making anything obvious, so I tolerated him.

One evening a couple of weeks later James and I were visiting together in Barberton, just sitting and talking about life. This is where he came out and opened up to me about being gay. I played ignorant, as though I had no idea, and was totally surprised. I said, "Oh really?" with a lump in my throat, and my heart racing. I was so uncomfortable but trying to stay the course.

"Wow, that's interesting," I said. I tried to subtly start in on the questioning as to how and why. Things like, when did you first know? Have you been discriminated against? He was both black and gay, a double whammy in our society. He was straight behind the eight-ball. I coolly played it off as though I was totally OK with him being gay and that it in no way even bothered me. I was lying straight through my teeth. I did enjoy his company and conversation, so once again, I tolerated him.

As our friendship grew the only thing I didn't really care for was the affection that James displayed when we parted ways after being out somewhere together. He loved giving long and very tight hugs. I didn't. They made me so uncomfortable. To not hurt his feelings or be offensive, I embraced it. Had I let being homophobic get the best of me, I may not be alive today. Meeting James would end up being more living proof to me that nothing in life ever happens by coincidence.

In June, I started working for the Barberton Parks and Recreation summer program. I was responsible for running the summer program activities for the youth at Edgewood Park. During that time I was going through a sort of application process to appear on MTV's *True Life* series. I was very familiar with MTV programming back then. *True Life* was a show that was always very interesting and featured people from many different walks of life. I thought my story was every bit as interesting, if not more, than the ones I had been watching on MTV.

I reached out to Lucia Engstrom, a producer at MTV. I explained a little bit about myself and she informed me of what they required of me to be featured on the very popular *True Life* series. I would need to do some interviews, film myself answering some pre-written questions, and explain my story on film. This required making another trip to Haiti to film what my life looked like down there. I thought that this could be the break I had been waiting for. If I could get my quest in Haiti made public, maybe I could draw some interest from people around the country, willing to get involved and back me financially. I bought a ticket to Haiti for August. Everything was set.

At the end of July, I suffered a severe sprained left ankle with some ligament damage while playing basketball on the job with the high school kids at the park. I was to be leaving for Haiti to film for the *True Life* episode in the coming days but now I was on crutches. I wasn't going to be denied this opportunity, however, because of an ankle injury. On the day I left for Haiti in August I discarded the crutches and wore an aircast. I was hobbled. Getting around would be tough, but I was not going to let this hold me back. I went to Haiti armed with my mom's home video camera.

For the next two weeks I filmed my own documentary of what life was like for me in Haiti. I filmed in Port-au-Prince, in Cite Soleil, and in Jeremie. I filmed myself swimming out to the top of the submarine at Anse d'Azur in Jeremie. I took video out in the ocean on a fishing boat. I used to go out with fisherman and jump in the crystal clear waters of the Caribbean to swim around. That was a refuge for me. I filmed myself swimming in the Grand Anse River in Jeremie. I filmed on a small plane ride to Jeremie. I filmed on a boat back to Port-au-Prince with Sabine. I filmed inside of Jeremie's Catholic cathedral and in the main cemetery. I did all of this running around, producing my own documentary, while in tremendous pain on one foot. I got away with it because I had an obsession.

I was hell bent on making something happen in Haiti. Back then, outside of taking care of John and Sabine, from time to time I would send money to four other young kids and their families that I knew in Jeremie. I sent the funds through Western Union to John and then he dispersed it. While filming this piece for MTV, I went and rounded the four of them up to film them with John and Sabine. I presented them as the disenfranchised kids that I was working odd jobs to support, paying for school, clothing, and food. Even though during this time I was no longer involved in church, I presented Haiti as my own personal church. I saw God in the faces of the Haitian children. This proved to be one of the most intense, action-packed two weeks that I had ever spent in Haiti.

When this *True Life* episode finally aired in October of that same year, my piece was the last segment of the thirty-minute- long program titled, *True Life* "Spirituality." They had condensed everything I had filmed into just three minutes. It was good but I was very disappointed because they didn't devote enough air time to it. Other stories covered that night were not very good at all. I was less than impressed and almost a little embarrassed that they would put some of those other ridiculous stories in the same show with mine. The next day Lucia from MTV called me and said her boss told her that the piece she produced about "Zeke in Haiti" was the best part of the show that night. That made me feel good but it was of little to no consolation, knowing just how much time and effort I had put into it, grinding it out with an injured ankle.

I now waited to see if anything came from it. Would there be any sort of national response? Certainly, I thought, viewers somewhere in the world were moved by this. Somewhere, somebody would want to get involved, I hoped.

Interesting to note: Although I did good things for all those kids and their families, I went straight Haitian with no conscience whatsoever, rounding them up for what amounted to a photo op in hopes of acquiring aid. Similar subtle changes in how I did things would start to become more evident and more glaring. Ultimately, nothing would come of it and I was left very bitter.

Outside of the filming for MTV, this trip in August would end up changing the course of my Haiti life. While in Jeremie filming, I stopped by Johane's grandmother's place in Lasous to see the family. I was sitting in a front room talking with Johane when a beautiful girl appeared from a back room. I looked at the girl, then I looked back over at Johane, and I said, "Dodoche?" Dodoche was Aslyne's nickname. Johane responded wi, yes. Dodoche looked at me with a big smile. I hadn't seen her since October of 1993. I didn't see her on my trip to Jeremie in 1995, or my previous trip to Haiti back in the spring a few months before. Roughly five years had passed since I last laid my eyes on her. I thought, "My good lord, is she beautiful." She had just turned fourteen in July. She looked so grown. I had to pick my jaw up off the floor, I was so surprised. Regardless of what my relationship was or wasn't with Johane, I still always tried to keep in touch with the family. I shared great affection for all of them. I could have never have imagined Dodoche's transformation. A caterpillar into a butterfly. It was incredible.

In December of 1998 I called Johane's grandmother's house during Christmas time. I had been half-heartedly trying to salvage a relationship with her, still not knowing how things were going to shake out with Leonne. I was pretty sure by then that I wasn't going to stay with Leonne long term.

When I called, Aslyne answered and told me Johane wasn't home. When I asked where she was, Aslyne innocently responded, "Oh, she left with some guy." I was so pissed. I cut her off right then and there for the last time. Haitians learn early that even the walls speak in Haiti. They learn to keep personal business quiet. They keep things from their own family members. They even keep secrets from themselves. Aslyne had offered up that information to me about Johane because she had no clue that we were still talking. Johane didn't even know that I had sent $350 for the family when her mom passed because her oldest brother never told her. I was frustrated to no end with certain members of the family. I thought that I had been really generous with them over the years and none of them could even return to me some sincerity on any level. It was this night that I decided for good that I would start taking whatever I wanted in life without hesitation. And I now wanted Aslyne, who with the greatest of affection I called Dodoche.

I spent about twenty minutes talking to her on the phone that evening. I said, "I miss you so much. I'm gonna call you tomorrow."

184

Tomorrow came and I called and she was waiting right by the phone. I told her that I loved her and that I wanted to be with her. She was star struck and immediately became timid. She normally had such a great open personality that I could sense her getting really shy right through the phone. I insisted that she relax and not worry. I reassured to her that I loved her. I said, "It's very important that we keep this between us," and she agreed. Going into the new year of 1999 we would stay connected by continuing to talk regularly by phone.

JANUARY OF 1999

By the end of January, I embarked on another brand-new phase of my life. I wanted some tattoos. I had always flirted with the idea of getting tatted up but never went through with it. But I was now going through a transformation inside and out. I saw a story in the *Akron Beacon Journal* about a tattoo artist named Dino. He seemed reputable so I said to myself, "It's now or never. That's where I'll go to get my work done."

One cold evening I went to Dino's parlor on North Main Street in Akron but was told that Dino was not available. He was downstairs tattooing someone, but another person named Justin Wright could help me. I was very nervous. My teeth were chattering. Justin wasn't featured in the newspaper. How could I trust he was any good? He was young and newer to the tattoo game. He didn't really have any portrait experience and I wanted my first tattoo to be a portrait of Sabine. I wanted to get it on my upper right arm. On my upper left arm I wanted the Haitian statue, Neg Mawon, the unknown slave. I wanted that tatted with "Zeke of Haiti" around it. I almost walked out and left because I was dead set on Dino being the guy to do the work on me. But I had come all this way on the bus, so I said, "Fuck it, let's do this." Justin seemed excited and got me prepped. He went right to work.

About five to six hours later, I walked out of that shop with two brand spanking new tattoos that looked great. Although they hurt a little bit, I was so used to needles that I was pretty unbothered by it. When I returned home and showed my family they were all speechless. Even my dad was impressed. I felt like a new person. I loved it and would soon be addicted to getting tattoos.

In February, during a conversation with Aslyne, I said, "You know what, I'm going to call your older brother, Hantz." By that time, Hantz was living in Montreal with a woman from Canada that he had married. She was much older than him. I felt in my heart that Hantz would be okay with me asking his blessing for me and Aslyne to be together. He had been the one to call me when their mother died. Surely he'd understand.

It took me several days to work up the nerve to call. Hantz answered the phone and for a couple of minutes I beat around the bush. Then, finally I spit it out. I said to him, "I love your youngest sister, and she loves me too. I am seeking your blessing for me to have her."

Of course, Hantz was well aware that I had been with his sister Johane, and he also knew that I was considerably older than Aslyne. I was soon to turn twenty-six, and she was fourteen, turning fifteen in July. Hantz also knew that in his country, relationships with this type of age difference was very common.

He seemed to be a bit tongue-tied and slow to respond, but he ended up saying, "OK, I guess it's possible."

I said, "Great," hastily thanked him, and got off the phone quickly before he could change his mind.

A few moments later the phone was ringing and it was Hantz's Canadian wife. She went straight in on me and asked what my problem was. Who did I think I was, talking about Aslyne in this manner, and having the nerve to ask her husband's blessing.

I went right back at her. "You don't even know Hantz's family like I do. Mind your own fucking business. Your husband's mother loved me."

She then said, "What are you, some kind of pedophile?"

That really pissed me off. I said, "Fuck you, you ugly old bitch. The only reason your husband is even with your sorry cracker ass is because he wanted the hell out of Haiti and needed a visa out of the country."

That was the end of the conversation. I called Aslyne right away to inform her that the phone call I just had made to her brother didn't go as planned. I said, "In the meantime I will leave you alone. I still love you, never forget that."

186

Aslyne responded, "I love you too, Zeke," in a very soft and sad tone. I wouldn't talk to Aslyne again until May. After that phone call with Hantz and his wife, I really started to grow angry. Going forward I wasn't very nice to Leonne, or any of my family and friends.

One night in the month of March I went to play basketball at a church with two of my childhood friends, Jay Belkey and Jason Hance. During one of the games I broke my ring finger on my left hand. I was playing so hard, trying to win against these high school and college kids this night. I was diving on the floor, killing myself competing. Late in the final game of the evening I threw a pass to Hance that ended up getting stolen and converted into points for the other team. I was incensed with Jason and I started cursing him and his lackluster effort. I yelled, "You got to come back to get the motherfucking basketball. Fuckkkkk!"

Then I turned on everyone in the gym and cursed at all of them. The gym fell silent and all the men were in a state of shock. Apparently, it wasn't often that a total stranger playing church pick-up basketball games went off on a tirade. I was still cursing as I walked out of the gym with a final "Fuck all of you." I was starting to become a different personality altogether. I was not happy with my personal life, I had just broken my finger, and I was missing Haiti terribly. My personal relationship with Jason suffered a blow. We didn't talk again until a year and a half later. He went home that night and cried like a baby. I had badly embarrassed him at this church where everyone knew him.

Years later Jason filled me in on what kind of negative impact that night had on him and how much it hurt him. How I conducted myself that night spoke to a very dark side of myself that was coming to the surface.

That May I went back to Haiti with my finger in a splint. Although I broke it in March, I didn't have it addressed until many weeks later. It required surgery to have a pin placed into it. Sprained ankles, broken fingers . . . regardless of the inconvenience these would be in a tough environment like Haiti, nothing stopped me. On this trip I took Sabine, who was soon to turn seven years old, to the U.S. Consulate to try and acquire a visa so I could take her to the States with me. I told the people I knew on the inside that I was just trying to take her for the summer months and then I'd return with her. I brought her mother, Masline, along with us. The folks were about to stamp her passport with a visa when a white lady working inside said, "Hold on a minute, I'll be back." She then came out with a light-skinned, pleasantly plump, Haitian woman who started to grill Masline on why was she letting Sabine leave with this white man.

Masline told her that Sabine looked at me like a father figure – the only father she had ever known, and that she called me "Papa." And that she didn't have the means to take care of her. When Masline said that I knew we were fucked. We were denied the visa and I walked out of that place pissed off. I was angry at the well-to-do mulatto woman that put us in this situation of great disappointment. But I was also very angry with Masline for being so blatantly ignorant that I wanted to punch her right in her teeth. I cursed her while walking all the way back down to Grand Rue to Phaubert's Aunt Milly's house. I was enraged with her. I called her every vile word in both English and Creole that I could think of. I was even making up new curse words I was so angry. That devastated me. The plan was to get Sabine out of Haiti, and once in the States, I would adopt her with Leonne's assistance. That was the only way my relationship with Leonne was going to be saved. Had my plan worked to get Sabine out of Haiti I might have ended up staying with her. But it wasn't in the cards.

We went back to Jeremie and I went by Aslyne's grandmother's place to see her. It had been close to three months since we last spoke. She was very surprised to see me. She was very elated. She said she had to make a phone call at the Teleco station to Hantz in Montreal to ask him to send money. She insisted I accompany her. At the Teleco station there were several motorcycle taxi drivers sitting outside on their bikes, waiting for some customers. When they saw me walking with Aslyne, who stood out in a crowd due to her beautiful looks, the guys shouted, "Hey Zeke, is that your girl?" I didn't respond until Aslyne jabbed me with her elbow, telling me to say "yes." I shouted, "Yes," and that was it. She was now officially mine, and I didn't give a fuck what anybody thought or said or did at that point. Aslyne and I enjoyed our first kiss on May 13. I can honestly say that this was the very first time in my life that I was sure of something. I wanted to be with this girl forever.

Aslyne had a smile that radiated for miles. She lit up a room when she walked in. Her brown skin glowed. She had such a lovely personality. She was so graceful in her walk, and she could really dance. She loved to laugh and was full of life. We still had some obstacles standing in our way until we could be an official couple. And for the record, at that time, I no longer gave a rat's ass about our age difference. We were in Haiti. The rules of life and the rules of engagement were much different here. *Fuck what anyone thinks*, I thought.

I suggested to Aslyne that she tell her older sister, Poupette, that she wanted to be with me. Aslyne was afraid. She was scared to tell her older sister. For one, Poupette had a dominant personality. She was also a Haitian National Police officer.

Aslyne had also drawn romantic interest from one of her school teachers, and from a lawyer in town. Both these guys were older than me. She wasn't a little girl anymore. Men were trying to openly court her. She refused them, however. I stood on these facts. "Your parents are both dead. This is Haiti where it's dog eat dog." And she made it clear that she wanted to be with me only. We really had no other options. We had to devise a plan to get Aslyne out of Jeremie and into Port-au-Prince where I was now renting a place for John and Sabine.

I had to leave and go back to the States in the meantime. I once again worked the summer program for Barberton Parks and Recreation at Decker Park this time around.

Then, in early June, it started to turn ugly at home for me and Leonne. One afternoon when I was home on the phone talking with Aslyne in Jeremie, Leonne overheard some of my conversation. She stormed into the room to confront me. She swiped hard to grab the phone as I was still talking. Her nails left a gash on my hand. She continued, trying to get the phone out of my hand while yelling things in Creole I don't even remember. Aslyne was listening to all of this on the other end. This infuriated me to the point of war. I looked and saw that I was bleeding in two different places and I quickly hung up the phone on Aslyne without saying bye.

Leonne and I were now in a dogfight. She was very strong and well put together. Her passions were running high. She was flailing and scratching and hitting and kicking. I wrestled her to the ground and got up on top of her to subdue her. She grabbed my testicles and then I slapped her in the head violently with great force to get her to release her grip. She grabbed

189

and threw a VHS cassette tape from across the room that ricocheted off of my head. She then pulled a butcher's knife on me. We were both very fortunate that my brother, Jon, was there to come between us. He took the knife from her. I now had three different places on my skin where I was bleeding. Her nails ripped me open pretty good.

Although this would be the beginning of the end of our relationship, I had to do some smoothing over to help her understand that splitting up was best for both of us. She didn't see it that way.

I had planned a trip back to Haiti in mid-August with my brother Ben. I talked Leonne into going with us. I did my best to convince her that she could easily find a new boyfriend in Haiti. At one point, I even suggested to her that one of Phaubert's younger brothers, Foucorlt, who was an artist and really nice guy, would be a great match for her.

In late July there was a plan in place. I would send John back to Jeremie to get Aslyne. Aslyne had one of her closest friends named Petuelle coming along to Port-au-Prince with her. Petuelle also wanted to relocate and attend school in the capital. Her family was well aware of her leaving.

One early evening Aslyne and Petuelle both met up with John and hopped on a bus that made the overnight trip to Port-au-Prince. I was on edge about all of this. I knew it would scare her family, yet at the same time, I knew she would be safe. The plan worked. They left undetected that night in July and never looked back. Aslyne contacted her family as soon as she arrived to her destination in Delmas 31. She let them know that she was with me and that she was safe, even though I still wasn't yet in the country. Her sister, Poupette, who worked for the National Police and was married to a police officer, was very upset. But ultimately, she let it go. She was well aware of the hardship that each and every one of her siblings were going through since the death of their parents. She saw that this was what Aslyne wanted, and she let us be. Aslyne and I had pulled off our own coup of sorts. It was all coming together and I couldn't actually believe it.

On August 16, Ben, Leonne, and I set off for Haiti. This was Leonne's first trip back since she left three years earlier. She went off on her own with her cousin, Yolette. Ben and I went our own way. The plan was for us to meet back up with Leonne on the morning of August 26 to fly back to the States. Those ten days spent with Aslyne were special. We made love

190

but not full intercourse. Having sexual relations with a fifteen-year-old girl played much different on my psyche. For a young girl like her, the loss of virginity is painful, and I didn't want to hurt her.

Ben and I went to Cite Soleil a couple of times to play basketball in the different neighborhoods. Soleil 19 was always a favorite of mine. Playing ball in the ghetto like that with my brother Ben was special. Fifteen years earlier we were playing against all the black kids from the ghetto in Norfolk, and now all these years and many miles later, we were still at it. That ten days went by so fast. Then we were gone.

Leaving Aslyne behind with Petuelle, John, and Sabine was difficult, but they were all safe and in a good place. Leonne seemed to have hit it off with Foucorlt so that was a win for me. I needed to get Leonne's focus off of me and on to another guy to gain true freedom and set her free. It worked.

I continued living with Jon and Leonne back in the States. I went back to JR Engineering to work in security and their tool crib. Leonne returned to her housekeeping job at the hotel, and we started our divorce proceedings. We agreed to a dissolution to make it fast and simple. By the time October rolled around I couldn't take being away from Aslyne so I made a quick three-day trip to Haiti. In the meantime, there was a new added stress to my situation.

John and Aslyne and Petuelle bickered over the money I was sending bi-weekly. Who got what and how it was dispensed was now an issue. At this point I asked Phaubert to come and stay with the four of them to oversee the finances. Phaubert came but it didn't last long. Trying to please everyone was difficult. Soon there was more bickering and Phaubert decided to leave. On this short trip back to Haiti I took Aslyne's virginity from her. She was now officially mine.

In mid-December I returned once again for a month until mid-January. I was always so fortunate to be well liked at all my different places of work over the years, with the people in management tolerating my trips to Haiti. On this particular trip, I went down on a mission. I was going to get Aslyne pregnant come hell or high water. She had told me she wanted a baby. I was well aware that if I did succeed in getting her pregnant that nobody would ever try to come between us. We had unprotected sex nearly every day for about three weeks. We would now wait and see the results in the coming days.

JANUARY OF 2000

Back home, while patiently awaiting news of whether Aslyne was pregnant, I worked two full time jobs. I was continuing to work at JR Engineering, and I took on another job in Akron up by old Rolling Acres Mall at a daycare that was open twenty-four hours a day, seven days a week. They were looking for a male to work evening hours especially. I worked second shift at the day care and continued working double shifts in security and the tool crib at JR Engineering during the weekend.

By the end of January, I got the news from Aslyne that she was, indeed, with child. I was so excited to know that I was going to be a dad.

At the daycare, I met an African American girl named Erica. She was a very spiritual gal. We had many deep conversations about life and religion. I found her to be very interesting. She was very committed to the things that she believed. Erica was the black woman that I mentioned earlier in the book who once told me that God revealed to her in a dream that when black people look at me they see themselves – I was just in a white body. I forged a close friendship with Erica. She told me that she wanted to start giving me money for Haiti. I was reluctant to accept it. When I refused she seemed to be offended. So I gave in and said OK, fine. She knew that Aslyne was pregnant, too, and she went out of her way to show me great generosity.

Sometimes people come into your life for a reason and maybe for just a season. Life is all about timing, and trying to embrace things that make you feel uncomfortable. I was uncomfortable accepting her offer, but long term, it turned out to be a tremendous blessing that I was very thankful for.

On April 24, 2000, Leonne and I went to the divorce court in Akron to finalize our dissolution of marriage. Our time together was now officially over. It was a sad day for both of us, but also a new beginning. We had spent the better part of the last four years together. In this life, however, I

192

would soon learn that nothing lasts forever.

A year later Leonne made a derogatory remark about me within earshot of my father. My dad looked at her and said, "You wouldn't have the life and enjoy the freedoms that you do if not for Zeke. Be careful with how you speak regarding him, even if he is a jackass."

Leonne would never speak to my dad again after that. If you ever want a Haitian to disown you, shame them. Haitians despise being shamed. They will hate you for life if you embarrass them, especially in public.

Leonne remained close to my mother and still called her mom. I personally took some solace in the words my dad expressed to Leonne that day. She was now free to live whatever life she wanted, dreamed of, and chose to live, and that was all because of yours truly. I leaned on that truth because I did feel guilty in how I went about ultimately separating from her. It bothered me. But I just couldn't live with her for the rest of my life. We didn't match, period. Unbeknownst to Leonne, I asked God for favor and protection on her life.

On April 27 I headed back to Haiti, this time for the long haul, or at least until Aslyne gave birth. When I arrived at the house and laid my eyes on Aslyne I was blown away. She had an extended belly and she was glowing. It was incredible to touch her stomach for the first time like that. I was excited yet very scared. Having a female pregnant in a place like Haiti would be a hell unto its own, as I would soon find out.

Often because of the stifling heat I slept out on the roof of the house in Delmas 31. But now that she was pregnant that changed everything. Aslyne and everyone else in our life said it was no longer a wise thing for her to be exposed to the elements at night.

"Dyab sa yo ki deyo a, yap manje pitit ou a wi," they said.

"The devils that are out there, they will eat your child."

This, of course, pissed me off. I was like, "Get the fuck outta here with that bullshit." I just refused to believe it.

So one night in early May of 2000 I got up late at night to go pee on the roof of the house. If I ever got up late at night to pee, the roof is where I relieved myself. On this particular night it had rained hard and not a soul was out and about. Nights like this were seen as prime for the dyab "devils" to come out.

193

I was standing by the edge of one corner of the roof where there was a big palm tree. I wasn't wearing my glasses, which I've had since the sixth grade, usually to watch TV or drive. There was only a little moonlight. I heard a rustling, which startled me. A large, dark object stood a few feet away. Then all of a sudden something that appeared to be and sounded like wings of a large bird flapped violently. This thing, whatever it was, rose straight up into the night sky and flew off.

I was shaken. "Oh shit, oh fuck," I said to myself. "What the fuck was that?" I had always heard stories about Haitians transforming themselves into different animals, but I never really bought into it, thinking it was bullshit Haitian folklore. This event changed how I viewed all of this. I decided that I was once and for all going to get to the bottom of how Haitian Vodou worked. Although in years past I had up close and personal access to the Vodou religion with members of Leonne's family, I never took full advantage of it. Now was the time. It was now or never.

I started asking questions of Haitians close to me. That led to a man that was a Hougan that lived nearby in Delmas 31. A Hougan is a male priest in Haitian Vodou that is charged by duty to preserve rituals and songs and maintain the relationship between spirits and the community. They are entrusted with leading the service of all the spirits of their lineage. A Hougan is also a bokor, a sorcerer.

Everything about my meeting with this man was secretive. I was never even told the individual's name. I only met with him a couple of times at night. But this man seemed more interested in how I could benefit him financially. I was searching for Vodou secrets and how transformation was possible. He said the answers to these things could only be found and obtained through a long secretive process that takes time and money. Initiation wasn't so simple. I didn't want to hear this shit. I was done with this dude. I said, "I will continue to do my own research." He seemed displeased with me but I didn't give a damn what he thought. I was trying to protect my unborn child, and to do that I wanted, armed with the knowledge of how this shit worked. I wanted antidotes and remedies for anything that could go wrong concerning Aslyne and the baby's health. I didn't give a fuck about this guy and his Vodou personally.

Later that month of May parliamentary elections were held in Haiti.

194

I spent the majority of that Election Day, Sunday May 21, 2000, running around the capital with my closest friends from Cite Soleil. We rode around in a truck with a press pass from Leslie Manigat's political party, RDNP, Rally of Progressive National Democrats. It gave me a really great perspective of just how small Port-au-Prince really was. It takes forever to get anywhere, usually due to heavy traffic in the capital on a daily basis. On election day there is always a ban on traffic from public taxis to private vehicles. We were able to go from point A to point B in just a matter of minutes, where normally it would take an hour.

On this day I had my first run in with Haitian authorities. It was late in the afternoon and we were driving in Cite Soleil, dropping off some food for RDNP party members that were working the day of the election in Cite Soleil. We were now getting ready to leave the Western Hemisphere's largest ghetto and head back up to the RDNP main headquarters in Delmas. That's when four SUV vehicles stopped us.

The back doors of three of these vehicles swung open and about a dozen Haitian National Police armed to the teeth with automatic weapons got out and roughed us up. They had some of the guys pinned with their faces on the ground and some of us, like me, pinned up against a cement wall. The officer that had his hands on me was a large man physically. He must have been in charge because he was doing a lot of talking. He was the only one talking. He was speaking to me like I was an animal, less than human. He said, "Sa sa ye la?" ("What is this?") I was the only blan, or white man, in the vehicle with a bunch of Rastafarian friends of mine. The other officers were jeering and insulting each guy they had pinned.

This man then picked me up from the back of my pants and dragged me to the lead vehicle's passenger side. The tinted window slowly rolled down. A dark black man in a suit wearing shades was sitting there with radio in hand. He dipped his sunglasses to get a better look at me. He then said, "Kiyes ou ye?" ("Who are you?")

I didn't respond. I just turned my head away. Then he said, "Kisa ou ye?" ("What are you?") He then pointed at the tattoos on my body and said, "Sa sa yo ye la?" ("What are these?") He continued pointing to my tats. He said, "I don't ever want to see these things again."

As he was talking, the large officer that was in charge and doing all the shit talking still had me by the back of my pants, going out of his way to make me uncomfortable. I looked around at all my friends from the hood that were left cowering silently, afraid for their lives. This made me angry. I then said to the man dressed like a mafia boss, "These tattoos can't come off and they won't come off. We've done nothing wrong here. We were only delivering food to Leslie Manigat's people."

He then said to me one more time, "I don't want to ever see these tattoos again." That was his way of telling me that I should disappear. I then said to him that General Hugh Shelton was my uncle. General Shelton had led Operation Uphold Democracy in 1994, returning President Aristide from exile. I said, "He won't be happy to hear about this."

The mafia boss quickly said, "Ann ale," ("Let's go,") and all the officers let go of us, hopped into the SUVs, and sped off violently, purposely kicking dust up into our faces.

All my friends said, "Yo Zeke, what did you say to the magistrate?" I told him that American General Hugh Shelton was my fucking Tonton "uncle," and they all instantly grew brave and cursed the officers and magistrate that had just left the scene. It was former President Aristide's Lavalas party that was currently in power, led by President Preval. After this incident I was pissed at Fanmi Lavalas, I had never had any real political affiliation whatsoever. I did once proudly wear a President Aristide t-shirt back in 1995, however. But outside of that I was only for the Haitian people, regardless of class, color, religion, or political affiliation. But now I had been violated, I was pissed.

Not long after that I went to see the former mayor of Port-au-Prince, Evans Paul, at the office of his new political party headquarters, Democratic Convergence. A friend of mine named Esteril Compere from Soleil 19 set up the meeting between me and Evans. Evans's old party, The National Front For Change and Democracy, is the party ticket that father Aristide came to power with in the 1990 elections.

Evans, along with many others in the NFCD political party, had suffered great persecution during the time of Aristide's three years in exile. Many of the Lavalas political party organizations members left the country during those years, joining Aristide abroad. Both groups had supported Aristide's rise to power. Evans split from Aristide due to the Lavalas partisans that he referred to as opportunists in the mid 1990s. Fanmi Lavalas was officially founded in 1996, and Evans, the former mayor of Port-au-Prince under Aristide, was not a part of it. Knowing these things, I thought maybe I could get people in Cite Soleil to back Evans. So I had a meeting arranged with him to see what he was all about.

I entered into his office and we shook hands. He asked me to take a seat directly across from him at the desk in which he sat. He said, "How can you help us?" referring to his political party. He noticed my tattoo of Neg Mawon on my arm that reads "Zeke of Haiti" and said to me, "You love Haiti I see."

I started to speak and he swiveled in his chair to place a book on a shelf behind him. He said, "I'm listening" while his back faced me. I said, "I've been coming to Haiti for nearly a decade, watching the Haitian masses continue suffering. I want to get involved in the political arena to help change the scope of what is going on." I told him that the guys in Cite Soleil and I could help him carry the Soleil vote in any election that he participated in. I told him Soleil was no longer for Aristide like it used to be.

Evans turned back around, smiled at me, and said that he was well aware that he had a following of loyal supporters. He then dipped his glasses, looked at me squarely and said, "Zeke, do you really think you understand what Haitian politics is all about? Eskew panse ke ou vreman koprann sak rele politik Ayisyen?"

I didn't really know where he was going with that question. But I said "Yes" with great conviction. He said, "Politik Ayisyen glise anpil, ou konn sa, pa vre?" ("Haitian politics are very slippery, you know this, right?")

After speaking with him for a little bit longer he said, "OK Zeke, I'm writing your name down on my list." He thanked me for coming."

I said, "Yes sir thank you. I'll see you soon."

We shook hands and I left. I'd never again return to his office.

I found him a bit uninspiring. He had all the makings of what a lot of guys become. The dreaded career politician. I wondered to myself, after leaving his office, if he could be a beneficiary of U.S. foreign policy that quietly used guys like him to make a viable opposition while trying to continue the conquer by dividing approach in places like Haiti. Paul

197

seemed far too comfortable for my liking. In my mind, he couldn't be the leader that Haiti really needed. I told my friends from Soleil that I had seen enough. I wouldn't be supporting Evans.

At the end of May, Aslyne and I started going to a clinic in the vicinity of downtown Port-au-Prince not too far from the General Hospital that had a doctor a friend of ours referred us to. His name was Doctor Jean Arold Danastor. He had a distinguishable lazy eye. After meeting him my first impression was that I really, really liked him. Aslyne had originally gone to a clinic in Delmas 31 before I arrived back in Haiti in late April. When she told me how the doctor there examined her with gloves on, and how he touched/fondled the inside of her vagina, I said, "Fuck this, you are not going back there." So we started seeing the new doctor and we were both pleased. He was really nice and respectful. An ultrasound revealed we were going to have a boy. We were excited. The baby was due in late September.

The next few months became a tough, slow grind. I spent many late nights sitting on the rooftop throwing rocks at cats. Often times the dyab "devils" that came out at night transformed into the body of a cat. I heard this throughout the years over and over and by this point, I finally believed it to be true. The dyab would try and kill the baby, even before its natural birth. After a baby was killed and buried the dyab would retrieve it from the grave.

A baby's skull is a hot commodity in the underworld of Haitian Vodou. Shavings from a baby's skull are in high demand. They are mixed with other ingredients in the making of what's known as the zombie powder that's used to sedate human beings. It makes them appear to be deceased, when in fact, they are still alive. Armed with this knowledge I would be proactive. I was ready and waiting to kill anything I thought to be a threat. This would start taking its toll on me mentally.

I tried running in the early morning hours to help clear my mind. While out on an early morning run in Delmas 33 in late July I came across a young female body with its head decapitated. The body was sprawled out, fingers and toenails all over the ground around where she lay. Her underwear was torn, showing signs of sexual assault. Her head lay about twenty meters away in some brush. A crowd gathered around the body and another crowd gathered where the head lay. I went over to look at the head. I observed the face of a young woman with her tongue hanging out to one side. It was absolutely gruesome.

Haitians would often say to me, "Zeke, Ayisyen pa jwe non." Translated it means, "Haitians don't play." I was living and learning this in real time while living amongst them.

A couple of weeks later in August, before I could even make it out of the house to go run, our neighborhood was abuzz about something awful that turned into a public spectacle. In Delmas 31 there was a young girl who had been decapitated. Her head had been placed high up on a telephone pole with one of her hands nailed to her cheek. This particular killing was made even more heinous by the fact that it was this young girl's father who committed this violent act. As rumor had it, the father was in debt to a dyab "devil," and the debt he was forced to pay was the sacrifice of his own seed. Once again, in the country of Haiti, nothing was ever as it appeared. I was on the brink of becoming a father for the first time. And now twice in a matter of weeks I'd witnessed the aftermath of attacks and two lifeless young faces – females killed in the most hideous, grizzly, and horrific manners. All of this wear and tear on my mind, along with the stifling August heat, became so taxing I was now in a very fragile place.

September was finally here. On the early evening of September 11, Aslyne came out from bathing and was holding her one side. She said after making a particular movement while bathing she both heard and felt a click in her abdominal region. She said that she felt OK but that she was going to go lay down. We had just been to Dr. Danastor two days before and he said he would see us in a couple of weeks for the baby's birth. The baby was due on September 23. Aslyne and I were so ignorant, naive, and green as to how this first-time baby stuff worked.

Later that night Aslyne woke up in great pain. She said, "I feel like I need to shit." So she went down to this little unsanitary outhouse we had. I was thinking, *My God, be careful.* I was worried the baby could pop out and fall inside this hole laced with lime.

At two a.m. in Port-au-Prince, Haiti, it wasn't as if we could just call the doctor or conveniently run to the emergency room. Home births are very common in Haiti. When she couldn't shit but still remained in great pain I grew scared that we might be having this baby at the house. I prayed hard to Jesus that night to see us through until the crack of dawn when we could get to the hospital.

By five a.m. we were knocking on the door of a neighbor they called Papi. He was a school teacher and had a car. By the time we got going it was six a.m. and the early morning traffic was already growing thick. We were leaving Delmas 31 to travel to Rue Chareron in Port-au-Prince to Hospital St. Francois de Sales. At one point during the car ride, Aslyne was crying out in pain, screaming that it felt like the baby was coming out.

"Oh Bondye pitit la ap vini wi, lap vini wi," she cried out.

I was telling her to "hold on cherie, hold on." My mind raced back to one of our previous doctor visits where they wanted to give Aslyne some kind of vaccination just in case the baby ended up born in the street somewhere. I refused, saying she would be fine, the baby wouldn't be born in the street. All I could think of in that moment was how, once again, I had managed to fuck something up.

We pulled up to the hospital at 6:45 a.m. after what seemed like forever due to the traffic. Papi was a Godsend even though it took us a miserable forty-five painstaking minutes on a drive that should only take ten minutes at the most. I was so angry. When I got Aslyne out of the car she laid down right on the side of the road in agony. I picked her up and I was cursing at everyone in sight. I laid her down by the hospital's front entrance. John was along with us and I shouted at him to stay with Aslyne. I ran into the reception area and gave the pager number of Dr. Danastor to the receptionist before she could even ask me how she could help me. I yelled at her that my girlfriend was outside the front entrance about to give birth.

"Page the doctor, hurry, goddammit."

She said that they required a certain amount of dollars before they could help me. I screamed, "I have money you little bitch," while pulling out a wad of cash. "Just do what I tell you to do, you fucking little bitch. Page the motherfucker right now, you fuck face." I was cursing this woman in English so she didn't have a clue what I was saying. Otherwise they might have removed me from the hospital grounds. I counted out Haitian gourdes and handed the cash over to the lady. She then methodically counted very slowly to make sure it was all there before finally paging the doctor. In the meantime orderlies were dispatched to retrieve Aslyne from the front gate to put her in a wheelchair and take her in. I rushed behind them, scared to death. They quickly got her into a room, and threw her up on a bed. As she was on that bed, crying out in pain, Dr. Danastor ran in. I was thinking, "How the fuck did he get here so fast? My God, did he transform into a bird and fly here?"

The room was filled with a controlled chaos of sorts with the doctor directing all the traffic inside. Aslyne was again screaming, "Oh Bondye, Oh Bondye, lap vini wi." ("Oh God Oh God he's coming.") I remember vividly the doctor snapping on his second medical glove and Aslyne arching her back with a final scream at the top of her lungs. I was standing right behind her, holding her, when Moses came flying out. Aslyne fell silent, everything slowed down, the doctor grabbed Moses before he could hit the floor. I was waiting to hear a baby cry, but nothing. The doctor was now holding Moses upside down. He smacked him on the ass and the first cry rang out. I lost it. I started to sob uncontrollably.

They say the most incredible thing in life is to witness the birth of your firstborn child. They were not lying. That was the most intense twelve hours, from the evening before until that morning, when Mo was finally born. The doctor and nurses had me removed from the room. After the door closed behind me I collapsed into John's arms and then went straight to the ground, sobbing like Michael Jeffrey Jordan after winning the 1996 NBA finals.

The most emotional moment of my entire life came at 7:10 a.m. on Tuesday, September 12, 2000, when Moses Jeffrey Petrie arrived in this world.

Moses was quickly moved to a room where all the newborns were kept. I posted John at the door to watch over Moses like a hawk. In Haiti, it's not uncommon for newborns to be stolen right out of the hospital where they are born, especially in the General Hospital of Port-au-Prince. Although St. Francois de Sales was a much safer environment, I was now a nine-year veteran of Haiti and I didn't trust anyone or anything by this time. I left John and entered the room that Aslyne had just been wheeled into. She was so drained and exhausted. She was looking up at me with her big brown eyes as if to ask me, "How did I do?" I told her that I was so proud of her. She could barely utter a word. I told her to go to sleep and that I would be here. Steven Curtis Chapman's "I Will Be Here" played in my mind in that moment. She closed her eyes and immediately drifted off into a deep sleep. I just stood over her, just us in the stillness of the room together. I was watching her skin glowing in a radiant color, and thought of what a beautiful angel this girl was, and how lucky and fortunate I was to have her. I cried as I ran my hand over her head and through her hair. It was truly one of the most intimate moments of my life.

We stayed the night in the hospital while John and I took shifts watching the door to Moses' room. The next morning we were discharged. For the next few weeks I was a stressed out mess. Trying to take care of Aslyne and her overall health was a great priority. She had been torn by scissors during the birth process, which caused that arching of the back and final scream during labor. I had missed that because I was trying to hold her down and comfort her from behind. That fresh wound she now had could easily get infected if not cared for properly. She would stay bedridden for a while. Standing guard over the house at night became very taxing on me emotionally. I was running at, chasing down, and throwing rocks at every cat I saw on the rooftop. It felt like I was starting to lose my mind.

I was required to venture out into the streets to take Moses for a couple of doctor visits and vaccinations. I was very on edge about that. I had to take Moses on public transportation that was absolutely filthy. Dust thick in the air was not ideal for a newborn to be breathing in. I had purchased a car seat to put him in and ended up holding the car seat with him in it in on my lap because most of the Haitian taxis didn't have working seat belts. The bad roads in Haiti make the car rides extra bumpy. I was trying my best to keep Moses's little head from shaking too much.

One of the times I had Moses out on a doctor visit we ended up switching vehicles. We got out of one taxi on the main Delmas strip and had to walk a little way to get to the Delmas 31 entrance. While doing this a big truck sounded its horn and nearly blew out my eardrum. I was cursing the driver while carrying the baby. Finally, I gave Moses to John and I walked in front of them to protect them from people traffic as well as car traffic. It was always a shoulder to shoulder mass of people walking in the streets. I was throwing myself in front of people and cars so they didn't come anywhere near John and Moses. I was ready to kill someone and die over protecting my son.

Looking back now and pondering these things, it was during this time that a really dark change happened in my life. Having a baby for most Americans is usually a joyous occasion. For me, it was anything but that. My only objective now was to get Moses the hell out of Haiti as fast as I could. I couldn't leave him behind in Haiti. The dyab would have eaten him right from underneath Aslyne's nose. She was so young, so ignorant, and so naive through no fault of her own. I had to get my son the hell out of there.

So I set out to the American Consulate in downtown Port-au-Prince to see about getting Moses a passport. I was no stranger to folks at the Consulate. I had prior dealings with them before concerning both Leonne and Sabine. From time to time I stopped in just to see a couple of guys that worked there that I had met on previous visits. Networking and having contacts like this was a big deal, as I would soon find out and benefit from.

Just days after Moses' birth I had a Haitian birth certificate made for him. I took that along with me to the Consulate to get information on having his passport made. One of the guys in the Consulate that I was cool with happened to be working on this particular day.

"Hey bro do you remember me telling you that I was soon a father to be?" I said.

"Yeah man, how is Yes doing?"

Months earlier, I had mentioned to this guy that I was gonna name my son Yes YourMajesty. He loved it and thought it to be a really cool name. My mom, family, and Aslyne were not as thrilled. To this very day people in Haiti still ask me how Yes is doing.

I said, "He is great but his name is Moses now."

He then told me to bring Moses to the Consulate. I agreed and brought him in a few days later. On October 3, I took little Mo into the American Consulate and everybody inside lit up. They thought he was so handsome. To my great surprise everything was expedited without any issues. They made a Consular Report of Birth Abroad certificate for Moses and I was not even required to take a DNA blood test to confirm he was mine. That kind of testing would have taken more time and money that I didn't have so I wasn't complaining. I was thrilled. I then secured a U.S. Passport for him. Now all that was left was to get plane tickets, and somehow get Aslyne to agree to let me leave the country with him. I hatched a plan that involved lying to her and I did it quickly.

I told her that I was going to take Moses to the states for ten days so that my parents could meet him. After a lot of persuading she reluctantly agreed. During that entire stretch from the birth of Moses and until we left the country, my mom, my sister Jennie, and brother Ben all chipped in financially. I was very fortunate they helped because my funds were all depleted. When the day arrived for me to leave Haiti with Moses the calendar read October 6, 2000. I had a guy come take some pictures for us as mementos, because I knew Moses wasn't coming back. I mentioned to Aslyne that while I was abroad I would get her paperwork started to acquire her visa to the states. Many tears were shed that morning. Finally me and Mo set off for the airport with John. When we parted ways with John all I said to him was to look after Aslyne for me. "I'll send money soon."

Just like that Mo and I were gone.

Boarding the AA jumbo jet with my son was surreal. I had never changed a diaper in my life. I had never fed him, never bathed him or changed his clothes. I was so lost and out of my league. It was scary for me but I managed as best I could.

When we got home to Barberton around midnight I went to my parents' home, the home I grew up in. It was so cold. I had been in the Haitian heat for the last five and a half months and now I was shaking in Northeast Ohio's chilly October night. Moses was starting to cry. He had just pooped. I laid him down on the dining room floor to change him. His little body was shivering from the cold. He was crying so loudly it woke my parents up. My mom came down to see what was going on. A few minutes later my dad came down. They were both tired and not very pleased with me during that time in my life. But this child of Haiti was their first grandson and on this night they both fell in love with him. My mom and dad would spoil Moses rotten. He was now the love of their lives.

A few days after bringing Moses home from Haiti my father went to a picture studio with my mom and Moses' cousins, Hunter and Grace, to get pictures taken. My dad was really emotional, especially after he was told that Moses' middle name was Jeffrey. It was a show of respect to my father, which resonated deeply. The picture my father had taken that day while holding his first grandson is still hanging up in my mother's house.

Ten days after bringing Moses home to Barberton Aslyne called to ask when we were coming home. She said they had expected me that day.

I said angrily, "Aslyne, I am not bringing Moses back to Haiti. Surely you know that Haiti is no place for a newborn. The dyab will take him from you and you know this. If you really love Moses you would never agree to let him return to Haiti."

Hearing my words, Aslyne fainted on the spot with the telephone in hand. John told me she went down like a ton of bricks. She soon got over it, though. She had no choice. It hurt me to hurt her but sometimes in life that's what is asked of us. I did what I had to do for the welfare of our son.

For the next two months I lived with my parents. My mom and my sister were a big help to me during those days. Whether it was changing, feeding, or bathing Moses they were ready and reliable. In December, I moved with Moses to an apartment in downtown Barberton next to Lake Anna. Moses' full care now fell on my shoulders. I had gone back to work at JR Engineering since returning home. The owner of the company, Louis Bilinovich Jr, once told me that I always had a job at his company whenever I needed one. While working security back in the winter of 1999 I had saved his plant from burning to the ground when I found a fire burning inside of the building in an area where there were some really hot furnaces running. So whenever I needed a job that's where I'd go.

The security department, however, soon suffered cutbacks. I was offered a job in another department but I declined it. Then I went to work at the Boys and Girls Club of Summit County at their Barberton location. Whenever I had my back to the wall I always hustled hard. Moses was my first priority but I still had people in Haiti depending on me, including Aslyne. I had to make do.

JANUARY 2001

One night in early January 2001 Moses was up late crying and nothing I did could get him to stop. He cried relentlessly. I tried everything I could to settle him down. It was unnerving. I finally grabbed him from his crib, snapped him to attention, and yelled, "Shut the fuck up" at the top of my lungs. He stopped crying instantly.

I scared myself. I always heard of shaken baby deaths. On this night I think I was on the verge of something disastrous like that. Nearly four-month-old Moses, with tears in his eyes, was whimpering and sniffling as he looked up at me. I observed him and felt so pathetic and so not worthy of the air I was breathing. How dare I grab my infant son in this manner and lift my voice to him. All he was doing was looking for some comfort from whatever he was being tormented by. Not having his mother there was very difficult. Some things can only be remedied by a mother's love and touch. I put little Mo back in his crib and I just stared at him and wept. I then buried my head into a pillow and wept aloud. I felt that I was at a point of breaking.

I hope this episode speaks to young fathers. Never ever shake a baby.

Between late January and late March I started to practice a very destructive habit. When I moved back in December with Moses my mom had given me one of the family cell phones. Having an infant with me, I needed it for communication. Often, while watching TV late at night, I came across some seductive commercials advertising local chat line numbers. They were local, and free to call. Each of these numbers would give you a free trial membership. Some were up to an hour long, and some only a half hour. One in particular gave you five hundred free minutes. You could chat with local singles to meet up or just talk. I had no experience with anything like this. I didn't even know if it was real. It seemed to be like the old 1-900 numbers back in the day that charged you four or five dollars a minute for phone sex. But these numbers were free. So I started calling them habitually.

It soon became a destructive addiction.

In early April I headed back to Haiti to get Aslyne. I had started her paperwork to come to the United States in October, and by April the process was complete. Just like when I brought Leonne to the states, Aslyne had an interview to receive her visa at the U.S. Consulate. Her visa was secured and we were good to go. Knowing all that we had gone through to finally see this day to its fruition was very emotional. (It is paramount that I be transparent in telling my story. I got Aslyne pregnant when she was only fifteen years old. She gave birth to Moses when she was sixteen. I knew that I couldn't just show up at the U.S. Consulate with a girl this young, presenting a birth certificate that showed her age to be sixteen. So I did what I had to do.)

In countries like Haiti you can do whatever you want if you have the right contacts and money to meet the price for said service. I needed a birth certificate for Aslyne. We never had her original birth certificate in the first place. We needed one that showed that she was at least eighteen years of age. I reached out to a guy who had those sorts of contacts and he took care of it for me. He gave her a birth certificate that said she was nineteen. Subconsciously, this was another event that made me feel invincible and untouchable. I could do whatever the fuck I wanted in Haiti, and that I'd surely do. Haiti was comparable to the Wild Wild West. Anything goes!

A Haitian man once said to me, "Haiti is such a sweet country. (Yon peyi dous li ye.) You can do whatever you want here. (Ou ka fe sa ou vle la.) That, my friend, is why everybody loves Haiti so much."

He said if you want to kill someone and get away with it easily, this is the place to do it. The system here is shit. The only thing that speaks in this country is money, that's it. You could buy and sell people in Haiti. He said Haitians will sell and kill their own for a mere hundred gourdes. That's twenty Haitian dollars. Haiti was in such a fragile state during my years there. Writing about this reality is heartbreaking even though I benefited from its chaotic structure and lawlessness.

Aslyne came home with me to Barberton on April 12, 2001. When she walked through the doors of my mom's home she saw Moses in a jumper, jumping up and down and smiling. She hadn't laid eyes on him in six months. She was overcome with great emotion. Tears strolled down her face. She admired him from a few feet away. Then she bent down slowly to his level. Moses was staring back up at her, just smiling away, almost as if he knew his mom was home. Aslyne embraced him with an embrace only a mother can share with her son. I'll never forget the sights, and sounds, and smells from that beautiful moment. We were finally all back together again. Certainly, my life would now be fulfilling and have some concrete direction, or so I thought.

We married in a courthouse wedding on June 1, 2001. We only lived at the apartment downtown by the lake for a few months before we left to go live with my sister Jennie on Wooster Road across from Portage Elementary School. That is where we were living when the events of September 11, 2001, happened. That particular day I was back working first shift at JR Engineering in a new department that I didn't much care for, where we produced semi-trailer truck rims. Over the course of the next few days I was forced to listen to a bunch of white factory workers in all their false bravado talk proudly about how the United States was going to kill them a bunch of sand niggers in retaliation. I grew tired of that type of white racist American rhetoric, and the factory environment as a whole, and I quit the job.

END OF DECEMBER 2001-2003

In December, I went to work for a cleaning company that serviced the National City Bank at the Cascade Plaza building in the heart of downtown Akron. This is where I would work for the next nine years.

In 2002 Aslyne started working at the same building, doing first shift hours as a day matron. It was her very first job. She was very well liked there. That helped my cause both among the employees at my job and financially. Two incomes were better than one. Soon we moved from my sister's and got our own place with a new financial independence we had never before enjoyed. We moved to an apartment on 2nd Street that ran off of Van Buren in Barberton.

After working in cleaning for about six months I started working in the security department as well. I would work both jobs for a few months. However in January of 2003 a new security company took over the account at the plaza and decided that it was a conflict of interest to have me working both jobs in the same building. I left the cleaning job to stay with the security team full time. With a young child at home, I worked my schedule so that I was pulling forty hours over the weekend. From Friday night until Monday morning I worked a full-time job. I started at eleven p.m. Friday night to seven a.m. Saturday morning. Then I would come back Saturday at three p.m. and work until seven a.m. Sunday. Then back Sunday at three p.m. until Monday at seven a.m. That way I was off all week and we didn't have to worry about daycare other than when Aslyne worked on the weekends the same time I did. We had my mom and my sister to fall back on for daycare so it worked out favorably for us.

It was during this time my addiction to calling the chat line flared back up. While my wife was gone during the day and Moses was sleeping, my idle hands became the devil's workshop. I would either be using my cell phone or our house phone to talk to all different kinds of local girls. I was having phone sex with total strangers on a daily basis. On one occasion, I invited a girl I met on the chatline over to our apartment to have sex. She was a very attractive white girl that was addicted to crack and needed fifty dollars. So, I took advantage of the opportunity. I had put Moses down for a nap in his crib in our bedroom upstairs. I took the girl down to the basement to fuck. It didn't last long. I handled my business quickly, gave her fifty dollars and got rid of her.

I felt filthy afterwards and jumped right into the shower to scrub the dirty feelings off of me. I had used protection but even with that, I still felt compromised. I didn't ever want to harm my wife so I was trying to take extra precaution even while being reckless. It was controlled chaos, just like Haiti. When I went to Haiti I turned the switch on. When I came back to the States I turned the switch off. At this point the switch remained on twenty-four/seven.

This was because Aslyne was so pure, and so clean, and so lovely that it became difficult for me to be aroused by her. For me, sex started to turn into something much darker. My conversations on the chatline started getting more vile, and more vulgar. I was having phone sex with women of all ages, colors, and nationalities without discretion. The common theme among all these females was that they were either looking for phone sex or

209

real-life hookups in person. Each time I got on the phone the conversations were pushed to new limits. I was often speaking with women who were far more sexually mature than I was. I was learning on the fly. Some of these sexual conversations could make grown men blush. Then, when I spoke with women who were much younger, I would greet them with a sexual maturity that they were not used to. On the chatline, people could be whoever they wanted to be. It was a sort of fantasy land. It had the potential to be something that was very dangerous, especially for young women.

In the spring of 2003 I had started my own small business venture. A long-time friend approached me with the idea of importing manufacturing items from Asia. On and off for the next five years we collaborated on various opportunities to import building products, manufacturing machine parts and miscellaneous materials from overseas. All home-based. We were mildly successful but the Great Recession of 2008 forced my business partners primary business into bankruptcy, and us, right out of business. It supplemented our income and provided us with extra money. Extra money for the people we supported in Haiti, and also for the selfish and sinful lifestyle I was leading.

We moved into a house on Washington Avenue in Barberton. This was our third move in two years. I was working full time in security at Cascade Plaza in Akron and Aslyne was now working full time at Giant Eagle in Barberton. We were doing pretty well. I was missing Haiti badly by this time and I decided to take a trip back in July of 2003. I went to Jeremie with John and Sabine to visit all of our old friends and folks we viewed as family.

While visiting in Caracolie I came across some old friends from way back during my time at Yvrose's orphanage. I ran into a young girl named Mamoune. I had known her and her siblings from years past. I asked for her mother. She replied, "My mom died, Zeke" with a look of great sadness. I felt sick to my stomach immediately. The last time I had seen her mother, Gertrude, was in May of 1999. I had stopped by to visit at her home in Caracolie. On that day she asked if I could look after her daughter, Mamoune, if anything ever happened to her. Mamoune was only twelve years old. I thought it an odd request, but I said, "Sure thing, you know I

210

would do anything within my power to help you and your family." I had no idea then that she was suffering. She didn't tell me that she was sick. She died from cervical cancer.

I then asked Mamoune about her father. She told me that he was now living in a place called Bonbon with a much younger female, having kids, and starting a new family. By this time her father was now in his fifties. I could see and feel the desolation in her face and hear it in her voice. She felt betrayed by her father. She said she lived with her oldest sister Gerda, her husband, and their daughter. Mamoune was now sixteen years old. She looked so beautiful. We embraced and I told her that I would always be there for her. I was staying in Borde at the hotel La Cabane. I told her to be sure and come visit me.

That entire two weeks in Jeremie we were inseparable. Our birthdays happen to be a day apart. Hers is March 6 and mine is March 5. We are both Pisces. That made us feel a strong connection. Back in the early '90s Mamoune visited me at the orphanage with some of her siblings. She was all grown up now and I started looking at her much differently. Initially I wanted to sincerely help her and be there for her. She had gone through so much. But I had no discipline whatsoever, and I quickly succumbed to emotions that were running high. I was not the slightest bothered by the fact that she was young. I told her that I wanted her for me. She agreed, even though she knew I was married. She remembered Aslyne from years earlier in Jeremie.

It's important to note that in Haiti back then it was common place for Haitian men to be with younger girls, married, and have girlfriends and mistresses on the side. Haitians who are in positions of power often exploit and take advantage of this part of the culture. Politicians, judges, police officers, pastors, priests, doctors, teachers, lawyers, businessmen, etc. I'm not justifying it, but that was the reality, and still is to this day. My evolution into being more Haitian than the Haitians was becoming more evident. This was part of the culture I wanted to indulge in fully. I would definitely take advantage of these no-holds-barred rules. I was well aware that the "King of Rock and Roll," had taken Priscilla Beaulieu at the tender age of fourteen. If Elvis could do such things, why couldn't I? Besides, in Ohio the age of consent was sixteen years old.

211

I told Mamoune that somehow, someway, "I will be back to get you out of Haiti." In the meantime, I told her sister, Gerda, that if they were at all interested in me taking Mamoune to the states, that they needed to get to work on a birth certificate with a date of birth stating she was at least eighteen, because she was only turning seventeen on her next birthday. I couldn't appear at the U.S. Embassy with her unless she was eighteen. Then she needed a passport. So, they got to work on it and made it happen.

I went back to the States and continued on in my marriage and daily life as usual. By then, however, I was really starting to neglect Aslyne. Physically, spiritually, and emotionally. She must have felt so isolated and lonely. She had come to the United States to be reunited with her husband and son, full of dreams for her future. After being in the country for almost two and a half years we were now living in our own place, but we might as well have been living a thousand miles apart.

I was continuing to become more of a chatline addict by the day and I had a new fresh love in Haiti. With the way I had manipulated my work schedule during the weekends, in a twenty-three story building, with many offices and an unlimited amount of telephones, I lived on the chatline. It helped pass the time for me during those long hours. I was a full-blown addict. If I wasn't on the chatline late at night I was sleeping.

I chalked it up as sticking it to the man. I felt that I was underpaid. I felt that the shit family insurance plan they offered to me was a bunch of bullshit. They were gonna pay me a tax, and that tax was in the form of me doing what I wanted when I wanted. I made my own fringe benefits in a system that kept people oppressed by paying them low wages by design.

JANUARY OF 2004

In late January of 2004 I made a short trip back to Haiti to see Mamoune and discuss with her how I was going to go about getting her a visa and bring her to the States. She came to meet me and stayed a few days with me outside of the capital in Bon Repos. We stayed together at a hotel called Adam & Eve. There, we made love. Mamoune was a virgin. Just like I was with Aslyne, I was very gentle and conservative with her. I promised her

212

that I wouldn't penetrate her until after I brought her to the States. In my mind, I thought if I penetrated her and left her alone for several months in Haiti, she would, at some point, need to fulfill a desire. That would mean possibly finding someone else while I was gone. Haitians are very sexual creatures, which is something learned on the fly and deeply embedded in the culture. In Haiti, you cannot trust your girl to be around other males, even your best friends. There are no limits and no boundaries when it comes to sexual relationships in Haiti. Class, color, political affiliation, religion, educational background, age, marital status, none of it matters. It's every man and woman for themselves. If a Haitian man sees something he wants, he shamelessly goes and takes it.

This is what I transformed into during my years in Haiti. I saw Mamoune. I wanted her. I took her, just as I had done with Aslyne.

In the few days I was there I went to Cite Soleil to see a friend of mine named James Petit-Frere, also known as Billy. I had met Billy years earlier through two brothers that were very good friends of mine named Enso and Jean-Robert. I talked with Billy for a good while. Billy's hero was Che Guevara. That's who he wanted to be like. At that time the country was really starting to heat up with political tension. Anti-government, and anti-Aristide demonstrations were mounting. I talked with him about being extra careful during these times and to make sure that his circle was tight.

I told him not to trust anyone, including President Aristide and his Lavalas chieftains. I said, "These guys are gonna use y'all until they don't need you anymore. What you gonna do when they don't need you anymore? You remember what they did to Amiot Metayer about four months ago in Gonaives?"

"I have no choice Zeke," he replied.

I hung with Billy until his brother, Winston Jean-Bart, also known as Tupac, showed up. Tupac's hero was legendary African American rapper Tupac Shakur. All he wanted to do was rap. He loved to play basketball too. Pac had just gotten out of prison during a jailbreak earlier that month where he had been held on kidnapping charges but was never convicted. Pac and I went and played some hoop in Soleil 19. We loved to play some ball together. Pac talked a lot of shit just like me so we enjoyed each other's company. I told him the same thing I told his brother, don't trust anyone. Pac said to me, "Yo Zeke you know me bro, fuck Haiti, and fuck Aristide baby, fuck him." Before I left that day, I told the guys that I loved them.

That would be the last time I ever saw them alive. Fuck Haiti.

I went back home to the States and by the end of February watched the rebellion against President Aristide take flight. I was at work early Sunday morning, February 29, watching it play out on CNN in one of the bank offices. I felt so helpless while I viewed the events in real time. It had been thirteen years since I had first stepped foot on Haitian soil and I still had never realized to this point for what reason I was called to Haiti. This would start to become a sore spot with me that slowly began eating away at my overall morale. I still had a beautiful trophy wife and a healthy handsome son. And I was now prepared to bring my new girlfriend to the States to join me. I was winning. But I was also getting really greedy really fast. I wasn't even sure of just how I was going to pull this off. How I was going to juggle two females without even having a vehicle was a pressing issue. I didn't care. All I cared about was meeting my own selfish needs.

My wife and I both took the bus or got rides to work and shopping. All these years running back and forth to Haiti, it never really benefited me to have a car. I didn't need or want a monthly car payment, or to be paying monthly insurance. Besides, taking the bus kept me in touch with the commoners. Riding the bus over the years helped me to better relate to poor folks in my own country. Without that experience, it would have been very easy to take things for granted. Did I like taking the bus? Hell no! But in these times it fit my narrative, so I continued on making due. Even though I was poor myself, I never saw it that way because I was living the life I wanted to live. I was poor financially by choice because I was a river to others in Haiti with my own meager finances. I was rich in my mind, and as long as you are bourgeoisie in your mind, you can never be poor.

I started acting as though I was untouchable and above the law. As our lease was coming to an end that spring of 2004, I had decided that we would not sign a new one. I told my wife that I was going to send her and Moses to live with my mom. Earlier in the year my father had moved up to Cleveland to be closer to where he worked. He was tired of the commute to and from his job every day. The traffic was always terrible and it exhausted my father stress wise. He was a veteran of three heart attacks, an angioplasty procedure, double bypass surgery, and had a defibrillator placed in his chest. He could do without the stress. He would come back to Barberton every other weekend. This opened the door for me to take advantage of the situation, so I sent Aslyne and Moses to stay there. I informed family members that I didn't want my mom living alone, and that it would also help us to save money for a nicer place to live in and enable us to get a car. I managed to get everyone to buy in – for a while anyway.

I mentioned to my wife that I was now helping a young girl named Mamoune from Jeremie that she knew. I said Mamoune's mother had died and she was now fending for herself. I said, "Surely you can empathize with her because you know what it's like to live through the same exact experience. I'm going to try and help her come to the States."

I left out the all-important details such as, "Oh, by the way, when she gets here, I'm going to use the money that I used to pay our rent with, and pay rent for her."

Everything was set. We moved out of the house on Washington in May. It was now June and I was setting off back to Haiti to try and pull off the unthinkable. Getting away with having wives and mistresses was one thing in Haiti. To do it in the States, on limited income, and no car, was another.

I met with Mamoune in Port-au-Prince and we went to the U.S. Embassy and secured her a ninety-day visa. I had no idea how any of this was going to play out but I didn't care. Those in my inner circle knew of my plans and they all tried to talk me out of it but I had tunnel vision. It was my way or the highway. I loved Mamoune, just like I loved Aslyne. But I probably loved myself even more. I was going to have my way regardless. In my own mind I had already done my wife the greatest service by bringing her to the States. I was now doing the same for Mamoune.

What could either of them say or do about it? It would be ungrateful for either of them to protest my plans and subsequent actions.

On this trip to take Mamoune away from Haiti something happened that altered the course of my very existence for the next sixteen months.

One morning after sleeping on top of the roof where I had always stayed in Delmas 31, as the sun was rising and I was waking up, I felt

215

and heard a click and a snap in the top of my gums on the upper right side. That's all it was. I thought nothing of it. It didn't last long and didn't even hurt. It was just a bizarre sound and subsequent numb feeling in my mouth. I didn't realize at the time how devastating whatever just happened would become.

On the day Mamoune and I were leaving Haiti to go back to Ohio I was very nervous and started to feel uneasy. These foolish and selfish decisions were always met with my conscience trying to hold me accountable, keep me honest, and on the side of what was right. When we got to Barberton it was very late, past midnight. Our first stop would be my mom's house. Aslyne was waiting up late for me. She knew I was due home on this night. I went into the house and she greeted me with a hug and a kiss. She was happy to see me.

I don't even remember what and how I said to her that Mamoune was outside and I was leaving with her to find somewhere to stay. She just looked at me with a lost and lonely stare. She could not believe what she just heard come from my mouth. Tears started to well up in her eyes. She grabbed my arm and said, "Please don't go." I said, "I have to go, I'll be back some time tomorrow."

She followed me out the door in her robe and slippers. She watched me go to Mamoune in so much pain and under so much duress. I could have given a damn.

My brother Ben had once said, "You came home from Haiti one time and when I looked at you, your eyes were black. He said I swear your eyes had turned the color black. Like your spirit had been overrun by a demon." This is important to point out because rational human beings do not do and act as I did. Nothing that I was doing made sense to anyone close to me. They all thought I was crazy.

That night I wounded Aslyne deeply. Yet she still loved me and refused to turn me away. She was an angel sent from God, surely she was. I ended up calling my friend Jason Hance, the one I had cursed out at a church for not diving after a basketball. Jason was gracious enough to open his doors to us so that we could stay the night, but by sunrise we would have to go. Jason and his wife both knew Aslyne, so he didn't want her to find out what I was doing with this new girl from Haiti.

216

The only thing Jason said to me that night about the situation was, "YOU ARE AN IDIOT!" He was angry with me for sure. He couldn't fathom what was going on in my mind, and in how I thought I could pull this scheme off. Again, Petries are all in, or all out. That's what I preached. That's what I lived by, and it would be no different now. Before the sun came up that morning we had already left. I don't think Jason's wife ever even knew that we were there that night.

From there, we would go to another childhood friend's house, Frank Jennings. Frank wasn't real thrilled about what I was doing either. He had tried to talk me out of it weeks earlier. But he tolerated me as a brother he grew up with and was still close to. Frank thought I was nuts, but he also thought I was pretty darn cool, too. We stayed at Frank's for the next three days until I could find a one-bedroom apartment for rent in Akron. That's where Mamoune lived for the next three months. I got her situated with the help of both Jason and Frank, who helped to move my things into the new apartment. They might have done it out of pity. I didn't know and I didn't care. Business was taken care of and that's all that mattered. Quietly, I was telling Aslyne that once I found a good situation for Mamoune, possibly with her distant relatives in another part of the United States, we would be back together full time again. "Just be patient," I told her.

For the next three months I would go between the apartment in Akron and my mom's house. I was having sex with Mamoune, then I would have sex with my wife. On some occasions, I went between the both of them multiple times a day. I had never desired sex more with my wife than at that point. I was king of my domain in my world. I was having so much sex with the two of them over a couple of weeks' period that I was at the point of exhaustion. My body felt like it was going to shut down on me. My orgasms were producing nothing. I was completely on empty. When I went to work on the weekends I took Mamoune with me and had sex with her there at my job, too. And while she slept at my place of work I was on the chatline talking to other females. I was obsessed. I was an addict. I was sick. My lifestyle hurt Mamoune just like it hurt Aslyne. I was sometimes leaving Mamoune all by herself for two or three days at a time in that apartment in Akron. She was so young, and so scared, yet so in love with me that any hardship was worth it to her.

217

During one weekend at the job very late at night Mamoune and I were greeted with a surprise visit by my ex-wife Leonne and Aslyne. They had gone out to a club. Leonne had her own car and she picked Aslyne up and they went out together. They had started talking when all this was transpiring. Leonne knew Mamoune and her family from back in Jeremie. At one point, Leonne loathed the sight of Aslyne. But now, after finding out what I was doing, she quickly joined forces with Aslyne to confront me and Mamoune. I don't know who reached out to who, all I knew was that my ex was now with my current wife and they were looking for a confrontation. On that night the three of them all stood across from me in one of the bank offices on the first floor that I watched television in. It was also where Mamoune slept, up under one of the desks, on the nights she came with me.

Both of them scolded Mamoune verbally and said that she knew I was married, so she should have never come here with me. Of course, Aslyne knew I was married to Leonne also, but did the same thing she was accusing Mamoune of doing. I defended Mamoune and told them they had to leave. I'm sure that Leonne was now advising Aslyne to leave me or take her own course of action against me. I think she probably encouraged Aslyne to start seeing other people because of what would happen the following weekend. Nobody ever saw it coming, not even me.

The following Friday night I was at my job as usual with Mamoune. I was trying to get a hold of Aslyne but she would not answer. I called my mom and she told me that Aslyne had gone out with some friends. This pissed me off because she didn't tell me beforehand. It was starting to get really late and she was still not back home. I continued calling and texting with no response. By now it was 1:30 a.m. so I called an Akron City Yellow Cab to come get me and Mamoune to take us to Barberton. I just left the building on auto pilot. I had the keys and nobody ever came in that late at night. Anyone of importance had their own swipe cards to access the building so I said, "Fuck it we are out of here."

When we arrived at my mom's Aslyne was still not home. My heart was pounding in my throat. I kept calling her phone to no answer. My blood was now boiling. I was cursing profanely. Finally, I heard something out by the side door of the house. I raced down the small flight of stairs from the kitchen that led outside and there she was, standing in the yard, just looking at me. She had listened to my voicemails, screaming at her and at this point she was scared to death. I said, "What are you doing? Get in here now. Where the fuck have you been and why were you not answering me?"

She was unresponsive at first but then said to me that she had gone out to see a movie with some white guy. I think he was a foreigner, but he was white. Hearing this I snapped. I grabbed her by the head and yanked her up the stairs. I dragged her into the living room and threw her onto the couch. I took my belt off from my security uniform and began to whip her with it. She tried to cover up in a ball and I started whipping her hands, the top of her head, and anywhere else I could get to. My mom came down the stairs with Moses after waking up from all the commotion. Moses was crying. Mamoune was watching from the dining room, horrified. My mom immediately called my brother Ben to come over. Ben was not too far away in the Akron area. I had flogged Aslyne so savagely that I was soaked through my clothes in sweat. I became dizzy and faint. Ben arrived, I told him what had happened, then had the nerve to ask him for a ride back to my job with Mamoune. I was now officially on the brink of going mad.

September was fast approaching and I had a big decision to make. Mamoune's visa was only good for ninety days and would be expiring by the third week of September. I could either have her stay indefinitely as an illegal with me. Send her to live with distant relatives in Massachusetts or Florida and let them worry about her illegal status. Or send her back to Haiti. I no longer wanted to continue how we were living. And I didn't want to send her back to Haiti. So I suggested sending her to stay with distant relatives that had already agreed to house her if she so chose to go live with them. When I asked her about going to join relatives her answer was a emphatic no. She said that she was not comfortable doing anything but staying with me or going back to Haiti. I couldn't leave my wife and son for her, I just couldn't do it. It was almost as if I went to test drive a car that I wanted. Then after I drove it I decided it wasn't for me. I had given her a taste of living abroad. I took her virginity. Then I informed her that this just wasn't going to work out. I said, "If you do go back to Haiti, I will

219

support you financially. You can stay with John and Sabine." I'll be damned if that's not what she chose to do. She went back to Haiti.

Before Mamoune returned to Haiti, my friend, Jason Hance, invited us to speak to the high school kids he taught at Max Hayes in Cleveland. He said, "Come up and share with my students about Haiti. They will love it." I agreed and thought it would be a fun experience so we went.

The day before we headed up to Cleveland to speak I had set up a rendezvous to meet a black girl named Kendra that I had been conversing with on the chatline. We exchanged numbers and kept in touch for a while but I had no car, and I was already juggling two females. I really liked her. We had some great phone sex and she was very raunchy and taboo in her sexual tone. It was something I was new to but very much digging. I worked it out that after we spent the day at Max Hayes, I would have Jason swing me by her place. I told Jason that an old friend of mine lived in the area and I just wanted to take advantage of the opportunity to say hello in person, knowing I most likely would never get back up in this area any time soon. Jason agreed.

We got to Kendra's apartment. I jumped out and said I'd be right back. My heart was pounding as I headed over to the door to knock. It was basically like my first blind date. She opened the door and greeted me with a big smile and a hug. She looked good and smelled good. We talked for a few minutes. I told her that I just spoke at a local high school and that I was on my way back to Akron with my teacher friend. I didn't give to her any intimate details about my life. I was keeping her in the dark the same way I was keeping Jason and Mamoune in the dark about what I was really doing there. Certainly I would see Kendra again. Or better yet, I would have her come see me. I was getting ready to ship Mamoune back to Haiti and Kendra was now right on time to be her replacement as my mistress. I was living fast and furious. This train was rolling and showed no signs of slowing down.

When the time came for me to get Mamoune back to Haiti I flew with her down to Miami. We stayed in a hotel together and had a nice dinner. We waded in the ocean on South Beach. I wanted to make love with her one last time but it didn't happen because of some major pain I was having in my mouth. I needed to get to a dentist soon.

220

The next day I saw Mamoune off on an American Airlines flight back to Haiti, and headed back to Ohio on a flight of my own. I started having excruciating pain in my mouth on the top right side. It felt like I had an abscessed tooth. When I got back to Ohio I made an appointment with Dr. Azam Qadri of Village Dental Hudson immediately. I was in tremendous agony. I had a root canal but the pain did not subside. After a few more days of suffering I returned to Dr. Qadri again, begging him to just pull the tooth that days earlier I had a successful root canal done on. He X-rayed it and assured me that nothing was wrong with the tooth.

I said, "Listen doc, this pain is killing me. Please pull this fucker out of my face. Just do it, I'm begging you." And pull it he did. Upon extracting the tooth he said to the lady assisting him, "What is that? I have never seen anything like this before." Some type of discolored liquid gushed from where the tooth was moments earlier. He said, "This is very strange." But he did not know what to make of it. For me it was out, and that's all I was worried about. I left the dentist office that day thinking wow, this is finally over. I'll be able to sleep tonight.

As the days passed the pain remained. Frustration set in. The only way to appreciate such agony is through experience. If you have never had an abscessed tooth you wouldn't understand. In my case it felt like the entire upper right side of my face was abscessed. I'd get violent pain that would suddenly go away. I was taking a lot of Ibuprofen. On occasion, I ran four or five miles to help clear my mind. I think the exercise helped combat the pain. Sometimes it was just a matter of not minding that it hurt. This sort of suffering would lead me on a never-ending search from doctor to doctor, specialist to specialist, and many visits to the ER all in the hopes of finding out what was wrong. It helped in leading me to a much darker place in my life.

I was now living back at my mom's full time with Aslyne and Moses. Of course, I had to do a lot of smoothing things over after what I had done to Aslyne in the last three months. That kind of mental and physical abuse took a toll on her and us as a family. I never stopped to take into account how all of this was affecting Moses, too. I begged Aslyne for forgiveness and let her know that I sent Mamoune back to Haiti. I told her that I wasn't going to let Mamoune come between us. I told her that I loved her more than Mamoune. The real truth was that I was never really going to leave Aslyne for Mamoune. I gave Mamoune a test drive. It didn't work out. I couldn't choose her over my wife. I still loved her. I still remained committed to taking care of her financial needs in Haiti going forward.

Clearly, at that point, my reality was altered. I was living by my own set of rules and regulations. Aslyne welcomed me back with open arms. I continued on living the same way, however. Not much had changed. I was very fortunate that Aslyne was so young and naive.

As the days passed I continued talking with Kendra over the phone. She had no idea that I was married and had a kid. I was sure to keep that hidden from her. One night in the fall of 2004 I arranged for Kendra to pick me up in Barberton. I told her that I was having car issues and that if she really wanted to see me she would have to come down here. Kendra was really into white guys so I had that going for me. She picked me up at Walgreens on Wooster Road and we made our way up to her place in Cleveland. It was on this night that I would breach new lines and sexual boundaries that would have once been considered heinous by me.

Although I had my suspicions after some of our communications via the chatline, email, and cell phone, I couldn't for sure be positive, and I really couldn't believe it. It was something I had to see for myself. On the drive to her place I noticed her hands were larger than that of a normal female. But she was looking and smelling hot. I had my hand between her legs the entire drive to her apartment. On this night I confirmed that this beautiful black girl named Kendra was indeed born a male. She was a transsexual.

This revelation did not turn me away. I was very intrigued. I had only seen stuff like this on Jerry Springer. It was around this time that the movie Alexander had come out in theaters. In that film it highlighted Alexander's relationships with "ladyboys." During the age of the Greeks this behavior was culturally accepted. With Alexander being one of the all-time greats that I was raised on, I thought, "If he did it, why can't I?" I was aspiring to be like him anyway, so let me be it all and consume it all.

This night with Kendra was some of the best sex I ever had in my life. How was it possible? I was turned off sexually at the very sight and thought of another male with me. In this case Kendra had the appearance of a very beautiful black woman. She walked, talked, smelled like, and kissed and caressed like a female. She was taking hormones for her voice and breasts. She looked great to me and I desired her. All I had to get over was the fact that she had male genitalia. Not minding that was the key. I had to play it off in my mind as though it was just a large clitoris. The hormones she was taking made it difficult for her to get an erection. I went Alexander the Great on Kendra this night. I was the aggressor and the penetrator. She was a bottom. She was the receiver just like any other female was sexually. I took her with no shame. The visuals she provided, the sounds she emitted, that's all I needed to be comfortable. Men are very animalistic.

Having sexual activity in a much more physically aggressive manner was a new outlet for me. I could unleash aggression without worrying about any consequences. I was trying to inflict pain. This type of sex I much preferred.

YEAR OF 2005

My relationship with Kendra continued into the year 2005. The next two times I saw her were at my job on Saturday nights really late. I had sex with her on both of those occasions. I ended up getting oral sex from another TS girl that was Puerto Rican. I met her on the chatline, too. She came to my job one late Saturday night, dropped to her knees and serviced me. I was verbally assaulting her as this was taking place. I was living out my own debauched fantasies.

In those days while I was working weekends I wore my security uniform during the day. Once it got to be eleven-thirty p.m. I changed into some nice dress clothes. I did that when I had arranged to see a girl from the chatline. I told the women I was a building inspector from Chicago and that I was just here for the one night. If it was someone I ended up seeing multiple times I just let them know that I was again back in town for only one night.

One Saturday night I left the building on auto pilot and took a cab to see a girl that lived on West Market. I talked to her for the first time that night and she invited me to her place. There was a snow storm that particular evening so I didn't worry about leaving the building empty. Nobody in their right mind would be out on the roads. The girl buzzed me into her apartment. I go up to the third floor and she had her door slightly pushed open. She told me candles would lead me to her bedroom. I followed the candles into her room, where she was laying on the bed with her back to me. When she rolled over I saw she was wearing a cat mask. It was something out of the movie *Pulp Fiction*.

I walked over to her bed. She immediately reached for my belt and started to unbuckle me. She was very aggressive and gave me oral sex without any questions asked. This girl wanted me to reciprocate the act on her. But when I saw how unattractive her vagina looked, I just wanted to get the hell out of there. I said, "Oh shit, I left the doors open and unsecured at the building I just came from. I have to go. I'll be back in the morning."

I never saw her again. I became so desensitized, treating women like objects, that it was no big deal, business as usual. On another occasion I hooked up with a girl that was pregnant and had a big belly. After my encounter with her I desired more sex with pregnant girls. As the days, weeks, and experiences I had passed, normal sex didn't any longer do anything for me. There had to be something more to turn me on. That's why the sex at home basically became non-existent. It got to the point that I needed Viagra to get an erection with my wife.

My wife was a good looking ten on a scale from one to ten. That gives you some perspective on how bad it got for me. I was suffering from a new disease. I was a sex addict. But not just any sex. The sex had to be debauched, taboo, freaky, kinky. There had to be a certain kind of perversion for me to get an erection.

As the winter of 2005 marched on I was still continuing to battle and suffer tremendously from the aching hurt in my mouth and my face. I continued going to the ER. They would send me to the doctor. The doctor would send me to a specialist. Every visit I hoped and prayed I would finally find out what was wrong. And every time I left frustrated. I was feeling more disheartened and more helpless each time. I was way too young to be suffering like this.

I tried to run and exercise to combat the pain. I was consuming Ibuprofen and Advil like candy. Living with that type of discomfort every

224

day really started to take a mental toll, and it really started to make me an angry individual. I was making everyone around me miserable.

"If I'm going to suffer, why not let everyone else partake in it with me to see what this death march feels like," I said. I think part of my reliance on the sex with total strangers was so I could unleash a punishment on them because of the constant torment I found myself in, something that I could never enact on my wife. It was a sort of therapy. This type of therapy would have me crossing some dangerous lines.

One girl I had met off the chatline was a very pretty, well-built light skinned African American. She was thick and big breasted. She came to see me on a Saturday late at night. Meeting her and enjoying each other's company led to oral sex. I saw her a second time and the third time we headed upstairs to one of the higher floors, into the ladies' restroom that was fitted with a nice lounge area. We started making out and before you knew it our clothes were coming off and we were pleasing each other. In the midst of sex she started saying that she wanted to go back to her place. I told her the same song and dance as everyone else: "I'm a building inspector from out of town. I'm on the job, I can't leave." This girl was looking for a relationship and she had no idea that I was married with a child. She said, "Let's go, I want to go now."

I didn't have any clue why she was now so insistent on going back to her place but I didn't really care. I was saying, "It's OK, baby, everything is going to be fine, just relax."

She grabbed my arms and tried to stop me from continuing. I responded with a show of force to remind her that I was the superior individual here. I was now thrusting even more violently. Then she started to scream "No." I kept on. I was met with another scream of no and a no again. She yelled out to stop it and tried to push me off of her. At this point I got really aroused. I wasn't going to stop. She was trying to push me off and I was pulling in as hard as I could. Push, pull, push, pull. As we were locked in a violent position of push and pull I silently exploded in orgasm but didn't let her know that. I said, "OK, let's go back to your place. Let me go get changed in the men's room."

She gave me her address and I walked her to her car. She left, and then I went to sleep for the remainder of the night. I never saw or spoke to her again after that encounter. How many men are in prison because of similar situations? I think that white male privilege entered into the equation. Had I been black she may have taken recourse against me.

What I did wasn't cool. But back then, I was going to do whatever I wanted to do. I was king of my domain. I rationalized it and made it OK.

She came to me, for the third time. She wanted it. We got undressed. She brought the condom that she watched me put on, then moments later, she changed her mind. With no spiritual discipline in my life at that point, that situation played out the only way it could. I wasn't sorry. I even grew angry thinking about it. Technically I just raped a female because she said no.

At any point, if a female says no, regardless of the fact that you've already started having intercourse, you as a male have to respect that. That was tough for me to swallow. Even more disturbing, I enjoyed it.

In the spring of 2005 I started speaking to my friend, Jojo more frequently. Jojo was cousins with Phaubert. He was the one who took me to the General Hospital when I was suffering from typhoid fever. Jojo hailed from Duchity in the Grande-Anse region. I was trying to convince him to run for a deputy seat in Haiti's government. I was still searching for my Haiti calling. That never left me. It was a burden I carried with me everywhere I went. I was encouraging Jojo to lead a real revolution together with me in Haiti. We talked passionately about it over the course of several months. I told him that I would take a bullet for him and defend him to the death.

"I will deliver to you all of Cite Soleil and every ghetto stronghold in the country. All the guys in Cite Soleil are looking for a revolutionary leader to follow."

He said, "I believe you can do that Zeke, I really do."

Jojo was very outgoing, very well spoken, well educated, and had great charisma. Overall, he was very popular. He lived in downtown Port-au-Prince. He worked as a teacher at College St. Pierre in the capitol. His education and background were in sociology. He was well liked and well thought of everywhere he went. He had a following in Camp Perrin, Beaumont, and Duchity, his birth place. I begged him to run in the elections scheduled for that fall. I said first a deputy, then a senator, then you'll be president of Haiti.

Jojo said to me that I reminded him of the great John Brown who was an American abolitionist. Brown believed in and advocated armed insurrection as the only way to overthrow the institution of slavery. Ironically, John Brown grew up in Ohio, about twenty minutes from where I grew up. His first wife died during childbirth. His second wife was only sixteen years old when they were married. That's how old Aslyne was when she gave birth to Moses. He had suffered failed businesses and acquired debt. We had things in common. He also lost several of his children to sickness and disease. He knew what it was like to suffer.

Haiti is one of the only countries in the world to recognize Brown for Harpers Ferry. On December 2, 1859, Brown was hung for his raid on the Federal Amory of Harpers Ferry, Virginia, now modern day West Virginia. Seven people were killed, and ten injured. Brown had intended to arm slaves with weapons seized from the arsenal. Brown's men had fled and were killed or captured by U.S. Marines led by Robert E. Lee. Brown refused to have any pro-slavery clergymen at his hanging, which was attended by Stonewall Jackson and John Wilkes Booth. Before he was hung he said, "I, John Brown, am now quite certain that the crimes of this guilty land will never be purged away but with blood. I had, as of now think, vainly flattered myself that without very much bloodshed it might be done." Famous writers such as Emerson and Thoreau praised Brown. Malcolm X once said that white people could not join his black nationalist organization of Afro-American unity, but if John Brown were still alive, "we might accept him."

I wanted and longed for that type of reverence by the masses in Haiti. That mattered to me. Brown was often referred to as a madman. People have referred to me as the same. Some considered him stubborn, egotistical, self-righteous, and sometimes deceitful. Yet, at the same time, they'd refer to him as great. His actions were spun to fit the view of whatever narrative was stressed. Abraham Lincoln called Brown insane. Frederick Douglass wrote, "His zeal in this cause of my race was far greater than mine. It was as the burning sun to my taper light. Mine was bounded by time, his stretched away to the boundless shores of eternity. I could live for the slave, but he could die for him."

These words from Douglass would pinpoint my relationship to Jojo and most of all the Haitians I was close to. It is ultimately the main reason, while after being seven years exiled from Haiti, that I have no real desire to return. I can't want something for Haiti stronger than the Haitians want it for themselves.

There is a street named after John Brown in Port-au-Prince. Before Jojo had mentioned him to me I didn't even know who he was. I was now learning about American history from a Haitian. This wouldn't be the last time I would learn about my own history from a Haitian man.

Jojo would never toss his hat into the Haitian political ring. He knew all too well that if he entered into it, life would never be the same. Living in fear all the time is Haitian politics personified, and he wasn't having any of it. Our relationship would never be the same because I saw him having great potential to do something for his country but letting fear keep him from his destiny. Frederick Douglass had said it best. Jojo didn't want it as bad as I did, period.

Summer of 2005 I went back to Haiti, yet again. I had sent a few thousand dollars for John to purchase a truck from our income tax money several months earlier. The idea was for him to turn it into a tap tap taxi to be used to generate income so that I could stop sending money every couple of weeks. All John needed was to get his license and he would be good to go to start driving and making money, finally becoming self-sufficient to provide for both him, Sabine, and Mamoune. Aslyne only agreed to let me send that much money at one time because I guaranteed her that this would be the last time we would have to send money to Haiti. The ironic thing is that we ourselves didn't yet even own a car. Part of me wanted the vehicle so I would have my own transportation in Haiti. I kept that to myself. This trip to Haiti was simply to see how this operation was unfolding.

When I got there, I found out that John had been in an accident. He had kept this information from me because he knew how infuriated I would be. The truck was still serviceable, but this was not the result I was looking for. I wanted to see him driving every day, bringing in money. I also needed to sit and talk with John and Mamoune about the constant bickering between them, which was the main reason I invested in this truck in the first place.

228

How the money I sent monthly was disbursed became an issue between them.

I also started to hear whispers about Mamoune possibly having a boyfriend. This was treasonous as far as I was concerned. It would start to become the beginning of the end of my love affair with her. We started to grow distant. I ended up leaving her behind in our apartment in Delmas 31 as I left for Jeremie with John and Sabine to visit Sabine's mom. While in Jeremie I was going through a period of tremendous pain in my mouth and face. Sabine's mother at that time was staying downtown in a place called Anba Lavil in a home right down by the ocean. I was in so much pain during the nights spent there I would swallow about eight Advils and sit outside right by the sea. I was starting to hallucinate, the pain was so intense.

We left Jeremie prematurely because of my suffering and I headed back to the states.

This affliction that originally started in my mouth had now infected the entire right side of my face and had made its way up into my head. It had now been well over a year since I started suffering. I had been to many different medical professionals. It was exhausting. My spirit was deflated. It was haunting my every waking moment. By the end of the summer I was now at my breaking point. I was on the verge of going completely mad. When going through a painful stretch I would put ice on my face to numb it. Then I would try a heating pad. The ever-present torture now had me slapping myself as hard as I could in my face. The pain would unleash hell for hours at a time. Then it would subside for a while, only to return again. It was the beginning of the fall months when it got so bad I was on the brink of killing myself. I was too young to live in this manner. For fifteen months I was tormented with no relief in sight.

One night at the end of September I ended up downstairs on my mom's dining room floor. We were still living there and a couple of my mother's sisters were in town visiting, so I was sleeping on the couch in the living room. It was storming late this night. I was woken from my sleep with the excruciating pain vibrating through my face into every corner of my physical body. When one part of the body hurts like that, it reverberates throughout the entire being. I got up and started slamming my head against the walls downstairs. From there I began slamming my face on the floor. I was thrashing and flailing, cursing and crying out. I snapped. Nobody upstairs could hear me because of the rain and the thunder. I then took my aggression in a verbal assault towards Almighty God. I began cursing Him. I cursed His Son Jesus. Then I started in on His mother Mary. I continued to cry out in tremendous grief. Flashes of lightning were lighting up the inside of the house briefly before another roar of thunder shook the house. Heavy rains continued to pour down. I wanted to die. I begged God to kill me. I didn't know how to kill myself. I swallowed two dozen Advils at once, hoping that would do it. After lying there in my own sweat and slobber while shaking uncontrollably I finally fell asleep. Jacob wasn't the only one that wrestled with God.

The next day I spoke to my friend James, a homosexual. I was telling him about what I was going through. I could talk to him about anything. He was the only who knew that I had sexual escapades with transsexuals. He made his living listening to people share their private struggles and issues as he worked in the field of mental health counseling. I told him I wanted to die.

About a week or two later in October he called me with the news that would save my life.

"You're not gonna believe this but I just spoke to a female colleague of mine. I was explaining to her about what you've been going through. She said that she had a friend that suffered from that same condition. She said the name of it is trigeminal neuralgia. There is no cure for it but it's managed with a medication called Carbamazepine 'Tegretol.' Tegretol is a medication that people who have epilepsy and suffer from seizures take. It's a very strong medication. One must be weaned on and off of it."

As James is telling me these things I was tearing up because I knew finally I had some closure and I could now find some relief. I turned on the computer at my mom's house to quickly do my own research. This was it. This was what I had. I didn't even make an appointment to be seen by the specialist in Barberton. I walked right into his office on Barberton's East side unannounced the next day and shouted, "I know what I fucking got. It's trigeminal neuralgia. Get me the doctor, and get me some fucking carbamazepine right now." My God I was so grateful that James had mentioned this to his friend. Otherwise, I may no longer be here.

Thank you so much James. Thank you for tolerating me. I'm forever in debt to you.

Trigeminal neuralgia is a chronic pain disorder that affects the trigeminal nerve. It results in episodes of severe, sudden, shock like pain in one side of the face that lasts for seconds to minutes. Groups of these episodes can occur over a few hours at a time. It's one of the most painful conditions known to medical science and can result in depression. Trigeminal neuralgia is called the suicide disease because 25 percent of its sufferers commit suicide.

Taking the medication Tegretol wouldn't be easy on me, though. The doctor said I was only to be on it for three to six months maximum. "It's very rough on your liver," he said. It gave me nausea, made me dizzy and unbalanced, and sometimes made me vomit. It did the job, however, and my pain was gone not long after. Every time I went back to see the doctor I lied to him that I was still in great pain. I was so terrified that it would come back that I did this for the next three years. I didn't finally wean myself off of the Tegretol until 2008. When I asked the doctor what caused it he said some sort of head trauma. The only trauma I had ever suffered was when Steve Thomas hit me with the football on my right ear when I was back in elementary school. In recent years, I have found out that it can also be caused by a tumor compressing the trigeminal nerve. This hellish period of my life was over. This was now five of my nine lives used up.

YEAR OF 2006

As the new year of 2006 was upon me I still didn't have a clear vision of where I was going in life. My vision and focus should have been getting me, my wife, and my son into a place of our own and seriously seeing about getting a car. Unfortunately, that was not what interested me. My focus was still totally on myself. I was still seeking out my "why" as far as Haiti was concerned. No matter what happened, I'd always go running back to Haiti. My lifestyle was anything but healthy, especially for the people around me. It was as though my very existence would damn anyone close to me from my family to my friends.

One Friday night in the summer of 2006 I was on my shift at work sometime after 11 p.m. My dad showed up with my brother Ben and our childhood friend, Frank Jennings. My dad had been drinking and had already consumed several beers. He was really pissed off at me. He came to see me face to face. He let me know that he was planning on taking both Moses and Aslyne away from me. My dad loved Moses more than anything in the world and he was not going to allow me to continue to abuse his mother. My dad understood that it was a privilege for me to have such a beautiful family and he thought I should appreciate this and not throw it all away. I told Ben and Frank to "get this son-of-a-bitch the fuck out of here. I'm not gonna permit him to do this at my place of work."

The next time my dad came back from Cleveland to spend a weekend in Barberton we got into another argument. This time it was about to go down. I went straight in on him for not holding any moral high ground to throw stones at me. "I remember seeing you slap my mom in her face right in front of me when I was little in this house I grew up in on Lloyd," I said. "My mom waited on you hand and foot my entire childhood. You smoked and drank away thousands of dollars over the years that you could have used on your family instead."

I cursed him for smoking in the house and in the car we rode in as kids with the windows rolled up and the air-conditioner on. My brother, Jon, happened to be present on this particular afternoon and he jumped in quickly, agreeing with a lot of what I was saying. Then emboldened by the fact that Jon was now an ally I crossed a fine line. I went in on his mother, my grandma Grace, cursing her and saying that she couldn't even come sit with my siblings so that my mom could stay with me in the hospital back in 1978. I said she was a selfish bitch, "just like you." He was like, "You really feel that way?" I said, "You're goddamn right I do."

He once again had been drinking and he tried to put his hands on me. At that point my dad was pushing 63 years of age. He could no longer tangle with me. I got on top of him and said, "You're an old man now, just stay the fuck down." I had him bent over the sofa. I called over to my brother Jon to get him. I could literally feel just how much stronger I was. I didn't want to hurt him.

My dad then called his brother, Gary, to inform him about what I had to say about their mother. This was the same Gary that had basically been left out of the Petrie family will. He had caused my grandparents so much grief over the years. The inheritance he received was pittance compared to my dad's portion. My dad said, "Me and your uncle Gary want to meet up with you sometime."

I didn't even let him finish and I said, "Fuck you and your crippled brother. I'll beat the fuck out of both of you."

My dad's brother was seven years his senior. As a kid my dad worshipped his older brother. Gary was a real tough guy. He was dishonorably discharged from the United States Army. My dad had told us years earlier that he wasn't able to tell us why he had been discharged other than it was something really dishonorable. Gary was always in fights, and always in trouble. Gary had kids with multiple women and had been married four different times. My mom would always say that I was going to end up "just like my Uncle Gary." Gary was a drinker and a smoker just like my dad. He frequented the bar scene and was a regular at the Bar Shannon in Barberton. People didn't mess with Gary. He had a tough guy reputation. If Gary came into a bar, and you were in the seat that he normally sat in, you got up without saying a word.

Many years earlier Gary had suffered a stroke and was paralyzed on one side of his body. But that didn't stop him from getting around. He used a cane to support his bad side. Even after being paralyzed nobody would ever dare cross him. He was that mean.

I had been to see Gary a couple of times as a kid in hopes of seeing his son, my cousin Greg. Greg was never there, however, much to my disappointment. Gary was married to a lady named Brenda, and I was fond of them both. Gary never stayed in one place long. He was always moving around, kind of doing whatever he wanted, just like I was now doing. My mother's voice echoed even louder now: *You're gonna be just like your uncle Gary.* These Petrie men were damn fools if they thought they could tussle with me now, but they were all in just as Petrie lore would have it. This would mark the beginning of my estrangement from my father that would last a little over the next three years. Other than an occasional hi and bye, and maybe being at the same function for my son Moses, we barely spoke or communicated.

Later in the summer my wife, Aslyne, became a U.S. Citizen. On the day she was to go to Cleveland to get sworn in I didn't feel like getting out of bed on time to go with her. So I stayed back while my mom, my sister, and Moses accompanied her. I was so selfish and so self-consumed. This was a really big deal for her. Here this beautiful young Haitian girl had given me a handsome and healthy baby boy. She put up with all the mess and fucked up shit I put her through for the last seven years. She worked her ass off to study and pass a test in a foreign language to become a citizen of this country. And on the day she was to be sworn in and honored for her achievement, I decided that it didn't fit into my schedule.

God had yet to finish dealing with me as He did with Job, so that I could see that my very existence could be looked on as detestable to Him.

Revolution was the only thing on my mind concerning Haiti. Aslyne was my trophy wife. She would always be there. I would see about taking care of her needs when I was finished seeing my Haitian destiny through to its fruition. As the days and weeks passed I was becoming more and more abusive to her. Not physically, but verbally. And I wasn't paying it any attention at all. My mom was starting to warn me, "You better be careful. She's going to get fed up one day and leave you." I blew my mom off. She wasn't going anywhere. I was Zeke of Haiti. Everything was under control.

In September of 2006 I told my supervisor I had to go back to Haiti for six weeks to take care of some personal business. I had even suggested to some of my inner circle that I was going to Haiti and I may not return. I was madly searching for my purpose in Haiti. My family and friends saw me as a crazed madman. Most everyone close to me had a healthy fear of me because of it. But I was well liked at the Plaza where I worked security, so they agreed to let me have the time off. My absence was a great strain on the company. Trying to find coverage for my forty hours from Friday night to Monday morning wasn't easy. Most people wanted their weekends off. I was fortunate, however, that they managed and I was good to go.

I was back off to Haiti once again, leaving Aslyne and Moses to fend for themselves. They had my mom so they were all good. I was so fortunate that my mom tolerated my behavior but she was starting to run out of patience. By this point I was renting a place for John and Sabine in Delmas

48. I spent the next six weeks in and out of Cite Soleil. U.N. aggression in Cite Soleil was heating up.

One day, as I was coming out of Cite Soleil, I watched as Brazilian soldiers talked to and treated Haitians like animals. They were talking to the Haitians like dogs. I was enraged by what I witnessed. Making me even more angry was that Haitians, in one of their biggest inferiority complexes, would root for these same Brazilians in the game of soccer. It was just another in the long line of social ills in this country that was so sick. I could never wrap my mind around the fact that Haitians would care more about a foreigner than their own blood. Before leaving in October I made one last trip to Cite Soleil. I spent a few hours speaking with two of my closest friends, Aristil Jean Smith, also known as Nasson, and Zaro. I told them that I was going to send money from time to time, and not just for them, but for some kids too. I instructed Zaro to give the money to a dance troupe run by a guy they called Bouchonka. I was all for anything that gave young people something positive to do with their time. I was all for it. I was going to be leaving Haiti with no return date in sight. I told everyone close to me that I loved them, and that I would see them one day soon.

The day that I was due to leave Haiti I was running late to the airport and I missed my flight. I nearly missed my flight again the very next day and I was the last one to board the plane. I had been late both days because I was having sex with a Haitian girlfriend of mine. On the second day I was running tardy I got a fortunate break because of a small delay in the plane's departure. And since I had no bags to check they allowed me to board. In this case a girlfriend of mine who worked for American Airlines got me through. As I boarded the plane and headed back to find my seat I was greeted with dozens of eyes fixed right on me. As I approached the one empty seat on the plane to sit down I was surprised to see this beautiful blonde woman sitting directly in front of me. I seemed to recognize her face from somewhere. I had years earlier seen a story about a former playboy playmate that had started an orphanage in Haiti back in 1994, only three years after I had arrived on the Haiti scene. Her name was Susie Krabacher. Years earlier I had thought about reaching out to her about possibly working together in Cite Soleil, but I never followed through with it. I thought, "If it is the will of God, someday our paths will cross."

As I sat in the chair right behind her I had to ask. I tapped her on the shoulder and said, "Hey there, are you Susie?"

She turned around with a big smile on her face and said, "Yes I am."

I introduced myself, told her how I knew of her, and we had a short chat. When the flight was over I spoke to her again as we were walking out of the plane together. We ended up exchanging contact information. She had told me about a book she had coming out and that she would email to me the redline edit so that I could get to know her story a little bit more in depth. I thought to myself, "Wow, maybe this is it? Maybe this was my why in Haiti?" I mean, I was supposed to be gone the day before. In my mind I couldn't reason that as coincidence. It must have been God's doing. If I could convince myself it was from above, then I was always all in. Meeting Susie was destined to happen in my mind.

The initial thrill of meeting Susie and possibly finding out my purpose didn't last long. When I arrived back home I was greeted by my mom and my wife, both telling me it was over. My mom told me that I would have to leave her house. Aslyne told me that she wanted a separation. It was a double whammy for me, one which I never saw coming. I had been living with a veil over my eyes for so long. The October weather was cold, dark, and rainy and that made my current state of affairs even more miserable. I took refuge in my brother Jon's apartment in downtown Barberton. I was in real trouble. I begged and pleaded for Aslyne to take me back. I cried like a little bitch at her feet for several days. I promised her that I would change. I said, "Let's go find a house and get a car."

At this point in my life I still didn't have my license. A good friend of mine named Donny Pavlik assisted me in getting a vehicle. I went and took my driver's test and officially had my license. It wasn't a very big deal at the time. In my mind, I was seemingly giving up my Haiti life going forward. I had a new car with a monthly payment and insurance to boot. I had avoided bills like this for all these years for a reason. A friend of mine that I did business with gave me an advance on some money and I went and got us a house on Evergreen Street in Barberton. The rent was expensive, at $700 a month, but it was a really nice place. All this leg work impressed Aslyne enough to have her believe that I was serious and I was now taking the necessary steps to make real changes.

Saying and doing were night and day.

I had never before given her any reason to ever believe me. I would always do what I wanted in the end anyway. A $700 rent payment, a $300 car note, insurance, gas, electric, cable, and internet. I wasn't getting away from all this and running back to Haiti anymore. Aslyne took me back. I was so relieved. I was really on the brink of losing her and I did not like how that felt. I was her first and only love. I had known her since she was eight years old. She used to sit on my lap. I had all that history on my side. I was so lucky because I believe that level of familiarity and comfort was the only reason she continued to tolerate me. All Aslyne ever wanted from me was my time, my love, my attention, that's it. She never asked for much. I promised her all of it and said this was a new beginning for us. I had shamelessly called on God in this circumstance to bail me out and He came through.

Feeling as though you always have God's hand resting on your shoulder bestowed with His almighty favor can be a scary thing. I always felt like this gave me a false sense of security. I could do what I wanted, and God's favor would reign in the end. Besides, I was taking care of the poor. That James 1:27 verse again. I rode that one particular scripture my entire adult life.

END OF DECEMBER 2006
BEGINNING OF JANUARY 2007

By December we were living in our own home and had a new car. A month later in January of 2007 we found out that we were expecting a baby. In my life things could change so quickly. On a drop of a dime, just like that. At the end of January, Susie called to say she needed my help in Haiti. I never expected to be seeing Haiti again that soon. I talked my wife into agreeing to make me available to Susie and her organization, which helped the disenfranchised children in her homeland. This trip would be on Susie's dime. It was of no consequence to us financially, and was only for about four days in the early part of February, so Aslyne gave me her blessing.

This time when I arrived in Haiti there was an operation by U.N. troops in Cite Soleil. They were going in to apprehend gang leader Evens Jeune, also known as "Ti Kouto," or "Little Knife." Rumors swirled that Evens carved up his victims with a knife, henceforth the nickname. What most people never knew, however, was how he really got his nickname.

Evens had a three-year-old child that was killed by a cat. It was a mystical killing. It was for that same reason I watched over Moses so tenaciously. Evens began killing every cat he saw after that. He would carve them up into pieces.

My first stop was at the hotel where Susie was staying to check in with her. Then I went straight to Cite Soleil with John. U.N. Troops had cordoned off most of the entrances into this ghetto, the largest in the Western Hemisphere. John and I went in on foot via back channels that we knew. We were truly rats of the corridors in the ghetto. Gunfire rang out in the distance. *Pop pop pop pop pop. Tat tat tat tat tat.* It echoed nonstop. All my guys in Soleil were under siege. Boston was the main focus because that's where Evens' Jamaica base was. Armored personnel carriers were everywhere. There was constant thunder from a helicopter up above. Back in December, these same U.N. troops, led by a Brazilian contingent, had committed and carried out a massacre of civilians, which the international community largely ignored. It was almost two months later and they were back at it. I finally got to where I was going inside of the 34 katye, "neighborhoods," and came upon my closest friends in battle positions. Normally gangs would fight against rival gangs in these neighborhoods. But in this case, all the gangs had reason to come together to fight a common enemy, the blan.

My friend Zaro's eyes lit up when he saw me approaching. He said, "Zeke, sa wap fe la man? (What are you doing here man?) We are at war I can't believe you would enter here now."

I said, "Are you kidding me bro? I wouldn't want to be anywhere else than right here, right now."

Zaro said, "Come quick, check this out."

We walked through an alleyway into a corridor where a half dozen brand spanking new M-16 machine guns were lined up against a wall. I said, "Oh fuck bro, where did you get these?"

238

Throughout the years my closest friends in Cite Soleil, from Billy and Pac, to Zaro and Nasson, to Esteril and Enso, had begged me to smuggle weapons into Haiti for them so that they could protect and defend themselves. I had seriously considered it at one point but then ultimately decided against it. I couldn't have the blood of innocent victims on my hands. I always stood strong on that principle. Guns to fight revolutions was one thing, but all the other bullshit a lot of these young men would get into, I refused to support.

Zaro looked at me and said, "We got these guns from U.N. soldiers." He explained how they dumped a bunch of them in a pile purposely. The outside world would never know intimate details like this. The U.N. needed justification to be able to go in and randomly mow down innocent people. Because that is, in effect, what they were doing. For every real dangerous gang member they caught or killed, they maimed or killed three civilians. So the U.N. decided to arm the gangs. They would claim that the Haitian gangs stole these weapons from the United Nations' troops. In all my years in Haiti dealing with guys identified as gangsters inside of the thirty-four neighborhoods that make up this ghetto of Cite Soleil, not one of them outside of maybe Amaral Duclona had any real money to even have weapons like this. Amaral had an immaculate house in Belikou compared to all the other houses in this ghetto full of tin shacks. These guys did not get the quality of weapons in their midst at the local gun shop.

Important to note: Not all of these guys in Cite Soleil were true gangsters as labeled by Haitian and Western media. Amaral, for example, was a very smart young man. He had the mind and imagination of a crafty businessman/entrepreneur all the while being a community activist. He was a natural born leader. Amaral was used as the right arm for Fanmi Lavalas in the Belikou neighborhood of Cite Soleil. He was well liked by his peers and the poor people, who he served in a Robin Hood type capacity. When he was no longer needed by government officials he became a liability and was used as a fall guy. This is how things in Haiti worked. The U.N. had a plan and they implemented it with success. They made it appear as justifiable, going into and shooting up these neighborhoods while looking for a couple of gang bosses.

I stayed with the guys until the cover of nightfall. That's when John and

I slipped through the cracks and crevices of several dozen corridors in the darkness as the sound of automatic gunfire rang out. That was the last time I ever saw Zaro alive. He was arrested and sent to the Haitian National Penitentiary, and inside of those walls he died. After a few days in Haiti helping Susie with some things I headed back home to the states.

That spring, Susie asked me to assist her with a group from Denver that was going to Haiti. I gladly signed up for that. Once again, it was on her dime and it continued to afford me the chance to return to Haiti. On this trip I met a nineteen-year-old girl named Alexandra who worked for Susie in the orphanage. Alex, as I called her, had been in an orphanage since the age of ten. When she turned eighteen she started working for Susie.

Alex and I grew very close. We started up a relationship unbeknownst to Susie. I really loved her. She was a classic tomboy and I was very attracted to her personality. We kept our relationship a secret. That same trip I met another beautiful girl who was still in school named Marc Dana. I started up a relationship with her, too. I couldn't help myself. I loved Haitian girls, and they loved me back. I desired to be loved by all of them. For me, Haitian girls had no equal. This same trip I met Julie Kartrude and Jennifer Sehnal Yaeger. Through the both of them I ended up meeting two Americans who would play a big role in my life three years down the road. I would learn through them that networking was a powerful way to really get things done in life. I became really good friends with Julie. I spent time with these ladies and others that were in the group doing mission work as their translator. I left Haiti on this particular trip with new contacts in hand.

In early August Susie had Jennifer Sehnal Yaeger phone me from Haiti. Jennifer said to me, "Susie really needs you in Haiti." I asked when and Jennifer replied, "Five minutes ago." I was like, "Oh shit." Aslyne was eight months pregnant at the time. I knew she wasn't going to be thrilled about me leaving for Haiti at this stage of her pregnancy. Once again, however, I sweet-talked her into letting me go. Susie put me on a plane the very next day in first class. I never rode first class anything before. I was a fish out of water. I didn't even know what to do with the things they were giving me in first class. It was definitely an eye-opening experience to how the upper class get down.

240

John picked me up at the airport and we went straight to see Susie at her hotel. Susie had sent me the redline edit of her book, Angels of a Lower Flight. While reading about her personal story growing up it was evident that she had suffered a lot as a young girl. That sort of suffering and pain never really goes away. Add to that the stresses of Haiti and the work she was doing there. Plus she had just lost one of her dogs that was like a baby to her. She was in a real emotional state.

I think what Susie saw in me was a counterpart that understood a little bit about what it was like to really suffer. I think she really appreciated what my presence meant to somebody like her in Haiti. After the spring trip months earlier, one of the team members from Denver told me that Susie's husband, Joe, thought highly of and had nothing but nice things to say about me. I really liked Joe as well. I found him to be very personable and down to earth. I spent some time over those couple of days talking with Susie, trying to be of some comfort to her. Misery loves company. I knew that better than anyone.

As September 12, 2007, approached we were very excited over the possibility that our baby boy, Spartacus, might be born on the same day as Moses. Several months earlier, when finding out that we were having another boy, Aslyne was visibly sad. I, on the other hand, was thrilled. I only wanted boys. I tried to convey to her that having a healthy baby was all that mattered. She had longed for a baby girl so much that she became a little depressed. We worked through it and by the time September rolled around, Aslyne was looking forward to the baby's arrival. The twelfth came and went, no baby. September 13, however, wouldn't disappoint. We spent the majority of that day in Barberton Citizens Hospital. On that night around the ten o'clock hour Spartacus would finally show up and show out. Aslyne had been in labor for a good while.

In the moments before Spartacus was born everyone stepped out of the room for a quick second including the doctor and nurse. I was standing alone with Aslyne in the room right across from her. Then all of a sudden she felt it happening and cried out. I ran to the door and yelled, "Somebody fucking get in here, the baby is coming." The nurse ran in to grab Spartacus as he was coming out. She got there just in the knick of time, otherwise yours truly would have been the one to deliver him. The female doctor credited with the delivery wasn't even present in the room when Spartacus Sejour Petrie came out kicking and screaming.

Nobody in the family wanted the name Spartacus. I told them all to stand down. "Spartacus is one of the greatest names in world history and it shall be his name," I said. The country of Haiti was often considered the Black Sparta. Spartacus was a rebellious Thracian, a gladiator, an accomplished military leader that led the first revolution in world history against the Roman Empire. Where he failed, the Haitians were victorious. The Haitians would become the first people in all of history to win their freedom in a successful slave revolt. This was a perfect name for my second son.

The name of my first son, Moses, means "drawn from the water." He was born on the island of Hispaniola where Haitians were always drawn from the water as refugees. Moses in the Bible led the Israelites from captivity in Egypt. My first son's name was legend, and so now, too, was my second son's name. I was very content with the names of my boys.

In December of 2007 we took our first and only family portrait. We all wore number 21 Washington Redskins Sean Taylor jerseys with the Haitian flag in the background. The Redskins were my favorite team from my childhood dating all the way back to 1982. My father took me to see the Redskins play the Cleveland Browns in 1985 at old Municipal Stadium. The game was broadcast on CBS. We sat in the famous dog pound bleacher seats. The Redskins won the game 14-7. I was twelve years old. In the fall of 2012, twenty-seven years later, I took my twelve-year-old son Moses to see his Redskins beat the Browns, 38-21, at FirstEnergy stadium. Those father and son memories made with my dad and my son will forever be priceless.

JANUARY OF 2008

By January of 2008 I was trying to steer Moses into playing basketball. My Haiti days and my endless plight in searching for my "why" had seemingly come to an end. Susie and I grew distant, we no longer communicated, and it seemed like my love affair with Haiti was over. I thought OK, let me try and be the best father I can be to my sons, and the best husband to my wife who I had failed far too often.

For me, part of being the best dad I could be meant pushing my son in the game of basketball. Moses was already showing signs of being a really good athlete. He had played a little bit of soccer in previous years but never really seemed to fall in love with it. It seemed he much more preferred playing basketball than soccer. I then decided that we would invest all of our energy and efforts in training him to become a great basketball player. Where I had failed, I hoped and dreamed of a much different outcome for him.

I ended up crossing paths with a guy named Chris Harrison. Chris had done a short stint in the NBA with the Utah Jazz. I had him working with Moses to start off. Chris became a good friend. I cherished his experience, advice, and wisdom. He got Moses headed in the right direction.

I continued searching online for basketball training that I could take Moses to throughout the year in our local area. That's when I came across the Cleveland Basketball School. CBS was founded by Steubenville native and legendary basketball coach Paul Haught. Coach Paul is a family man, married, with four kids. He is one of those white guys that has soul and has many close relationships with African Americans. I liked him from the jump. When I first took Moses to work out at coach Paul's CBS training facility in Medina at a place called Pinnacle Sports, his youngest son, Robbie, was helping him train all the young kids in attendance. I really enjoyed our first experience there because basketball wasn't the only thing being taught and stressed to the kids. Coach Paul was in the business of teaching kids about real life outside of basketball, and he was serious about it. I really liked his old school style and mannerisms. Coach Paul and I became close friends. So close, in fact, that on occasion I had Moses stay the night at the Haught family home in Brecksville. I looked at his wife, Shelly, oldest son PM, son Joey, daughter Leah, and son Robbie as family.

I immersed Moses into this game of basketball around so many great basketball minds and people with great work ethic. Working forty-hour weekends had me free all week long. Moses and I went to the local Barberton YMCA at six-thirty a.m. nearly every morning to practice and get up shots. At a very young age Moses was becoming advanced. He was

243

handling the basketball better than most kids that were two and three years older.

That summer we met a young man named Cedrick Middleton who hailed from Chicago. He was a former basketball player at the University of Akron. He was one of the hardest working athletes I had ever come across. He had real passion. Ced and I developed a friendship that would ultimately lead to him training Moses. It was my hope that he would be able to instill all of these great qualities into Moses' psyche. It was great for us too, because he was local in Akron at the JAR Arena.

We also met a coach named Steven Culp. Culp taught sixth graders at Jennings Middle School in Akron. He was an assistant coach for the Akron Zips back in 1994, and he was also an assistant coach on Keith Dambrot's staff at St. Vincent-St. Mary High School when a young man named Lebron James showed up on the scene. Steve and I hit it off right away and soon became close friends. Consuming Moses with the game of basketball had brought so many newfound relationships into my life. More importantly, it gave me some much-needed structure, and I needed lots of that. I felt a strong purpose now to guide my sons through athletics.

In the fall of 2008 I started to have some really bad low blood sugar episodes at night, much greater than what a normal low blood sugar felt like. I remember when I was younger my mom told me that they found Jamie Montgomery's mother wandering outside on Norton Avenue one morning wearing only her robe. I quickly charged that she was just doing that for attention. Now I was learning that I couldn't have been more wrong. These low blood sugars hit me especially hard when I hadn't received enough sleep, combined with being physically out of shape, and having a terrible diet. I went through a period where almost weekly I had a bad spell. I would wake up in the middle of the night and do something crazy, like pee in Moses' dresser drawers. I literally thought Moses' dresser drawer was the toilet. I would act out crazily and talk like I was drunk. I would only know what happened after the fact because Aslyne and Moses would recount to me the crazy happenings of the night before.

I once drove Moses to school while experiencing one of these devastating low blood sugars, and honestly, I can't fathom how I got him to school and me back home safely. It was bad. It was something that I battled then and also a few years down the road. Nothing in my life ever came easy. It's always been a dogfight.

NOVEMBER 2008

By November I decided to take a trip back to Haiti to spend a week feeding into my selfish indulgences – staying in a nice hotel, eating good food, and having lots of sex with several girlfriends I had outside of my marriage. My small business venture was on the verge of folding so I used my business credit card to pay for everything. That way my wife would never know the difference. In the past, I had flown off to Haiti on a moment's notice doing jobs for Susie, so it was easy for her to believe I was doing the same thing. She would never question me. This was the first time in all my years traveling to Haiti that I was going for no other reason than to be as self-absorbed as possible. I was going to take advantage of the remains of my failed business. I went to the VISA Lodge. I knew the Carvonis brothers that ran the place. I really liked them a lot. And it was close to the airport and very convenient in every way imaginable. I spent the majority of that week staying in my room, mostly having sex with about five different girls around the clock. When I was done with one another came in. I had John on the lookout for me. We'd communicate by cell phone. He would let me know when one showed up. There were times where I literally would be finishing up with one as another one was arriving. Needless to say I worked around it, and made it work for me.

I had the time of my life but it soon turned into one of the great regrets and shames of my life. I'm embarrassed and disgusted looking back on it now.

To make it tolerable to my conscience, I would say to myself, "Look at all you've done to help the disenfranchised. All the sacrifices you've made, the risks you've taken over all these years to help poor people. Certainly for someone who has done so much, for this week in Haiti, you are more than deserving of such pleasure. If anyone has earned it, you have."

Surely all the good I had done over the years had bought me some good credit with God? My good deeds would cover any wrong doing would they not?

That's exactly how I played it out in my own mind, never stopping to think about the negative affect it could have on these young women. I was very selfish!

A month later I started to scratch an itch in my groin area. My groin had been irritating me for a few days but I just chalked it up as jock itch. As I examined myself closer I saw what appeared to be a tiny black mole I didn't ever see before. I looked close, tried to scratch it to see if it was a piece of lint or something. All of a sudden it took a different shape, a different dimension. Little legs appeared out of nowhere.

I jumped up, my heart pounding, and thought to myself, "Oh my god, I have crabs."

I had always heard about STDs and crabs, but never had one before. I remember laughing when hearing of others who had them. And then, as though they were all hiding like the munchkins in *The Wizard of Oz*, all of these little tiny black mole spots appeared from every corner of my groin region. My wife was right outside of the bathroom at the time and I hurriedly jumped into the shower to wash them off, or so I thought. I yelled out to her that I was taking a quick shower. I then frantically tried to scrub away all the tiny dark spots. I scrubbed hard for about 20 minutes to no avail. When I got out and dried off they were all still there. I was beside myself. What was I going to do? I had to keep this from my wife.

I wondered which one of these girlfriends had been unfaithful to me and cursed me with these crabs. I took no responsibility for it. All I could think was which one of these little bitches betrayed me? I was furious! I raced to Kmart to buy shampoo to kill the crabs. I got in the shower again, this time telling my wife that I decided to do her a big favor and remove my pubic hair for her comfort, even though we barely ever had sex. My wife was such a beautiful girl but I spent more time having sex with other women than I ever did with her, and with females who were nowhere near the caliber of female my wife was. It was truly a sickness on my part.

I showered with the shampoo but still could not remove all these crabs from my groin area. I was infested and somehow never fucking knew it. I had to come up with a plan and do it quickly.

I decided to come clean, but only half way clean. I only gave her half truths. I finally called her in and said, "Look at this, Aslyne. You're not

246

gonna fucking believe this. I have crabs."

She looked at me in bewilderment. Again, she had only ever heard of STDs. She had never witnessed anything like that with her own eyes. I started to verbally bash my place of work. I said, "Yeah I got these from one of the toilet seats at my job."

I handed her tweezers and she started to pick and pluck away one by one. She picked them off my testicles, she plucked them out of my asshole. It was quite painful and humiliating. I really couldn't tell if she was mad or not. I must have had a hundred of these little fuckers on me. I was so pissed but relieved at the same time that Aslyne seemed to buy my excuse as legit and seemed oblivious to how, in fact, one contracts crabs. I'm sure in her heart of hearts she started to realize that this wasn't the dream marriage she had always wanted. She seemed cool with everything so along we went.

Aslyne tolerated me for a long time. She had always said she didn't get married just to get divorced. She loved me, she loved our boys, and I was the only man she had ever known. That December of 2008 running all the way through to December of 2009 would change everything forever. Our marriage would deteriorate for good. Crab-gate officially became the beginning of the end of our tumultuous eleven years together. It was like being woken out of a dream to the nightmare reality that I was soon to face.

BEGINNING OF 2009

As the new year of 2009 commenced I started to spend every waking moment with my two sons. I was so invested in Moses and making him the basketball juggernaut that I never became. I was pretty focused, and borderline obsessed with making Moses great. I was taking him all the way up to Cleveland regularly to play on a travel basketball team. Moses was in the third grade, often playing against kids that were in the fifth grade. He was really being pushed and challenged to compete hard. As the year progressed we were spending many late nights at the JAR Arena in Akron, working hard with Cedrick to get better. Everywhere we went Spartacus rode shotgun with me. I was hoping that Spart would follow right in

Moses' footsteps as he grew older. When we were home I made Moses do pushups and sit ups every day to strengthen his core. I was pushing him to the max and needed to show him what greatness looked like. On the morning of Sunday February 8, I asked my father if he'd like to go watch the Lakers versus the Cavs in person at the Q. I said Aslyne, Mo, and Spart and I were going and we had an extra ticket. Although he and I weren't really speaking, he agreed so he could spend some quality time with Moses Jeffrey, his pride and joy.

As we were walking around inside of the arena pre-game, Spartacus ran ahead of us and stopped directly in front of a man standing at the end of one of the tunnel exits. This guy was giving Spart a high five. To my astonishment I realized it was Derrick Kosinski from MTV's *Real World/Road Rules Challenge* shows. He was really cool. We talked for a few minutes, sharing a little bit about our backgrounds and where we both hailed from. We took some pictures together and then went our separate ways. Kobe's Lakers would go on to win the game. Kobe had played sick that day and I used it as a motivating example for Moses to heed.

At the same time I was pushing Moses to be great, I was neglecting myself. I started to put on some weight. I ended up reaching 205 pounds. That isn't where I wanted to be as a five-foot-ten-inch, 36-year-old diabetic. My OCD behaviors were now back in full effect.

It was also during this year that Aslyne got on the social media site called Facebook. In those days I was very private so I avoided Facebook like the plague. I made her run everything by me before she posted a picture. I wasn't thrilled about private pictures of our family going up on a board that anyone anywhere could view. I was very controlling, and I talked to her as though she was more my kid than my wife. I had taught her to drive a year or so earlier, and at that point we had two vehicles, so she was starting to become more and more independent. At every turn I was trying to control her.

I was also under the impression that Aslyne was always going to stay the same person. It never ever occurred to me that we were growing farther and farther apart by the day. My mom was always quick to remind me, "You better watch how you treat her. She'll end up leaving you." Aslyne was starting to grow into her own as a woman, and all the while I was treating her as this young girl that would always be dependent on me, and who would never leave me. As we grew apart I grew closer to my boys. I was with them all week long outside of when Moses was at school or when I was at work during the weekends. By this time I had slowed down on the chatline, even though I was still having phone sex. Once in a blue moon my wife and I were intimate, so I was hanging on for dear life to the masturbation while having phone sex on the chatline to relieve myself.

My wife started going out more frequently with her white friends from work. It was something that really kind of bothered me. I became angry about it. I once said to her angrily, "Why do all of you suck ass Haitians continue to lift up white people on a pedestal while demeaning your own?" It was cowardice in my eyes. I cursed both the whites who my wife hung out with, and the Haitians like herself who not only tolerated whites but continued to play the role of sou sou – suck asses, for them. I absolutely despised seeing her with these people.

On one occasion, she was heading out on a particular night with some white friends of hers. This didn't fit into my plans or into what I had going on for that evening, so an argument ensued. I was still estranged from my father. I had to constantly listen to him say to me how I was going to kill Moses' gentle spirit by pushing him too hard in basketball. All my family echoed his sentiments. This made me feel isolated. I was working a shit dead end security job that gave me no fulfillment and meant nothing to me. My business ventures had folded so there was no more extra money. Haiti seemed to be no longer in my future. Aslyne was distant and her entire demeanor began to change toward me. She said something about being fine without me and her tone made me very upset. I went off on her.

In the same manner I had cursed Almighty God, in the same manner I had cursed my father, I now was cursing Aslyne. I approached her and in close quarters said, "You little fucking Uncle Tom nigger bitch, who the fuck do you think you're speaking to?" I knew using the word nigger would cut her deeply. I berated her in every way possible. I said, "You do nothing but suck the assholes of white people just like all those bitch ass Uncle Tom nigger cowards in Haiti."

The only times that I ever referred to blacks using the word nigger, was when I viewed them as Uncle Toms. I did not tolerate an Uncle Tom, ever!

249

She responded in a disrespectful tone and I slapped her. She hit me back and tried to hit me a second time and I turned away. I was so angry at this point but I knew I could not hit her. So, I spit on her. Even after all this, I apologized, and we continued on with our lives as usual.

I was now on the brink in the coming year of 2010 of suffering a coup of my own.

JANUARY 11, 2010

It was the late evening of January 11, 2010. My wife was working second shift hours and didn't get off until 11 p.m. We only had one vehicle now which I had at home with me. I was taking her to and from work. On occasion, she got rides when it was late like this so I could let Moses and Spartacus sleep. I called her to say that I could come pick her up, but she insisted on me staying home with the boys, that she was okay. She would get a ride.

By the time she got home it was almost midnight. The car pulled into the driveway and nobody got out for several minutes. I went to the window to look out and then texted her, asking her what she was doing? She texted back that she was coming. It took her forever to finally come in to the house. By this point I was mad and it led to us arguing. The clock ticked midnight and now it was January 12.

This day would change the course of the rest of my life.

Aslyne said we need to talk. She came over and sat on the couch next to me. She said, "I want a divorce." I couldn't believe what I was hearing. She said, "We can still be friends but I want a divorce. I can't live with you anymore."

"Whatever," I said, "this is bullshit. We are not going to do this to the boys."

She said, "I'm serious I am done." She got up from the couch and went to the bedroom. I ended up going to bed a few minutes behind her, just not in the same room. I was sleeping in Moses' room at the bottom of the bunkbeds. Aslyne slept with Spartacus in our bedroom.

JANUARY 12, 2010

I woke up in the bottom bunk in my son Moses' bedroom. Moses was still asleep on the top bunk and I could faintly hear Aslyne talking on the phone in our bedroom. My youngest son Spartacus had been sleeping with her in our bed since practically the day he was born so I was banished to the bottom bunk in Moses' room. My marriage at that point was all but over.

Aslyne got out of bed to go to the bathroom. I jumped up quickly to go into the room to find her phone, which was under her pillow. I navigated to her most recent calls and texts. We both had blackberries so I was able to do it efficiently. Her most recent call just moments earlier was from Nivek. Her most recent text also was from Nivek. I'll never forget it, the text read, "I Love You So Much!" My heart almost came out of my chest. I immediately felt sick to my stomach. I hurriedly took down Nivek's number and placed Aslyne's phone back under her pillow and left the room. She came in from the bathroom and went back to bed.

I went down to the basement and started to dial "*67" and then Nivek's number. Dialing *67 blocked my number so that whoever Nivek was could not see my digits. I dialed, it rang, went to voicemail. The voice on the other end was that of a young guy named Kevin. Nivek was Kevin spelled backwards. She had it in her phone that way in case I ever came across it.

Then it all hit me. The times it took her forever to get home from work. A young homely looking dude named Kevin that worked at the same place who was on her Facebook page. The times late at night when I heard Aslyne up late texting and talking. This was going on right under my nose and I never even noticed it. I didn't leave a message. I hung up. I went upstairs and got on the computer. I went straight to her Facebook page after having a flashback of her always being on the computer and sending messages on Facebook, and I found some messages between them that she forgot to delete. I quickly deleted him from her friends list and blocked him. This was the guy who was behind my wife asking me for a divorce.

I grew enraged. I was thinking, "How could a pathetic looking little fuck like this be messing with my wife?" I slipped into Aslyne's room as she slept and grabbed her phone. I went to the living room and called this Kevin directly. Certainly, if he thought it was Aslyne who was calling him he would answer, and answer he did.

I yelled, "Hey you little fuck face, I'll kill you if you don't stay the fuck away from wife. She's married motherfucker. I'll beat your cracker ass you little faggit."

Aslyne ran in. I said, "Stay the fuck away from my wife," and hung up the phone. She screamed at me to give her the phone. I held her phone in my hand tightly, saying, "What are you doing talking to this little nineteen-year-old kid?"

Funny how that worked. For me it was OK to get her pregnant at fifteen, but she couldn't talk to a nineteen-year-old because he was just a kid to me.

I said, "You little fucking bitch, you're an embarrassment to your sons. I blocked that little fucker on your Facebook too."

She then went to the computer and added him back as her friend on Facebook. We continued to argue back and forth throughout the day before she left for work. She had a friend take her to work that afternoon. Before she left, however, I saw a piece of paper on the table that had some scribble on it. The name of a female lawyer, the name of a local women's shelter, and the number for Children's Protective Services. Aslyne had put her plan of escape into action.

"You fucking bitch, you're gonna go out of your way to make me look like a villain."

Her ride was waiting. She said nothing and walked out the door.

I immediately called two of my friends back to back. Donny Pavlik and Jason Hance. I needed ears to listen to me in that moment of tremendous grief. I was in tears crying out to my friends, looking for them to wave a magic wand to make things better. They both gave it to me straight. I was going to have to buck up and take whatever it was that I had coming my way. I was in a mentally fragile state where I was already starting to plan out how I was going to kill both Kevin and Aslyne.

I came to find out that Kevin had just come out of a relationship with a girl that was cheating on him. Of course, Aslyne had been in a nightmare relationship with me for about eleven years. They both found each other one day at work and started talking. Phone records would later indicate that Aslyne started having phone contact with Kevin in early December. They didn't officially start their own relationship until around about January 4. She asked me for a divorce a week later on January 12.

I also found out that she had already started a silent campaign against me, advising members of both my family and her family, and also some of her close friends including Kevin, that I was verbally and physically abusive, and that she was now in fear of me and what I might do to her. The verbal abuse I was guilty of, probably since day one of our relationship. The physical abuse was something that maybe happened once in a great blue moon. There were a few times throughout the course of the eleven years that I had slapped her. I never hit her with a closed fist. I spit on her a couple of times. I had wrestled her to the ground on a couple of occasions. I had, of course, once whipped her with a belt back in 2004. All these things were now coming to my mind. I was trying to somehow justify my abuse as not being that bad. I stood on the fact that if I had been all that bad she would have never stayed with me for eleven years.

Had it just been her wanting a divorce it would have been one thing, but now, with the knowledge of her seeing a young guy, that was an entirely different pill to swallow, one which my pride would not allow me to do. This new revelation of her being the unfaithful one was devastating to my ego. The fragility of the male ego is a very dangerous thing. I could not digest the fact that some little punk ass 19-year-old kid was going to take my wife from me. I was going to kill him first.

I remember saying, "I am going to show this motherfucker what being a Haitian is all about."

Then, as fate would have it, the heavens shined down on both Kevin and Aslyne at 4:53 p.m. that day. I had taken Moses to his basketball practice that started at five p.m. I was helping Jim Dippel coach. Jim's son, Jayce, played with Moses on the mini Magics travel basketball team in Barberton. As practice was letting out sometime around seven p.m. I turned my cell phone back on, anticipating messages that concerned my family crisis with Aslyne. The entire practice I kept thinking to myself, "Where do I go from here?"

As my phone vibrated on it started buzzing with one text after another from close friends, asking me if I had heard about the 7.2 magnitude earthquake in Haiti.

Time just froze.

I hurried home with the boys and turned on the television. I stood in disbelief while watching CNN's coverage of the quake that shook Haiti just a couple of hours before. When Aslyne came home later that night I asked if she had heard about the news in Haiti. She said yes but didn't have much interest in discussing it. She remained steely focused on one thing and one thing only, that was being liberated from me. She knew me all too well though. That was never going to happen without a fight.

She did take a step back, however, in the next twenty-four to forty-eight hours after the quake. An eerie silence had fallen over our house that night. The next day I took a phone call from childhood friend, Tim Widner. He said, "Yo bro, are you going?"

I said, "Going where?"

He said, "Haiti man! This is what you're made for, you're built for something like this."

He reminded me of all the services I could provide people in need down in Haiti during this crisis of epic proportions. He said, "Who knows, maybe this is your reason why?"

A few minutes later my friend Matt Levitch called me from the West Coast. I had met Matt through Jennifer Sehnal Yaeger. Matt was a freelance photographer living in Los Angeles at the time. He asked me if I had heard anything from our people in Haiti. I said no, nothing yet.

Back in the summer of 2009 Matt had gone to Haiti to document Vodou through his photography. While in the capital of Port-au-Prince he stayed at the place I rented in Delmas 31 with John, Sabine, and Lithana. Lithana was a girl that I had supported in years past. I had sent for her in Jeremie to come stay with John and Sabine. Sabine had been ill in the beginning of the year so Lithana came to help take care of her. I loved her and trusted her. I knew I could count on her to do anything I asked.

So Matt said, "Man, I wish that I could go down there right now."

I said, "You want to go?"

"Heck yeah, I want to go."

"Then let's fucking roll!"

Just like that I felt a new life come over me. I had a new purpose. This new purpose would help take the focus off of Aslyne and Kevin, and in fact, spare their lives. The earthquake in Haiti saved them, but it also saved me from myself. It spared my boys a life of agony. What became one of the worst disasters of biblical proportions in the modern age saved my life.

That same day I called Julie Kartrude to tell her about Matt and me going to Haiti. Julie, Jennifer, and I had all met through Susie Krabacher. That power of networking was now coming together. Julie then told me about a guy named Mike Keister who she had before mentioned, but I had never met in person. He had his own air ambulance service that was going to be involved in this theatre now taking place in Haiti. Mike would be providing transportation in and out of Haiti for people all over the world. She put me in contact with him. I got on the phone with Mike right away and informed him about our plans. We worked it out so that the three of us met in Miami on the afternoon of the fifteenth. We would go to Santo Domingo that evening, then fly into Haiti the next morning with Greg, one of Mike's pilots. In the meantime, I was making plans with my boss about getting the time off of work to go to Haiti. The people of the National City Center at Cascade Plaza were so generous. People on the 15th floor at Roderick & Linton, people on the bank floors, they all took up funds and handed them over to me to use at my discretion for my trip.

Then the day I left, *The Akron Beacon Journal* ran a front-page story about me, Aslyne, and the boys, much to her chagrin. I had received a call the day before from Katie Byard, one of the staff writers at the Beacon. Katie had informed me that Pat Barger from the International Institute had given her my number. Katie was looking to do a story about us for her Haiti earthquake coverage. I told Aslyne about it and she seemed OK with it until we were asked to pose for a front-page photo. She then said that she didn't want any part of it. She couldn't be on a campaign against me in private while showing publicly that everything was OK and that we were still a tight knit family.

I called Katie back and said I wasn't sure that we were going to be able to go through with this story because it was a very rough time. I said, "My wife really does not want to do it." Katie said she totally understood but kept insisting we go through with the story, as any good writer would do. She persuaded me to ask Aslyne again. Katie was not at all aware of what we were going through, nor was anyone else, outside of close family and a few friends. I finally said to Aslyne, if you don't want to do it, fine, I'll do it with the boys myself. That put pressure on her to not look bad so she reluctantly agreed.

I spoke throughout that afternoon with Katie, and then a Beacon Journal photographer came over to take our picture as a family at my mom's house. The next morning we graced the front page of the paper as I was already headed up to the airport in Cleveland to catch my flight. I traveled lightly. I left with a heavy heart not knowing for how long I would be gone and even more importantly, not knowing what I would come home to or not come home to.

That I might witness horrific scenes in Haiti for the next five weeks was the last thing on my mind and the least of my concerns. I could feel that my family as I knew it would never be the same. It was over. I was worried about being separated from my boys more than anything. The mere thought of it was death to me.

PART FOUR
LIVING AND DYING

*A*lthough the plan was for me and Mike to rendezvous with Matt in Miami on our way to the Dominican Republic, we both decided to go through Fort Lauderdale instead. We would meet up with Matt in Santo Domingo. I arrived in Fort Lauderdale on the afternoon of January 15.

I'm now on the lookout for Mike. I had never met him in person. I saw this guy approaching the boarding gate with a big smile on his face. As he got closer, we both started to extend our hands towards one another. I said, "You're Mike," and he said, "You're Zeke," simultaneously. I liked him right away. His illuminating spirit was infectious. We met up with Matt in Santo Domingo later that night. Matt had been routed through Miami and Puerto Rico via L.A. Matt was more stoic, quieter, but I already had a level of comfort with him because, over the course of a couple of years, we had several long phone conversations. It was almost as if we were already the best of friends.

Mike got a room for all of us to share together. We had dinner that night at the hotel restaurant. It was teeming with white people that were all trying to head over into Haiti. We overheard conversations what mode of transportation people were going to be using to get into Haiti. Some were taking private cars while others were taking public buses to the border between Haiti and the Dominican. No planes were allowed to land in Haiti at the time. One guy at a table next to us said that he and the group he was with had gone over to Haiti in a plane earlier that day and were refused the right to land by U.S. Special Ops on the ground, which were now running air traffic control. Seventy-two hours had passed since the quake. We were bracing ourselves for what we were about to be immersed in. I didn't sleep well at all that night. I was still reeling about my family falling apart back home.

The next morning, we were up early and headed to the airport. There, one of Mike's pilots, Greg Smith, was waiting for us. Matt, and Greg and I started loading up a light twin-engine Beach Craft Barron that the three of us would be flying in. A last-minute female aid worker was also added. We would be the second of many sorties flown in and out of Haiti over the next several weeks by Mike's pilots. For history's sake, the first arranged flight out of Haiti just hours after the quake was arranged by Mike for some U.S. Embassy personnel that were headed to Dulles Airport in Virginia. They flew out somewhere around midnight on January 12. A request had also been put into Mike about delivering some Satellite phones to the U.S. Embassy as soon as he could get them there. I grabbed a quick photo with Mike before boarding the plane. Matt was already in work mode snapping photos and documenting this historic event. We were off!

The approach to the airport in Port-au-Prince from the air became a fascinating listen. I was in the cockpit with Greg wearing a headset. I listened intently to the U.S. Military personnel on the ground, directing all inbound traffic. They kept turning around one plane after another, denying them clearance to land. We continued on ourselves in a kind of looping pattern, waiting for the actions of a Gulf Stream jet in front of us. Greg then moved to put the plane down. That's when the U.S. Special Ops started asking Greg to identify himself.

I looked over at him as the voice said, "Ident yourself immediately." The voice ran through some names and numbers and said, "Ident yourself, goddammit." The voice then said, "He's not responding. Son-of-a-bitch is not responding."

I kept looking over at Greg, wondering if he was ever going to comply. Greg sat there, going about his business, unannoyed, unbothered, as cool as the other side of the pillow. He landed us right there, smack dab in the middle of all that chaos. I liked him. I said, "Hell yes, brother."

As we removed our headsets, he looked at me, smiled, and said, "They're amateurs."

I said, "You're a bad man Greg, fuck yes," and I saluted him. That was the kind of stuff you only see on Netflix. We got off the plane in the grass

260

by the runway. Greg slowly and methodically made his way over to speak to the U.S. Special Ops that were on the ground. Matt and I watched from a distance. It looked as though Greg was the one in command. He handed over a piece of paper. They handed it back and saluted him. I said, "Yo Matt, he's CIA, bro."

Matt said, "Get the fuck out of here."

I said, "Yes sir that's a bad dude right there. I'll tell you all about it later."

Greg came back to the plane and when we finished getting our stuff out, he said, "Well fellas, good luck." He got back on the bird, and just like that, was gone.

Matt and I were now just moments away from entering into the shit, literally. We carried everything we brought with us. We walked from the runway, through scores of U.S. military personnel, all the way out to the front of the airport grounds into the throngs of total devastation, where hundreds of black faces greeted us with desperate eyes. I had used my cell phone to call John upon our arrival. I still didn't know if he was alive. When he answered, I was thrilled. I quickly asked about the girls. He said Sabine and Lithana were fine. I said, "I'm at the airport with Matt, come to us quickly."

Upon John's arrival at the airport we shared a long embrace that Matt captured on film. I looked to the heavens and said, "Thank you!"

The three of us walked from the airport to a hotel in Delmas 31 called Habitation Haat, which we were to call home for the next few weeks. After we got our things situated at the hotel, we headed out to go get the girls. They had been living in the same house that Aslyne and I lived in when Moses was born.

We came upon the place and found it in ruins. It was previously a two-story building. The three of them were fortunate to escape with their lives. As we looked around the rubble John informed us that before he came down to the airport, Sabine and Lithana had gone up the road to try and find some clean water for us. Instead of waiting for them to return we went up the block to look for them. In a matter of moments off in the distance we could see them running in our direction. Both of them mobbed me with hugs and kisses. It was another special moment that Matt caught on his camera. We returned to where the house once stood and the three of them rounded up what they could salvage from the collapsed structure. We then headed over to the Habitation Haat Hotel, which fortunately wasn't too far away.

Matt got a room for himself and I got one with John, Lithana, and Sabine. This was where things got really emotional.

Before leaving the States, I had my Blackberry phone turned on for international use. I also had access to Aslyne's Facebook account on my phone, unbeknownst to her. So now I was in Haiti following along with her Facebook activity. On one of the posts I came across a guy questioning Kevin, saying, "C'mon man, isn't she married with kids?"

I lost it right there. I immediately called home and told my mom and my sister all about it. I informed them of this guy named Kevin. I then called Aslyne and had Sabine speak to her for me. They had spent time in Haiti together in years past. Surely Aslyne would come to her senses after listening to Sabine plead her papa's case. Aslyne wasn't having it, however. As much as Sabine passionately pleaded on my behalf, Aslyne told her that she could no longer live with me. At this point I had no clue how much of a bill I was running up on my phone, but I didn't care. I was in this theatre of one of the most devastating disasters in modern history, where approximately 300,000 people were snuffed out in a matter of forty-five seconds, and I was a complete mess mentally because of my wife. It was unbelievable.

That night in the hotel the girls were very comforting to me. I ended up laying down and drifting off to sleep for a bit. When I woke, all I could hear was a fan running. In one bed John and Sabine were sleeping. Next to me in the bed was Lithana. She was wide awake. We started talking. She had observed how distraught I was earlier. She went out of her way to try and make me feel better in every way possible. And right on cue I took advantage of the affection she showered on me. I wrapped her in my arms and made love to her right then and there. I did it shamelessly. I had financially supported Lithana, her sister Maculanie, and from time to time helped other members of their family over the course of a couple decades. Even though she was now twenty years old, it was a line I shouldn't have crossed. I broke a code. But this was Haiti, and that's what I did. I was helping the poor. My good deeds would outweigh my bad ones. I tricked myself into believing that.

Looking back on it now, I'm ashamed. But in that particular moment I needed to feel like a man again. Here I was, amidst all this chaos, tragedy, and misery, having sex. I truly was a selfish animal.

Ironically, when the earth shook days earlier, there were many people found dead in hotels, their bodies still locked in sexual positions together. A few minutes later, Lithana and I were finished, the earth shook again. It was an aftershock. We all got up and ran out of the hotel. We were on the second floor and you could literally feel the building sway.

Very early the next morning John and I headed out to find Aslyne's sister, Poupette, and her family. When we arrived at the address we had for her, and were able to confirm that she was alive, I hurriedly called Aslyne back in the states, hoping this would lead to brownie points. I gave Poupette some money and begged her while on my knees to convince Aslyne to stay with me. She assured me she would do that. It made me feel much better because I knew how much Aslyne feared her big sister. It at least put my mind at ease for the time being.

John and I left Poupette and went directly to the airport where Mike already had one of his planes inbound that we were to receive. I was in sporadic contact with Mike via email on our smart phones. My friend, Donny Pavlik, was back in Tallmadge, Ohio, helping to coordinate flights and times with different people in the United States that needed to get into Haiti after the quake using Mike's Air Ambulance Services. Having Donny as sort of liaison was really helpful. If I couldn't get a hold of Mike, I'd go through Donny and he would relay messages to Mike concerning people wanting flights in and out of Haiti. Donny was basically running an emergency travel program, coordinating and connecting different folks with Mike's services out of his basement. Mike had a young nineteen-year-old pilot named Jan Derrick Lynch, a.k.a. Janny, a.k.a. Captain Cupcakes. Janny was flying a single engine Cessna 206. He was transporting doctors, journalists, batteries, and rice from Pompano Beach, Florida, to Port-au-Prince daily. It was about an eighteen-hour round trip with stops for fuel in Exuma or Inagua. Janny was landing on roads from Port-de-Paix to Jacmel. He did that for about three weeks. He also flew the Santo Domingo to Port-au-Prince route for a few weeks. For a nineteen-year old, Janny had nerves of steel. I was very impressed by his daring exploits. They don't make nineteen-year olds like him anymore.

The other pilot Mike had flying for him needed no introduction. His name was Clyde O'Connor. This trio of pilots, Greg, Janny, and Clyde were making multiple sorties in and out of Haiti daily, transporting doctors, surgeons, nurses, engineers, aid workers, missionaries, and foreign journalists from all over the world. Mike was also flying in shipments of water, food, and medical supplies. He even sent cash on occasions for whatever else we might need.

This day, the seventeenth of January, began one of the most intense mental, and brutally physical stretches I would ever do in my life. I was only sleeping two hours a night. Every day I was at the airport receiving people and supplies off flights Mike had coming in. Early on, Mike came over from the Dominican capital to tour the devastation, and to drop the satellite phones off at the U.S. Embassy. It was emotionally devastating for him to witness. He had brought with him a box of masks for us to wear to protect ourselves from the toxic air we were all breathing in. I felt embarrassed to wear a mask because most Haitians didn't have access to them. If they weren't wearing them, I wasn't going to wear them. I started to distribute the masks out to people in the streets until they were all gone.

At one point we made a stop at the Visa Lodge Hotel near the airport to drop someone off. It was here a man from the State Department said to me that he had been in Vietnam and Afghanistan, but he had never seen anything like what he was now witnessing in Haiti. He said it looked like they dropped a nuclear bomb on the capital of Port-au-Prince.

The Toyota John and I had wasn't very reliable so I enlisted the help of a friend named Orel. Orel was a former officer in the old Haitian military. He lived in Tabarre and he had a real nice reliable and serviceable truck that would be of great use to us. Orel, John and I were now a hot commodity. Our services, which were in great demand, came at a price of (U.S.) $250 a day. The U.S. military personnel at the airport had given to me full and unfettered access to the grounds there. I was running shit and doing it efficiently. This was an advantage and luxury I had that nobody else was given.

It was January 17 or 18 when the NBC News crew began to descend on the Habitation Haat Hotel. They took over the entire place. The owner of the hotel informed us that he was going to have us exit our rooms but that we could still stay on hotel grounds down and around the area by the pool. This actually worked great for us because now we had free lodging. We were accustomed to roughing it anyways. This was no big deal. I met guys like Lester Holt, Kerri Sanders, and Ron Allen. I had watched all three of them on the nightly news. The first night the NBC team came in I had the opportunity to sit with Kerri Sanders and Ron Allen and have a candid conversation with them about my life in Haiti. They were both very inquisitive and seemed to genuinely take interest in my story. Ron said, "Zeke, you're a very fascinating individual." Kerri concurred.

The NBC News crew was led by Bureau Chief Stephen Wende. Wende was a veteran of Baghdad. He was running all over the place, getting people and things moved where they needed to be. He was also handling security operations. Wende was no-nonsense and all business. The guy was a real pro. NBC News had enlisted the help of men that were known as fixers. Fixers were guys that could provide transportation, help with logistics, translation, and security services. The best fixers could do it all, especially providing access to people and places that the foreign media might not otherwise be afforded. Many of the men doing the fixing jobs after the earthquake were deportees – Haitians that had once lived in the United States, had committed a felony crime, and were sent back to Haiti. Guys like this who knew the English language and lay of the land in Haiti were invaluable. These guys had checkered pasts, but they were also guys who were resilient, and that had major street cred. That was very important. Scores of media members from around the world were now hiring deportees as their fixers.

Jean Dube and Marc Petion were two fixers embedded with NBC News at the Habitation Haat Hotel that were both deportees. Jean, who would end up being one of the late Anthony Bourdain's fixers later that year for his show *No Reservations* introduced me to his cousin, Cliford Kernisant. I brought Clif on with my team that also included John, and Orel. Clif had an SUV, and we needed another vehicle badly because of the demand on our services. The NBC team had asked me about coming along with them to work as a fixer but I had to decline. I had a much bigger operation I was running than just being a fixer. I had one deportee tell me the earthquake was the best thing that ever happened to him. He said that he made so much money. The average dollar a day amount after the earthquake charged by fixers was (U.S.) $250. The man told me that he was praying for another earthquake to happen. This would be the same sentiment shared by most of the NGOs and different organizations that came to Haiti after the quake. Not in word but in deed.

"You will know them by their fruit, you will know them by their deeds."

Almost ten years later, everyone is still asking where all the money went.

After crossing paths with Wende on so many occasions in and around the hotel grounds we finally bumped into each other and struck up a dialogue. He had overheard some of his security guys talking about me, so he approached me and together we made proper acquaintance. He asked me what I was doing in Haiti. After giving him a brief summary of my life in Haiti and what it was that I was doing, he said, "Zeke, how could I get some laundry done quickly?"

Without asking hotel management if it was OK, I offered to him the services of Sabine and Lithana. I said, "They can start washing your clothes and all the clothes of everyone here at NBC right now, today, if you wish."

He said, "Perfect, please come with me." He took me to a room on the second floor of the hotel where NBC had their command center stationed. He opened-up the door to the room and inside was nothing but electronic equipment staffed by a couple of people. They had their own satellite system set up. It was very impressive.

Wende said to the guys in the room, "This is Zeke, whatever he needs or asks for, get it to him." Moments later he appeared with a bucket of dirty clothes. We were now in the laundry business.

For the next week the girls were paid handsomely to wash clothes by hand. Since they were under my care and watchful eye however, I pocketed the money and held onto it. Every morning NBC News personnel dropped off their dirty clothes to us in a room at the hotel that we just kind of accommodated without even asking. Our laundry business worked great for a week until the hotel owner caught wind of it and shut us down immediately. He called me into his office, made a side deal with me, and then the laundry business was turned over to his hotel employees. This was how the hustle worked in Haiti.

Also arriving around the same time as the NBC people were Asger Westh and Jan Dago, both from Denmark. Jan was an award-winning photojournalist and Asger a writer for one of Denmark's largest selling newspapers, *Morgenavisen Jyllands-Posten*. During the late nights at the hotel after long hours working in the hot sun I observed and studied how all these journalists went about their craft. The photogs would go through 3,000 photos they had captured on that day, only to select one or two for the story they were going to run for the next day's newspaper. Many of these guys were from the other side of the world. Watching them work at a frantic pace to meet deadlines was fascinating. They were artists, working at the highest level. It was incredible to watch them perform under the pressure of these harsh circumstances. Many of their photos were nightmarish in nature, yet important for sharing with the world.

One night while sitting with several of these foreign journalists I got into a long conversation about life. Most of them took interest in me, especially Asger. He took me aside to speak privately and asked me if he could run a story about me for his paper back home in Denmark. Although I was very tired and droopy eyed, I agreed. I answered all of his questions. Around midnight we did an impromptu photo shoot right there on the hotel grounds where we were camped at, off to the side of the pool. Jan took several photos of me as I laid on my stomach with my eyes barely still open. A few days later a story about me titled, "The White Haitian" ran in the *Morgenavisen Jyllads-Posten*. This began a lifelong friendship with Asger.

So much was happening at lightning speed after this catastrophic event. All the days, dates, and times seemed to run together.

Early on in this madness Mike called me and said, "Hey, there are some former Israeli soldiers that are coming in to fly drones. I need you to take care of them for me." One female and two males were waiting for me at the airport when I arrived. They had been helicoptered in. They were accompanied by an American named Marc Stewart. Marc had worked for the United States Naval Department. I was really fond of Marc. He handled himself like a real pro. The Israelis, however, looked at me funny. The sight of a white man covered in tattoos and speaking fluent Haitian Creole threw them for a loop evidently. This crew was no nonsense and steely focused. They were not much for making any small talk or conversation. They told me what they wanted and needed, and it was my job to make things happen.

As we rode in Orel's truck, to break the awkward silence, I started a conversation with the leader of the group whose name to this very day I still don't know. I brought up the West Bank and the Gaza Strip. Collectively their eyes lit up, and I now had their attention. I started to speak to them about Yasser Arafat, the Palestinian people, Hamas, and the great city of Damascus. I let them know that my childhood hero was Lawrence of Arabia. They were in disbelief over what was coming out of my mouth. I then said what a glorious day this was. "I'm in a vehicle with my two favorite groups, Haitians and Israelis. It doesn't get any better than this."

That broke the ice, to say the least. I felt the need to let them know that they were not in the presence of just anyone on this day, and to appreciate and respect what I brought to the table, and to their cause.

I stopped short of asking them to free Gaza and to free Palestine. I was no dummy, I still needed to get paid.

The Israelis had put in an initial request to go to Jacmel. We started out to Jacmel but after coming across a giant split in the road on route National 2, I suggested against it. I, for one, didn't want to go all the way to Jacmel in the first place. My understanding was they were here to fly drones and search for potential survivors. They never confirmed that to me, however, and I thought it suspect when they inquired about Jacmel. The Israeli man in charge said he wanted an elevated position. He insisted we take them up in the mountains. Putting million-dollar drone planes up in a densely populated country like Haiti and landing them safely was not easily done. At one point I told Orel to stop the car. I turned around and suggested a different location. I said, "What you guys are asking and what you want done is not so easy to make materialize. Pulling this off could be an issue."

The man in charge looked right at me and reminded me that they were paying me handsomely. "We are going to the location of an elevated position that we asked of you – make it happen."

I got out of the truck and walked ahead several paces out in front of the vehicle to call Mike. "Where the fuck did you find these guys, man?" I said.

He said, "Who, the Israelis?"

I said, "Yes these arrogant pricks."

"They're great, aren't they?" he said. I could hear him laughing aloud on the other end. I got back in the truck, looked at Orel and in Creole said, "Motherfuck, who does this guy think he is?" The man was reeking with arrogance in the way he walked and talked. He was not used to being told no, that was evident.

Orel, being an old military officer, got a grin on his face and said, "Well, let's give the man what he wants, let's go."

"Orel, I hope you have somewhere in mind," I said. Orel then gave me the Lebron James "Silencer" push down of both hands and said, "Relax, I know a place."

Let history record that Orel made that "Silencer" gesture famous before Lebron's debut of it on March 20, 2013. (Coincidentally, I was at Quicken Loans Arena – since renamed Rocket Mortgage FieldHouse – that night with Jay Belkey, his son Jayson, and both my boys Moses and Spartacus when the Miami Heat won their twenty-fourth straight game against the Cleveland Cavaliers.

I said to Orel, "Yo bro, next time can you chime in quicker, c'mon man."

He laughed and said the foreigners were fascinating to him and apologized. We then headed up towards Kenscoff.

We finally arrived at a location in Kenscoff that fit their needs. They got all their equipment out of the truck, set up, then put their drone in the sky. It really was one of the more interesting and unique things that I had ever witnessed up close.

Still, putting the drone in the air was one thing. Landing it was an entirely different story. Nearing the landing spot they crashed it into a cement structure. I immediately looked at Orel with a gleam in my eye and said, "You see, sonbitch, didn't want to listen to me."

Orel laughed aloud and shook his head. I knew the lay of this land. Putting up million-dollar drones in a place like Haiti, that's one thing; landing them, a totally different beast. I had advised them with my expertise, but they would not take no for an answer. In any event, they

269

got some incredible video of the destruction from the air and they were able to salvage the drone and put it back together. They next sent it up in a location I suggested in Croix-des-Bouquets. Things went much smoother this time around.

I then took the Israelis to CNN's command center at the Le Plaza Hotel in downtown Port-au-Prince. There, we met CNN correspondents Anderson Cooper, Sanja Gupta, Gary Tuchman, and Ivan Watson. I had an interesting conversation with Ivan that afternoon. He was special in his field of work. It was humbling to be afforded the opportunity to meet so many of the personalities that I would normally only ever see on TV. But I was no groupie. Not for CNN, not for NBC, and not for the Israelis. They were all in my house, this was my turf. When it came time for the Israelis to leave, we got them, and their belongings situated on a helicopter. Instead of the initial cold shoulder greeting 48 hours earlier, I was given a heartfelt embrace, by all of them. I had won them over.

On January 21, I greeted an American couple that had come looking for their Haitian son that they were currently in the process of adopting. Noel and Lori Tugwell didn't much know what to think of me when I retrieved them from their plane, and they were informed that I was going to be the one responsible for their welfare and safety. They were assured however that I was Zeke, and I was the guy to help them. We secured their orphan named Louis, then headed directly to the U.S. Embassy. There was an incredibly long line of a thousand people standing outside the Embassy that day. When the Tugwells sought the line for American citizens, they were directed to the end of that same line. They both looked at me discouraged. I was probably more pissed than they were. I, for one, was not trying to hang out at the embassy all day. I told them to hang tight, that I would try to get them in quicker.

I went to the very back door and proceeded to tell the individual manning the door that I was there to see a guy named Pius Bannis. Although I had never once met Bannis in person, I was aware of who he was, and what he did on the inside. I told the individual manning the door that Pius was expecting me and who I had with me. The individual left and returned, saying that Bannis was waiting for me. I put the Tugwells through with Louis and then waited patiently. While the Tugwells were inside I got acquainted with the U.S. Marines guarding the embassy. They had come from Norfolk, Virginia, my old stomping grounds. One of them was from Stow, Ohio, not too far from where I grew up in Barberton. They were asking me what it looked like on the outside.

I said, "It's a real shit show out there, fellas. It's ugly."

They wanted to go outside of the embassy grounds so badly. I said, "It's a real shame you guys have to follow orders, otherwise I would show you around my house."

They seemed envious. I can't think of anything worse than being a United States Marine and having to guard the shit U.S. Embassy in Port-au-Prince, Haiti, while stuff was going down outside those walls. After a while the Tugwells emerged from the embassy doors all smiles. They had secured Louis's passport and all his travel documents. We whisked them back to the airport and they were off on a jet back to the States. Five hours was all it took.

My friend Tim had said, "You were born for this." He wasn't lying. Thank you, Pius.

Coming right behind the Tugwells the very next day was a man named Wes Gardner, his cousin Jerry Dillon, and friend Joel Thomas who was also traveling with him. Wes had ties with the Tugwell family. He had come to Haiti on behalf of a family in Minnesota that was in the process of adopting a young Haitian boy named Fauberson. On the day Wes arrived people were growing even more desperate. We exited the airport grounds and drove through a sea of humanity, looking for any help they could find. At one point we had to stop. There were so many people that we could not safely continue forward. I got out of the car and started barking orders at everyone in the crowd to move the hell out of the way. I was drenched in sweat while yelling at the top of my lungs to steer clear of our truck.

We finally got through, found Fauberson and then headed to the U.S. Embassy. I did the same thing for Wes as I had for the Tugwells. I told the guy at the back door that Pius was expecting my delivery while pointing over at little Fauberson. Pius Bannis, for a second time unbeknownst to him, was our ticket inside. It was a good thing, too, because the long lines outside the embassy were no joke. Wes and company were traveling with 10k in cash, x-ray film, and medical supplies which we were to distribute at

Heartline Ministries and Hospital Espoir in Delmas 75. (I had the chance to meet Gladys Thomas on this visit. She oversaw operations at Hospital Espoir, and I was very impressed by her.)

On this occasion, it took much longer than five hours. It was from sun up to sun down until we finished securing all of the travel documents, Fauberson's passport, plus dropping off the cache of supplies. We hurried Wes and company to the airport as darkness was settling in, got them on a jet, and they were off. This really made me feel accomplished. Not just anyone could pull this kind of stuff off. I knew that, and I was proud of it.

The longs days in Haiti after the quake all seemed to run together. It was like being in a Hollywood film, seeing and smelling death every day. We drove by rubble, watching camera crews filming while people were digging out survivors. In some cases, they were looting. It was reality TV playing out right in front of our eyes.

One night back at the hotel I was sitting across from NBC News anchor Lester Holt. I was exhausted. I had the stench of death lodged in my nostrils and down deep inside my chest cavity. No matter how much I tried to wash my face or brush my teeth the stench remained. I could not get away from it. I got up, walked out of the hotel, and headed down the street. I looked up into the sky. I was thinking about my life and everything I had lived through up to this point. I was thinking about home. It scared me to think about what was going to happen when the day came for me to finally return to Ohio. I dropped to my knees in the darkness and vomited all over the ground. Overwhelmed, I laid there alone in a heap, drowning in throw up and tears. I hadn't cried like that since the birth of Moses. Once again, it was a Michael Jeffrey Jordan Father's Day weep. When I tried to stand up to go back to the hotel, I was so dizzy I fell back to the ground and laid there even longer. I grew cold. I was so tired. I had not slept for days upon days. My head and my body ached that night.

It was in moments such as this that I never felt more alive. The physical and emotional pain forced me to feel all the feelings a human being could possibly experience.

The following day I went inside the ruins of the Catholic Cathedral in downtown Port-au-Prince. I had been inside once before since the quake. This time, however, I was there to loot it. This earthquake in Haiti would be on record as causing one of the greatest losses of human life in any one disaster or event in world history. I was going to take a piece of it home with me. When the roof of the Cathedral collapsed many artifacts came crashing down from the top of the structure. I took both metal and wooden pieces I found on the Cathedral floor. I commandeered the microphone from the pulpit in front of the church. I took some flowers that were strewn around on the floor. I wasn't going empty-handed. My God, I witnessed some gruesome stuff. It was especially difficult hearing and seeing young children in great agony. At one makeshift tent clinic in Delmas I held a young boy who was eight or nine years old, roughly the same age as my son Moses. They were getting ready to remove a leg due to an infection that was getting worse by the day.

I put my hand on his head, fighting back my own tears, telling him it was OK to be scared, it was OK to cry. "Let it out, scream, you're a beast, you're a man, grab my hand and squeeze it as hard as you can. Let's go, let it out." He was so scared, yet so brave. He was old enough to really understand what was going on. I hugged him and whispered into his ear to squeeze me hard. I don't think I will ever be normal again. In August of 1991 I had cemented that fact. I needed to live through all these emotions, however. It was a refining process. Earlier that month I was contemplating killing my wife and her new romantic interest, and for what? I was a terrible husband that didn't deserve her anyway. What a life this was!

I left Haiti on Valentine's Day. Mike sent the legendary Clyde O'Connor to get me. From January 16 to February 14 of 2010 I lived, and died, and lived, and died again. I was spent physically and emotionally. Before I boarded Clyde's Cessna 206, I looked back onto the airport grounds and I could see Matt Levitch's ghost on his stomach snapping photos of U.S. military choppers. I was leaving one sad mess to go back to another.

Clyde and I stopped in Exuma for fuel, then headed to Fort Lauderdale Executive Airport. I was Clyde's only passenger. It was an honor to fly with such a legend. Clyde was the man who had taken over for Barry Seal at the CIA. He took Seal's role and changed the game. He was multi-versatile, playing different roles for the CIA and the DEA. If Barry Seal was Dr. J, Clyde was the Michael Jordan of this field of work. Dealing with the Pablo Escobars and the Joaquin "El Chapo" Guzmans of this world, you had to be a bad dude. Clyde proved time and again that he was. He had once been shot out of the sky by a Dominican Air Force pilot. Clyde had the audacity to flip his middle finger to the Dominican just moments before machine gun fire pierced his plane's engine. You know someone is next level when they are in the position of a David, while looking up at Goliath, showing no fear, as Clyde did on that occasion. After being pulled from ocean waters off the Dominican coast he was handed over to the Dominican military. Without getting into details on how, he was eventually released. He is as tough as they come. No nonsense, brash, cocky, arrogant, and animated. I loved who he was. He was a real-life, modern day Indiana Jones. Growing up, he's exactly what I wanted to be. Anytime you get afforded the chance to be in the presence of someone with Clyde's resume, you embrace it.

When we arrived in Fort Lauderdale, customs asked me to explain the contents of a huge sack that I was toting around from the Catholic Cathedral in Haiti. I responded that these were things from my wife's house in Haiti, even though she didn't have a house in Haiti. I was not going to say that I had just looted the Catholic Cathedral in Port-au-Prince. Only a complete savage would do something like that. Greg Smith came and picked me up from the airport. He dropped me off at Julie Kartrude's mom's house in Fort Lauderdale where I stayed the next couple of days before returning to Ohio.

While there I visited Little Haiti in Miami with Mike. I stopped by Mapou Book Store and a couple of other boutiques on the same block. This is where I met Kim Ives. Kim is an editor of *Haiti Liberte Newsweekly*. He also hosts a weekly show on WBAI FM Radio. He's a filmmaker who has helped produce several documentary pieces about Haiti. I was searching for and eager to learn from people like Kim. He had a vast wealth of experience with great perspectives on all things concerning Haiti. The night before I left South Florida for Ohio, I had dinner with Mike, Greg, and Clyde. On this night I really felt at home with the company that I was keeping. I was sitting at the same table with men of action. Men that were risk takers, men that lived fearlessly. These guys had walked with presidents and generals from all around the world. That resonated with me. I wanted to bottle up those feelings in that moment and hold onto them forever. For I was well aware that what awaited me in Ohio wouldn't treat me so kindly.

When I finally arrived back to the February snow and cold in Ohio, I felt as though I had been transported in a time machine. I just spent nearly five weeks in a theatre that most people only ever watched on Netflix. I was now trying to adjust back to normal life, with the knowledge that I was going to be a single father. It was hard for me to fathom. I made one final attempt at reconciliation with my wife. When I was gone, she had been staying at our house, my mom's place, and Kevin's house. When she was asked about whether there was another guy in her life by my family members, she lied and said no. Who could blame her? She didn't want anybody to think less of her, which is human nature. When I pulled up to our house on Evergreen nobody was home. The house was dark and empty. I went over to my mom's where I found her with the boys. She was getting ready to go out somewhere. I gave her a hug. Moments later while I was playing with Spartacus, I caught her in the corner of my eye, staring at me with those big brown angel eyes. That gave to me an inkling of hope that I could still try and salvage our relationship. So, I went out of my way to call a meeting of some close friends from all walks of life. We were to meet together at the Chapel in Akron, Ohio. I invited these friends to have a sit down with my wife and me so I could have people we both knew hold me accountable for the way our relationship had deteriorated. I wanted to be transparent with everyone we knew about what was going on with us. When that evening rolled around my wife was a no-show. She was out with Kevin again. I was left there to come clean all alone, and that I did. It was an emotional evening. For all those that were in attendance that night I will forever be grateful: Ben Petrie, Donny Pavlik, Larry Bach, Steve Culp, Chris Harrison, Cedrick Middleton, Shaundel Berwick, Marcell and Tasha Harris. I thank all of you, I've never forgotten.

―――――

WINTER 2010 - HOMECOMING

So, this is where the idea of a book about my life story was born. One night while sitting alone my mind drifted back to Mr. Ricks. I started putting pen to paper. As fate would have it, I ran into my dad at my mom's house and we started talking. Unbeknownst to me, my dad had been moved to tears by the article that the *Akron Beacon Journal* published about me after the earthquake in Haiti. My dad's friend and co-worker would reveal this to me months later. I asked my dad if he would read what I had started writing, to let me know his thoughts. I gave to him the opening stanza to my life story. My dad was an intellectual. He was not easily impressed. After reading it he said, "Wow, that's really well written." His words imparted great confidence, and served as a healing gesture for our relationship. Our father-son relationship was now reborn. We started talking once again.

While back at my job at Cascade Plaza on the weekends, my dad called me and began giving me some reminder quotes from *Lawrence of Arabia's* masterpiece, The Seven Pillars of Wisdom. He said, "Son, all men dream, but not equally. Those who dream by night in the dusty recesses of their minds, wake in the day to find that it was vanity: but the dreamers of the day are dangerous men, for they may act on their dreams with open eyes, to make them possible."

I felt like a million bucks, and it was timely, because I was still aching physically and mentally from my impending separation with my wife.

One day my wife and I were talking. She said, "I didn't leave you because of other women. I left you because of how you treated me." Knowing that it was now inevitable I agreed to a dissolution of marriage. I did not want to get divorced, but she deserved a fresh start at life. There's nothing worse and more pathetic than trying to hang on to someone who does not want to be with you. I asked her to set up a meeting between us and Kevin. She agreed without hesitation. I needed to sit and talk with him if he was now going to be living with my sons.

She then said this, and I can still hear her saying these words. I've heard it every day of my life since then: "I love you Zeke, I've always loved you, and I will continue to love you forever. But I don't trust you, and I can no longer be with you."

The day came for us to meet and get acquainted. We agreed to meet at Olive Garden in Fairlawn, Ohio. I took a girl with me named Katie Measell. Katie had babysat the boys for me on occasion, and I didn't want to be the third leg at the table. Katie remembered Kevin from high school and

276

couldn't believe that my wife had ended up with him. Katie said, "What does she see in a dork like that?"

I said, "Well, I gifted that dork my wife because of how I treated her. She would have never left but for the way I treated her. It was my fault, I was to blame, I brought it all upon myself."

The entire time sitting at the table during dinner I anxiously awaited for Kevin to just look at me the wrong way, or to say the wrong thing. I was praying and begging for him to give me a reason to maul him right there. I told Katie if he dared to even look at me the wrong way while in my presence I would knock him into kingdom come. I left dinner that night kind of disappointed. That was all God's doing. Kevin was respectful, kind, quiet, humble, and just happy to be there. I was the one that ended up very grateful however, because had my wife chosen a guy that was cocky and arrogant like me, it would have ended all bad.

On March 25, 2010 my wife and I headed to the divorce court to finalize our paperwork. I walked ahead of her with Spartacus in my arms. My wife snapped a photo without me knowing as I carried Spartacus on my way into the courthouse in downtown Akron. I think she wanted to send out proof to all her people, including Kevin, that she actually had the courage to see this through. In the meantime, we had agreed to continue living together and slowly transition to her eventually moving out. We did it for the boys. At this point she wasn't officially dating Kevin publicly. It was still a secret to most. She kept that quiet for a while. She was very concerned with how people were going to view her, and was well aware that for many, it would not be acceptable.

I had met a Haitian woman named Mimi Douze on the flight from Fort Lauderdale to Santo Domingo after the quake. We exchanged numbers after chatting for a bit. She had just lost her mother in the earthquake. She was a single mother with a degree from Florida University. She had one son named Bryan with a former member of the Florida Gators who once played football for coach Steve Spurrier. Mimi became a really good friend and close confidant. I also had a romantic interest in her. She was much older than the females I was used to talking with and a lot more educated. I spent hours on the phone with her after returning home from Haiti in February. Mimi was now going to be taking over all of her mother's affairs in Haiti. She was also doing some of her own humanitarian work, helping those who were in great need. I planned a trip back to Haiti in the month of April to do some leg work for a block company that Mike Keister wanted to start to help in the rebuilding of homes. I chose to fly through Fort Lauderdale to meet up with Mimi before going on to Haiti. She picked me up at the airport, put me up in a hotel room, and then drove me to the airport the following day to catch my flight. My relationship with Mimi was welcomed and it comforted me through a rough stretch. That trip to Haiti was very productive and set the stage for my return to live there once again.

Upon returning to Ohio my wife had a change of heart and wanted to hasten her departure from our house on Evergreen. At this point she was pregnant by Kevin, although no one had been told, which moved the process along much faster than I would have preferred. She told me that she could no longer live like this, and that she was leaving to go live with Kevin. She agreed to let me keep the boys, which was really her only choice. No one in my family was going to allow her to run off with the boys and move in with a nineteen-year-old.

The first day of May 2010 was a Saturday and I was working at the Plaza. Late in the afternoon I fielded some phone calls from family members asking whether I had spoken to my dad at all that day. They informed that he was missing. My mom said that my dad had called her at about quarter to twelve that morning. My mom and my sister were waiting for him to come to Barberton from Cleveland. They had all planned on leaving together to go to Massillon to watch my six-year-old nephew, Solomon, golf in a tournament. He told my mom he was on his way. When the clock struck one-thirty, my dad was nowhere to be found. He was not answering calls or texts. My mom's gut instinct told her that something was wrong. My mom and sister headed on out anyway to see Solomon golf. Between five-thirty and six p.m. they met up with Ben, his wife Michelle, and Solomon at Durban's Ice Cream on Wooster Road in Barberton. All of them had been calling my dad throughout that entire afternoon to no avail. They were all hoping to find him at the house on Lloyd when they got back.

I was immediately sick to my stomach. My eyes started to mist. It was like I could feel a disturbance in the force – I had the same feeling of Obi-

Wan Kenobi when Alderaan was shot out of the universe by the Death Star in *Star Wars*. I knew it was bad right away. It had now been two or three weeks since I last spoke to my pops. I had just returned from Haiti and hadn't yet connected with him.

My brother Ben went to look for him with his friend, Joel Matos. Around nine p.m. on Euclid Avenue, right down the road from his apartment, they found my dad in the driver's seat of his vehicle, slumped over, cold and stiff as a board. Somewhere between the time my mom talked to him at eleven-forty-five a.m. and twelve-thirty p.m. he stopped off at a liquor store to get some beer for later that evening. After purchasing the beer and putting it down on the floor of the front side passenger seat he prepared to start the car and before he could even turn the key, God called him home. He suffered a massive heart attack. He had just received a new defibrillator a few months earlier. He had been experiencing some issues with it and suggested to my mom that he really didn't think it ever worked correctly. It didn't work on this day!

And so, on May 1, 2010, my father, who once bounced me on his lap while we watched Secretariat run the greatest horse race in history, died of his fourth and final heart attack. He laid there in his car all day, unnoticed by the passersby. Even if anyone did notice him, they did nothing about it. When Ben called to tell me I was so angry. I just kept saying "No, fuck no!" I paced the Cascade Plaza lobby for the remainder of that night in total disbelief. My father and I had been estranged. We barely communicated for a few years leading up to the earthquake in Haiti. The earthquake saved my relationship with my father. It restored us, and we were finally going to make up for lost time. And just like that he was gone forever.

At Cox Funeral Home, they let us in to see his body. I took pictures with him and my sons. It had been so long since we had a photo together, this was my last chance and I embraced it. He was to be cremated. In my final moments with his physical body I put my hand on his head and tried to draw strength from him. There's never any getting over a lost loved one. No matter what anyone says, there's no getting over it. It hurts.

In my father's wallet were a few pictures. He had a photo of Moses, Spartacus, and my wife and I. All the other pictures were of his pride and joy, Moses Jeffrey Petrie. I was his favorite child, and Moses was his favorite grandchild.

After my dad's death, I was able to find some great comfort in conversations I had with his co-worker and good friend, Alberta Jones. Alberta said to me, "Your dad always said that you were his favorite. No matter how much grief that you ever caused him he would always say, 'Jason's my favorite'. " When the story ran about me in the *Beacon Journal* after the quake, she said, "He was never before so proud." He cried in her presence over it. She said that he told her that article made his life worthwhile. One article changed everything. The tribute I paid to my parents in that article was all my dad was looking for. He was well aware that we had not been speaking. He never realized that even though we were not speaking that I still believed in who he was, and what he had meant to my life. Once again, this earthquake in Haiti really saved me. It afforded me a few more intimate conversations and moments with my dad that I would have never otherwise enjoyed.

In 1989 my dad gifted me a new Bible. On the inside cover, he wrote the verses Romans 8:38-39: *For I am convinced that neither death nor life, neither angels nor demons, neither the present nor the future, nor any powers, neither height nor depth, nor anything else in all of creation, will be able to separate us from the love of God that is in Christ Jesus our Lord.*

Cathy Widner, the mother of childhood friend Tim Widner called Tim the day after my father's funeral and said that was the best funeral she had ever witnessed in person. The service was officiated by Father Rick Kramer and assisted by Paul Howe with some scripture reading. Some of the family got up to speak, including myself. We talked openly, honestly, and transparently about my father's many faults, vices, and transgressions. My father would have frowned upon us had we executed his funeral service any other way. Frank Sinatra's, "I Did It My Way," echoed through the Cox Funeral corridors on the evening of May 5. My dad was made proud that night once again.

Legends Live Forever!

SUMMER 2010 - A NEW LIFE

As the summer months rolled in I knew that I was no longer able to live and function normally in the United States in my current predicament. The idea of the block business in Haiti gave me something to focus on and run towards. In early July I quit my job of nearly nine years at the Cascade Plaza building in downtown Akron. I told the people closest to me that "I gotta get the fuck outta here." I mentioned to my ex-wife that I needed to sit and talk with her and Kevin one last time. They agreed and had me over for dinner one evening in their backyard on Washington Avenue in Barberton. I just laid it out to them. "I'm handing over the boys to you guys. Don't fuck it up."

Kevin was not one to ever really look me in the eye, and that probably worked out for the best for everyone involved. He turned out to be the best thing for my ex-wife, so I had to move on. I helped move the majority of all of our belongings to Kevin's house. One day I found Aslyne at the place on Evergreen packing up boxes to take over to her new dwelling. She was on her knees, looking out a window with tears running down her face. She said, "I never wanted to get married to get divorced."

Emotions were now flowing through her as she was thinking about all the memories, both good and bad, that we had shared over the years. Aslyne is special, she really is. We shared a final moment there together and hugged. I told her that I was so sorry, and that I would always love her.

After that I sold my car, I cashed in my life insurance. I got some more tattoos done by Justin Wright. Then I made my final plans to get the hell out of Dodge. Before I left I had one last visit with Moses and Spartacus. Spart was too young to know what was going on, but Moses knew and understood. We had a good cry together as Aslyne stood just feet away, watching and fighting back her own tears. It was an emotional time. I was not mature enough to handle it. I ran away, back to the only true love that I had ever really known, the country of Haiti.

Before I returned the first week of August, I stayed a couple of days in Miami, and got a tattoo of the Haitian statue Neg Mawon on the left side of

281

my face by a tattoo artist named Alex Heter. My closest friends were telling me not to do it. They said that would be the end of my life; I'd never be able to work again. My response to all them was, "Fuck it. I don't give a fuck. I'm a true rebel." This was my way of sticking it to and thumbing my nose at society. Besides returning to the states every September for my boys' birthdays, I didn't plan on ever coming back here to live or work again.

Tim Widner was with me the night I got the tattoo in Miami. He said, "You are fucking crazy man, but I still love you. We are Hoodsmen. For life." He was referring to our childhood gang growing up back home in our North End Barberton neighborhood.

I was now off to Haiti to live and make a new life. Mimi told me I could stay at a place in Delmas 75 where she stayed every time she went to Haiti. Mimi's mom's best friend was a lady named Mommy Pierre. She was like an aunt to Mimi. It was Mommy Pierre's private residence that I descended upon with John, Sabine, and Lithana. I don't think either Mimi or Mommy Pierre were big fans of the team that I was traveling with. They would have been much more content had I come by myself.

While staying at Mommy Pierre's house during that month of August I had the chance to work with and meet some influential women: Sonali Fiske, Eli Omar, and Regine Theodat. All were businesswomen and humanitarians – movers and shakers – that I really admired. Mimi was the same way. I tried to learn from all four of these incredible females of action who got things done and did it all with tremendous grace. I was always trying to steal knowledge from people with great life experiences and add it to my own arsenal.

At this time, the main thing on the agenda was meeting up with one of former President Aristide's closest confidants, a man named Toussaint Hilaire. Toussaint was the director of Aristide's Foundation for Democracy. Mike Keister was well connected. His lawyer, Steven Weinger, was one of Ira Kurzban's partners in a law firm. Ira was President Aristide's lawyer. Mike and one of his business partners from the Cincinnati, Ohio, area, Leonard, wanted to start a block company in or around the capital of Port-au-Prince. The business plan was to run three shifts around the clock non-stop. They needed land to lease. Ira told Mike about a piece of land owned by President Aristide in Tabarre not too far from the U.S. Embassy.

282

A meeting was set up between me and Toussaint around September 3. Neither Mike nor Leonard could be present for the meeting and neither of them spoke any Creole anyway. I was to be their eyes, ears, and feet on the ground for this potential project.

At that time President Aristide was still in exile in Durban, South Africa. We met at Aristide's Foundation in Tabarre. I got there really early. My dad always stressed being punctual. He said, "If you're late it's like you are telling the other person that their time is not important." I let myself in and walked around the interior of the facility. My dad also taught me that when you show up, do it with confidence as though you own the joint. I found myself upstairs in a large conference room in which hung a very large portrait of President Aristide. I stood in front of his picture and thought of how many people had died following this ex-priest-turned-politician. Many of my old friends were among the group that was now deceased.

I thought it something similar to Saddam Hussein in Iraq. Hussein had his portrait hanging in all four corners of his palace in the former Babylonian kingdom.

I was gazing at the portrait when Toussaint startled me from behind. "You like that portrait?" he said.

I said, "Oh yes, very impressive. How is President Aristide doing?"

"You know, he is missing home." Toussaint then asked me to have a seat. He proceeded to sit down at the head of the conference room table positioned in the direction of Aristide's portrait. Before long we were talking and debating Haitian politics and the current state of affairs of the Haitian masses. We talked about pretty much everything except the land for lease. I wanted to make it clear to Toussaint that I was against the illegal U.N. occupation of Haiti. I told him that I frowned upon all the white people that lived in Haiti. They were living high off the hog and benefiting from an environment that squeezed the life out of Haiti's poor masses. I stressed to him that I was against the governments of Canada, France, and the United States of America. The racist foreign policies of these three governments had crippled Haiti over the decades. I think this kind of rhetoric coming from me emboldened Toussaint to speak freely and candidly. He gave a passionate speech, detailing the problems, the struggles, and the fight for true independence. He grew louder and louder in his tone. This fiery speech, given to an audience of one, right in front of President Aristide's likeness gave me goosebumps.

We then went to visit the piece of land. I walked around the roughly two acres that had a few structures still left standing after the quake. The largest structure had collapsed in its footprint. I was emailing pictures of the place to Mike in real time. After finishing the tour, I thanked Toussaint, and told him it was a pleasure. He said, "Likewise my friend," and we parted ways.

On September 9, I left Haiti and returned to Ohio for Moses's and Spartacus's birthdays. After a short sleep, I drove my mom's car to somewhere northeast of Cincinnati to meet with Mike at Leonard's home. I was so tired on that early morning from traveling the day before. During the drive, I was beginning to fall asleep at the wheel. I turned the music up really loud to stay awake. If I felt that I was starting to drift off to sleep I would smack myself in the face.

Shortly after leaving Columbus I was in the left lane of the expressway and fell asleep at the wheel. The car veered off to the side of the road. The only thing that brought me back was the shaking of the vehicle as I hit a rough patch of the median strip while going 70 miles per hour. The car bounced up and down violently to jar me awake. God must have sent an angel from heaven to take the wheel. When I came to, I cried out, "Oh Jesus," and grabbed onto the wheel. I pulled hard, swerving to the right to get back on to the expressway. My heart raced. It took my breath away. I kept driving – it scared life back into me and I was no longer sleepy. This was now life number six of nine used up.

I made it safely to Leonard's place to visit with both him and Mike. We discussed the block-making plant business venture in Haiti. Ultimately it never came to fruition for several reasons. At the end of the day nobody goes in to business to lose money.

As the next few years unfolded the majority of the businesses and NGOs that came to work in Haiti post-earthquake took a lot of heat and criticism for what they failed to accomplish, and monies wasted. Mike's decision to stand down on the block making plant proposition turned out to be very wise. I felt I advised him in a manner that was very respectful and heartfelt. I said to Mike, "If it was my money personally, I wouldn't do it. I know Haiti too well, that's why I'm suggesting you stay away from going through with it." Although we were disappointed, we would be justified down the road.

About a week after celebrating both my sons' birthdays I was invited to another birthday party of my brother Ben's friend, Paula DeJournett. I took Spartacus along with me. While at this party I met former heavyweight champion of the world, Akron's own Michael Dokes. I saw him staring at me from across the room and then he motioned in my direction. I immediately went over to sit next to him. Before I could introduce myself and Spartacus, he said to me, "You're different." He said he was told I came from Haiti.

I explained a little of my story and he said, "I know. I could tell you were different from the moment I walked in," as he kind of bobbed his head up and down in approval.

His speech was somewhat labored it seemed, and he spoke soft and slowly. I told him of my friendship with former professional boxer and founder of The Good Shepherd Boxing Club George Jacobs. George was contemplating making a trip to Haiti with me before his untimely death in November of 1994.

I said, "It was a pleasure speaking with you champ." I had Spartacus salute him, and we left.

Dokes died of liver cancer less than two years later. He had just turned fifty-four. RIP Champ. RIP George.

After spending about five weeks with the boys I went back to Haiti. On the plane ride from Miami to Port-au-Prince a seventy-six-year-old, light-skinned Haitian woman who was very nice sat next to me. We shared a long conversation on the plane. She said her niece was married to Charles Henri Baker. Baker, also known as Charlito, was running for president of Haiti. She wanted me to meet him. I gave her my contact information, which she passed along to the Baker family.

Meanwhile, my relationship with Mimi fizzled out for a variety of reasons but we remained friends. When I returned to Haiti this time I took up lodging in a zone called Silo which is part of Delmas 33. Phaubert's brother, Jean Maurice, a police officer in Haiti, had lost his wife and youngest child in the earthquake. He had also attended my father's funeral while visiting the United States during the spring. He arranged for me to stay at the apartment of a female friend. I think maybe she had agreed to take me in, hoping a romantic interest would be sparked or maybe for some financial gain. In any event this time around it was just me and John. I sent Sabine and Lithana back to Jeremie to live with their mothers in the meantime. Things were too unstable for me during this period. John would now be the only one with me. I needed to find real work so I could sustain myself in Haiti over the long haul.

And just like that, right on cue, Matt Levitch reached out to me. He told me about a website that photographers all over the world used as a networking resource. He told me about an Italian named Dario Mitidieri who was looking for a fixer in Haiti. Matt, knowing I was back in Haiti, thought I'd be perfect for this job and referred me to him. Dario was coming to Haiti at the end of October through the first few days of November to cover Fet Gede, "The day of the Dead." Shortly after speaking with Matt I received an email from Dario. It was all set. I was now officially in business as a fixer. My experience doing the fixer work after the earthquake really put me in a great position to succeed in this type of job.

The going daily rate for a fixer in Haiti during the fall of 2010 was (U.S.)$150 a day plus $50 for gas. I undercut that price and charged $100 a day plus gas. I needed the work and I had to build a clientele that would refer me to other journalists. Dario came into Haiti on October 30. Before that, however, on October 29, I met up with presidential candidate Charlito Baker's son, Charles Henri II, in his dad's factory located off of Airport Road. Charles Henri received me well and we had a really nice discussion in one of the factory offices. He took me on a tour of the place. He gave me a detailed rundown of the family history, which was really fascinating stuff. I learned things about his father, Charlito, that I would have never otherwise known. I started to look at the wealthy, light-skinned Haitians in a much different light after this meeting. I was now on board Charlito's bus and actively campaigning for him and his Respect Party Of Haiti (Pati Respè).

Baker's declaration was "Nou Bouke (We Are Fed Up)." He said there was a place for everyone on his bus, and that through order, discipline, and providing jobs he would alleviate the suffering of the poor masses. I knew

286

in my heart he was the man to get Haiti going in the right direction.

The next day Dario arrived. John and I went to pick him up in an old four-door Toyota that was barely serviceable. It's all we had. I was embarrassed about it, but Dario said he loved it. He said that he'd much rather blend in with the natives than drive in a fancy car that stood out. While Dario was in Haiti I was on top of my game. I was always punctual. I provided him great access to people and the stories of their lives. While I was working for him in a variety of capacities, I had John watching the car and Dario's equipment. Many fixers that worked alone were not as effective or efficient with their services. In a place like Haiti you need extra eyes, extra hands, and extra feet to get stuff done. Some fixers didn't have a mode of transportation so they would hire either a driver or a moto taxi to provide the transportation. John had been with me for a long time. I could trust him. We worked well as a team.

Dario covered a story of a little girl named Christela who was born the day of the earthquake. Her mother, Cala Ferival, was killed when the Catholic Cathedral crashed down at 4:53 p.m. that day. I was asked by Christela's father, Fritz Robert Pierre-Saint, to be Christela's godfather and I accepted. We then went to Belikou and the projects in Cite Soleil where Dario was able to capture some great shots on film. I took him to the Grand Cemetery in downtown Port-au-Prince on November 1 when the Day of the Dead festivities were in full throttle. On Dario's last evening in Haiti we went to a peristyle in Petionville to cover a Vodou ceremony. This particular ceremony included many animal sacrifices. All in all, Dario was pleased with the services I provided him. It was after he departed Haiti that my email started to explode. I was referred by Dario to many other journalists from around the world.

Dario stayed at the Plaza Hotel downtown while in Haiti. Around this same time I met a photographer named Antonio Bolfo who was lodging at the same hotel. I believe he was on assignment for *Newsweek*. Antonio was a former NYC police officer who was tough as nails. I thought highly of him. This was also where I met Jacques Richard Miguel. I affectionately called him Rich. He was a fixer too, and much different from most of the other fixers I knew. Although he was a deportee you would never have known by the way he looked and conducted himself. He was a seasoned pro. Unlike the majority of Haitians who are always late, he was always extra early and on time. He was no nonsense and straight to the point. I was taken aback with how arrogantly direct he spoke to people. I respected him. He had been through a lot of shit in his life but continued working his ass off to make ends meet and find a way to survive. Anyone who grows up in the States gets kicked out and sent back to a place like Haiti to fend for himself is a survivor. A real badass in my book. I knew all too well the Haitian terrain and just how dangerously slippery it was.

Through Richard I met award-winning photojournalist Les Stone and *Rolling Stone* magazine reporter Janet Reitman. Janet was working on a big story for *Rolling Stone* about how the world had failed Haiti. The piece centered around the up and coming one-year anniversary of the earthquake and just how little progress had been made in rebuilding the infrastructure of the country.

On Sunday, November 14, I went to the Kinam Hotel in Petionville to do an interview with her for the story she was working on. It was around 8:30 a.m. when we got started. As she commenced and asked me the first question, she pulled a recorder out to tape my comments. This was a first for me and something I was not very comfortable with. I was so uncomfortable, in fact, that I requested that we do the interview with no recorder and off the record. She quickly grew frustrated and annoyed with me and understandably so. What she didn't know, or was maybe indifferent about, was that in a country like Haiti, when you're on record, and it's made public, you're now in harm's way.

I finally just said, "OK, fuck it, let's go, next question." I told her that I thought Charlito Baker was the man to lead Haiti out of the turmoil she was in. I focused my answers more on how Haitians had failed themselves rather than how the world had failed her. I was pretty candid with my responses to her questions.

At the time of the interview I didn't think much of Michel Martelly. I knew he was a great musical artist and an even greater Vagabond Sal "Dirty Rascal." The sexual connotations in his music, whether visual or verbal, were offensive to many. His hatred of former president Aristide and Fanmi Lavalas suggested to many that he didn't care for Haiti's poor masses. This view changed a few days later after I watched him absolutely destroy other presidential candidates like Manigat, Neptune, and Voltaire. Martelly embarrassed all of them on a national television debate. You could hear Haitians erupt with cheers as Martelly responded to questions and especially when he started to mock the others and go straight into his showmanship mode. It was goosebump incredible and it really appealed to the younger generation of voters. I emailed Janet and told her how impressed I now was with Martelly, and that I thought Charlito Baker should make him his prime minister after he was elected president.

During Janet's stay in Haiti that November I also accompanied her to the main wharf in Port-au-Prince where she went to interview a gentleman who was in charge of operations there. I took her to Belikou in Cite Soleil to interview my friend Raymond Duclona, a.k.a. Tcheke. Raymond was the brother of Amaral Duclona. At the time Amaral was in prison in France after being apprehended and extradited in the Dominican Republic. Amaral had been charged with the murder of French citizen and diplomat Henri Paul Mourral. On November 18 I was supposed to go with Janet to interview Sean Penn. I was obliged to decline, however, because Charlito Baker was making a campaign stop through the heart of Cite Soleil and I wasn't going to miss that for the world.

Baker's other son, Sacha, who was a former U.S. Marine, led his father's security detail armed to the teeth. I walked out well in front of them as the point man. The long walk through the heart of the ghetto went pretty well until we went into the Belikou neighborhood. As we headed in a couple of large stones flew towards us and bounced and ricocheted right in front of me. Loud bangs started ringing out all around us as rocks continued to rain down on top of the tin shack roofs that littered the entire vicinity. Baker, encircled by his security detail, was rushed out of harm's way. A couple of Haitian police officers that were onsite working this political march ran down into the area from where rocks were thrown and fired several shots into the air. I was cursing the people for this violent gesture towards Baker's presence in their neighborhood. Some of the men standing within ear shot hurled slurs in my direction. One of them cried, "We didn't know that you were really a Macoute, Zeke. You switched up on us." To which I responded "No, no I didn't." The class violence I would have once supported no longer made any sense to me.

I yelled out to the men, "When President Aristide was in power, y'all lived in shit. Since Preval has been in office, y'all have continued to live in shit. Let's give the mulatto a chance this time and see what he's all about. It can't get any worse than what y'all are already living in. Tomorrow you're going to wake up in this same shit anyways. You have nothing to lose."

It was around November 24 that I started working with a photographer from the states named Jeff Trunell. At the same time my journalist friend Asger Westh from Denmark reached out to me about a photographer colleague of his, Ben Kürstein. Ben was currently on the ground in Haiti and needed some help. He was taken advantage of by some other fixer before I swooped into the rescue. Both Jeff and Ben were covering similar stories, so I juggled both of them together with John's help. It was with these two photographers that I was working when a higher destiny calling came my way in the form of a young little brash black kid from the Bwa Néf ghetto of Cite Soleil.

It had been a long day of weaving in and out of the chaotic maze of Port-au-Prince with Jeff and Ben in tow. The late afternoon sun beat down on us as we crossed the street and into a tent city that sat just a couple stone throws from the Toussaint Louverture International Airport. We were pretty close to where I was staying at the time in a Mais Gate neighborhood.

I was weary from a day full of navigating and translating. My stomach growled while I smelled the smoky, sweet BBQ chicken that one of the nearby machanns – street vendors – was plating up for a customer. I glanced down at my sweaty, dusty self.

I was a fucking filthy mess. I picked up my pace a little to hurry Jeff and Ben along but had to pause for every photo op they desired. Ben was particularly meticulous. I turned around to find him on his stomach trying to capture a certain perspective on film.

"Eske li ka pran foto'w?" ("Can he take your picture?") I'd ask those residing in this makeshift city on a pile of dirt. There were times that I'd hate the job I was doing. The pay was good, but in this line of work, I often felt like I was pimping poverty to the highest bidder. I drove, handled logistics, and provided translation and security services for foreign journalists that were in Haiti to cover news.

Nearly every time I was contacted for a job opportunity, the stories most journalists were intending to capture painted Haiti in a negative light. Post-earthquake stories, cholera, natural disasters, demonstrations, and political violence were usually the focal point. What bothered me the most about this type of work was the verbal abuse, and threats of physical violence that were hurled in our direction while out covering these stories. The jeers, taunts, and trash-talking were constant. I was serving as a human shield for the journalists, and for the most part, they had no idea of the extent of these threats.

To make it tolerable to my conscience, I often gave a portion of my earnings to the poor people whose pictures were taken by these photographers/journalists. I began to walk ahead again, to passively signal that the $150 they had paid me for the day had run out. Just as my patience was wearing thin, I heard someone yelling my name over the crowd. "Zeke! Yo Zeke! Zeke." I turned and saw this little short black kid coming towards me, weaving through the traffic jam of gaudily painted tap taps and men selling ice cold bags of water on their heads. Who the fuck is this kid, and what the fuck does he want? For nearly the last two decades in Haiti I had kids coming up and asking me for food or money daily. I usually engaged them in conversation, but on this particular day, I wasn't having it. I just wanted to get the fuck back home. He sauntered up to me with a big, flashy smile, hat spun backwards, raggedy pants drooping off his little ass, and an oversized pair of shades. He looked me dead in the eye as he extended his hand to greet me. I firmly shook his hand before he could say a word. "Kisa ou fucking bezwen la?" "What the fuck do you need?"

Without batting an eye, the young boy said to me, "Zeke, I want you to be my manager," to which I replied, "Manager for fucking what?" "Manager poukisa?"

"I'm a rapper," he replied.

A rapper?! Are you fucking kidding me? And he wants me to be his manager? Oh, this is fucking rich. I yelled at him in English at the top of my voice, "Get the fuck outta here or else you better get to rapping something real quick goddammit!"

Still unfazed, with the biggest grin on his face, and the confidence of a young Tupac Shakur, this kid let loose a rap in Haitian Creole that I had never heard before. And he let it drop like he was performing a concert for thousands of cheering fans, yet here he was rapping for an audience of only one. His lyrics were edgy, and he carried himself like a man twice his size. I was stunned and completely mesmerized at what I had just witnessed. He was shockingly good, and I didn't know how to respond at first. In fact, I forgot how annoyed I was just a few minutes before. Who is this kid? He has the nerve to approach me in the middle of all this madness to bust a rhyme and show me what he was made of...despite all of my negativity. "What's your name, kid?" "Yo, Zeke. My name is Sperlif Omeus."

I bent down to his level, taking one of my Neg Mawon business cards from my pocket and handing it to him. "Here's my number. Don't fucking lose it. Listen, kid, I don't know if I can be your manager, but you can roll with me anytime....By the way, how did you know my name?"

"I'm from Cite Soleil-Bwa Nèf. Everybody knows who you are, Zeke." I extended my hand to him again-this time a smile crept over my face.... and you better call my phone Sperlif ti neg Cite Soleil. He nodded his head at me and spun around, looking content with what had just transpired. I kept watching him as he walked away, with all the swagger in the world, momentarily forgetting that I just wanted to get home. That was incredible. HE was incredible! As I turned back around I froze up. My thoughts drifted to my own two young sons back in the states. I had spoken so harshly to little Sperlif and he never even blinked. I could see my kids' faces and I just started to weep.

That was one of the single greatest moments of all my years in Haiti. About two and a half weeks later Sperlif would come live with me.

As Election Day in Haiti approached, I ended up back at the Kinam hotel once again. I had just finished up a long day with Jeff Trunell and Ben Kürstein. Jeff and I walked into the hotel's restaurant and there he was, sitting at a table with a bunch of light skinned wealthy Haitians, none other than Wyclef Jean. I went right over to him without hesitation and said, "Yo, what's up Clef?"

He immediately rose to his feet to embrace me while sizing me up and down with a big smile on his face. As we began to chat, I mentioned Billy and Pac of Cite Soleil. He quickly said, "Shhhh, don't say that too loud in here." In recent days Clef's bid to run for President in Haiti was quelled by the folks in power. He had not officially been living Haiti for the previous five years that led up to the election. It was one of the qualifications that candidates needed to meet for the right to run for the country's highest office. Current President Preval and his Unity Party were well aware of Clef's popularity amongst the younger generation in Haiti. Being an international superstar, his music resonated with hundreds of thousands of people the world over. Although Preval smiled at Clef when in his presence publicly, behind closed doors he moved to have him disqualified. Clef would have most likely won the election of 2010 otherwise. He was now learning on-the-go how things in Haiti really worked. You couldn't trust anybody.

During our brief conversation, I mentioned to him that I had seen him perform at the House of Blues in downtown Cleveland back in January of 2008. I told him how impressed I was with the show. For me personally he's arguably the most talented human being that I've ever met in my life. But just like his fellow Haitian brothers and sisters, he seemed more concerned about fitting in and getting his. He was doing what was best for him and his family, just like everyone else. In other words, he wasn't trying to suffer or die for the cause. He'd live for it, but he wasn't trying to die for it. And in my opinion, he in no way shape or form was anywhere close to being prepared to become president of Haiti. Clef asked me for my card. I gave it to him, and I never heard from him again. Interestingly enough, his Haitian lawyer at the time was a man named Jean Renel Senatus.

While getting ready to exit the hotel that night I noticed a face staring at me from across the room. I had remembered seeing this same guy several days earlier when I did the Rolling Stone interview. It was Patrick Elie, political activist, commentator, presidential adviser, and former defense minister. Evidently, he remembered seeing me wearing a "Charlito Baker for President" shirt. He didn't like that, and he took advantage of the opportunity to let me know about it. Of course, Elie probably thought he was about to shake down some white Joe Blow in the crowd that didn't know anything about Haiti. I blitzed him verbally in Creole in front of everyone present in the room. He wasn't aware that I was fluent in his language. His jaw fell open and he became furious. We stood toe to toe, going back and forth in a verbal battle. As we separated, he was still running his mouth in good ole Haitian fashion. Elie was left standing there that evening not knowing exactly what had just happened. But on this night, he wouldn't soon forget the white American with the tattoo of Neg Mawon on his face.

For the day of the election I worked it out that Jeff Trunell would be embedded with the Baker family for the entire day. He spent the time documenting the day's events through some incredibly intimate photos, only to have them stolen from him in the street chaos later that evening. I had been in the streets during the election, running around with Jan Dago and Ben Kürstein. While out and about a contingent of Israeli soldiers working with the U.N. waved us to stop and come over to them. We obliged. The group requested a picture with me. Jan took a few shots of us. I'm still waiting to this very day to lay my eyes on those photos from nine years ago. By the end of Election Day all hell broke loose with accusations of voter fraud, the election ultimately favoring president Rene Preval's protégé, candidate Jude Celestin and his Unity Party.

That night I was up in Petionville at the Karibe Hotel where there was a meeting of several presidential candidates that were denouncing the events of the day. I ended up on foot separated from all the other guys I had been working with all day including John. As I was walking down from Petionville, Sacha Baker and a man named Patrick, who was another of Charlito Baker's security detail, picked me up. They were driving in a bullet proof car. We traveled down to their headquarters on Airport Road. There was a sense among the three of us that the people in the streets that night wanted Martelly as president. Martelly was not a poor man nor did he represent the poor. He did, however, represent the current Haitian culture and the sentiment of its time to get rid of all these old criminal politicians even if that meant putting a vagabond like himself in power. The people loved the way Martelly mocked all the current politicians.

I said to Sacha and Patrick, "God, no, this won't be good for Charlito's chances." There was no relationship between Baker and Martelly as far as I knew.

The next day in the late afternoon Isabeau Doucet of Al Jazeera

Washington reached out to me. She asked if there was any way I could get Charlito Baker to come down to the Le Plaza Hotel in downtown Port-au-Prince to do a live interview with Al Jazeera. After several emails and phone calls back and forth with Baker's people, Charlito agreed to come down. When he showed up under the cover of darkness with his armed guards led by his son Sacha, he looked at me and said that he had already shut it down for the day. But once they said "Zeke" that's all he needed to know, and he was there.

I walked with him to the far end of the hotel and up the stairs where Lucia Newman, formerly of CNN, waited to interview him. Baker said to Lucia while pointing over to me, "That's Zeke, he's more Haitian than most Haitians." Al Jazeera only wanted to speak to him. None of the other candidates interested them. This was a coup of sorts for me to pull off. I was exhausted. I busted my ass trying to get Baker elected and because he was the real deal in my estimation. Baker had been going into cholera camps while campaigning at great risk to his own health. In my opinion, the U.S. government would never want someone like Charlito Baker as president of Haiti because they would not be able to get away with manipulating him like they do guys like Martelly. And how right I would be. Baker was the man to lead Haiti at that time, and U.S. involvement fucked it up again.

After the election I had another couple of days working with Ben on a certain project in a very poor neighborhood in the capital. The rapport I had built over the years with the Haitian people afforded a guy like Ben intimate access. He was doing a follow-up story on one of his post-earthquake pieces. He was given the opportunity to follow a couple into an isolated area that could only be accessed by crawling on the ground and through a hole. It took him inside this claustrophobic area where a candle was used for light. He was able to photograph the two of them bathing out of a bucket together. When Ben finished, he got into the car and looked at me with great wonder.

He said, "Oh my god thank you! That was incredible."

There were a lot of fixers in Haiti, and I mean some really good ones like Jacques Richard Miguel, Jean Dube, Marc Petion, Gregory Senatus, and Yvetot Gouin. But I was as good as it got, and I knew it! I was cheap, and more affordable than many of the other fixers. That was to my advantage.

But this type of work had its downsides, too. It meant long hours, very early mornings, hostile environments, and usually concern covering poor disenfranchised Haitians who were becoming increasingly hostile and annoyed by foreign journalists. Taking journalists into cholera camps was something I didn't like doing at all.

A young girl that I was taking care of from Cite Soleil named Whitney had fallen victim to cholera. Whitney is one of the daughters of the late Haitian Tupac. Pac also has a daughter named Taina. Whitney's mother, Yolen, was a friend of mine. When she called me to tell me that Whit had cholera I was in disbelief. She was taken to a cholera camp in a place called Sarthe. I hurried over there and went right in to see her. I walked straight over to the bed she was in and said, "What in the hell are you doing here missy?" She gained new life upon seeing me and quickly moved to embrace me. The people working on the inside ran over, saying, "No, no, no, no, don't touch her, don't touch him. The disease is so contagious." It was really unnerving being in there and having someone I loved infected. It was one of the more uncomfortable experiences of my life. I had no protection to boot. But I didn't really even care. What a life I was living.

On December 7, 2010, things start to deteriorate in Haiti's capital city. On this night former First Lady Mirlande Manigat representing the Rally of Progressive National Democrats party (RDNP), and Jude Celestin of the Unity Party were declared the two candidates who would go on to the runoff elections set for January. With allegations of fraud running rampant, the opposition, consisting of majority Michel Martelly's Haitian Tet Kale Party (PHTK) took to the streets in violent protests, burning tires, and setting up roadblocks across the city. Their slogan was that the educated men in vests have done nothing for this country. "Now, let us take our chances with the Vagabond, the Legal Bandit," referring to Martelly. The next morning a thick cloud of black smoke hovered over the roof of my apartment in the Mais Gate neighborhood overlooking the airport. Businesses and schools stayed closed. All flights in and out of the country were canceled, and the international airport was closed down. The protesters set fire to the headquarters of Preval's ruling (UNITY) coalition. Enraged Martelly supporters tore down and hurled stones at election posters of Manigat and Celestin. The local Haitian police were overwhelmed by the number of protesters in the streets. U.N. peacekeeping troops were barely visible. One U.N. helicopter flew above the city, monitoring the events from the air.

I called Claire Martin, a photographer from Australia that I was now working with. Days earlier I was with Claire covering a violent protest in downtown Port-au-Prince. I asked her if she was trying to go work. She said yes and I went to get her. She was staying at Walls International Guest House in Delmas 19 that I could get to off of Airport Road. As John and I took to the street that morning of December 8, the Haitian sky was pitch black. There were roadblocks set up everywhere. I needed to get out and work because I needed the money badly.

We approached a fiery roadblock on Airport Road. Before we could stop the car, rocks were hurled in our direction. Two Rastafarians quickly approached us and were cursing at us, telling us we couldn't pass. They said, "Get your car off the road or we are going to set it ablaze."

This made me irate. I jumped out of the car and ran towards the men, cursing them. There were approximately a hundred men manning this particular street barricade. In Creole, I told them that I was in Haiti when all of them were still in diapers. I removed rocks and bricks and other pieces of metal they had aligned together in the street and threw these out of the way.

One man in the crowd yelled out, "Boulel," meaning, "Burn him."

I replied, "Ou met, m nan hell deja frem," meaning, "You can, I'm already in hell."

I became even more incensed and I was cursing all kinds of awful and ungodly things. I cried out, "I'm going to work today you motherfuckers, watch me."

That's when the beautiful sound of "Zeke, Zeke," came from across the street. A few guys ran over saying, "Yo man this is Zeke, he is Cite Soleil, he's good, let him pass through." All the young men began removing remnants of the blockade.

That morning my heart skipped a couple of beats. Those young men were enraged and ready to do some damage. As I turned to see where John was I found him cowering inside the car, scared for his life. He couldn't believe his eyes when he witnessed the men removing the obstacles from our path. With his eyes wide as sausages he says to me, "What did you say to them?"

297

"I told them that I must work today fellas, and if you're lucky I may come back later with some cash and buy y'all some drinks."

"Really?"

"Get the fuck outta here man, let's go to work!"

When we arrived to pick up Claire, I decided to leave the car at the guest house and proceed on foot the remainder of the day. On this day Mike Keister emailed me that he may be flying Sean Penn into Haiti. He asked me if I could pick Sean up at the airport with armed security. I responded that I was all the security that Sean would need. "The people are my security," I confided.

Mike was trying to desperately get a hold of the legendary Clyde O'Connor to fly Sean in. In the meantime, Dave Perez, who was the chief operating officer for Sean's Jenkins/Penn Haitian Relief Organization had called me and asked me if I was available to get Sean. He asked for an assessment of things on the ground. I said I would get Sean and safely land him at his destination. Ultimately Mike couldn't get a hold of Clyde, and Sean was brought in by another outfit.

A few days later a photographer from Indonesia named Andri Tambunan came to Haiti. A Haitian friend of mine named Vladimir was getting married towards the end of December. Another friend of mine, Yvetot Gouin, was "The Godfather" of Vlad's wedding. I asked Andri if he would be at all interested in photographing a modern-day Haitian wedding. He said he was all on board for that. Because I was already strapped for cash, and I didn't want to spend money on a gift, I came up with some original and unique ways in which to provide the greatest of gifts without spending a dime. Andri would pay me to be his fixer for this wedding. So I was getting paid to attend my friend's wedding. Then, Andri would send me the wedding photographs and I would present them to Vlad as my gift. To have a pro taking your photos for free was a great luxury for such a wedding.

To top it off I took a girl named Nathalie with me, who I was dating in a roundabout way and who was a great singer. She sang for the couple in the church during the ceremony and it was really nice. Without spending a nickel, I provided Vlad with two of the best gifts someone could give to him on his wedding day. The reception was held at the Le Plaza Hotel where Vlad worked as a bar tender/cashier. That evening I spoke with Yvetot and met his wife, Isabelle. I told them that they would soon be with child. I found out later Yvetot's wife was already pregnant at that point, unbeknownst to them. I was spot on. They had a son in 2011. Yvetot once filmed a music video for Wyclef Jean. He's been CNN's main contact on the ground in Haiti whenever they enter the country to cover a story. I was glad to know him.

Because I was a river to so many people financially, I never had enough money. No matter how much I made working with journalists it never sufficed. I had just purchased a tan colored Toyota 4Runner from my friend Clif for $8,000 in cash. I needed a more reliable vehicle if I was going to continue my fixer work. Fixer jobs required a trustworthy car that could go outside of the capital into the mountains and the countryside. The old, rusted tan color, four-door Toyota we had been using was no longer serviceable for such jobs.

This was now our third vehicle in Haiti. This car had a system in it so we could play some loud music. It also had tinted windows and air-conditioning. But it would soon put me in financial strain. The upkeep of a vehicle in Haiti is financially taxing. So I reached out to several people that I had been close with over the years in Haiti. I sent a message appealing to anyone who felt moved to contribute to what I was doing in Haiti to contact me. So I did something I didn't normally do and I asked. It was basically a SOS distress call at the end of the day. One person responded with action, just one. His name was Wes Gardner. Wes and I had some history together during the days after the earthquake. Wes told me he'd like to help out. He started wiring me money around the first of every month. This gesture by Wes was a life saving grace for those I was providing for. I had been doing for so many poor people that I had no money left to give. I was up against it financially.

During that month of December Sperlif came to stay with John and me in Mais Gate. The beginning of January 2011 Les Stone came to Haiti to continue his documentation of the Vodou religion. Les, Sperlif, John and I all went to Gonaives. We were guests at one of Haiti's grandest Vodou sites in all the country, the legendary Lakou Badjo. Dorsanvil Estime, the man responsible for this Lakou, was a gracious host to us on this trip. Les was photographing the services to the Kongo Lwa. Lakou Badjo is one of the three grand Lakou Ginen of Gonaives in the Artibonite region of Haiti. Every time a new president takes office in Haiti it's always a custom for that person to visit this Lakou.

While on this trip with Les I spent most of the time hanging out with Sperlif and John. Les was an old grizzled vet of Haiti. He was the easiest job for a fixer like me. He worked so independently of me it was almost as if he really didn't need me at all, other than to provide transportation and on occasion some translation. Les could always be seen with one of his trademark cigars. Sperlif loved the smell of those things. I asked Les for one of them and he gifted me two. I still have them sitting in my dresser drawer at home untouched all these years later.

Upon returning to Port-au-Prince I met a little girl named Fimee and her family while working with Hadler Carsten and Detlev Konnerth of N24 TV from Germany. Fimee had lost one of her legs during the earthquake. While working with the guys from Germany I took Detlev up to the hills above Port-au-Prince to interview Charlito Baker at his private residence in Boutilier for another story they were covering for N24 TV in Germany. Spending time at Baker's home was really nice. I have nothing but respect for him and his entire family. After leaving Baker's place I went down to the Sylvio Cator soccer stadium with Detlev. He wanted to document on film the Franklin Graham Crusade. Security was really tight. Neither of us had any credentials other than the big camera he toted on his shoulder. We were late arriving as it was.

I said to him, "We are good. I'll get us in. Just act as if. Pretend you're filming me while I walk us through and right in past security."

It worked. We walked right on to the stadium field. The stadium was jam packed. Michael W. Smith's voice rang out. He was performing on a stage they had set up. I had listened to Smith's music since I was a youngster. His song "Friends" was the song we sang at my high school graduation. It was surreal to now be this close to his legendary voice.

Moments later in a corner entrance a mob of people pushed in. It was Franklin and a whole host of his personal security flanked by Haitian

300

police officers, some in plain clothes. I knifed through this entire mass of bodies and walked straight up on Graham with my hand extended. His eyes got really big.

I said, "Welcome to Haiti Mr. Graham, I'm Zeke, and it's a pleasure to meet you." We shared an embrace while his security detail stared at one another in bewilderment. Franklin grabbed the guy next to him and told him to give me passes and he pulled two all-access passes, making Detlev and me official. Franklin then headed up on to the stage to speak. Detlev came over smiling. I asked if he got it on film and he said he didn't. He was too busy watching my interaction with Franklin, just like everyone else in attendance.

As we left the stadium that afternoon, I had a really bizarre encounter. I had been waiting for Detlev when a couple of big white buses rolled out from inside the stadium parking area. I could see nothing but very pale white faces. Many were young children. They were all staring at me. It looked as though they were in a trance. The windows on these buses were very large. All these people that were visible to me appeared to be trapped in silence. Many of them had their hands pressed up against the windows while looking out and about. Their eyes had a black color to them. It was really eerie. I thought, "My good lord, it looks like something out of a horror film." I didn't know where these people came from, or where they were going.

The next day I took Fimee to get fitted for a new leg at Bernard Mevs hospital. I asked Les along to photograph the day's events. It was one of the coolest things I ever had the opportunity to make happen. So many times, foreign journalists came to cover stories of poor disenfranchised Haitian people that were living in great suffering. After the cameras departed, however, these people were still left to continue on in their sufferings.

That's where I would step in. Helping Fimee to get a new leg was nothing more than me taking the time to care, and using my network of contacts on the ground. Finding her a way to receive a new leg made me feel alive again. It made me less hard on myself for all my past transgressions. It was as if I was always paying penance for my many former sins and pay them I would.

JANUARY 2011- DUVALIER COMES HOME

On January 12, 2011, the one-year anniversary of the earthquake, I met Sean Penn at the Karibe Hotel in Petionville. I greeted him with a handshake and told him we had just missed running in to each other on a couple of previous occasions. I sat with Haiti's country director of the Pan American Development Foundation, Jeff Kerzner right in front of Sean as he gave a speech that day about what his organization had accomplished since the quake. In my opinion, Sean and his entire team would have been much better off had they had access to me from day one. That I do know and stand on with a hundred percent certainty.

On January 15, I took Susan Philips, a reporter from WHYY-91FM radio in Philadelphia, to Cange to visit Paul Farmer's Partners in Health medical facilities. We were to stay there for a few days. I had never been there, so I was looking forward to it. Sperlif, John and I geared up, picked Susan up, and went on our journey. Before we arrived at our destination, we stopped off above Lake Peligre to take some photos. It truly is one of the more magnificent sites in all of Haiti.

When we finally arrived at our destination Susan went inside to find a lady named Cate Oswald. Cate is Haiti's senior program officer for Partners in Health, who situated us in our lodging. I remember walking up and down several flights of stairs while at this place. We when got to these guest rooms that they were going to house us in, I looked around. It seemed as if they had plenty of space for multiple visitors and guests. Cate showed Susan to her room and then she took Sperlif, John, and me to where we would be sleeping. There was a slight problem, however. She had us arranged to stay in a room with some other Haitians that we didn't know. If we didn't know them, you could be damn sure we didn't trust them. In a place like Haiti it's hard to trust your own family and friends, let alone total strangers. Desperate people do desperate things, and most Haitian patients and their families at Partners in Health were living desperately. Over the years in Haiti I experienced personal theft and each of our vehicles had been vandalized. On this particular occasion I had money and phones. I was hoping to be comfortable while on this trip.

Cate left the room and I said, "Yo, all these rooms and they're making us share a room with these strangers? Fuck that, hold on."

I ran back out to find Cate, and she was already gone. When I finally tracked her down in her office, I asked why she was rooming us with strangers when there was plenty of other space available. I said to her, "Do you not know Haiti? You're putting me in a precarious situation."

Cate didn't much seem to care what I had to say and quickly grew frustrated with me. She said that we were welcomed to leave if we didn't want to stay. That really pissed me off. Of course, we couldn't leave, that was not an option. I had to get paid from Susan. She wasn't going to pay me if I abandoned her all the way up in Cange. Leaving her would cost me business in the long run. I looked across the room at Cate seething and said to myself, "You little bitch." For the record, Cate Oswald is a wonderful person. I just wasn't in any frame of mind to deal with total strangers staying in the same bedroom with me and my belongings. I ultimately stood down. Cate was very fortunate that day. I was on the cusp of cursing her to her face in Haitian Creole. I walked out of the office, cursing Cate under my breath. I cursed Partners in Health, and Paul Farmer, too.

We stayed that night but as fate would have it the next afternoon, I received a phone call from an old friend that was a staunch Duvalierist. He told me that Jean Claude was in Haiti on this day of January 16, 2011. He requested my presence for the president's arrival. He said, "I would like for you to stay close with Jean Claude for the first couple days of his return. Please do that for me."

At first, I thought he was joking. It wasn't until I ended up confirming this news with a couple of other sources that I really believed this was happening. I said to both John and Sperlif, "We are outta here, President Duvalier has come home today." I was forced to break this news to Susan. I said, "Look, I know you planned to stay here another day yet, but I have to leave within the next hour. You can either go back with us or fend for yourself tomorrow. President Duvalier has come home after being in exile in France for the last quarter of a century. Fuck Partners in Health. The story covering Duvalier's return will be much better. You can give live updates on your radio station back in Philly tomorrow." Susan agreed.

Did I do the right thing professionally? No, I didn't. Did I care? No, I didn't. I had spent a lot of hours reading about the Duvalier family when I was a teenager. I wasn't going to miss being a part of this history in the making. On the way back down to Port-au-Prince we passed Lake Peligre once again. Sperlif and I both jumped from the vehicle to get one last souvenir photo. We raced back to the capital that evening. I was informed that Duvalier was at the Karibe Hotel. We immediately headed there and went inside while John took Susan back down to the Le Plaza Hotel to get a shower, and retrieve some of her things. Sperlif and I went right over to the Duvalier entourage. Duvalier was leaving from the restaurant area of the hotel as we arrived. He was walking into the lobby to get on the elevators. The press was hounding him. Flash bulbs were lighting up the entire hotel lobby. He was surrounded by security. I headed straight for him with Sperlif next to me.

As we came up on his security detail I yelled out, "Mr President, we are glad you are home. It's a great pleasure for us to welcome you. This is Sperlif. He is from Cite Simone."

It would be Duvalier's first intimate interaction with any Haitian child on Haitian soil in twenty-five years. Cite Soleil used to be called Cite Simone, named for Jean Claude's mother Simone. Jean Claude looked at me, grabbed me, and gave me the biggest bear hug. I whispered in his ear who had sent me to stay close to him for a couple days. He said thank you. Then he proceeded to bend all the way down to Sperlif's level and give him a big hug, too. It really was a surreal moment for us. I can't stress enough that so many of my pre-Haiti day readings were about Jean Claude. This was really a historic moment for me personally.

Sperlif, Susan and I stayed that night in the Karibe Hotel lobby. The next day I accompanied Duvalier to the courthouse downtown. That morning I saw an older white gentleman with a full head of gray hair head upstairs to see Duvalier. It was none other than Lynn Garrison. Regretfully I didn't get an opportunity to speak with him. At the time I was waiting to speak with CNN's John Zarrella who was doing a live spot outside of the Karibe. At the same time this was happening, Sperlif was rapping a song he composed for President Duvalier to his Chief of Security Rodny Tancrede. Rodny loved it. My brother, Ben, sent me a message: "Yo bro, I just saw you on the TV on CNN standing behind Zarella."

At one point, I ended up sitting on a grassy area out in front of the hotel. NBC's Kerri Sanders, who I had met a year earlier to the exact day, came over to say hello and asked me if I could get him access to interview Jean Claude. Simultaneously I fielded a call that President Duvaliers' entourage was ready to roll. I slipped back into the hotel to join the president and his team. There's a YouTube video online showing Sperlif and me in the back of the Karibe Hotel with Duvalier's security detail, which we were a part of, along with a good dozen Haitian police from special units. Some of the guys in these units had masks covering their faces. One of them called out to me by my name. He removed his disguise and said, "You don't remember me, but I remember you, from Jeremie."

In 1993, when the Neptune sunk, this guy was just a kid. He told me when he was young how much he used to look up to me. He was very surprised to see me looking as I did. Back in those days I had no tattoos. Here it was, eighteen years since this young man had last laid eyes on me, and he remembered. For me that was a great thrill. I can't put it into words, but it was confirmation to me that I had lived a life of great meaning regardless of my many sins.

Finally, we left for the courthouse and drove past the throngs of media members and Duvalier supporters who were running alongside the motorcade. After President Duvalier was finished seeing a judge, he left the proceedings at the Paquet in Port-au-Prince to make his way through a mass of humanity waiting for him outside. While walking slowly and methodically among all this congestion of bodies I was right behind Jean Claude with my hands on his back. The circle around him was very tight. He was a large man that had a great presence about him. When we came upon the vehicle that was going to take him away, I was with Jodel Chamblain. I literally placed him inside the vehicle and shut the door behind him. I graced the front pages of *Le Nouvelliste* and Haiti Liberte newspapers in the following days.

In all the news broadcasts on television later that day and into the next day I could be seen walking with President Duvalier. By that time my cell phone was ringing off the hook with people saying they had just seen me on the TV.

I believe it was the next day when I saw Susan Philips off to the airport. She was very gracious. She was a real professional. I was fortunate that she tolerated me cutting her time at Partners in Health short.

My next job was with Jacob Kushner of the Associated Press. Jacob contacted me and said he needed a fixer for a job up north in Port-de-Paix. He said he was bringing along two photographers, Rodrigo Abd and Nicolas Garcia. It was a secretive investigation. Jacob was interviewing individuals involved in some orphanage where abuse was suspected.

In the early morning hours of January 26, we journeyed up north. We were met in Cabaret by a violent anti-government protest. The main road was blocked off and barricaded. I jumped out of the vehicle and told John to take over the wheel. Rodrigo and Nicolas followed close behind. A Haitian SIMO Unit showed up simultaneously armed to the teeth in full body armor with shields in place. As I approached fairly close to the protesters with the SIMO Unit, rocks the size of baseballs and softballs were hurled in our direction. Each stone hit either right in front of us or right behind us. Some stones were landing on the tops of tin roofs with a loud banging sound, almost like cannon fire. The thunderous bangs from each rock thrown made you very aware that this was real, and one could easily be killed as too often happens in Haiti.

The SIMO Unit huddled in the middle of the road in a tight circle, covering up with their helmets and shields. I didn't have the luxury of the protection they were afforded. I got down beside one of the men where we discussed their objectives and plan of response to the rioters. It was now beyond just a protest. Rocks continued crashing down as I looked to one side of the street and noticed Rodrigo, who appeared to be dancing as he captured all this on camera. He had a smile on his face to boot. I thought, "Wow, these photojournalists are really incredible. They go about work like this in hot conflicts around the world every day and do it with such grace and courage." This courage would be on full display in 2012 while Rodrigo was covering the war in Syria. He was awarded the Pulitzer Prize along with four other AP Photographers for their gripping images of that

306

brutal civil war.

The leader of the protesters in Cabaret was a young guy named Nasson. Nasson was the one who hurled the first rock that nearly hit me after skipping off the pavement. I needed to pee badly, so I slipped off into a corridor which led me to another corridor and into a backyard of a residence where I ran into a young lady. I startled her. She said, "Oh God you frightened me." I said, "Oh I'm so sorry sweetheart, I just have to pee so bad."

She got me a bucket to pee in and as I relieved myself with her back turned, I told her there was some motherfucker out there called Nasson that almost hit me with a stone. "He's leading this gang of thugs."

The young woman replied, "That thug is my brother. He is a hot head by nature. " She assured me he was a good guy and meant me no harm. She then explained briefly what the protest was about. Of course, always being one to side with the underdogs, I quickly changed my tone. Nasson's sister then led me on a back trail down the road to where the protesters were now held up. She kept me out of the line of fire as SIMO troops launched the tear gas canisters. When both of us appeared in front of the protesters led by Nasson, his eyes lit up. I said, "Yo motherfucker, you almost hit me with one of those boulders you were hurling. What the fuck man?"

He held his hand over his mouth and said, "Yo blood, I'm so fucking sorry" in his broken English. His sister was grinning from ear to ear as she was the one responsible for bringing us together. I then explained to Nasson and his men what the plans of the SIMO were. I told him that I had three foreigners with me along with a Haitian driving my Toyota 4Runner. I implored Nasson to not do anything to any of my guys. He assured me he would look out for them.

As the SIMO Unit started to close the gap and back up the protesters, I almost bought it. I took up a position on the side of an old rundown school bus. From there I placed a phone call to Charlito Baker to inform him of what was going on that morning in Cabaret. As I was speaking to Baker, a large stone rifled off the bus with a monstrous bang about three feet from where I was kneeling. I said, "Motherfuck" at the top of my lungs.

In Haiti violent skirmishes get started frequently. They can escalate quickly, and innocent lives are easily lost. After what seemed like forever the SIMO Troops and local Cabaret police got the protesters to scatter and break up. The five of us on my team were finally reunited and back on our way to Port-de-Paix.

Jacob and the guys finished their work and on the morning of January 28 I took them to the small airfield in Port-de-Paix. I put them on a U.N. Helicopter back to the capital. I drove with John all the way back to Port-au-Prince that same day, making one stop in Gros Morne. We drove that night with only one working headlight, and brakes that were shot to boot. I beat the shit out of my car that trip. The roads were so bad it just killed my shocks and brakes. For the money I made it almost didn't seem worth making the trip. Especially after putting the income back into the vehicle for repairs.

The next day we took the car to a mechanic in Delmas 48. After looking at it the guy could not believe we actually just made a round trip to Port-de-Paix and back. He said, "You have no brakes, they're completely gone." This entire trip was life number seven now used up. God kept me safe, He really did!

In early February Les Stone came back to Haiti in anticipation of former President Aristide's return from exile in South Africa. On February 10 while sitting at the Le Plaza Hotel Les opened up a Facebook account for me. I had avoided Facebook like the plague. Les talked me into it. He said it would be great for communicating, business, but most importantly, to keep in close contact with my sons. Les looked out for me just as I had for him while working together. He grew very fond of having Sperlif around. He loved Sperlif and Sperlif loved him. Les was definitely our favorite.

I spent some time hanging out with Les and Reed Brody on February 11. Reed is a human rights lawyer who was trying to see justice served concerning the accusations against former President Duvalier.

February 12 I went with Les to visit Bobby Duval at the Cite Soleil Athletic Fields. Bobby had spent time in the notorious prison called Fort Dimanche during the Duvalier regime. He had some soccer fields and basketball courts where young people could play in Cite Soleil. Meeting and hanging out with both Reed and Bobby was a real educational experience for me. I loved to learn from people with their kind of life experience.

I was in Delmas 40B on February 22 when I ran into Edouard Laventure

308

Ernest aka "Moloskot." Moloskot was a very popular radio personality. His program, "Les Grands Dossiers," was big among the masses. I listened to him live every evening at nine p.m. on Nouvelle Generation 94.1FM. When I saw him sitting in a vehicle on the side of the road I took advantage of the opportunity to make his acquaintance. I told him that I was a big fan of his show. We hit it off right there on the street. He invited me to speak on his radio program that night. I was flattered. I couldn't turn it down.

That night at nine p.m. I went live on the radio with him, introducing myself in Creole. He started a question and answer session with me. This led to me speaking freely about Haiti and all her social ills. I touched on the divisions between light and dark-skinned Haitians. I spoke about the divisions between rich and poor Haitians. I elaborated on the divisions between Haitian Christians and Haitians who practiced their Vodou heritage. I went in deep on how many Haitians are affected by the Uncle Tom syndrome and how they kneel at the base of the pedestal they put white people on. I spoke against the governments of the United States, Canada, and France. I lambasted the illegal occupation of Haiti by U.N. Troops, reminding people of the massacres committed in Cite Soleil, and the cholera they had introduced to Haitians that killed thousands. Can one even imagine such a philosophy? Send in foreign troops to a country that's not at war to keep peace? All they did was kill Haitians and make them feel like second-class citizens in their own nation. Even worse, the Haitian people tolerated this.

By this time, after all the political jockeying between Haitians and international players, Martelly was ruled the winner over Celestin. I discouraged the masses from participating in the upcoming second round of elections between Manigat and Martelly. I declared any elections run by the foreigners was nothing more than a divide-and-conquer strategy. "Do not vote. Stay home," I pleaded. "Otherwise you will be feeling the effects of this for years to come."

My sentiments that evening would be proved right and make me look like a prophet of old.

My friend Mimi was listening back in the states that evening. She sent a message telling me how proud she was of me. That meant a lot. When I got ready to walk out of the radio station, my head was on a swivel. I feared going out into the dark and all the way back to the Mais Gate neighborhood where I was currently spending most of my nights. It would be on this night that my life in Haiti would forever be altered. I had turned full activist, freedom fighter, and revolutionary for disenfranchised Haitians.

The next day in Mais Gate scores of people came by the apartment I was staying in to let me know how much they loved and appreciated the things I said on the radio the night before. Moloskot himself called me and said that President Duvalier had called to say how impressed he was with my words. President Duvalier asked how it was possible that Zeke knew Haiti better than most Haitians? Jean Claude told Moloskot that he would like to sit and talk with us sometime. It was a real defining moment for me.

SPRING 2011

On March 17, 2011, I took a job in Carrefour picking up plastic bottles to be recycled by the bag with a guy named Charlie. Charlie had worked security for Sean Penn's team and was dating American Holli Griffiths. Holli had also worked for Sean's organization. San Francisco's own Lisa Mcfadin, who had been working in Haiti since after the quake, was dealing in recycling and it was through her the job was set up. This all came about because of the networking I had done post-earthquake.

I spent that entire day collecting bags of plastics in schools and places of business. By day's end we were exhausted. John, Charlie, and I were just on the edge of leaving Carrefour when Charlie said he forgot something at his mom's place and we had to go back. I was so pissed off. I was tired and hungry and just wanted to get the hell out of there. I turned the car violently to the left and started to head down the rail in Carrefour. I was so pissed because taking Charlie home meant going all the way up to Petionville. I'd have to do that before I could ever get back home to Mais Gate in the first place. With late afternoon Port-au-Prince traffic, that meant I wasn't getting home anytime soon. I was looking at another couple of hours sitting in the hot car with my foot going on and off the brake pedal. The thought of that was painful enough.

PART FOUR - LIVING AND DYING

As we made our way down to Lamentin 52 I caught a young female out of the corner of my left eye. She was trying to cross over from the middle of the road. She had an uncanny resemblance to my old girlfriend, Mamoune. I thought it was Mamoune actually. I looked back, straining my neck to see if it was her. I hit the gas to head toward Lamentin 54's turn-around and went back. I floored it hard. I wanted to see if Mamoune was in Carrefour and how was it possible that I didn't know about this. I hadn't seen her since 2008. I was yelling at both Charlie and John to have their eyes peeled for this girl. I was afraid I had lost her in the crowds of people alongside of the road. When we finally stopped and got this girl's attention, I saw it wasn't her. But I gave this pretty young lady my number. She was so shy and timid. She had a dumbfounded look on her beautiful face, yet a flattered glow all at the same time.

I said, "Don't forget, I'm waiting for your call tonight."

She called later that night and we talked for a couple of minutes. She said her name was Wiseline and that she was nineteen. I prayed she didn't have children, but she had a sixteen-month-old daughter. I desired no female with kids, none.

After I got off the phone I looked at Sperlif and said, "Yo Sper, this chick has a daughter, scratch her off the list, son."

Sperlif laughed. He had now been living with me and John for about three months. He had witnessed me bringing home a few different girls. I would even take Sperlif along with me to the house of a gal I was seeing, named Fedeline. Sperlif was always trying to talk me in to going back with Moses' and Spartacus' mother. He wasn't aware or could not comprehend that a guy like me could be dumped by a female as my ex-wife had finally proved possible. For Sperlif I walked on water. He looked up to me. He thought I was the coolest show in town. He and I Skyped with Moses and Spartacus. He was like a son to me and he looked at my boys like his brothers.

In the meantime, I wasn't being a very good fatherly example to Sperlif. When I brought a girl home he would always put his ear to my bedroom door to try and hear what we were doing. One girl, Anaelle, who I really liked, would get really loud when we were having sex. When I emerged from the room in a victorious strut, Sperlif would say, "Yo Zeke, you're

311

the general of this country" with a big smile. He wanted to be just like me.

Earlier that day before I started the job with Charlie, he had introduced me to a young gal from Carrefour named Nerline Pierre who was his next-door neighbor. I knew she was young, maybe seventeen, but I wasn't trying to ask her age. I didn't care one way or the other. Nerline was very mature beyond her years. She was very bright and very talented. We sat across from each other talking for about a half hour. She never took her eyes off me. At one point she came over and sat on my lap and we kissed. This girl was very aggressive and had no fear – none – and I loved that. She was far more my type than Wiseline. But for a variety of reasons a long-term relationship with Nerline was not in the cards. There was something inside of me telling me that Wiseline was possibly the one. Nerline would go on to become a female rap star in the Haitian hip hop Creole movement going by the name of UX-Unik Xpert. She was featured in a hit single by Haitian rap star Trouble Boy Hitmaker titled *Trouble Love Story*. We remain friends.

On March 18, President Aristide returned to Haiti from exile in Durban, South Africa. In late January I was in close contact with Mike Keister about the whispers of the former president returning to Haiti just like President Duvalier had done. Mike's lawyer, business partner, and good friend Steve Weinger worked with President Aristide's lawyer, Ira Kurzban. Mike was in a good position to be the one charged with flying Aristide back to Haiti. In 2004, Aristide had been removed from his home in Tabarre, and placed on a plane by a U.S. Special Operations Unit. He was flown to the Central African Republic against his will. Mike was the one that came in after all that and brokered a deal handling the flight arrangements and crew via Pacific Jet that flew Aristide back to the Western Hemisphere in Jamaica. I was trying to set up Les Stone to be the photojournalist to document Aristide's return. If he was not available, Antonio Bolfo was next in line. I sent an email to Ira Kurzban on behalf of Mike on February 20, 2011, letting Ira know that Mike would indeed be able to fly Aristide back from South Africa. At the time Mike was tied up with some affairs on the continent of Africa and was not available so I was acting in his behalf.

Ultimately it was the government of South Africa that foot the bill to bring Aristide back to Haiti. This afforded Aristide the luxury of having his entire entourage along for the voyage back to his homeland.

Sperlif and I went to the airport to greet the former president upon his return. We arrived a bit tardy to the airport and that cost us the chance to board the shuttle that took press members on to the tarmac before the South African plane touched down. We went along behind the presidential motorcade, however, to Aristide's private residence in Tabarre. The front entrance was very congested, so we scaled the walls of his home and on to the grounds of his property.

While inside I ran into Toussaint Hilaire. I briefly saw and spoke to Henry Ceant. Walking around the grounds of the former president's estate I ran into many of Aristides' old supporters from Cite Soleil. It was a *Fanmi Lavalas* reunion to say the least. The car carrying Aristide and family drove him all the way up to the front door. When the small framed former priest emerged from the vehicle the place went bananas. It was euphoria. I had never been a part of anything like that in all my years in Haiti. I had goosebumps. Even though there were a few things that I didn't like about Aristide, to be in his presence was electric.

Two days later I worked the pretty much non-eventful second round of the run-off elections between Manigat and Martelly.

A few days after that I took on a job working with Victoria Lim and Jon Kilb of Bright House Sports Network out of Tampa, Florida. They were doing a story about the life of a professional Haitian-born soccer player, Pascal Millien. Pascal was from Leogane so that's where we went for a couple of days. We had the chance to visit Pascal's family and his soccer academy for kids. It was a joyful experience and Pascal became a life-long friend.

And then came April 4. There was great anticipation on just who would be declared the presidential winner from the second round of voting. When the announcement came that Martelly was the winner the top blew off Port-au-Prince. Hundreds and thousands of people took to the streets singing and dancing. It was a madhouse.

I had no time for any of that mess. All those cheering people would be looking to chase Martelly from office soon enough, I thought. In Haiti, it's always "long live" to a particular person until the masses grow tired. Then

313

the ax comes down via the dechoukay (uprooting).

I was off to the Dominican border under the cover of darkness to retrieve Antonio Bolfo. With me were John, Sperlif, and my good friend Jean Maurice. Again, Jean Maurice was a police officer and one of Phaubert's brothers. They had the same dad but different mothers. I had him along for added security. He was always armed. When we arrived at the border everything was closed, and it was pitch dark. I was in contact with Antonio via my Blackberry phone. He told me that he was paying a runner to sneak him across the border. When he finally appeared to us from out of the darkness, I noticed he had his hand wrapped in a makeshift splint with white gauze. Just days earlier while working in New York he had been attacked by a guy and suffered a knife wound to his hand. Antonio is a tough guy. A former New York City police officer now turned photographer, he had a wealth of life experience to lean on.

Over the next four days we went into the landfill dump just on the outskirts of Cite Soleil. Bolfo was doing a big story about this place for a paper back in the states.

This was the toughest assignment I ever worked. The environment we were in was very toxic. We put our own selves at risk. All of the human waste and trash collected in the capital was dropped off here. The mounds and mounds of trash were always burning. The smell was absolutely disgusting. Witnessing how people actually lived in and around this dump was mind blowing and humbling. Seeing street kids flock to this wretched place to scrounge for food and scrap metals to resell was incredible. Mothers with little babies lived in this environment. It was horrific, it really was.

The people of this landfill were not fond of foreigners, especially those wanting to take their pictures while living amongst this heap of filth. Threats were made towards Antonio during this project. I kept the people at bay as long as I could. On the fourth and final day, however, things got heated. Antonio was persistent on getting some key shots for the piece he was working on. He was laser focused on capturing certain scenes from this theatre. This didn't sit well with one of the grown men that frequented the dump. The man cursed at Antonio. The guy had his posse with him as he jeered and made threats in Bolfo's direction.

The man looked right at me and said, "The only reason I don't kill him right now is because of you, Zeke."

"Well," I said, "he is with me. I brought him here and yes, he's paying me."

"It's a pretty fucking shitty deal, right?"

I said, "Relax, I'll give you something when we are done. Leave him be, let him work."

He then pointed at Bolfo and said in Creole, "You only get to live today because of Zeke."

Antonio finally broke his silence. He said, "Are you talking to me, sir?" He had Antonio's attention now.

"AB," I said, "this guy is jealous of you bro', he thinks you're much better looking than him."

The guy had no idea that Bolfo was a bad man and could handle himself. The man and his crew reluctantly backed away as he continued to talk trash to Bolfo off in the distance. This job was exhausting physically and emotionally. I would never want to do it again.

By the second week of April I finally set up a meet and greet with Wiseline. Her nickname was Darline so that's what I chose to call her. We had hit and missed with phone calls for a few weeks. I took the initiative to say, "OK, let's finally get together in person and talk."

Darline was sort of timid, so she brought her cousin Nadege along with her to make her feel more at ease. They took public transportation all the way to a place called Gerald Bataille, where I picked them up. It was an intersection not too far from where I was staying in Mais Gate. When I arrived and pulled over to the right my eyes caught a glimpse of her in the crowd. Time stopped! I just stared at her. I said, "Wow, she's the one." I lucked out. I had been through several really pretty girlfriends in recent months but this Darline gal had a look to her that had me smitten. She had an incredible ass, too. When we got back to my place, she told me, "The day you gave me your card, I was going to throw it away. My mom told me not to and encouraged me to hold onto it."

Darline told me that about two weeks before our first encounter she was very depressed and sad. She was a nineteen-year-old single mother who was no longer in school and going nowhere in life. She got down on her knees and she cried out to "God in Heaven" to send her someone who could help her and share a life. After our encounter she thought, "Could this white man with all these tattoos be the one I prayed to God for?" It wasn't until I had asked Darline to come see me that she started to dare to believe this was an answer to her cry.

John, and Sperlif and I had just recently moved from one Mais Gate apartment to another right across from where we had been staying. I called Darline and asked her to come live with me. Selfishly, I said, "You can leave your daughter at your mom's place in the meantime. She will be fine." I still didn't want any more kids. She agreed.

During that time John's girl Nathacha was pregnant so he got the OK from me to let her come stay with us, too. And just like that we had a house full. When Darline arrived to move in, I said emphatically to her that we were not getting married and we were definitely not having any kids. She looked at me with the cutest smile on her face. I said, "What's so fucking funny?"

She said, "You don't get to decide those things, God does."

I quickly responded, "Well God already told me hell no."

At the end of April I flew back to Ohio to see my boys after not seeing them for more than six months. After spending a week or so with them I left for Colorado to go visit my friend Wes. Wes and I had been growing closer as friends and I looked to him as a big brother and spiritual mentor. He was a real blessing to me in an abundance of ways. I wanted and needed the time to talk with Wes, learn from him, and express my gratitude for the financial help he had given me.

While in Colorado I went to visit the business Wes owns and met a few of his employees along with some of his closest friends and family. One afternoon we went to his sister Gretchen's house and ended up in a really competitive game of horseshoes. His brother-in-law, Harry, was a serious horseshoe player. Harry's friend, George, was also a serious player and he happened to be there. I was surprised when they asked me to play, being that I had never thrown a horseshoe in my life. Wes and I teamed up to play Harry and George. I felt a little pressure after seeing how talkative and competitive both Harry and George were. My first couple of throws

316

were awful and Wes said I could do much better than that. Wes is very competitive himself.

Although it took me a bit to get used to it, before long I was doing really well and trash talking myself. Of course, I was the biggest of trash talkers, but as a guest, I was trying my best to be quiet and humble. The games grew extra competitive and contested. As the sun started to set Harry maneuvered an ATV out on to the stretch of grass where we were playing, so we could have light. We went back and forth until finally Wes and I were victorious. Both Harry and George were quite sure that Wes purposely brought me all the way from Haiti because he knew I was a great thrower of horseshoes and wanted to team with me to beat them.

A month before I was in a landfill dump with some of the world's poorest inhabitants. And here I was throwing horseshoes at a private residence in Colorado.

I really admired that Wes was self-made. He became a wealthy businessman by starting at the bottom from scratch. While becoming wealthy he remained very humble. He shared his wealth with others. The biggest imprint he left on me was his devotion to prayer. He didn't do anything without praying first. He is a true man of God. I appreciated this more than he ever knew.

Wes gave to me one of the greatest compliments I've ever received in my life. While sitting outside the Denver airport he said to me, "Zeke, you're more comfortable in your own skin than anyone I have ever known." That meant a lot to me coming from him.

I said, "Next time we go to your ranch in Montana."

He said, "You bet." We prayed, embraced, and I was back off to Haiti.

SUMMER 2011 - BACK IN HAITI

Shortly after returning to Haiti I went through a tough two- to three-week period of being very sick with flu-like symptoms. I was stricken with fever, diarrhea, and suffered from really bad low blood sugars at night. On one occasion, I was found naked down by the toilet in a hallucinogenic state lying in my own piss, shit, and vomit. Darline and John didn't know

317

what to do other than make me drink coke. Unfortunately, this was a sign of bad things to come. Some new revelations were on the horizon and would shake my mental health to its core. My mental well-being would take a tremendous blow.

In early to mid-June of 2011 I was contacted by Isabeau Doucet for a job. She wanted me to take her to Leogane where she was working on a story about some shelters used for school children. The Clinton Foundation had put these in place. These "hurricane proof" trailers were found to be structurally unsafe and laced with formaldehyde.

Isabeau was assisted in covering this story by Canadian journalist Isabel Macdonald. I didn't particularly like every job I took, but an investigative one like this, which took some real get up and courage to do, I liked a lot. Clinton had announced this project as his foundation's first contribution to the Interim Haiti Recovery Commission, which he also co-chaired. His foundation described the project as emergency shelters that could also serve as schools, to ensure the safety of vulnerable populations in high risk areas during hurricane season, while also providing Haitian children a decent place to learn.

These trailers, according to the Clinton Foundation, would be equipped with power generators, restrooms, water, and sanitary storage. The trailers turned out to be anything but. There were a host of problems with these trailers from mold, to sweltering heat, to shoddy construction. Most disturbing was that they were manufactured by Clayton Homes, the same company sued in the United States for providing FEMA with form-aldehyde laced trailers in the wake of Katrina. Air samples collected from twelve of the trailers in Haiti detected worrying levels of this carcinogen in one, according to laboratory results obtained as part of a joint investi-gation by the Nation, and the Nation's Institutes Investigation Fund. This spoke to the fact that people in countries like Haiti were looked at and viewed as third-class citizens.

In other words, we give the Haitians our trash – stuff we wouldn't use in our own country. The Haitians would gladly receive it. They are poor. They are begging. They can't be choosy, they can't be picky. This occurred far too often and still is the case in Haiti. Give it to the Haitians, they'll use it. Give it to Mikey, he likes it. It's a real indictment on the mindset and

318

mentality of giving Americans.

It was during the month of June I began to hear some whispers about John. Whispers of things John had done, and in some cases, was still doing. It's funny how things have a way of finding their way out of the dark and into the light, regardless of time or space.

One night I found myself in a conversation with John when he revealed to me that he, too, once had the sexually transmitted disease crabs. I asked him when and he said in 2008. That seemed odd to me, being that I, too, had crabs then. During this conversation, I mentioned how much I thought Darline favored my former girlfriend, Mamoune. He slipped and said he once was with Mamoune sexually. He got caught up in the moment and referred to her using a nonchalant sexual innuendo. This was, of course, startling news to me. When he noticed my surprised reaction he quickly backtracked while stuttering his way through a lie he was clearly feeding me.

He and Mamoune having sex was treason of the highest level to me. Throughout the years I had always taken John's side. Regardless of who he had issues with – Yvrose, Phaubert, Phaubert's father Boss Claude, members of Leonne's family, Aslyne, Petuelle, and countless others. I trusted him more than anyone. From 1995 until 2011 I often entrusted to him thousands of dollars.

Evidently, when Mamoune had returned to Haiti from the states in September of 2004 she didn't get along with John. John started to manipulate the situation, giving Mamoune things she wanted in exchange for what he wanted and desired. I think Mamoune was probably of the same mindset in thinking she could manipulate John to get from him what she thought should be hers. Surely Mamoune knew that she'd be inconvenienced with giving him sexual favors, but she went through with such things regardless.

Of course they both knew that it wasn't in either of their best interests for me to ever find this out. John kind of enjoyed a free pass to do whatever he wanted with impunity. Hindsight is always 20/20 – I reflected on two occasions that were very suspicious, when I should have known, or at least suspected. Once Mamoune went through a period where she fell ill. Being stateside I had no idea what was going on other than what John told me.

319

I spent a lot of money on her during this period. John told me on one occasion that Mamoune had run out into the street naked, like some crazy person who had lost their mind. Truth be told, years later, she had become pregnant by him. He made her abort the child, and then she had to deal with the aftermath on her own.

On another occasion, John was a passenger in a car accident and suffered some pretty good bumps and bruises. He was really hurting and had been hospitalized. Mamoune asked me to send money. Days earlier I had just sent money. I angrily said, "No, I'm not sending another dime until two weeks from now just like I normally would do." She got really upset, which I found highly unusual, almost as if she was too worried about John's welfare. It wasn't a life-threatening situation, and knowing those two never got along I thought it very strange. I never thought any more of it, however.

I subsequently heard more whispers from people that had been close to both me and John over the years. I was asked by an individual if I knew that John had said this and that about me. I responded, "That's funny because he told me the same things about you." John was very jealous of anyone getting too close to me. I was his blan, I was his papa, he called me Pa. He was fearful I'd be taken away from him. He would go out of his way to come in between me and others and disrupt any harmony I might have with other people. He may have said to Phaubert, for example, "Zeke said he really didn't like you all that much. But you can't tell him I confided this to you." Then he might say to me, "Phaubert never has anything nice to say about you. He says you're greedy. But please, you must not tell him I told you these things."

Because Haitians keep secrets John was able to get away with such lies of great discord. These are small examples, but by the month and throughout the years this web of lies grew larger and larger the more threatened John felt. John once mentioned that if I wasn't with him, I wouldn't be with anybody in Haiti. At the time he said it I laughed, thinking about how funny it was. But in fact, he was threatening me. I wasn't aware of it, however, because at that time I wasn't privy to the things that were now whispered about.

Then came another stunning revelation. Through another channel I

320

was informed that John had also been having sex with Lithana during the time she stayed with John and Sabine. I was beside myself and furious, even though I was guilty of committing the same offense. One day out of the blue John said that Darline favored Mamoune in an all too-affectionate manner. I immediately took Darline outside and said, "I don't want you anywhere near John, ever!" I told her that I didn't trust him anymore and to stay clear of him.

As fate would have it, on the night of June 19, 2011, just eight days removed from the birth of John and Natacha's baby boy, things exploded. Several people were sitting across the street one night in the dark looking at somebody's cell phone. There was no electricity at the time, so this turned out to be the neighborhood's evening entertainment. They were all bunched together, trying to get a view of what was playing on this mobile device that had everyone's attention. I walked over to see what was going on, and found Darline sitting right next to John as she looked intently at the program. Had she forgotten I passionately directed her to steer clear of him? I almost threw my heart up out of my chest. I called her over to me. She didn't respond as she was laughing along with everyone else at the comedy taking place on the telephone screen. I finally went over to her and yanked her up by her seat.

I dragged her into the house and said, "What the fuck did I tell you?"

She was looking at me in the darkness, dumbfounded. I said, "What did I tell you about being close to John? You're going to pay me the price right here and now or I'm sending you back to your mother's house first thing in the morning, and we are done. You choose."

I violently ripped her top off. She spun around, grabbed my hand, and said she was sorry.

"If you're going to be with me then you're going to fucking learn to listen when I tell you something," I said. She started to whimper, saying, "I'm sorry papi I didn't mean to do that. I didn't even notice him amongst all the people sitting there."

"I don't give a fuck if you're sorry or not. You're getting this belt or you're going home tomorrow for good and I never want to see you again."

I removed my belt, grabbed her left arm, and forced her to the floor on her knees, facing the bed, and started to unleash hell. The entire time

I thought about John, who was very short in stature, gap toothed, and not in the slightest way appealing to the eye. He was a coward at heart. He was lazy. He never had a job in his life. He wasn't smart enough to finish his schooling that I had paid for. He wrecked the first truck that I bought for him. He could never get along with anyone I was close with. This little lying fuck that I took from the streets when he was an abandoned kid; the same kid that had been kicked out of an orphanage and found homeless, how was it possible that he, of all people, was the one causing me the most grief? He had me so enraged that I punished Darline like the Romans flogging Jesus before his crucifixion. Everyone outside was now standing at the front door of my apartment trying to see what was going on. I yelled at all of them to mind their own fucking business. Darline had transgressed against me and this was the result.

Early the next morning Darline revealed to me something Sabine had recently mentioned to her in confidence concerning John. Darline had never yet met Sabine in person but because of my father-daughter type relationship with her, Darline desired to know her in a more intimate manner. So, they often conversed on the telephone. Sabine made Darline swear that she would never speak of this secret to me. Well, Darline caved and told me. Five years earlier John had raped Sabine. He placed a knife underneath her pillow and threatened to kill her if she dared ever tell me. This particular revelation sent me into oblivion. I went downstairs to where I normally bathed to gather myself. As I stood down there, I thought about how I was going to do it. How was I going to kill him?

Lawrence of Arabia was called on to take a man's life that he once originally saved. Now, I believed, so must I.

I started back upstairs as Darline was coming down. She crossed directly in front of me and with my left hand I smacked her without hesitation right in the head. I then smacked her again, and shouted, "Damn all of you."

I continued on a warpath headed straight for John and found him seated, messing around with some play station games that I had bought for him. He had made a small business venture using the Play Station 2 and all the various games I had purchased. Neighborhood kids would pay to play when there was electricity. I came up on him and landed a blow so viciously to the side of his head that he was thrown airborne from the

322

chair. He tried to get up and I leveled him again.

John always had a healthy fear of tussling with me. I was too big and too strong for him. In that instant I wanted to kill him. The civilized white guy moment that would overcome me right then saved his life for sure. The second you have or show pity on a Haitian, that's when they will eat you alive.

I had my hands on his neck, prepared to choke the life out of him, but I let him go. I spit on him and walked away. Minutes later this damn fool threw a huge rock through the house at point blank range and missed. He did this while his brand-new baby boy laid on a bed in the next room. He ran back outside of the house. I gave chase and exited the house as another huge rock flew at me. By this time the entire neighborhood was running over to see what was going on. I took shelter back inside the house. Moments later I heard my 4Runner start up. I ran back outside to see him tearing off in my vehicle. His girlfriend, Nathacha, had snuck out a side entrance of the apartment with the baby. She took the spare key to the car and they got away.

At the time I thought for certain that John would notify the Haitian authorities. I was surely going to end up in prison. I got on the phone right away with Jean Maurice. I made him aware of what just took place. He informed me that he was on duty at the time and that he'd stop by later. He was the one Haitian police officer that I knew well and trusted.

Darline and Sperlif were now sitting on my bed in total shock from what they just witnessed. Jean Maurice came by later that night. There had been no word from John, and he never came back to retrieve any of his belongings. The next morning, we were unable to reach John by phone. He had taken refuge at a private residence in Carrefour where he hid my car. He was now in a precarious situation himself. He, his girlfriend, and their baby depended on me financially. Jean Maurice's involvement really helped to alleviate the tension. We finally got a hold of John, and Jean Maurice was able to talk some sense into him. Jean Maurice said this was a no-win situation for anybody. I needed my car to work and make money to live in Haiti. John needed me because, otherwise, he would have absolutely nothing.

That morning Jean Maurice and I traveled to Carrefour on his motorcycle. Fortunately, I was able to retrieve the car. I took John, Nathacha, and their baby back with me to the apartment in Mais Gate. That was an uncomfortably awkward ride to say the least. This, however, was the beginning of the end of our eighteen-year father-son relationship. It was now only a matter of time. When the right time came I was going to leave for good. John and I were through. He betrayed my trust on too many occasions. It was tormenting me because he was the one I had trusted the most.

I could no longer stomach the sight of him.

On July 26, 2011 I was invited back to speak on Moloskot's radio program Les Grands Dossiers. He was now working at RFM 104.9 at nine p.m. every night in Petionville. Jacques Richard Miguel heard me on this night and called me the next day. He asked me if I was interested in working alongside him and Erik Niva, a well-known sports journalist who covered soccer, and award-winning photographer Magnus Wennman, both from Sweden. They were coming to Haiti to do a story about a young girl named Madeleine Delice. Madeleine played for the girls Haiti 17U National Team. She had lost her mom, dad, and sister during the earthquake at its epicenter in Leogane. Rich didn't have a working vehicle at the time so he reached out to me. He told me that we would split the profits right down the middle. I said, "Sure thing, I'm in."

Rich and I started working with Magnus and Erik at the beginning of August. They were a lot of fun and very engaging. This job took us out to Leogane to see where Madeleine was from. Haitian girls' soccer is what we were force-fed over the next few days whether we liked it or not. On one of the days during this assignment at a soccer field in Tabarre, Rich and I shared a give and take exchange which made us laugh harder than we ever had before. I really liked him. During this particular job, I no longer had or needed John running as my sidekick. Sperlif tagged along with us instead, and he brought lots of joy to both Magnus and Erik.

At the drop of a dime, it all changed on the final day of this gig.

We were wrapping up and about to get paid. Rich and I started to disagree over a measly fifty dollars. Rich was of the mindset that I was a white American, and that fifty dollars was no big deal. For me, however, money was very tight. I was soon looking to be traveling back to the states for my sons' birthdays in September. For the rest of August, I didn't have any jobs lined up. It was going to be a tough stretch for me financially. Out of the $150 cash paid daily we split it $75 apiece. But I was losing money out of my $75 to pay for gas.

So, I felt strongly that the fifty dollars belonged to me, and he felt that it should be his. We weren't budging and started cursing at each other. The day before it was laughter; now, less than twenty-four hours later, it was anger. I stood down, though, and let him walk away with the money. He had a seven-month-old daughter at home and said he really needed the money. We went our separate ways that day with some hard feelings towards each other.

Later that night at a send-off dinner at the Pizza Garden in Petionville for Magnus and Erik things grew uncomfortable. Rich and I sat across from each other trying to avoid eye contact. I got up, said my farewells to the guys, and to try and salvage the friendship with Rich, I made a peace offering with him, telling him that I would take the guys to the airport the next day. Rich said no and waved me off. He was still very angry. I apologized to Magnus and Erik and I left. I proceeded to another restaurant called Muncheez along with Sperlif to get a bite to eat. Rich called me a few minutes later and agreed for me to take the guys to the airport in the morning.

Hoping to draw a laugh out of him I said, "Did you forget that you don't have a car and that's why you called me in the first place?" I tried to keep an open mind that he was a deportee. He was grinding out a way to survive daily in the third world. I was also conscious of the fact that, in a roundabout way, because of him I had met some really cool people such as Les Stone, Janet Reitman, Antonio Bolfo, Joe Mozingo, and now Magnus Wennman, and Erik Niva. I thanked him and we hung up. We wouldn't speak again until about a year later.

On September 7 I returned to the United States. I stayed the night at Julie Kartrude's mother's home in Fort Lauderdale. I went to get another tattoo in Miami. This time I tattooed the names of Moses and Spartacus on my face bordering the Neg Mawon statue where they connected at the last letter s. I went back to Ohio to celebrate their birthdays. I was so happy to be with them. Haiti had exhausted my physical and mental being to its tipping point. I stayed the next three months at the home on Lloyd that I grew up in. I did nothing but dive right into research on all kinds of things that have happened right underneath our noses as Americans. Encouraged by my brother, Ben, and childhood friend, Frank Jennings, I went in deep. From the Kennedy and King assassinations, to the Gulf of Tonkin in Vietnam, to the events of September 11, 2001. I started to uncover real hardcore truth. I would never be the same again.

On the morning of September 20, I met up with Katie Byard of the *Akron Beacon Journal* for some coffee and catching up. This was actually our first ever meeting in person. Unbeknownst to us, it wouldn't be the last. It was the first of many, future get togethers.

In early December, right before I left to go back to Haiti, Marion Coblentz invited me over to his home in Hartville, where I met a guy named Joshua Harsh. Josh was due to go down to Haiti for the next three months to work at the Heartline Ministries Guesthouse in Clercine. I had a job coming up in January working with a group of doctors and master's level development majors. These folks were participating in a Haiti Natural Disasters Conference led by Dr Mark Plaster and his son-in-law Jondavid Landon. They were due to stay at the Heartline Guest House. I thought it a good idea to connect with Josh in advance.

I had sent my son Moses to the Akron Zips University basketball camp in the summer of 2008. While there I met one of the players, Eric Coblentz. After speaking with Eric, I realized that we both had a common bond, the country of Haiti. Eric had done missionary work in Haiti with his father, Marion. Shortly after the quake I contacted Eric, anticipating that his father would most likely be making a trip to Port-au-Prince since his son and daughter-in-law, Jared and Jalayne Coblentz, had recently moved there to start a girls orphanage. Sure enough, Marion was driving from Sarasota, Florida, to South Beach, Florida, with loaded suitcases of food and over $10,000 in cash strapped around his waist. Grocery stores and banks had collapsed so food and cash were in hot demand. Marion had a one-way ticket to Santo Domingo.

I told Eric about Mike Keister and his pilots. I said if his pops wanted in, they were the way to go.

326

When Eric called his dad, Marion's first question was, "Can we trust Zeke?" since all he remembered were photos that he had seen of my many tattoos. Knowing that I had been heavily involved in Cite Soleil, a place well known and touted as the most dangerous slum in the world, left him reason for concern. Eric and Marion both went with their gut instincts and decided that I was a Godsend because Marion had no idea how he was going to get from the Dominican capital to Port-au-Prince. Through Mike, I was able to help Marion get into Haiti. Janny, one of Mike's pilots, met up with Marion in Santo Domingo and flew him over.

After spending three grueling weeks in Haiti helping people find food and shelter it was time for Marion to return to Ohio to his family and business. Marion hitched a ride back into the states illegally on a cargo plane that was not cleared to carry passengers. He received some much-needed help to get through customs and boarded this cargo plane when a U.S. Marine stepped in and cleared the way for him, which ultimately saved Marion's life. Within forty-eight hours of arriving back in Hartville, Ohio, he became deathly sick and in just thirty-six hours, he lost thirty pounds. He was admitted into Aultman Hospital. There he was diagnosed with malaria. The doctors were pretty excited about this diagnosis because they had not seen a malaria case in over seventy years. For a brief time, Marion was sort of a local hero. The doctors told him had he waited around another twenty-four hours without getting medical attention, he would not have made it through to see another day. Over the course of the seven days spent at Aultman Hospital they found a massive tumor in Marion's stomach. He was sent to the Cleveland Clinic to have it removed. It was an extraordinary case in which one of the world's greatest disasters saved a life. God's miraculous way of turning a disaster into a blessing.

On December 7 I traveled back to Haiti. Three days later I had already found a day's work with world renowned photographer, humanitarian, and activist Lisa Kristine. Lisa's photography has documented indigenous cultures and social issues such as modern-day slavery in over a hundred countries around the world. This job was set up for me through a mutual friend named Bobbi Dunphy. I spent the day with Lisa visiting several Cite Soleil neighborhoods. Lisa turned out to be the most mesmerizing human I have ever met in my life. She's arguably the greatest human being I know.

I feel fortunate to be able to call her my friend.

Magnus Wennman returned to Haiti on December 16 to do a story about me and my life in Haiti for a publication in Sweden called *Afton Bladet*. On December 20 I saw him off to the Dominican border. At the end of December, I met with Arnaud Robert, Paolo Woods, and Ben Depp for an interview and photo shoot in Bwa 9 Cite Soleil. Arnaud interviewed me about my life and experiences in Haiti over the course of two decades. Paolo and Ben did the photography for the piece. A year and a half later I appeared in Arnaud and Paolo's published book about Haiti entitled *State*. I was one of the only Americans in Haiti featured in their book.

In the beginning of January 2012 my car was vandalized in the Carrefour neighborhood I was now spending a lot of my time in. Since returning to Haiti in December I moved with my girlfriend Darline to where her mother Monita was staying in Lamentin 54. Their rent was due, so I paid it, and moved in. I hadn't communicated with John during the three months that I was in the States. I hadn't even notified him to let him know I was back in Haiti. Haiti is a small place, however. It didn't take long for him to hear that I had returned. Needless to say, he wasn't very happy.

When we finally spoke on the phone, I let him know that I was putting our relationship on hold for the time being. I reminded him of all the things that had happened, the things he had done, and expressed to him that I needed time away from him to heal. That was a bullshit answer, of course. I didn't want him anywhere near me ever again. I had no plans of ever taking him back into my life under any circumstances. He was dead to me. Even though he didn't know where Darline's mom's place was located in Carrefour, in the back of my mind I wondered whether he had sent someone to vandalize my vehicle. He still had the spare key for the car and if he knew where I was staying, he most likely would try to steal it himself. He, his girlfriend, and their new baby were always dependent on me to take care of them. Now they were on their own to fend for themselves. Desperate people do desperate things.

My head was on a swivel 24/7. I started parking my car in a private residence about a quarter mile away to keep it safe from vandals and from John. The car was my lifeline for work. Without it I couldn't continue to live in Haiti.

PART FOUR - LIVING AND DYING

My next job was with that team of doctors, and master's level development majors led by a man who once saved former Vice President Joe Biden's life, Dr. Mark Plaster. Plaster is an emergency medicine physician and military veteran. He has his own emergency medicine magazine. For this entire group one car would not suffice. I enlisted the assistance of an American friend of mine named Steven Parker Shaw to help drive. Steve had a truck, so it worked out perfectly. This group was staying at Heartline Ministries Guesthouse in Clercine. I stayed with them. Since Steve lived closed enough in Mais Gate, he slept at his own place. With this group of highly educated individuals, I found myself in some very deep conversations discussing life, religion, politics, and world events. I prided myself on being very bright and well educated. Although I was self-educated, I could hold my own in a discussion with anyone, from anywhere, no matter how many diplomas or degrees they had. Hanging with this group would really challenge me. Listening to the different thoughts and ideas shared by people with such extraordinary educational backgrounds was exhilarating.

On January 10 I picked up Dr. Plaster's team from the airport. Later that evening we were at the Hotel Montana overlooking the city of Port-au-Prince. Seeing the city from that perspective is really incredible. It was on this night that I received a phone call from a guy in Cite Soleil telling me that JhaJha, a.k.a. Mackenson St Fleur, had been arrested and taken back to the Haitian Penitentiary. Jha was an evader of prison after breaking out when the earthquake happened. After being on the loose for two years the Haitian authorities finally caught up to him. Jha was like a little brother to me so I took the news hard. I was currently going to be on this job for several days to come. There was nothing I could do for Jha at the time. I had to focus on what was in front of me and try to forget about things that were out of my control.

On January 11 we visited Samaritan's Purse headquarters in Titanyen. From there we went to have lunch and a conversation with Bill and Susette Manassero at the Child Hope Orphanage in Delmas 75. After leaving there we headed to the U.N. Building to visit with Senior Policy Advisor for the U.N. Office of the Special Envoy to Haiti Nancy Dorsinville.

The following day, January 12, the two-year anniversary of the

REACH AND FALL

earthquake, we traveled to Leogane to visit The Notre Dame Program led by a biologist, Father Tom Streit. Notre Dame is affiliated with St. Croix Hospital in Leogane. Together they were fighting and trying to eliminate lymphatic filariasis, a.k.a., elephantitis. During a sit-down question and answer discussion with the group and Father Tom, a certain topic he addressed made me enter the fray. I knew he was wrong, not because he wasn't sincere, but because he didn't know any better in this case. That's where I stepped in to correct him.

Father Tom is a living legend. It's usually against protocol to cross a line like that with a man of his resume. But he was in my house (Haiti), and I was going to make sure that on this day, I was the teacher.

In the room sat two Haitians, a guy named Jean-Marc and another named Louis Rigan. I could see the twinkle in their eyes when I spoke up. When I suggested to everyone in the room that I was correct while staring over into the eyes of Jean-Marc, I waited for him to confirm that what I was saying was spot on. I pointed over to him and said, "Ask Jean-Marc, he will tell you I'm right."

Jean-Marc, not wanting to disagree with Father Tom had no choice but to tell the truth. He said, "Zeke is right. He is right."

Often throughout my twenty-one years involved in Haiti I had to set many a foreigner straight concerning Haitian affairs and the ways of life in that country. It didn't matter to me if they were living legends like Father Tom Streit with Notre Dame, or Father Tom Hagan with Hands Together in Cite Soleil, or Father Rick Frechrette with St. Damien's Hospital, or even a guy like Dr. Paul Farmer himself. Not one foreigner who has ever stepped foot on Haitian soil has ever become more intimate with the Haitian people than me. My pride would make sure that I made everyone aware of this at all times if need be. If not for anything else but order. Without order chaos reigns.

The four gentlemen previously mentioned are living legends. Make no mistake about it. The contributions by these to their fellow man are immeasurable. Surely their treasure awaits them in the life hereafter.

On January 13 it got even better. We went to discuss Haiti's current state of crisis with World Bank Lead Disaster Risk and Management Specialist Joe Leitmann. We discussed the Haitian Reconstruction Fund amongst a host of other topics. I wanted to sit in on this meeting to learn. I really loved Joe's candid answers. I thought that he would give vanilla answers with little substance when the meeting first began, but I couldn't have been more wrong.

Joe was very frustrated by the lack of progress concerning the reconstruction of Haiti post-earthquake. He was passionate about it too. He was very critical of a lot of big names, both Haitians and Americans. That turned some heads in the room and had everyone now looking on him with great favor. His pure honesty was a breath of fresh air.

On January 14 this job took me back up to Cange, to the exact place I had a run in with Cate Oswald a year earlier at the Partners in Health facilities. I was not going to be staying the night this time around, however. I went out of my way to avoid seeing Cate. I really felt bad about how I talked to her the year before even though, on principle, I thought I was correct. From there we went to see the brand-new hospital that Dr. Paul Farmer was building in Mirebalais. There was a South African man overseeing the project. I started up a very candid conversation with him. I looked straight at him and asked how much this state-of-the-art project cost. He said $17 million without batting an eye. I was blown away by that small figure. I found it to be a very low number. I was expecting him to give a much larger dollar amount. The place was still under construction, but we were given a full all-access tour. After my request to see the roof we were permitted to go up on top of the building too. It is now Haiti's best medical facility. Had the reconstruction of Port-au-Prince post-earthquake been done in the same efficient manner, like this new medical facility in Mirebalais, the capital of this 1804 Republic would look much different today. It's a credit to Dr. Paul Farmer and his people.

On January 15 we went up to spend the day at the Karibe Hotel. While at the hotel a lady named Lisa Nuccio, a total stranger, walked up to me like she had known me from years past. She was just staring at me with eyes wide open. "Do you know you're a prophet?" she said. I just looked at her and smiled. She said, "You're a prophet, yes you are, and you know it." We talked for a couple of minutes and exchanged contact information. She was on to something. I felt like she had been sent into my path for a reason.

A few moments later I met a guy named Jonas Belizaire, a.k.a. Haitian

Jonas of Oncamera media group. We hit it off right away. I said he needed to meet Sperlif and I set up a day to bring Sperlif to do an interview with Jonas at the Karibe Hotel. Sperlif did a great interview and Jonas put it on YouTube. This gave Sperlif his first real break in some publicity. Jonas, just like Lisa, had come into my path for a reason. This would become evident in the very near future.

On January 16 I saw Dr. Plaster's group off on a ferry that took them to La Gonave. This was the end of the job for me. It was arguably the best experience of my time doing fixer work in Haiti. I was very thankful for this group and I often times think of them to this very day.

To Dr. Plaster, his daughter Whitney, her husband Jondavid, Rashmi Sharma, Hollyn Romeyn, Maya Bahoshy, Danielle Fuller Wimbush, Katie Sprinkel, and Katherine Dillon, thank you!

About two and a half months later Katherine tagged me in a post on Facebook, saying she spoke to someone in Jacmel on Skype who heard stories about me four times in the past two weeks. She then asked how it felt to exist somewhere between rumor and legend.

I had never been to Jacmel, but even there, people knew who I was, or who they thought I was. You think you had it bad when someone circulated a rumor about you in school. Think about a rumor about you that spread across an entire country, cutting into it like Moses through the Red Sea.

It was now time for me to focus on Sperlif's musical talents. The kid was a born rapper, a genius. I reached out to one of my longtime friends from Cite Soleil named Luisgens Jacinthe, a.k.a. Gagòt. Gagòt was himself an artist in the Haitian rap Creole industry.

The three of us wrote a song called "Nou Mele." Sperlif spit three verses on this track with a fourth and final verse by Gagòt. The lyrics were tremendous. We went to Gremateck Studio in Carrefour in February to record it. A guy who goes by the name Gremateck Gregory Beatmaker was the individual who produced it. It was Sperlif's first hit single. It played consistently on local radio stations in Port-au-Prince. Many CDs of this single were made and passed out for free in Cite Soleil. That was something Gagòt and I did to push Sperlif's popularity amongst the young population. The song played over and over again throughout the thirty-four Soleil neighborhoods.

This was just the beginning. Sperlif was destined to be a rap superstar in the country of Haiti.

Gagòt, Sperlif, and I went to visit Yvetot Gouin in Petionville to discuss the possibility of creating a music video for Nou Mele. I took a copy of the CD and played it for Yvetot. He loved it. He always had a very busy schedule with film making and producing and said when he could fit it in to his schedule, we would start working on it. He was very gracious to us. We already had the grandest of visions of Sperlif being filmed in different Cite Soleil neighborhoods and spreading these powerful lyrics that we hoped would ignite a fire in the people. It was only a matter of time.

Towards the end of February, I was in contact with my new friend Lisa Nuccio. My birthday was coming up on March 5 and together we planned for me to visit her in Naples, Florida. My mom would bring Moses and Spartacus down with her from Ohio so we could all spend my birthday together. We had about five days of good bonding time while in Naples. We explored the Everglades. We rode on an airboat and saw lots of gators. We traveled through the swamp on a buggy, seeing and learning all kinds of things about the history of the land. This was my first time swimming on the gulf side of Florida's southern tip. We traveled around in a rented car jamming to Sperlif's new song. The boys loved it, especially because Sperlif expressed his love for them at the end of the track.

Finally the boys presented me with a cake and sang "Happy Birthday." It was special. My mother and Lisa did me such a great favor by making that happen on my 39th birthday. I was so very grateful.

By mid-March Wes Gardner was coming back to Haiti with a couple of friends, Kent Sump and Mike Jeronimus. Wes and I had many conversations over the phone about ways of really sustainably helping Haiti's poor. I conveyed to him that hey, if you are going to come back down to Haiti, why don't you see as much of the country as you can in the few days that you will be here. The three of them wanted to view the deforestation of the land from an elevated position to possibly start some sustainable farming. Mike was a forester in Colorado. I reached out to Yvetot about arranging a helicopter trip for the guys to see Haiti up close and personal. I knew

333

he had contacts on the ground that could make this happen. After seeing the landscape from above and visiting Cite Soleil, Mike said that Haiti's greatest export was misery. He was spot on.

A day after Wes and the guys left, I had been emailing back and forth with a man named Jae Evans about my availability to be a fixer for him and two other men named Chris and Eric who were due in Haiti on March 20. I was originally put in touch with Jae via a young man named Francesco Raphael DeMeo.

I met Francesco in Delmas 75 back in October of 2011. He was cool. We hit it off and kept in touch. Networking like this once again led to a new opportunity.

Jae was the founder of Outside the Bowl. His organization specialized in running Super Kitchens in poor areas of South Africa, Mexico, and Haiti. When they began their work in Haiti it was up north in Port-de-Paix. For certain reasons things didn't work out at that location so they decided to find another place to set up shop. This led them to venture down to the capital. These kitchens are designed to feed thousands of hungry mouths daily. The impact they have is a huge deal with the poor and disenfranchised.

Unfortunately, the day Jae arrived he caught me at a bad time. I wasn't feeling well physically, and I really didn't want to go anywhere on the days he was suggesting, especially after the few days I had just spent with Wes and his guys. I had every intention of blowing him off until I received a phone call from Susette Manassero. Susette asked me to please come up to Delmas 75 and at least hear what Jae and his partners had to say. For Susette and Susette only, I agreed to do it.

I hung up the phone with Sue, looked at Darline, and said, "Fuck! I hate this shit man, these fucking white people are going to be the death of me."

I begrudgingly got into the car and went up to Delmas 75 to see them. God works in the most mysterious ways.

I showed up in a bad mood. I was not doing a very good job of hiding or keeping it concealed. Being polite and professional meant everything in this line of work, but at this point I no longer cared. I sat with Jae, Chris, and Eric intently listening to their story about why they left Port-de-Paix

334

essentially, and how they wanted me to drive them up to see a location in Kenscoff that was to be a potential site for this new kitchen. I started to feel myself coming unglued.

I immediately went in on white folks in Haiti and all the things I loathed about them. At the top of my lungs I said, "You have all these Christians who come to Haiti wanting to do this and do that, but only do said things in the most comfort possible. Good deed doers with limits to what they were willing to do. If Jesus was here, where would he be?"

Complete silence fell over the room. The three of them were now looking upon me, surely feeling the rage and the fire that was burning deep inside of me.

"And you guys want me to take you to fucking Kenscoff? I'm not going to Kenscoff. I will take you to Cite Soleil. Down there in the heart of the largest ghetto in the Western Hemisphere is where the people are the hungriest. That's where Jesus would be. You guys decide, I personally don't give a damn what you do."

As the three of them sat there looking at me, Jae finally spoke up. He said, "I trust your judgment and understand your sentiments." He reminded and made clear to me that their mission was to serve Christ throughout the neediest places in the world. He agreed to make the trip down to Cite Soleil to see what the possibilities were.

I said, "OK, suit yourselves, I'll be back tomorrow morning to get you guys and take you. There you will have an opportunity to experience an avalanche of gut-wrenching sensations. You will enter through gates that take you into the bowels of hell on earth. A place that the Devil himself would only visit after smoking crack cocaine. It's a volatile community of a half million tormented souls. Enjoy!"

The next day I arrived early in the morning to pick the guys up for our trip to Cite Soleil. I spent the next several hours showing Jae and the others what the reality of being the poorest of the poor really looked like.

I so badly wanted to trust white people in Haiti, but I never could. I wanted to see them place the Super Kitchen model in Cite Soleil with all my being but I don't think I had any delusions that these men would really come through with a Super Kitchen in an area that the United Nations once listed as the most dangerous place on the planet.

335

REACH AND FALL

I remained pessimistic about Jae's group after the Cite Soleil visit.

Before Jae left Haiti, I told him that I would oversee the operations of it, and work it for free at no charge to him. This is when I reached out to Wes about Jae and Outside the Bowl. I put Wes in contact with Jae and before long Wes was traveling to go meet Jae in person. I was now having a new and very optimistic look about what we could all do if we worked together to make this happen. A Super Kitchen would be something that a place like Cite Soleil had never seen before. It would be unprecedented. I felt at this point in time that God was using me to have a great impact on the lives of the less fortunate on a much grander scale. I felt like a modern-day Errol Flynn, a.k.a. Robin Hood.

2012 . . . THE TIME OF RECKONING IS NEAR

In my last year in Haiti, Child Hope, located in Delmas 75, run by Susette Manassero and her husband Bill, served as a refuge for me. Sue knew that I lived in the ghetto amongst Haiti's masses and she showed great compassion towards me, inviting me up on occasion for a weekend to get away from the harsh reality I was living in. It was really life sustaining for me in the last year. It gave me a chance to breathe a little bit.

Sue and I had some great conversations over the course of that final year. On this Easter weekend of 2012 I took Sperlif and the late Haitian Tupac's daughter Whitney with me. Sperlif had been up to visit Susette with me before and he loved it. He loved her daughter Ari. He had a really big crush on her. He was also very fond of Sue's adopted Haitian children, daughter Frankie and son Kenny. He loved interacting with other white people and the Haitian kids his age at the Child Hope orphanage. I enjoyed watching his interactions with all of them. It was a simple pleasure for me.

Sperlif had become like a son to me, standing in the gap for my two sons back in the states. Delmas 75 was like a little American neighborhood in Haiti. Going there made Sperlif feel like he was a legit world traveler with an invisible passport. A kid from Cite Soleil was not accustomed to seeing white people showing so much love to black people. His limited experience with foreigners was with the United Nations military force that

336

had occupied Haiti since 2004. The UN Troops who constantly patrolled the Bwa 9 neighborhood that Sperlif was from treated Haitians harshly and with great arrogance, like they were beneath them and it showed.

In those days I was still reeling from my divorce and separation from Moses and Spartacus. I was very rarely ever happy. So anytime I had the opportunity to spend a weekend with Sue and her family I welcomed it with open arms and a grateful heart. This visit would be much different, very emotional, and very special all the way around. For Whitney, it was her first time ever being around white people other than myself or the U.N. troops as she lived in Soleil 19 in Cite Soleil.

That Saturday on Easter eve we all sat down to watch *The Passion of the Christ*. I had seen it once before, but for Sperlif and Whitney it would be their first time viewing anything like it.

Two very powerful things happened in the next few hours. One was seeing both Sperlif and Whitney moved to great emotion as they watched the brutal treatment of Jesus by the Jews and the Romans. His betrayal, arrest, mockings, beatings, and subsequent crucifixion was overwhelming, especially for Whitney. The scene where Jesus fell down while carrying the cross as the camera panned to his mother Mary, envisioning him falling when he was a little boy, was absolutely devastating to her.

She was crying while watching this theatre play out on a small color TV, and trying to mask it so that nobody would notice or see her so vulnerable. Where she is from in Soleil 19 young girls her age didn't cry. Being the daughter of Haitian Tupac, a rapper, a gangster, she was supposed to be tough, and she was well aware of that. She carried herself with a hardened exterior all the time, always acting the part. I was sitting next to her and I put my arms around her in that moment and confessed to her that I cried too. She glanced at me with a look of astonishment. She was baffled that I would admit to such a thing. Men definitely never ever cried where she came from. We just hugged and said no more. It was quiet as we sat there in full embrace. I never felt more alive than during intimate moments like this, regardless of who I was with. It was so real, hardcore, and special.

The opening scene in the movie, where Jesus was in the garden of Gethsemane praying to His Father in Heaven and asking for this cup to pass is where I was moved in my spirit. I remember thinking wow, my

337

good God, wow! I want to know what that felt like. As Jesus was in the garden sweating blood, feeling the weight, betrayal, and abandonment of man's sin against His Father, I thought to myself, "I need to know what that feels like, I must know this feeling."

They say be careful what you ask or wish for. A little over a month later my thoughts would manifest themselves into a brutal jarring to the senses reality. I was privileged to get a small taste of what that sort of betrayal and abandonment felt like, just a very small taste. The same people I defended my entire life would now be the ones treating me like an animal. I was on the cusp of learning a new type of suffering. Looking back now it's clear that it was my destiny playing itself out, and I'm very thankful for that experience.

God is Great!

On April 19, 2012, I was still spending the majority of my nights at a Lamentin 54 address in Carrefour. I was really close to the military base that eight former sergeants in the old Haitian military were running. Some old friends of mine were residing at this base: Sergeant Jean Fednel Lafalaise, Sergeant Yves Jeudy, Sergeant Larose Aubain, and Sergeant David Dorme. So I paid them a visit that evening. There was probably close to fifteen hundred former military and aspiring military men and women living at the base. Most of them were sleeping in tents. I went inside the base that night and had a long sit-down talk with the guys. I bought some drinks for everyone and I spoke candidly. I told them how impressed I was with something that I had recently witnessed. After a torrential rain that littered the rail in Carrefour with debris, I saw all these men in olive green uniforms the next day in the hot sun cleaning it up, led by Larose Aubain. They were not being paid to do it. It was done voluntarily. In Haiti something like this is a rarity. A scarcity. Haitians do nothing for free. It really never happens. At least not in all my years there. I immediately got goosebumps after laying my eyes on the men working. Cars were honking as they drove by. I thought, *wow, this is real, this is incredible.*

This could be what a new Haiti looked like.

During this time, anti-U.N. sentiment was at an all-time high. I told the former sergeants that since witnessing this one act I was now on board with them. Sergeant Lafalaise smiled and said, "We have always asked you to come train with us.

I smiled back and said, "Y'all don't want this."

He laughed and said, "Zeke, Haitians are far more resistant than the whites."

I said, "Yes you are correct about that, just not this white." That was greeted by a chorus of laughs by the men.

One of the young men spoke up. "A lot of us have stood up on the back wall of the base watching Zeke swim in the ocean," he said. "I believe what Zeke is saying to be accurate. We once watched him for well over two hours swimming in the sea. He is much different from other whites."

Of course, I wouldn't be able to prove that young man's sentiments correct until future events, but all the men in that base respected me. They looked to me for an extra voice in leadership, which I would provide come May 18. I went on to remind the men that I was in Haiti before the U.S. military intervention in 1994. Since that point there was always some kind of foreign military presence in Haiti. Even if it was in the form of foreign military police training Haitians. I was one of the handful of Americans that still could remember what it felt like during Haiti's final days of sovereignty. So seeing the men in the old olive-green garb of the Haitian military uniforms made me feel proud. It also made me feel a strong sense of anger towards the illegal occupation of the homeland by U.N. Troops. I was convinced now more than ever to be a part of the solution to Haiti regaining its sovereignty. My conviction was so great that when I spoke on the radio just a few days later I declared that it was time for all the foreigners to leave Haiti for good.

"Well Zeke, if that's how you feel, you're a foreigner, that would mean you leaving too," the show host said to me.

I responded, "You better fucking believe it, and I would leave. As long as the foreigners are allowed to continue to come and go as they please, you will all remain in a sort of extended captivity regardless, and more so mental than physical." I was all in now.

A few days later I traveled with Moloskot and his team to Camp Perrin to do his nightly radio broadcast for RFM 104.9 Radio on location. The program was in the form of a Haitian town hall meeting. Before leaving for Camp Perrin we stopped in at the military base in Lamentin 54 to see all the guys and have a photo op with the entire high command of the base. Moloskot was popular among the men and often talked about these guys on his radio program. He once visited the base in person to do some live interviews on the radio.

When we arrived at Camp Perrin we were well received. We visited the private home residence of the deputy of that region serving in the current government. Having the opportunity to address the large crowd that gathered for the town hall meeting was tremendous. The people in the audience were engaged. I was giving to them very animated answers to their questions. When I got back to Port-au-Prince a couple of days later, I had many people telling me that they heard me on the radio in Camp Perrin, and they loved what I had to say. I really started to feel as though I was making game-changing plays.

On May 1, 2012, the second anniversary of my father's death, I took a job with Betsey Chesler. Betsey is the founder of the Cameras for Kids Foundation. I was set up to spend the day working as her fixer by a man named Len Gengel. Len's daughter, Britney, was killed in the earthquake and Len was doing a book with his wife about Brit's story. Their book publisher just happened to be Betsey's father, Barry.

More of the networking that I learned was so very powerful on display yet again. I brought my good friend Clif Kernisant along with me for this job as extra security. Having lots of previous experience with Clif first-hand in the field of fixer work, I felt it necessity to make sure Betsey was safe. Clif's larger than life presence and the fact that he carried a 9mm was the extra-added insurance I needed to feel comfortable.

I took Betsey to several places. One of them included a drive through Cite Soleil so she could take in the sights and sounds of real hardcore poverty.

While stopped just outside of Soleil 17, Betsey captured a picture of me talking with my oldest friend from the ghetto, Nasson, and a couple of other guys. I didn't know that would be the last time I ever stepped foot in Cite Soleil, and subsequently, the last photo of me ever taken there. The day of my dad's death was now coupled with my last ever appearance in Cite Soleil. The ironies of life!

PART FOUR - LIVING AND DYING

The night of May 14 I once again went live on RFM 104.9 Les Grands Dossiers with Moloskot. I knew that a march on the capital by the Haitian military was imminent. I had personally and quietly reached out to some people looking for support of these men. I knew that with enough financial support this group could do some real work for the betterment of the country. At every turn, however, I failed to convince anyone else to get on board with this movement of the old Haitian military being revived. Although discouraging, I didn't let it get me down. I thought how fortunate Lawrence of Arabia was to have support by the British government even if covertly. I knew that had I been afforded such means it would have meant a world of difference. Speaking on Moloskot's program for the final time, I urged the Haitian people to come together as one on Flag Day, May 18, to make a statement against the illegal U.N. occupation of their land.

The next day I was asked by several of the former sergeants in command of the base at Lamentin 54 to take a couple of the young recruits with me to downtown Port-au-Prince and distribute flyers. These flyers telegraphed a march on the capital scheduled for May 18. We dropped these pamphlets off at key locations in and around downtown, especially at the faculties for the student population. There had been a hot internal debate amongst the old Haitian military members a few weeks before. It concerned all the former military personnel that were taking up camp in bases around the country. They aspired to make a show of force throughout the entire 1804 Republic by all the men in olive green taking to the streets in unity, as one. They wanted to go out of the way to exaggerate their size and numbers. This called for many of them to drive several miles in convoys together in a display of strength. I encouraged them to do it. I said it would give the appearance of having a much greater force than they had. After several discussions and debates about this idea they scratched it altogether. I think after consulting with Guy Philippe the men agreed to not see it through. I thought it a great opportunity wasted.

May 18 was coming, however. A few thousand of us would march on the capital. This was to be my moment to lead. I knew one thing, that if the masses marched with us, the U.N. Troops and Martelly government would be in big trouble. Even though president Martelly was said to have been in support of the Haitian troops, he was only ever playing politics trying to appease them. He knew ultimately that he answered to one entity, and that was the folks at the U.S. Embassy. They were responsible for getting him elected. He was now obliged to be their yes man. And the folks at the Embassy said an emphatic "No!" to the reestablishment of the old Haitian military.

What I asked for I received: members of the old Haitian military along with new aspiring recruits – numbers in the thousands – were planning to march on the capital demanding the restoration of FAD'H forces on Flag Day.

The late afternoon of May 17, 2012, I was waiting at the Hotel Veve in Carrefour, expecting Steven Parker Shaw. I had asked Steve along for the use of his truck. During the past few months since the job we worked together back in January, we grew much closer. I trusted Steve like no one else. He was a good friend. Having him around would only benefit me if things went sour, plus I enjoyed his comradery and leadership. Steve was an old grizzled vet of Haiti life. I wouldn't want to roll with anyone else. He had been bed ridden for a few weeks suffering from dengue fever. But he wasn't going to miss this show.

Back in 2008 a school collapsed in Petionville. Steve was one of the first people on the scene climbing underneath the rubble in the pitch darkness trying to find survivors. He worked alongside a guy from the U.N. that was forced to use a saw to cut a dead child in half so that the two of them could proceed forward in their attempt to rescue other children that were still alive. Steve was always helping poor people without any fanfare. He never wanted any credit for anything, never wanted to be interviewed, never wanted his picture taken. He was a rare breed. We were the exact opposite of each other. That's why we made such a great team.

We were the modern day version of Butch Cassidy and The Sundance Kid. On this occasion, his truck was really going to come in handy.

I opened up to Steve that night about some of my relationships with these former sergeants. I told him that a few weeks earlier I responded to Larose when he called asking me to transport a sickly woman at General Hospital to Leogane with him. The lady was on her last days in this life. Larose wanted to get her back to her family so she could spend her final days in peace. I personally wanted no part of this sick individual sitting in

342

my car. I had no idea what Godforsaken disease she had nor was I trying to find out. My OCD would drive me mad thinking about it. Out of respect for Larose I agreed to do it.

On another occasion, I had bought dinner for Jean Fednel and his young son at the base one night. I heard the youngster say to his father that he was hungry. I looked at both of them and said, "What do y'all want? I'm buying!" On yet another occasion, Yves Jeudy's wife was pregnant and needed a ride back up to Petionville from Carrefour. So I transported her myself. I did these guys solids because of my respect for them, and out of respect for all my old comrades in the Haitian military dating way back from my first years in Haiti during the early 90s. I also did the favors because I had a dream of a sovereign Haiti. A Haiti without foreigners running and ruining things for the poor masses.

As the night waned on Steve slammed some Prestige beers while I watched the Lakers vs. Thunder playoff game. He was in one bed, I was in the other. I said, "Look big bro, whatever you do tomorrow, if they ask, you're ex-military.

Steve replied, "You're goddamn right I'm ex-military, motherfucker."

It was the last night of sleep before our lives would change forever. As we were getting ready to retire for the night I said, "Yo, I just had a big argument with my girlfriend's mom. Then a couple of her aunts and cousins showed up running their mouths. I can't take it anymore. I'm getting the fuck outta there next week." I loved Darline, but I was done with her family.

Steve then said, "I'm about to call it quits with my girlfriend Nanoune too. I can't take it anymore myself."

Steve and I loved Haitian women. There was no shortage of supply. Who would be next?

The morning of May 18 and the day of reckoning was upon us. Steve and I were both up early and ready to go. Steve wearing his military fatigues made me feel somewhat under dressed for the occasion.

"You fucker," he said, "you're making me look bad."

By the time we arrived at the base just down the road from where we slept things were already abuzz with foreign and Haitian journalists. I stood nearby as I heard Sergeant Lafalaise proclaim to members of the press, "It's either the Haitian military or death. The day has come. We will see if President Martelly is serious or not."

I saw Sergeant Jeudy in passing and asked him if he had an extra FAD'H Haitian military shirt at his disposal that I could wear. He quickly dispatched an individual to go retrieve one for me. It fit perfectly. Now I was no longer feeling under dressed. It was the equivalent of Lawrence of Arabia wearing the Arab garb. When my grandfather, John Pierce Petrie, died he left his watch and Masonic ring for my father. When my father died I seized them both. On this day, I was wearing the pair. I wished they could see me.

Before long the military base was swarming with activity both inside and outside the gates. People by the hundreds were trying to get a look at all the men preparing to take to the street. At one point the central command of the base asked the foreign media to go up to the front gate because, in the back of the base, Sergeant Larose Aubain started a bonfire. This was to be a re-enactment of the August 14, 1791, Vodou Ceremony led by Boukman at Bwa Kayiman. It was the site where the first major slave insurrection of the Haitian Revolution was planned.

In a matter of moments hundreds of the men were all lined up in the back by this now raging fire. There were huge flames and men running to the rear of the base. Then someone shouted, "Zeke, ann ale, (let's go.)" I was asked to participate in the ceremony.

"I'll be damned," Steve said to me with a big smile on his face. He was well aware of what kind of honor was just bestowed on me. As I turned to head all the way to the back of the line a man up front said, "Yo Zeke, here man, come here." And just like that it was my turn to run through or jump over the flames.

Two Haitian journalists documented this spectacle. One was filming and was one snapping photos. I took off with a head full of steam and adrenaline rushing through my veins. I approached the flames and leaped up as high as I could to get over them. It was electrifying. I was covered in goosebumps. I was incredibly moved to be asked by these men to take part in the re-enactment of such a ceremony. A ceremony initiated in the first place to cut off the heads of their white French slave captors. I was treading on sacred ground and I felt it in my bones. The men were in a frenzy. It

344

was immediately a top-five moment of my life. I couldn't help but think of the scene in the movie *Glory* when the once-racist white soldier shouts to the black troops, "Give em hell 54." I was with all these men of color in the military base at Lamentin 54. For me this was my destiny fulfilled.

I was then asked by the eight sergeants in charge of the base to be in the lead vehicle for the march. I was told I would be flanked on both sides with several motorcycles. News had already come in that U.N. vehicles awaited us a couple of miles down the road. I proudly took the charge upon myself and agreed to lead the march.

Jeff Trunell had originally planned on covering this event but couldn't make it. Ben Depp, who was one of the foreign journalists present, requested that I transport personal things he had with him, which I obliged. Ben was a really good guy so it was my pleasure.

As we started out of the base that morning Steve and I were in the two lead vehicles joined by dozens of military men on motorcycles. Ingrid Arnesen of *The Wall Street Journal* was late arriving and in passing I told her I was asked to be the lead vehicle. Not too far down the road my eyes lit up. My girlfriend, Darline, was making her way across the street, eerily similar to how I originally met her. I called out to her and said come on, come with me. She told me her mom sent her on an errand and I said, "Fuck your mom, come on, you're coming with me today."

Darline knew wherever I was, "shit was happening." She once told Sperlif she loved going out in public with me because whatever the venue, "the shit was live when Zeke was there." She said being with me was exciting. She hopped in the front seat and rode shotgun with me.

As we got closer to the armored personnel carriers flanked by scores of U.N. troops on the ground we made the decision to keep going right through them. We had numbers on our side. The crowds of people in the street were now taunting and jeering the blue helmets, calling them all kinds of foul things. We were now in the thick of it. The shit was real. We left those U.N. troops behind in Carrefour and continued on towards Martissant. Soon we would pass by Portail Leogane.

As we approached Sylvio Cator Stadium all the former sergeants responsible for this march on the capital walked right in front of my vehicle, which was now overloaded. A car that seated five comfortably was

345

now hauling sixteen people. I had men standing on the running boards on both sides, and others clinging to the back standing on the bumper. Steve's truck behind me was packed down the same way. The closer we got to downtown, the more hectic things got. The crowds were in a frenzied state seeing all the men in olive green uniforms thumb their noses at the blue helmets. At one intersection past the stadium after the Grand Cemetery, five blue helmets were on patrol. They stood outside of their Humvee with their M-16s in hand. Rocks started to fly in their direction. At this point the crowds were so thick, we proceeded very slowly. I called Charlito Baker to let him know what was going on. I always tried to keep him abreast of current happenings in the country out of respect for his being a presidential candidate. I hung up with him and put the car in park. This is where my weakness of showing pity was in full effect.

I hurried across the street to tell these blue helmets to put their guns out of sight and to get the fuck gone. I said, "If you guys as much as show any aggression at all, y'all will die here today." They spoke Spanish and broken English. But they understood exactly what I conveyed. Five of them against all of us, plus the Haitian civilian population wasn't a fair fight. I was a man of honor who observed a code in this case.

Getting out of my vehicle to warn these guys was the worst thing I could have done in that situation, however.

Someone from the crowd hurled a large rock. It skipped hard on the pavement, hit my left shin, and ricocheted off my right shin as I turned back toward the vehicle. I was bleeding from my left leg and cursing at the crowd for reverting to throwing stones. I looked back over my shoulder and the blue helmets were high-tailing it the hell out of there, speeding off down the road towards the General Hospital.

I limped back to my vehicle, pushing my way through the crazed crowd of spectators that were now flooding the streets. I started the car and we continued on. Our planned destination was the front of the Presidential Palace that was still in ruins. As we got closer word came in that the exterior of the palace grounds were blocked off by dozens of U.N. troops with armored carriers. The sergeants in command decided against a confrontation with those blue helmets and stopped short of the Palace.

Sergeant Lafalaise gave a speech to the press and a wreath was laid at the statue of Dessalines at Champ de Mars. The men in olive green uniforms didn't stop there. They put on a marching display as the crowds cheered. I stayed behind in my vehicle with Darline and a couple of the Haitian troops, one of whom was suffering from a medical condition and having trouble breathing.

This is where things deteriorated.

I lost visuals on all of the men in command of these former soldiers and aspiring recruits. They disappeared from my sight after the marching display ended. Neither Steve nor I were going to leave our vehicles in downtown Port-au-Prince in the midst of this raucousness. The crowds continued to taunt and jeer the blue helmets and then rocks flew from every direction. The people were urging the men in olive green to confront the blue helmets. They wanted to see a fight. The last individual I saw from the base's hierarchy at Lamentin was Sergeant David Dorme. I ran over in his direction as soon as I caught a glimpse of him. David was one of the few that were actually armed, and he had his own team of security around him.

"What are we going to do from here?" I said.

"We are going back to Lamentin right now," he told me.

While we talked, crowds of young men were imploring the Haitian troops to confront the U.N. troops in front of the National Palace grounds. Dorme said, "We didn't come here for a confrontation."

In my mind, I was thinking that's not the message I received from the likes of Sergeant Lafalaise. He said it was the Haitian military or death. I remembered Sergeant Jeudy proclaiming that May 18 was the deadline for Martelly to reinstate the FAD'H Troops. I believed we were there to pick a fight. A fight where God would be our right hand.

I stared at Dorme, waiting for something more concrete. Before he could answer I said, "You mean we came all the way down here to just tuck tail and go back home?"

"Zeke," Dorme said, "we don't have the capabilities right now to stand up to this U.N. force. We didn't come for this we are going back."

I was taken aback by this declaration from Dorme. This moment of clarity – that the Blue Helmets had too much fire power coupled by the fact that they were also backed by The Haitian National Police Force – came a little too late for me. Dorme and others saw that we didn't get the push from the people that they we were hoping for and anticipating. Crowds came, people jeered and threw rocks, but the population didn't swell like that of an old President Aristide march in the early 1990s. Without that kind of support from the population it was a losing cause. We even lacked numbers of men in olive green. Hundreds of them didn't even show up for the march. I could hear Lynn Garrison's voice saying to me, "Zeke, Haitians are puppy dogs compared to Afghanies."

For myself I always had a heart like one of King David's Mighty Men. I would have been like Eleazar who taunted the Philistines into battle, and who, even after the rest of his men had retreated, kept on fighting until his hand was frozen to the sword. And won. I couldn't find a Haitian on this day who had that kind of heart. I was looking to pick a fight with the bullies wearing blue helmets knowing that God was my hammer. I knew that God was on my side, and just having the courage to show up He would swallow the U.N. troops just as He did Pharaoh's Egyptian Army in the Red Sea. Every warrior hopes a good death will find him. Perhaps that is what I was looking for? My twenty-one-year crusade in Haiti was about to come to an end. This was the last time I ever saw Dorme.

I went over to Steve to inform him that we were going back to Carrefour. I gave him the opportunity to cut and run and head back to his home in Mais Gate. I said, "You're good to go, bro, I no longer need you. Let these motherfuckers walk back to Carrefour." I was now waving people to get out of Steve's truck. Steve said, "No Zeke, I'm good, I'm good. I'll drive back to Carrefour with you." There was mass hysteria all around us. Rocks continued to fly and we heard gunfire just blocks over from us. We had stirred up the hornets' nest, and they were not going to let us walk away. It was now every man for himself.

As we started to head out of town Steve's black Toyota T100 pickup truck began to overheat and it was several minutes before he could find water to cool it down. By this time it was around three p.m. We got moving again, and then a tear gas canister hit my front windshield. Gunfire rang out. Then another loud bang, and another one. We had been given the gas from two different directions. More gunfire rang out. I immediately put the car in park and jumped out. I couldn't see anything. I started

348

coughing intensely. My eyes were watering. It was a suffocating sensation. We had been ambushed and never saw it coming. A special Haitian police unit called SIMO had surrounded us on both ends of the street we were traveling on. They gave the gas which disoriented all of our members, it wiped out any visibility, and then they overwhelmed us quickly.

A large hand came down on the back of my neck, forcing me to the ground. I shouted out "Pozew!" meaning relax. "Motherfucker, respect me, you let me walk," I said. This guy was probably six foot three, pretty well built, and had mitts for hands. He led me to a caged police vehicle and forced me inside with his hand on the back of my neck the entire way.

GOODBYE TO FREEDOM

Steve was taken to the ground and manhandled by SIMO members in heavy body armor. All around us this special unit was beating and tying up Haitians in olive green uniforms. I composed myself quickly as I sat down in this caged vehicle. They asked for the key to my 4Runner. I handed it over with the barrel of a shotgun right in my face. One after another of the Haitians in green uniforms were thrown into the enclosure with me. They all looked scared to death. Both Steve and Darline had been apprehended on the other side of the road. The officer that drove my vehicle allowed Darline the courtesy of riding up in the front passenger seat while Steve was laid in the back of his truck, tied up like an animal.

When they started to drive us away, I called Moloskot. He told me he was on a boat in the ocean coming back from La Gonave. I told him what happened and said, "Do what you can brother. Don't forget me."

We were transported to a place called Commissariat Pompier de Port-au-Prince, a police station, where the fire department was housed, and the offices of Secretary of Public Security Reginald Delva were located. Temporary holding cells for people taken into custody by Haitian police could be found here too. When we arrived at Pompier they made us all line up with our hands placed behind our heads. Members of the Haitian media were present and ran in to capture photos for their respective newspapers. Steve and Darline were farther up the line, and I was all the way in the back. One by one they frisked each person and made them remove their shoes.

When I finally got to the front one of the officers said, "Zeke, what are you doing here, man?" I told him it was a long story. Out of respect for me he didn't frisk me or require me to take off my shoes. Haitian special units had often seen me out in action alongside of them during times of crisis when I was working with foreign journalists. They had seen me with Baker, they saw me in Cabaret, they watched me walk with President Duvalier, they heard me speak on the radio. Some of them were dismayed by the fact that I was being arrested and treated like a common criminal.

Every Haitian in olive green arrested, including Darline and a couple of other civilians, were placed in the holding cells. Steve and I were abruptly whisked away and taken upstairs to Reginald Delva's office. In that moment neither Steve nor I had any clue who Delva was. Delva came into the office asking for any identification. They had already confiscated Steve's ID when he was frisked downstairs. I still had mine, so I handed it over.

Delva paused to look at my license. Then he bellowed, "Jason William Petrie from the Great State of Ohio."

Without hesitation, I responded, "You're goddamn right, you better fucking believe it. It's the greatest state in the union. You're fortunate to be in the presence of an Ohioan."

See, Uncle Tom Haitians are always bending over backwards to try and impress the white man. In this case I think Delva was trying to show off his English and his knowledge of my country back home. I wasn't impressed.

I then started to undress him verbally after I was made aware that he was indeed the secretary of public security. I went on a tangent in Haitian Creole telling him how he and those like him should be ashamed of themselves for the current state of affairs in Port-au-Prince. He was very surprised. Delva was taken off guard and blown away by what came out of my mouth. No ordinary blan was in his presence today. He grew angry and then went on a tirade of his own.

"I see that you are more Haitian than I am. You speak better Creole than I do. What do you say? I'm going to send for a judge right this minute. You can revoke your U.S. citizenship right now and become Haitian. That's what you want isn't it?"

350

Of course, Delva knew that had I been foolish enough to commit such an act, it would mean certain death for me. Delva then took a phone call in which he responded, "Yes, your excellence." He was now on the phone with President Martelly. He kept repeating, "Tout afe, all things, everything!" He mentioned having us moved so that the press wouldn't know where we were located. Then Martelly asked him something, Delva looked over at me, and knowing I was too fluent in his native tongue, hurriedly got up and left the room to give his answer away from my presence. As he exited, he placed a guard in the room with Steve and me. I told Steve to distract the man so I could make some phone calls. Delva was not aware that I had a cell phone. I told the guard I had to use the bathroom. Connected to Delva's office was a room with a toilet where I made phone calls. I called Susette Manassero. I told her what had become of Steve and me. She told me that she was currently with Soledad O'Brien of CNN. I asked of her about getting me some needles, insulin, and alcohol swabs. I said, "If you don't find us at Pompier, check the Canapé Vert station." I called Ben Depp and Seanna McLeod and requested the same. Finally, I called Louino Robillard from Cite Soleil. I told him what happened and asked if he could post it on Facebook for me so that everyone on my page could be made aware of my current situation.

Delva finally came back with a couple of other men to move us to Canapé Vert so the press didn't know we were taken. Unknown to Delva, I had already alerted the entire world. My gut instinct and suspicions of being moved to Canapé Vert were spot on. As we were led out of his office nightfall was upon us. While slowly walking down the stairs back to ground level I thought about quickly removing the memory card from my phone and hiding it on me. At this point I didn't know what was going to become of us. I didn't know if I'd be able to continue hiding the phone. In a matter of moments, they put both me and Steve through an extensive pat down. My phone was seized with the memory card inside. Delva overhead the men saying the blan had a phone on him. He was enraged.

The men working at Pompier that night got a real treat. They were given some great theater to take in. Steve and I gave them a small taste of Butch Cassidy and The Sundance Kid in our attitudes and the way we conducted ourselves.

Not soon long after we arrived at the Canapé Vert police station some of the people that I had sent out distress calls to started showing up. Ben Depp appeared with his wife. Seanna McLeod was Johnny-on-the-spot. A young man named Jack Strutner, who was at the time dating Susette's daughter Ari, also showed up. I was surprised to see him. I was expecting Sue and Soledad to come. I knew Jack, and I liked him, so it made no difference to me. Everyone brought life-saving necessities. Steve and I both thought that by next morning we would be released.

Not so fast.

The Commissioner of the Haitian Government came in, surrounded by his security and a female secretary. Jean Renel Senatus, a.k.a. Zokiki himself. Senatus was flamboyant and cocky in my observation. He called me and Steve out of the cell to answer a few questions. Steve went first. He answered the questions in a cooperative manner and was returned to the cell.

I was summoned and in no mood to cooperate. The personal secretary that Senatus had writing down our responses was very ignorant, in my estimation. I was quickly annoyed by her presence. As she was struggling to write my name correctly, I barked at both of them to give me the paper and pen to let me write the information they needed. "I have no tolerance for incompetence of this nature," I said. "Can we just do this in Haitian Creole to simplify everything?"

This really pissed Senatus off. I didn't care because to me, he was a little arrogant prick with weak credentials on his resume. I dismissed myself from the table we were sitting at and a guard quickly rushed over to put his hands on me to direct me back to the cell. Senatus instructed the guard to seize my necklace and earrings, but I refused to let him. At this point another guard came over to remind me that I was now under the authority of the Haitian National Police and that it would be in my best interest to follow instructions. My rebuttal to them was, "You already have a few things of mine back at Pompier downtown. My car, my license, my phone, and my girlfriend. I better get all of them back the same way you received them today." I said this with great authority as though I was the one in charge. I slowly removed my earrings and my necklace and said to the men in the room, "Am I not generous?" Knowing Haitians only respect brute force I blitzed them verbally. Feed them and beat them was how things were done in this country of Haiti.

Because Senatus was now good and pissed off at me, he was going to go out of his way to make everyone as uncomfortable as possible. Because of his contempt for me he ordered the guards at the Canapé Vert jail to hold Ben, Seanna, and Jack for the next twenty-four hours until they could be further questioned by authorities to see what their relationship was to me. This upset everyone, especially loved ones, which meant more pressure falling on my shoulders. I spent a long night on that hard floor not knowing what was coming the next day. On the inside, I was thinking the worst, but outwardly I portrayed all the confidence in the world that everything was going to be just fine.

During our time in the cell on Saturday I was running my mouth to the guards calling them Uncle Toms. Two Americans who were working for the U.N. police force in Haiti showed up to interview me and Steve. They spoke to us separately. I mentioned to them that I had verbally sparred with Reginald Delva the night before. That made both of them pause and glance at each other with a look of astonishment. One said to the other, "Man you don't want to piss Reggie off, oh man!" Well, it was too late for that. I missed that memo. Trenton Daniel from the Associated Press came over to talk with me and Steve. He recorded us and did a short film of our answers. I think that Trenton thought that we were potentially in deep water, as did I.

We awaited the appearance of Senatus at Canapé Vert on Saturday. He was busy running around the military base at Lamentin 54 with the Haitian police answering questions for the media. He also went out of his way to stop off at Pompier, where he went in specifically to ask for the girlfriend of this white man named Zeke. "The blan with the tattoos that everyone calls Zeke, show me the girl that is with him," he said. Officials at Pompier pointed to Darline in the cell. Senatus called her to stand in front of him. He looked her up and down and said, "So, you are Zeke's Zokiki." Jean Renel Senatus had gained the nickname of Zokiki, which refers to juvenile delinquency, because of his campaign against underage prostitution, clubbing, and men who had sex with underage girls. Darline was twenty, so he had no case against me. Remember, in Haiti nothing is ever as it appears to be. Senatus had a wife and three daughters living in the United States. He was no different than any other Haitian in a seat of power and influence. Knowing Haiti like I did, I knew that whatever Senatus fought against publicly, he himself was living privately. Do as I say not as I do. At one point the night before he joked about how he needed to get to the beach and relax. A Haitian man in a position of power was not going to the beach alone. Senatus could fool the ignorant, but he wasn't fooling me, and he knew this. His desire to cause me as much grief as possible was his main objective.

Finally, during the late evening on Saturday Senatus decided to show up fashionably late at the Canapé Vert jail. By this time the family and friends of the foreigners being detained because of me were all present and growing restless. One by one Senatus called them to a back office in the building to be questioned. After he was done with them, he called on Steve to answer questions. After what seemed like forever Steve came back to the cell.

It was now time for the "Main Event." The room where the interrogations were happening was filled to capacity by the time I got there. It was standing room only. Senatus was present. A judge was present. An individual keeping manuscripts was present. Two of Senatus' security team were standing directly behind me. Several of their lawyers were present. It was probably a 10-1 ratio bad guys to good guy. As the questioning got under way I was as defiant as I've ever been in my life.

Senatus asked me where I was residing while in Haiti. I simply responded, "When you are a chief, you never sleep in the same location more than two nights in a row. I said you already know this I'm sure. You are a chief, aren't you?"

I was not, under any circumstances, going to give him the address of where I was residing in Lamentin 54. I didn't want them raiding my place and getting their blood-stained hands on any of my personal things, especially my laptop. If they got my laptop they could get to my email. If they got to my email, they could get to messages soliciting support for the guys in olive green.

Senatus said, "So let me get this straight, you can be found wherever things are hot? Correct? That's where we can find you Zeke?"

I scanned the room over and said, "Surely this seems like unfair odds in your favor, doesn't it? I'm a guest in your country, where are your manners? Should I not be allowed a witness during this questioning? It's all of you against me in here. You all can just simply lie on me and I'd have no chance. Where is your honor you sons of Capois La Mort?"

And I recounted the story of Francois Capois, a Haitian officer in the Haitian revolution. He is mostly known for his extraordinary courage and especially his Herculean bravery at the Battle of Vertieres in which the French General Rochambeau, commander of Napoleon's army in Saint-Domingue (Colonial Haiti), called a brief cease-fire to congratulate him.

On November 18, 1803, Jean-Jacque Dessalines had ordered Capois to take Vertieres, a fort situated upon a mount. Capois La Mort advanced with a demi-brigade which, horribly mutilated, soon recoiled before the cannon fire coming from the fort. He led it back for a second time, but was again driven to the bottom of the hill by the mitrailleuse. Boiling with rage, Capois ran to seek other new troops. Mounting his horse, he advanced for the third time. Again, the thousand deaths that vomited from the fortress repulsed him and his brigade.

Now for the fourth time, he asked his men to follow him by shouting "Forward! Forward!" While he was at the head of his men, his horse was hit by a cannon ball. He fell, but Capois took his sword, got up, and ran to place himself again at the head of his black soldiers by shouting "Forward! Forward!" His cap, garnished with plumes, was carried away by a shot. He replied to the insult, which left him hatless by drawing his sword and again throwing himself into the assault.

Observing this, Rochambeau and his men shouted "Bravo! Bravo! Bravo!" The firing in the fort ceased. Suddenly, the battle was still. A French staff officer mounted his horse and rode toward the intrepid Capois La Mort. With a great voice he shouted, "General Rochambeau sends compliments to the General who has just covered himself in glory!" Then he saluted the Haitian Warriors, returned to his position and the fight resumed. The next morning, a French officer followed by his companions led to the headquarters of the Haitian army a horse caparisoned, and delivered with him these words: "The Captain General (Rochambeau) offers this horse as a mark of admiration to the 'Black Achilles' to replace the one of his that the French army regrets having killed."

On October 8, 1806, Capois was on his way to Cap Haitian when, near Limonade, he rode into a trap set for him, and was killed by assassins on the orders of Henri Christophe."

From Wikipedia

When I decided to go on this journey and write this book, I had a few goals in mind. One of them was to share this great story and to do it in proper context concerning all things Haiti. In Haiti, if you're a person of consequence, at some point the Haitians will destroy you. And they will do it when you least expect it. When you have a nation full of people that are in constant debt to the Shango, "The Vodou God of Thunder and Lightning" noted for his anger, it's the ones that are most visible, the ones with the greatest valor that fetch the highest price.

Se yon peyi trayi san – it's a country of men that betray their own blood. Creole pale Creole Fucking Koprann! Med!

I then said, "I shall be given a witness right now or I refuse to say anymore."

Senatus said with a hardy laugh, "Sure blan, you can have your witness."

I knew before I entered the room that CNN's Soledad O'Brien was standing outside. She had come with Susette to retrieve Jack. I was led out of the room by the security detail for Senatus to handpick a witness. I pointed to Soledad, who stood across the way from me. She wasn't going to turn down the opportunity, and she quickly agreed. While Senatus was playing checkers, I was playing chess. Senatus then asked me how often I had been over to the military base at Lamentin 54. I responded in Haitian Creole, "De tanz a tan," meaning, "From time to time."

He then said, "Where did you get this FAD'H military shirt you are wearing?"

"Sergeant Yves Jeudy gave it to me Friday morning."

"The same Sergeant Jeudy that told us you and Steve were both training the Haitian troops?"

I responded, "If, in fact Jeudy said that, he's lying. But I don't believe that he said that at all."

Senatus then said, "As often as you went to this base surely you were doing some kind of work in there."

I said, "First off, I only visited the base from time to time."

"Senatus said no, you just told us you were there often."

"I said no, the word often in your language is souvan. I said de tanz a tan."

We then had a heated exchange of words as Senatus was trying to manipulate the process. I slammed my hand down hard on the table and said, "G-- damn you all in this room for sitting there silent as this man is lying. Souvan is often, I said de tanz a tan, which means from time to time."

Senatus then quickly reprimanded me and said, "Do not raise your voice to the judge like that again or I'll have my guards put their hands on you. I know you want to jump across the table onto the honorable judge we have in our presence tonight. That's why I have two security agents standing directly behind you."

I kept scanning the room in disbelief that of all the Haitians present, not one would speak up and tell the truth. Finally, a light skinned Haitian lawyer in back of the room spoke up as he cleared his voice. He said to everyone in the room, "Let's be serious, Zeke is right, we all know what he is saying is true."

Senatus started to laugh aloud. He said, "Hold on hold on. Where did this blan come from? He knows my country better than I do. He speaks Creole better than I do. How can this be possible? He must be CIA."

Soledad, who had an interpreter of her own, was furiously taking notes trying to keep up. She then asked Senatus for permission to start running a voice recorder. When I heard this request, I became enraged. I was pissed off that she hadn't taken the liberty to start recording from the minute she stepped into the room. Nobody would have known the difference. As Senatus started to tell Soledad no, I said, "Ah hell, hell no! You've been in here all this damn time and now you want to start recording? Get the hell outta here." I was so angry with her. I then went on a rant to justify who I was.

I said, "I'm an individual who is about inclusion not exclusion. I'm friends with many of the men from the old military just like I was friends with the late Billy and Tupac from Cite Soleil. I accused the Haitian government of using young men like Billy and his brother Pac. When they were no longer of any use, the government would have them killed like dogs. "This emphatic statement was met by whispers in the room of people saying where does this man come from? He knows and understands how things work here. He knows Haiti!"

Senatus took this information and ran with it. He started accusing me of being a gangster involved in kidnappings, killings, and attempted murder of a Haitian police officer. He followed that with an accusation, and charges against me of wanting to overthrow the Haitian government. He said I was a threat to the security of the state. For this accusation I was probably guilty, but only because I wanted what was best for the Haitian people.

I looked at Soledad and said, "I can see where this is going. This is how Haitian politics and Haitian justice functions." I finally said, "I have nothing else to say."

I immediately stood so they could hurry up and take me out of the room. They gave me a pen to sign the paperwork concerning my interrogation. I defiantly signed it. When Soledad was asked to sign it, she refused, and said that she would need a full translation before doing so.

As I was heading out the doorway Senatus called me back in. He said, "Remove that shirt you're wearing with the FAD'H on it and give it to me."

I responded, "Well, just like the soccer players do after games we will exchange shirts. I'll give you mine and you give me yours. Since I kicked your ass in this debate tonight let me give you this shirt off my back. Surely your wife will like to have it as a souvenir."

He of course refused to give me his shirt. I went out of my way to reach

358

out to shake his hand and surprisingly, he took my hand and shook it. As I walked out of the room, shirtless, I said to Soledad O'Brien, "You must have a heart of steel to live with these people."

After the interrogation was over Senatus agreed to release all the parties being held because of me. Before Seanna McLeod left I called her over to my cell. I gave to her the Masonic ring of my grandfather Petrie along with his watch that no longer worked. I had been hiding them on me since I was taken into custody Friday afternoon. I asked her to please hold onto them for me. She agreed and prepared to leave with everyone else. I could feel that they were all pretty upset about the entire ordeal. I felt a lot of pressure because of this. I was really uncomfortable as I watched them all walk past my cell as they left. Ben passed by to offer his well wishes. It was difficult watching young Jack leave with the Manassero family. I felt the worst for them. No words – not even a look in my direction – as they exited the Canapé Vert jail. That was the first time I really felt alone in that situation, but I understood. I had put them through a lot of grief. They had all sacrificed reaching out to offer assistance in my time of need just twenty-four hours earlier. They paid a heavy emotional price for which I regret. It was on this night that I knew I wasn't going anywhere anytime soon.

Early the next morning Steve, another prisoner, and I were led one by one to a room next to our cell to bathe. There was no door and you bathed in full view of all the guards. I was the last man up and I needed to give my insulin. My sugar was high. I had asked to wash my hands first. The guard assigned to me wanted to play tough guy, and refused my request. I told him I was diabetic and needed insulin and had to clean my hands in this shit hole before I injected myself. This guard then put his hands on me to push me into the designated bathroom. He said you can wash your hands while you bathe. I stood my ground and we were caught up together in a violent struggle. I hadn't slept in two nights and had barely eaten anything. This guard had just shown up for the first time early that morning for his shift. He was in full gear with a club in hand. He got some leverage on me and shoved me down hard to the floor. Other guards ran over to assist and started yelling out, "Relax blan, relax man." I was hurting and angry. My fight was just beginning. I got my shower, finally gave my insulin, and went back into the cell to lay down.

Steve was in scramble mode this morning. He was able to secretively make a phone call from inside of our cell. A friend of his that came to visit passed it into him under the noses of the guards. Steve called some neighbors in the Mais Gate neighborhood where he lived to have them immediately remove a couple of firearms from his apartment that were not registered with the Haitian government – in effect making them illegal. Steve had nothing to hide so he had given Senatus the address to where he was staying. He forgot about the guns, however. Those guns were removed just in time because that afternoon the Haitian police raided and flipped the place upside down looking for evidence to use against Steve. Had those guns been found it would have really put us in a bad spot. I then took advantage of the opportunity to call a close friend of mine back in the states. I had him change my email passcode right away. If Haitian authorities were to get their hands on my laptop, I needed an insurance policy.

Next, two U.S. Embassy personnel came to see me and Steve. They asked us how we were being treated. They provided a list of lawyers. As they walked out I left them with some parting words for President Barak Obama. I said, "Tell Obama that he is very ungrateful. He was elected the first black president in the history of the United States, and yet never had the decency to come to Haiti to thank the Haitian people for bestowing upon him that opportunity. Without the Haitian fight for freedom there would have never been a Barack Obama. Tell Obama he is without shame. Tell him he is shameless. Do that for me!"

Before the day was over one of Seanna's friends named Lesli Zoe Petit-Phar brought me clothes, even though we weren't exactly the same size. I appreciated the gesture. It reminded me of what I learned back in Sunday school as a young kid. Matthew 25:36 says "I needed clothes and you clothed me, I was sick, and you looked after me, I was in prison and you came to visit me." Hebrews 13:3 reads: "Continue to remember those in prison as if you were together with them in prison, and those who are mistreated as if you yourselves were suffering." Thanks Zoe! I haven't forgotten.

Monday morning came and Steve and I were looking for something definitive to happen. I was growing more impatient. I started getting vocal in the cell towards all the police officers in the building. Especially towards the one who put his hands on me the day before. I started to rip them for their cowardice. I called them "Uncle Tom suck asses for the white man." I unleashed the same rhetoric and truth I had spit on the radio a few times before. Before I could finish, I glanced over at Steve. He was giving me a death stare and told me to shut the fuck up. Nothing else needed to be said. Steve demanded my respect. He was my elder, a hardcore veteran of Haiti, and he was only there because of his friendship to me.

It was late morning when a special unit of the Haitian authorities was sent to escort me and Steve out of the Canapé Vert jail. As we walked out one of Haitian police officers, an older gentleman, walked alongside of me and spoke quietly. He said, "I appreciated watching and listening to you over the last couple days. All of the things which you speak are a sad reality of my country. Let me apologize to you on behalf of my countrymen." He patted me on my shoulder as I was led away in cuffs. This gesture in that moment meant everything to me. I needed the encouragement badly. I was up against it.

We were whisked away back down to Pompier. After a quick stop there we were taken to the Paquet (Tribunal) in Port-au-Prince.

After arriving at the Paquet they put us in a holding cell. With the addition of me and Steve, there were forty-five men and eight women in there. All of us had been arrested on Friday afternoon and held in different locations. This cell, now occupied by fifty-three people, was divided into two sections. The men on one side, the women on the other. To my astonishment I heard Darline's voice. I was looking around and everyone in the cell was pointing over in the direction where the cell was split in half. Darline was looking right at me excitedly waving me over to her. I rushed over to her and kissed her through the dividing cell bars. That was such a delicious moment for me. Darline was a sight for sore eyes.

I heard my name called out again. In the very back corner of the cell sat Sergeant Larose Aubain. He was a shell of himself and was tended to by some of the other men. On Friday night he was beaten badly by Haitian police. When Larose and the men tried to return to the Lamentin base they were cut off and surrounded by Haitian National Police units and U.N. forces in a joint operation. Larose suffered blows to his abdomen and

361

testicles. He took a blow to his eye in the melee. That night gunfire was exchanged, and a Haitian police officer was assaulted. This is where Steve and I had the attempted murder of a Haitian police officer charge added to our dossier of charges against us.

Looking upon Larose in that instance I felt a sadness fall over me. Seeing such a proud soldier in that predicament was difficult for me to stomach. He recounted to me in detail the beating that was handed out to him by men that were most likely in diapers when he was a sergeant in the old Haitian military. This made me angry. Before I could share the details of my own arrest, I was summoned to the doorway of the cell by a security agent who placed cuffs on me. I looked at Steve and asked him to keep an eye on Darline for me.

I was led away with this agent's hand firmly on the back of my shoulder as he steered me to Commissioner Jean Renel Senatus's office. There were media posted outside his office door as I approached. I was led inside and made to sit across from the commissioner's desk. The armed agent had his hand on my back. Other people brought messages for Senatus as he fielded some phone calls. I sat for a few minutes going out of my way to make eye contact with him before he finally acknowledged my presence in the room. His first words to me were, "What is your relationship to Guy Philippe?"

Guy, from Pestel, was a former police chief in the late 1990s. In 2004 he led the invasion force that toppled President Aristide's government, albeit with an assist from American Special Forces. Guy was affiliated and close with many of the old Haitian military men although he himself was never formerly part of the old Haitian military. In 1992 Guy had received a scholarship from the Haitian Armed Forces to attend Ecuador's police academy where he graduated in 1995. By the time he returned back to Haiti the FAD'H had already been dismantled. He was assigned to the newly created Haiti National Police Force.

I responded to Senatus that I was friends with Guy on Facebook. I admitted that I had been to Pestel many years before and had been with the old military members when they were on the phone with Guy. But as for me and any relationship to him there was none. Guy knew who I was, I knew who he was, but we never once spoke. I was told that Guy had his suspicions that I was sent by the DEA to get coordinates on him since

362

he was a wanted man by U.S. law enforcement. Senatus said, "Ou manti, (you're lying)." I just laughed. I said, "Do you want me to lie? Is that why you asked me in here? Did you not get enough of me on Saturday night?"

Then Senatus received a note from a young teenage girl and made a phone call. I can only assume he was talking with someone in Haitian law enforcement on the other end of the line. He said the girl had informed him that her father was forcing her to have sex with him. He said the girl's father was currently at the home address and ordered him to be arrested. Senatus then said, "After you arrest him execute him."

He issued this order right in front of me, glancing in my direction. It was done to flex his muscle and show me who was boss and who was in charge.

When he got off the phone he returned to the question of where I resided in Haiti. I looked dead in his eye. I said, "I have no home here. Robin Hood sleeps only where the good folks that he takes care of give him to lay his head."

Senatus quickly motioned for the security agent to remove me from his presence. As I was leaving his office he again said, "Ou manti, you're lying!" I responded, "You can't handle the truth Zokiki."

We were all placed in the back of armored police vehicles that were sort of like paddy wagons, but much more sadistic in nature. The inside was very dark. There was no light and no air coming through. The feeling of claustrophobia was overwhelming. We were all sweating profusely. At this point we were not yet made aware of where they were sending us. The ride was very bumpy, and at times it felt as though the vehicle was going to tip during some of the violent turns made. The sirens on these vehicles rang out through the streets. When we finally arrived at our destination, I could feel that we were entering some sort of fortified structure. We went through one gated entrance that slammed hard behind us. It was only when they let us out of the armored vehicle one by one that I finally knew where we were. We weren't in Kansas anymore.

Steve and I were now guests at the National Haitian Penitentiary. Just two weeks earlier I was visiting Mackenson St. Fleur, a.k.a. JhaJha, a son of Cite Soleil via Jeremie. Jha was like a little brother to me. I was helping to take care of his needs while he was in prison. I gave to him a $100 on this

363

day. As I stood outside the prison that morning to see him, I asked Darline if she would stand in these long lines waiting to see me like all these poor women do every day. She said, "Yes!" I said no you wouldn't. In an ironic twist of fate we were now both standing inside of those same prison walls, as prisoners of the state.

Darline and the other seven females that had been arrested were moved to the Women's Penitentiary in Petionville later that evening.

Those penitentiary doors opened and swallowed us. I remember there was a big black female dressed in uniform filming us on her phone. The prison guards were having a field day. The guards were very loud and physically aggressive, throwing around and manhandling some of the guys while talking all kinds of shit. They were mocking the ex-military soldiers in their olive-green uniforms. I remember looking back at Larose and seeing a guard in his face demeaning him verbally and mock saluting him.

Then I felt a hand violently slap down on my neck and yank me over and the guard asked me what my problem was. The same guard then shoved Steve up against a wall. I looked at Steve and he at me. We both knew how fortunate this fucker was. Had we been on the outside this poor fella wouldn't have seen another sunrise. We would have killed him.

We were made to strip out of our clothes and our socks. They made all the men in green uniforms put their clothing in one pile. Then the guards went out of their way to verbally abuse us about what we'd have to endure sexually that night from the other men. This reduced some of the men to tears. The Haitian Penitentiary can be very intimidating for the most hardcore criminals and killers.

There were two holding cells they used for the forty-five of us. Steve and I were both placed in a twelve by fifteen-foot cell with twenty-four other men. A cell only designed for a handful of grown men. They jammed us in there good. Steve and I slept in shifts. One of us would sit crammed in a tight spot while the other one carved out a small spot on the cement floor to lay down. Feet in your face, feet kicking you in your groin area. Guys pissing in small bottles every so often. The stench of souring smelling sweat of men who hadn't bathed since last Thursday. It was miserable trying to sleep. We both now realized that the cell at Canapé Vert was like a five-star hotel in comparison. That was a long first night in the penitentiary.

364

PART FOUR - LIVING AND DYING

We had been arrested on Friday afternoon. It was now Tuesday morning. The adrenaline was still running high and that's what was keeping us alert. We had been running on very little sleep the last four nights. On this morning I heard someone calling my name. It was JhaJha calling out to me from another section of the prison behind some gates. He couldn't believe I was in there. He yelled over to me that he was going to fetch some toothbrushes and tooth paste for me and Steve. On this morning our prison dossiers were being put together. Things like our height and weight were documented. I measured in at five foot ten inches, 185 pounds. Steve measured in at a Lawrence of Arabia-esque five-foot-five, 125 pounds. Our entire torsos were photographed. Even the U.N. sent officers over to take photos of me and Steve. We were issued our prison numbers and these numbers would now be our new names. I was assigned number 12-05-208. Steve's number was 12-05-209.

When I had to go to the bathroom a guard led me into the bowels of the prison. I kept thinking *I hope they have toilet paper where I'm currently headed.* Then an inmate took me into a courtyard full of open air toilets, where dozens of half-naked men were doing their business in the yard. Time just stopped. All eyes were on me. It wasn't every day that a white guy showed up out of thin air in their yard. I slowly walked over to the open-air pit, and in that very instance the stench made me lose any desire to use it at all. I no longer had to go. Things were deteriorating by the hour for us. I turned around and went right back to where I had come from. I told Steve, "It only gets worse from here bro. You won't believe what it looks like behind those walls over there. It's like a small city inside there. The conditions are inhumane. Fucking animals, man!"

Later we were both greeted by an American who was working for the U.N.'s police force in Haiti. His name was Patrick. He was formerly a New York City cop from Brooklyn. He was of lighter skin and Haitian descent. He spoke Creole and English. Unbeknownst to me and Steve he was trying to play the role of private detective hero for the bad guys. We thought he was there on our behalf to see how we were doing. The American flag on his shirt and the fact that he spoke perfect English was misleading. In a matter of minutes we both realized that not only was this guy not on our side, he was proactive in blatantly working against us. He questioned both of us separately with a negative and disrespectful tone, badgering us for answers to his own premeditated questions.

Patrick asked me for contact numbers back in the United States. I gave to him the cell numbers of my mom and my ex-wife Aslyne. I was told well after the fact that one night my ex-wife received a call from an unknown number out of Haiti. The male voice on the other end told her not to go to the press about her ex-husband's imprisonment. I was only left to speculate that it was Camille. Patrick then rifled through our medications. I told him that I used syringes to inject insulin. He questioned the validity of that and started to examine me to implicate me or suggest that I was a drug abuser. Steve had been taking a narcotic for pain. Dengue fever had him bedridden recently. He had medication for cholesterol, acid reflux, and Tylenol for a bad tooth. Patrick claimed they were drugs and Steve was denied the use of them for five days. To add to this my brother Jon said that while at my mom's one day he happened to answer a phone call from the State Department. The individual asked my brother about my military service in the U.S. Armed Forces. Jon responded that I was diabetic and had never been in the military. The individual continued to press him for answers as though he was lying. By the hour the shit was getting deeper for us.

We spent Tuesday night cramped in those same holding cells. The next morning one of the elder statesmen from the old military woke up in the cell talking a bunch of bravado bullshit about dying for the Haitian flag. He kept on and on until I couldn't take listening to him anymore. I said, "Shut the fuck up! Do you actually think anyone gives a shit about you and your shit flag right about now? Do you? I don't want to hear another fucking peep about your fucking flag. Just pray to God your old ass gets the fuck out of here alive. Fuck that man!"

On this morning Patrick would return. I was led out of my cell by a female nurse who showed me the way to the infirmary so I could give my insulin. It only took the Haitian authorities five days to start taking my diabetes into half serious account. Up until then they were not allowing me to give my insulin at any set time and sometimes, I wasn't allowed to give it at all. It was very difficult. I ate and drank as little as possible. When I was able to give some insulin, I tried to give as little as possible unless my

366

sugar seemed to be running really high. Low blood sugars were my biggest fear. I couldn't afford that. It was a matter of life and death, literally.

Patrick accompanied me to get my insulin injection. He listened to other inmates from different corners of the prison calling out my name. One inmate housed in a section of the prison called the Brick caught view of me and yelled out, "Zeke, what's up my nigga." Patrick asked how it was possible that all the guys knew me. I said I'd been in this country a long time. As I waited for the nurse, JhaJha walked in. He made a peace sign gesture to me and I returned the same gesture back to him. Patrick immediately chastised me for throwing up gang signs to Jha. He continued to put pressure on me and made things uncomfortable.

That Wednesday afternoon we were all moved to a cell called the Gref. This cell was about sixteen by twenty-two feet with a ceiling fifteen feet high. After being moved into the Gref we once again realized that where we had just come from was paradise in comparison. Counting me and Steve, there were one hundred and eight men in this cell. It was our Haitian Hilton.

The Gref was really dark. The only light shone in from the front door and a far back window. The atmosphere was raucous. The inmates talked all kinds of shit to us newbies. In each cell throughout the prison there was a hierarchy of who was in charge. Steve and I walked all the way to the very back of the cell. There were several bunks stacked three high that were all full. There were many inmates on the floor. In the far left-hand corner the guy running things and sitting on the top bunk was a deportee from Dorchester, Massachusetts. Steve would call him Dorchester. This guy motioned for my meager belongings to be thrown up to him. He then said, "Blan get up here with me" as he hastily scrambled through my stuff. I slowly climbed the ladder up to where he was sitting. He motioned to two other guys in the top bunk to the right side of us to put Steve up with them. It was so hot, and so loud in that cell. Everything was happening so fast.

Dorchester asked if I had anything to give him and when I said no he said, "If you have nothing to provide me with then you go down on the floor with the rest of the maggots."

Larose was sitting across the room from me on a top bunk, watching to see how I would react. Dorchester was very loud and he went out of his

367

way to make sure everyone in the cell could hear him. He was running the cell and he made this clear. When he tried to throw the pillowcase with all my belongings on the ground I put my hands on him with force. I was afraid but said, "I'm not going anywhere. You invited me up here, and this is where I'm going to stay. Do you think I'm just anybody? Do you?"

Dorchester said, "I know who you are. I know you're JhaJha's big brother. But you need to know who I am, and you need to respect me. I run shit in here." I said, "Great, we will get along just fine then."

I had an overwhelming rush of emotion come over me. It was suffocating. Back during Easter at Susette's house in Delmas 75 I wanted to taste what it felt like to be in Jesus's shoes on that night in the Garden of Gethsemane. My God be careful what you wish for. It was hard for me to look at Steve. He was only in this predicament because of me. I felt badly that he was suffering on my account. This became a mental struggle for me. The first night in the Gref was a long one. It was loud and very dark. An inmate in this cell they called Anastasia, who resembled a female, had sex throughout the night with multiple inmates.

The later it got, though, the quieter it became, until there was nothing but silence. I laid there looking up at the ceiling thinking about my two sons. A tear rolled down from my right eye into my earhole. I had already witnessed several grown men cry since my arrest on Friday. This place was not for the faint of heart.

The next morning, we were awakened by a scuffle down at the entrance of the cell. In the early morning hours inmates with work privileges were out and about doing different jobs in this small city that was the penitentiary. A guy named Reggie in our cell had done hard prison time in the states, and he was deported back to Haiti. From the inside of our cell Reggie was having a verbal confrontation with one of the inmates that was out on work privilege duty. The inmate outside the cell had a shovel in his hand. He tried to strike Reggie with it through the opening in the bars of the Gref cell door. Reggie got a hold of the shovel and a violent struggle ensued. The entire cell erupted with sadistic cheers. They wanted to see blood. It felt as though I was a kid watching the gladiators fight in the movie Spartacus. Reggie ripped the shovel from the man's hands and then threw a bag of human waste at him. The man then opened-up the same bag of waste and bathed everyone near the cell door entrance with the contents inside the bag. This threw our cell into a frenzy. The man ran off to another area of the prison. He was very fortunate that nobody could get out of our cell. He would have been killed right there on the spot without hesitation. In the moments directly after the incident I spoke with Reggie at the back of the cell. I wanted to know exactly what happened.

He explained to me how the confrontation started and then said, "Yo, my name's Reggie. And you are Zeke I know. All the guys in the yard have been talking about you for several days now. You're a popular dude."

This was news to me and provided me with some renewed confidence, which I needed. Reggie then said something I will never forget: "Zeke, I would rather do three years in the penitentiary back in the states than to do three months in here. It's a struggle just to survive every day. You must keep your head on a swivel at all times. Don't trust anybody."

Not long after, Jha appeared at the cell entrance and called out to me. Jha was a very popular prisoner who also had privileges. He used certain privileges obtained over the course of his three years of experience in the penitentiary to come get me so I could take my insulin. We headed over to the infirmary where none other than Patrick stood there waiting on cue. Jha quickly said, "Yo I'm out, I don't like him." As I entered the room where my insulin was stored I was greatly surprised to see a young man named Pierre. I knew him by Ti Pierre. That's what we used to call him back in Jeremie a couple of decades ago. On one occasion during the early 90s Ti Pierre had a terrible toothache. It was killing him for several days. One day, in tears, he came over to Phaubert's house where I was staying. He was in so much pain and crying his eyes out. I gave him money for the dentist, who extracted the tooth. He came directly back to Phaubert's to thank me for delivering him from his calamity. Now all these years later our paths crossed in the National Haitian Penitentiary. However, this time it was I who needed him. Ti Pierre couldn't believe his eyes when he gazed upon me. He didn't believe it was the same Zeke that he knew from so many years ago. I didn't have any tattoos back in those days. He informed me that he currently worked in the prison's infirmary. He was responsible for overseeing inmates that were ill with diseases such as tuberculosis. Ti Pierre provided me with some life sustaining protein biscuits that my

369

stomach seemed to tolerate pretty well. I was very happy to see him and comforted by his mere presence.

I went back to my cell with Patrick accompanying me much to my dismay. He was annoying me and I was done with him and I let him know it. We both stood outside of the Gref cell entrance. He watched as scores of other inmates who were mingling in the yard came over to look at my tattoos. I was shirtless after giving my insulin injection in my stomach. Patrick looked on me with great disgust. In his arrogant contempt for me he said, "You're a superstar now. You got what you wanted."

I looked at him and said, "Fuck you, you dirty pussy ass Uncle Tom. Go to hell! I ain't got shit to say to you anymore. Don't come back here again motherfucker. You've been disrespectful to me and Steve. You're not here to help us, you've never been here to help us. So leave us the fuck alone."

He said, "You don't make the rules here." I said, "Fuck you!" At this point I had nothing to lose. They had already taken everything from me. Patrick laughed and went on his way. After re-entering the cell, I told Steve what just transpired. Steve said, "Fuck that piece of shit. If I ever see Patrick outside of these prison walls, I'm going to kick his fucking ass."

JhaJha came back to take me over to the Titanic building where his cell was. He was on the middle floor in a back corner above where the isolation cells were located. Jha had been in prison since April of 2007 when during president Preval's second term in office the Haitian police backed by U.N. Troops were routinely doing raids/sweeps of Cite Soleil neighborhoods indiscriminately arresting young men believed to be gang members. He was a political prisoner. He escaped after the earthquake. He spent two years on the run before he was apprehended in January. His popularity was not just with other inmates but also amongst the guards. This afforded me the chance to make it over to the Titanic and place an international phone call on an undetected cell phone in Jha's cell. I called my friend Tim Widner. I told him as much as I could in the short time I had to speak with him. I stressed to him, "You gotta get us the hell outta here bro. We will die in here." I pleaded with him to get with my brother Ben, and my friend, Donny Pavlik, and make something happen.

After returning to the Gref I was called out again. A prison official came to retrieve me and inform me that I had a visitor. I was escorted over to the same area that I used to come to when I visited Jha in prison. There stood Lisa Nuccio. It had been three months since I last saw Lisa in Naples for my birthday. Emotions rushed over me because the last time I was with her I was also with my two sons. I teared up. Lisa handed me a bag that had some shorts, toiletries, and a pen with a pad. She said she'd be back to see me the next day. I responded, "Tonight I will write you a letter to share with everyone."

That night I was the last one still awake in the cell writing into the early morning hours. I only had a small crack of light coming through the back window of the cell. I positioned myself just right on the top bunk to be able to see well enough to pull that off. It was an emotional twenty-three-page letter that to this very day I regret writing. I came off way too apologetic, way too humble, and way too pathetically sorry. I take it all back today. I said what I said in that letter to gain sympathy and support of those back home. In some instances, I told the truth for what it was, but I should have never portrayed myself to be anything other than what I already was, and that was a rebellious soul who was looking to be a part of some great history in Haiti. I wanted to help the Haitian masses rid themselves of foreigners in their country. It was that simple.

On the day of the May 18 march on the capital demanding the return of the old Haitian military, I never envisioned or even thought about ending up in prison. Not once did any of that cross my mind. I did envision, however, the Haitian people joining in arms with members of the old military. Kinnoch had once said to Gandhi, with respect, "Mr. Gandhi, without British administration, this country would be reduced to chaos." Gandhi said, "Mr. Kinnoch, I beg you to accept that there are no people on earth who would not prefer their own bad government to the good government of an alien one."

So, too, I thought, was the mindset of the Haitian people. I was dead wrong. The more I learned about Haitians the more I realized I knew nothing about them at all. Haitians have been brainwashed by the white foreigners since July of 1915 when the United States 19-year occupation of Haiti began. It's as simple as that.

Early the next morning, while sitting in the top bunk of my cell, the guys on the bottom bunk directly across from me yelled up, "Hey Zeke, Zokiki is talking about you on the TV." They were watching a small handheld radio/TV device. It was a replay of a press conference the day before given by Haiti's Prime Minister Laurent Lamothe, Police Chief Mario Andresol, and a host of other ministers including Secretary of Public Security Reginald Delva, and Commissioner of Haiti's Government Jean Renel Senatus. Steve and I had been alerted that they were looking to give us three years in prison. This was devastating news to me. Soon I was called out of the cell. Lisa was back to visit me again. I took the twenty three-page letter that I stayed up all night writing, folded it up, and put it in my pants. I was escorted over to the chain link fence where Lisa was standing. While staring across at Lisa I motioned to one of the inmates with work privileges on the inside to approach me. Lisa and I were being watched by a couple guards. Every move or gesture we made was scrutinized.

The guy came over to me. I said to him, "I need a service from you right here, right now. I'll take care of you later, just do this for me. I have a twenty-three-page letter in my pants. Come over here and just stand next to me really-close while I continue to talk with the white lady. Stay tight next to me and I'm going to slip this letter onto your person. Then take it over to the blan and give it to her in the same manner."

We were now practically stuck together. As I was sliding the letter underneath a long white shirt that he was wearing he said to me, "Zeke, I want a Walkman radio." I said, "OK, you'll get it. But only if she gets out of here safely with this commission."

He went around to the other side and successfully transferred the paperwork to Lisa. They frisked Lisa coming into the prison, but not going out. Lisa stuffed the bulky paperwork that was folded up right into her underwear. A few weeks later I bragged to one of the other inmates named Pequeno about how I snuck a letter out. He said, "Yo that's nothing Zeke. When my girlfriend comes to visit me, we kiss through the chain linked fence and she passes a Digicel SIM card from her mouth to mine. How do you think we get these cell phones to work in here?"

On Saturday morning Jha came to get me from my cell so I could give my insulin. After leaving the infirmary we made our way over to the Titanic. This gave me the opportunity to make some more phone calls abroad. My feet were really starting to swell so the chance to get out and walk throughout the prison was a godsend for me. The Titanic had its own separate yard where the inmates bathed, used outdoor toilets, and played soccer and basketball. They had a pole erected with a rim attached. There was no backboard, and no net, just a pole and a rim. It felt good to grab a ball and shoot. I started to run around a little bit in a pair of sandals that Lisa had bought me. The exercise was life breathing. Coincidentally on this day I had to use the toilet. I couldn't hold it any longer. It had been eight or nine days since my last bowel movement. Jha took me over to a building which sat across the way from the infirmary that housed nothing, but very ill prisoners contaminated with disease. It was sincerely one of the most grotesque situations of my life. It had a foul stench and housed every sickness and virus imaginable from HIV Aids, to cholera, to tuberculosis. Jha led me into where they had a private toilet. I could barely stomach to look at it. The smell was awful. Even worse I didn't have much toilet paper. Surely, I was not going to sit down anywhere close to it. I tried to half squat down and……….!

And then it happened, I let it all out. I got lightheaded and nearly collapsed because it was so hot in this stall. I was sweating profusely. I was completely drained. There was no soap, and no water to wash my hands. I would have to be getting very used to these types of conditions. In the past I was always OCD about washing my hands especially when I gave my insulin injections. In prison, luxuries like this were non-existent. Early on during my prison stay I wouldn't get out of my cell until late mornings to give my shots. In the evenings they wouldn't let me out of the cell to give my insulin at all. I was on one shot a day at that point.

On Sunday when Jha finally showed up to get me out of my cell in the Gref he told me he was taking me to the Titanic to bathe. This was my first official bath in the Haitian Penitentiary. I had one the Sunday before in the Canapé Vert jail with an audience of prison guards. This time, however, I would have an audience of dozens watching me bathe on the middle floor of the Titanic, right outside of Jha's cell. The men in the cell provided me with a bucket of water to wash my hair and bathe in. I stood there in my Batman boxers bathing in front of a few packed cells of inmates looking on. It was not common to see a white man bathing outside of their cells.

Probably a first in the history of the prison. The water felt so good running over me. That was the one bath I had in this life that I will never forget.

On the afternoon of Monday, May 28, things got worse. Steve and I were moved with all members of the old Haitian military into isolation (solitary confinement). Isolation is located at the very bottom of the Titanic. The outside door leading into isolation is always locked. We were led into a really confined area that had a row of about five or six cells going east to west, or right to left. Across from these tiny cells in the very middle of the space was a small area to bathe in and an outdoor pit used as a toilet. We were forty-five strong. They used three of the cells to house all of us. Steve and I were placed in a cell with fourteen other men. There were sixteen of us in a cell designed to hold two or three comfortably. Each and every time Steve and I were moved to a new cell it was worse than the previous one. We learned really quick to start embracing the suck in the moment that we were currently living in. The first night in isolation on that hard floor in pitch blackness was really miserable. The sixteen of us were jammed in there like sardines. There was absolutely no room to move.

Steve and I slept next to each other crammed up against the wall in this fourteen by seven foot cell. The entire night a foot would be in my face or slammed into my stomach. I slept with my hand covering my testicles to protect from being kicked. I spent the better part of that night cursing guys for how ugly and violently they slept. Steve tried to turn from one side to the other and I could hear all his bones cracking. I felt so bad for him. He was fifty-seven years old. He didn't need or deserve to be in this quandary. You could hear the rats running amuck throughout the night. They were as big as cats.

The worst of the worst in Haitian society were placed in isolation. Political prisoners were often placed in there too. In our particular cell was a photo of former President Aristide. It was carved into the wall with some device that would have had to been very sharp. The likeness of Aristide in the photo on the wall was incredible. Of course, you could only see it during the daylight hours with the little bit of light that illuminated the cell. I sat there underneath the photo of Aristide that first morning just thinking about all my history in Haiti. I thought about my good friend Zaro who died inside these same walls some four and a half years earlier. I

374

thought about my two sons Moses and Spartacus. I teared up once again. Steve consoled me. Had I been in Steve's shoes I would have most likely harbored some hard feelings towards me. But he didn't and he never once complained. I needed him to lean on. My time spent in the Haitian Penitentiary would have been much easier had I not been a father with young children back home in the States. For that I am certain. The great Jimmy Valvano once said that part of having a full day involved crying. I was learning this on a very intimate level.

From the day we first set foot in the penitentiary, many of the inmates looked at Steve and gave him the slit throat gesture trying to intimidate him. Early on some of them walked right up on him and told him they were going to kill him. One inmate that was really large in stature tried to take what he had from his pants pocket.

The man said to Steve, "Zeke is OK, he's one of us, but you're a blan, you're a dead man." I finally had to tell Jha about it. I said, "You need to make sure that all these fuckers know Steve is off limits." I looked at Jha straight in his eyes and said, "Yo, get it done. Don't fuck with me Jha, you tell these motherfuckers to leave Steve the fuck alone." Jha agreed and the aggression towards Steve was halted immediately. Steve could have really been bitter. Instead he was serving as a great comfort to me. They don't make them like Steven Parker Shaw anymore.

Later that morning when they let me go to the infirmary to get my insulin injection, I was greeted by one of the inmates on work duty. He had just been instructed to tell me that someone named John stole all of my personal possessions from the place where I was staying in Lamentin 54. John had shown up again, and this time he was playing the role of Judas Iscariot.

He had seen my arrest on the news in Haiti. Somehow, he was able to find out exactly where I had been staying in Carrefour by be-friending one of Darline's family members at the prison. John came to Darline's mother's place where I had been spending the majority of my nights on a day when only one of Darline's sisters was there. He told her my lawyer had sent him to retrieve my laptop and passport, and that it was very urgent. My laptop was in a case that also contained my passport and all of my money, even my Sogebank card. John knew this from all his prior years of experience with me. Darline's sister didn't know any better and she gave it to him. He made off with about 700 Haitian dollars, US$300, my laptop, my passport, my bank card, and my backup Blackberry cell phone. With Darline still in the women's prison in Petionville, and her mom Monita at work in a factory, John was able to make out like a bandit. It was the Judas kiss of betrayal. He left with all my stuff and made sure to tell people close to me that if I ever wanted my things back, it would cost me a lot of money. He then changed his statement saying if I didn't come up with the money, he demanded, he would turn my computer over to Haitian authorities.

When I heard this, I felt sick to my stomach. My mind raced back to the day this homeless young kid laid on a dirt floor in Jeremie, Haiti. I took pity on him and took care of him for eighteen years of his life. I needed to vomit. I was learning that being baptized by Haitian fire was the only way you could truly become one with Haitians. Jean-Jacques Dessalines was betrayed by his own, as was Capois La Mort. John disemboweled me with this act of betrayal. It was now just another thing that I had to stress over. The stress of prison is what they say will kill you in a place like the Haitian Penitentiary. A slow agonizing death is what stress like that amounts to.

The second night in isolation, as we laid in the darkness, one inmate was killing someone a few cells over.

A crazed man was laughing, screaming, howling, and making animal like noises. All the prisoners in the other cells were banging on the bars at the entrance of each cell while they cheered and begged for blood. I closed my eyes and thought about being a young kid back in 1981 watching the movie *Midnight Express* with my father. In that moment, with such barbarity taking place just feet away, I transported myself to a different place as though I was in a time machine. The howling of these savages finally faded into the night, and I drifted off to sleep while watching one of the all-time great cinematic features about the legend of Billy Hayes.

The really bad thing about isolation was that no one came to check on us, no matter what happened during the night. If my sugar were to go low I'd be dead. They didn't open the outside door that led into solitary confinement until about nine a.m. to serve breakfast. They wouldn't open that door up again until sometime around three p.m. when they served dinner. If you wanted to bathe, brush your teeth, or use the toilet you had to do it during these short time frames when the food was being served. So, for twenty-three hours a day we were closed and cut off from everything in a tiny cell with fourteen other grown men. Not an ideal situation for a type-1 diabetic. My only respite from this misery was when Jha came to get me so I could give my insulin. The folks in charge often just literally forgot about me. I would be left sitting there waiting for what seemed like forever. While on the outside with Jha after giving my shot, I usually tried and sneak off with him to either his cell or the recreational yard in the Titanic.

Several nights earlier back in the Gref I had encouraged Larose to step up and lead the troops. I felt the morale of everyone was really low. I said, "You being a leader of men doesn't stop now because we are in prison. In this moment these guys need you more than ever before." I told him that I always looked at him like a pastor who was leading his sheep. I said, "You have talent."

He looked over at me, sat straight up and said, "Thank you Zeke." He then called on the attention of all the military men in the cell. He gave a short speech and they all sang in unison, followed by a prayer. All the other inmates in the cell were looking around like, "What the fuck just happened here?" This didn't end in the Gref. It continued on in isolation. This caused all of them to bond and grow closer. The group of them preferred the sanctuary that isolation provided compared to being in the normal prison population where they were despised.

The old Haitian military had shot up ghetto neighborhoods many years before when a lot of the current prison population were young kids. So they felt much safer in solitary confinement. Steve and I, however, wanted the hell outta there. Different inmates who were from those ghetto neighborhoods kept asking, "Why the fuck are you with these guys Zeke?" After being placed in isolation I did everything possible to distance myself and Steve from the military men. Steve and I wanted to be moved. Preferably to the cell within the Titanic where Jha was.

Meanwhile back in the United States, my cousin Greg Petrie's fiancé Julie Tompkins was working the phone lines making calls to Doctors Without Borders and trying desperately to contact the U.S. Ambassador to Haiti, Kenneth Merten. Coincidently, Merten, just like the legend John

Brown, called Hudson, Ohio his home. But Merten was no John Brown. Not even close. I am still waiting for the day to see Merten face to face to let him know what I think about his exploits in Haiti. Merten doesn't belong in the same area code with the great John Brown.

Julie was able to talk with a nurse inside of the prison, and she spoke with Lisa Nuccio daily. My friend Donny Pavlik petitioned on my behalf to Ohio 13th District Democratic Congresswoman Betty Sutton's office. My brother Ben, along with friend Tim Widner were also maneuvering behind the scenes to secure a Haitian lawyer that we could trust.

My friend Jonas Belizaire put them in contact with a Haitian lawyer named Jean Philippe. He was in and out of the Boston area while he traveled between Haiti and the states. Jean Philippe was hired and paid a few thousand dollars. Ultimately this bastard tried to extort me and Steve for $20,000. He worked against us the entire time. It was very frustrating.

Enter John Shattuck. John was a businessman out of Chicago. Chicago was where my journey to this 1804 Republic started. He was a veteran of the Navy who was well connected. He was also a veteran of Haiti. One day John happened to come across a Facebook post by Canadian Seanna Mcleod. Seanna, of course, had been held for twenty-four hours because of me and was still holding my grandfather's Masonic ring and watch. Both of them had been discussing the case since about five days or so after my arrest. This led to John getting in touch with my brother Ben. Ben started the operation "Free Zeke" along with Tim Widner and Donny Pavlik. After a couple of phone conversations with Ben, John brought out the big guns. John's connections ran all the way up the ladder to people at the State Department. He had high level contacts across the country, and around the world for that matter. John called upon the Godfather for some assistance. Things were now set in motion.

The phone calls I was able to make abroad from Jha's cell phone provided us this information, so at least Steve and I had some kind of hope. Hope is what you need more than anything in a place like the Haitian Penitentiary. It's the best of things!

The next two days and nights in isolation were more of the same. I would have another run in with Patrick. He invited himself into the isolation area to start badgering Larose, and some of the other military

378

guys about who Steve and I really were, and what role we played at the base in Lamentin 54. Patrick was determined to try and hurt our cause as he played the role of Mr. Hero Inspector Clouseau. On the morning of June 1, our last day in solitary confinement, Larose came over to me and said, "I told Patrick nothing." Me and Zeke are friends, end of story," he told Patrick. I embraced and thanked him.

Later that day Steve and I were moved out of isolation and into the infirmary together. For several days there had been some petitioning going on about getting us moved into the infirmary, especially on my behalf due to the diabetes. Truth be told, neither one of us wanted to be anywhere near the infirmary, let alone housed in there. The infirmary was a place that many inmates would try hard to get sent to. The cell was big enough so that you could walk in and stretch your legs. It also had running water, a shower, a working toilet, a radio, and a television. Several inmates would fake an illness in order to be sent to the infirmary. For them it amounted to a two or three-day vacation. But Steve and I thought some of the men housed in there looked so disgusting that we wanted no part of it. It looked like a leper colony. We could have chosen to stay in isolation. But over the course of the last two weeks, with lack of movement, confined like a sardine, not being able to give my insulin in a timely manner, not being able to eat on a regular schedule, and the stress I was under put me in a no-win situation.

My feet were so badly swollen from beriberi. It was common for prisoners of the World War II to suffer from beriberi. If not treated soon enough it could be irreversible. The short walks with Jha to get me out of the cell to administer my insulin, or to sneak off to the Titanic to shoot some ball or make phone calls wasn't enough to keep the swelling in my feet down. Being squished into a very small space with many grown men for twenty-three hours a day was too much for me. My blood circulation was badly hampered. So, we were now reluctant residents of the Penitentiary's infirmary.

Steve and I weren't ungrateful, however, and we did count it great fortune that whenever and wherever we were moved, we always went together. We were never separated. When I was originally told that I was going to be moved to the infirmary, I was going to be moved alone. Steve was to remain in isolation. I made it known and was very clear about the fact that if Steve wasn't going than I was not going. I refused to go without him.

In the infirmary we were given a small bed to share. After two long weeks of no sleep, we finally had the chance to rest in a normal position. It was really ecstasy for the both of us. Several days later we were afforded the opportunity to watch game six of the NBA Eastern Conference Finals between the Miami Heat and Boston Celtics.

During the game that night I was able to slip off into a bathroom stall and place a phone call to Tim in the states. The infirmary, just like Jha's cell in the Titanic, had a cell phone that always remained hidden. You had to pay to use it. Phones like this are snuck in and sold to inmates by corrupt prison guards looking to make extra money. Being able to share information back and forth with Tim continued to keep our hopes alive. This was very important for our mental health.

Shortly after being moved into the infirmary I was given access to a radio where I could listen to Moloskot's radio program Les Grands Dossiers on RFM 104.9. He continued to address my situation on a nightly basis. He implored officials in the Haitian Government to be careful. He said they were holding someone of great significance and to be very clear, anything that happened to me, they'd be responsible for. "Whatever happens is on your hands," he exclaimed while addressing those in the government. One night he spoke of my relationships with guys in Cite Soleil, and the men from the old Haitian military. He proclaimed that Zeke should have every right to have friends from all walks of life. "We are all human beings," he said. As Moloskot spoke every eye in the cell was on me to see my reaction. This filled me with life-giving energy and strength.

In the infirmary we were housed with some guys from Cite Soleil. Wilio, the brother of former gang leader, the late Evens, a.k.a. Ti Kouto, was now a few beds down from me. Another guy named Roody from the Boston ghetto in Soleil was with us too. Roody had suffered several gunshot wounds. He was missing the big toe from his right foot because he couldn't get medical attention for an infection that developed after he was shot. It was either go get medical attention and risk going to prison, or try and suck it up and continue to evade capture. He chose the latter and was caught anyway. While being cared for in the General Hospital in Port-au-Prince, he tried to escape under police guard in his hospital room. He was handcuffed to the bed and somehow able to pick the lock to free himself as the officer slept. He was apprehended yet again. He was a real-life character of the *Wild Wild West.*

It was early on during our time in the infirmary when Roody exchanged some harsh words with a really big guy named Chandler. Chandler was a big bull with a really great personality. He was in the infirmary because his testicles were badly swollen. I think he was suffering from orchitis. As words were exchanged between the two of them little Roody rose to his feet. Roody grabbed his crutches and quickly scampered over to where Chandler was standing. He called Chandler out and they met face to face right in front of the bed Steve and I were on. Chandler towered over Roody. I looked at Steve, and then jumped up without hesitation to get between them. I put my hands on Roody and told him to shut the fuck up and go sit his crippled ass down.

Then I turned to Chandler, who by this time had a shit eating grin on his face. I said, "Yo bro, we can't be friends, man. Roody is from Soleil. You know how things work here. I'm rolling with him either way. So I'm across from you now, just know this." Chandler said nothing and went and sat back down. I tried explaining to Steve what was happening between the two of them. Steve was very fortunate. Often he didn't understand what was being said. His Creole wasn't nearly as fluid as mine. Ignorance is bliss they say. Sometimes I wished that I didn't know what was being said because it was usually never anything good.

A couple of days later everyone in the cell watched as Chandler mauled another inmate a few beds down from us. The inmate that got a beating was a real bad ass. He made the mistake of teasing Chandler about his elephant-sized testicles. After witnessing this happen from just feet away, I immediately walked over to Roody and said, "You best not ever, and I mean fucking ever, open your teeth to Chandler again." The entire cell grew quiet after seeing Chandler manhandle this other tough guy in the cell. You really always had to keep your head on a swivel in the Penitentiary. Inmates were always threatening each other with violence. Even in the infirmary guys looked to hurt one another. There was no safe place inside this Haitian fortress from hell comprised of some of its worst citizens.

One early morning an inmate in our cell followed Steve into the shower room. While Steve was bathing the guy stole money out of Steve's pants pocket. His pants had been draped over the shower wall. When Steve realized he was missing money, he quickly alerted me about a suspicious looking inmate who had been in the bathroom area with him that he didn't recognize. He said that he could point the guy out, however. The inmate who was responsible for running our cell was a guy named Jonas from Leogane. He was the leader of the cell. I went to him and told him what had happened. I called to Roody, Chandler, Wilio, Pequeno, Phillipe, Biggie, and a couple of other inmates Steve and I were fairly close with to tell them of what happened. We all headed to the very back of this cell. It was L-shaped and divided into two different rooms. At first Steve could not identify anyone, until they found a man trying to hide underneath one of the beds. Steve said, "That's him, right there."

Jonas announced to everyone in the room what this man was being accused of. He yelled, "Give back what you took from this blan." Before the man could even reach into his pocket, kicks and punches landed on his head, his back, and his entire torso.

The majority of the inmates in the infirmary issued the verdict with a violent beating of this man. Out in the streets in regular Haitian society this guy would have been killed for stealing. On this day he was fortunate to be in the Penitentiary. That was the only thing that saved his life. Inmates in the cell that had nothing to do with this situation made sure to come over and strike a blow on this dude. They all took advantage of an opportunity to let out some pent up aggression. This inmate took a drubbing that would kill most average men. I looked at Steve and said, "Well, we are gonna have to save this poor bastard or they are gonna kill him." It was like watching some savage hyenas on the plains of Africa devouring their prey. Steve, the victim in this case, finally had to plead mercy for the man, and he did.

On another occasion an inmate tried to kill himself by drinking Clorox that he was somehow able to get his hands on. He most likely did this in order to get moved to the infirmary. When he was placed in our cell, the other inmates battered him savagely. He was told next time to finish the job or they would. They said, "You're not coming down here to have a vacation, you filthy animal."

The barbaric nature of Haitian prison went on to include men having their penises operated on. They would have these little marble type balls placed inside of the skin of their shafts. They did this in prison in hopes of being better able to please a woman sexually once they were back on the outside. It was the equivalent of a dildo made with objects built on the outside to stimulate the inner walls of a woman's vagina. One of these operations took place right in front of me and Steve. The procedure caused blood to drip onto the floor profusely. It was like no big deal, business as usual. Both the inmate receiving it, and the inmate doing the surgical procedure went on about this affair, showing no emotion. It was animalistic in nature. But it made them feel like men, so they didn't mind at all.

On a day not long after being transferred into the infirmary, Steve and I were both summoned to an office in the front of the prison where we met a State Department representative who was accompanied by someone from the U.S. Embassy. They spoke to me and Steve individually and gave us the chance to make one phone call each to the states. The only person I was able to get a hold of was Donny Pavlik. I quietly told Donny that I had been in contact with Tim via some hidden cell phones throughout the prison. "Y'all got to get me outta here," I said. He told me they were doing all they possibly could.

Later that afternoon I had the chance to call Tim from JhaJha's cell. He informed me that the man named John Shattuck was making moves and coming to our aid. He said that Shattuck was sending someone important to come visit us. The phone line cut off so I received no additional details.

In any event, it gave us more hope.

The very next day we received a visitor. It was not just any visitor, however. It was the father. Not just any father, it was the Godfather! Godfather had been all over the world. He had walked with kings and queens, with presidents and generals, with Pope John Paul ll and Mother Theresa. He had a Haitian man with him, and they seemed to be working together. Why was he visiting me and Steve? We certainly had no idea. He asked us what exactly we were doing in Haiti and spoke in pretty good Creole much to my surprise. He came across as very pompous. We didn't like him at first.

Steve looked directly at the Godfather and said, "Do you not see this pointing down to my feet. Do you see how badly swollen they are? He's going to be in real bad shape if you don't get him out of here real soon."

Before the Godfather left he told us that he was going to see what he could do for us. As we were escorted back to our cell I told Steve how arrogant that little prick was. Steve replied, "Fuck yeah he was, little bastard," in his Boston accent.

Every day in prison guaranteed two things. The days were long and every day was different. I was always on my toes with my head on a swivel. The guards that worked inside the prison treated us like shit. One of the men in charge named Inspector Turriene was particularly rough on me verbally. He would walk over to me, size me up and down, and say things like, "What is a white man like you doing amongst all those filthy animals in Cite Soleil?" with great disdain and disgust in his voice. He viewed me as lower than dog shit. Several of the guards fed off his words and treated me with the same type of negative tone. On a daily basis some of them would put their hands on me with a slap or a push, or a shove to remind me who was boss.

This all changed one morning when I went into the room where I gave my insulin. Inspector Turriene came strolling in telling the nurse in charge that he needed her to check his blood sugar. I had no idea he was diabetic — somehow he missed the memo that I was. I started up a dialogue by saying, "Oh, so you're diabetic too?" His eyes lit up. Before he could respond I went in on about how tough an environment Haiti was to live in as a diabetic, and how someone like him deserved so much respect for grinding it out on a daily basis. Then I said to him with great conviction, "So you can imagine how much more difficult it is for a prisoner with diabetes in this Penitentiary."

He sat in a chair intently listening to me as the nurse pricked his finger and nodded his head in agreement. I continued on about how diabetes is a silent killer, and what it does to one's body if not controlled at a high level of consistency. I went on about the disease in detail educating him about things that he never even knew. I said, "You do know that it was this disease called diabetes that eventually killed Haiti's president for life Francois Duvalier? You know this, correct? Papa Doc's Tonton Macoute militia couldn't save him from that, could they?"

It was at this point Turriene realized that he wasn't in the same room with just anybody. Finally he asked me several different questions about diabetes, and what to do in certain predicaments concerning this illness of high and low blood sugars, and the balance one must find to live healthy. I had him now. I said, "My Grandfather Petrie was a Mason just like you are inspector." Turriene always had his Masonic ring on, something that didn't go unnoticed by me.

The inspector, getting a real chance to be up close and personal with me in this intimate setting inside this fortress, changed everything. The way he treated me changed immediately. Not only with him, but with all the other guards. The abuse came to an abrupt halt. The prison guards had all heard Moloskot speak of me on the radio. They were well aware that the prison population knew and looked at me as a heroic figure in the ghetto neighborhoods of Port-au-Prince. The guards now viewed me with the same reverence going forward. The treatment of me and Steve went from third class citizens to first class in a blink of an eye.

The next day on June 11 my girlfriend Darline was released from the women's prison in Petionville. When the news of her release reached me in my cell I cried. Being separated from the ones you love the most is tough. Being responsible for their suffering is even worse. I was so relieved.

The following day during the late afternoon I was called out from the cell. A guard came to get me and said I was wanted up front. I had no idea what was going on. Steve was not called out with me. As I headed towards the front of the prison, I got a glimpse of Darline. I didn't believe I was really seeing her. I was led through a gated area in the front of the prison where Inspector Turriene sat in a chair waiting with Darline. Visiting hours were long over with. The inspector said, "You're a legend in my country, and you should be treated as such. I know who you are, I've always known. I admire what you have sacrificed for poor people. So, I'm rewarding you with this visit from your girl" and he pointed over to Darline.

Darline and I embraced. She was tearing up. I fought to compose myself. After several seconds of us holding on tight to one another the inspector, who always walked with a long thin black cane, motioned that our time was up. He was making us mindful that he was still the one in charge. I was hoping that he was going to give us a moment alone to ourselves. We wouldn't be that fortunate, however. There was so much to talk about yet we couldn't really express what we wanted to. It was really a special moment nonetheless.

I thanked the inspector for his gracious gesture and told Darline I loved her. I was escorted back to my cell. This is where Turriene showed his full arsenal. Before I was even out his and Darline's sight, he began to ask Darline for her telephone number. He said, "I can provide for you first class service here at the Penitentiary." He suggested they exchange numbers and meet up at a hotel/restaurant for dinner. This was his way of saying, "I want you, and I will have you as long as you continue to want personal service like I've provided for you on this late afternoon."

Fortunately, Darline didn't utter a word about it to me. I would have come unhinged. Both Darline and Steve's girlfriend, Nanoune, would be forced to deal with men like this for the rest of our time in prison.

From that day forward Darline came to the prison every day to bring me clothes, food, drinks, and letters, fulfilling the promise she had made to me two weeks before our arrest. She would and did indeed come to stand in those long lines to see me and provide for me. Although she wasn't made to stand in long lines often. She was usually given preferential treatment and moved to the front without having to wait. So many of the Haitian women must provide sexual favors to these prison guards for any favors given to them. It's an unspoken rule. It's the same thing with Haitian police officers, and any man in position of power. In Haiti they say it's a give to give country. You give me, I give you, period!

A couple days later Jha came to get me out the cell. Again, Jha was a grizzled vet of the Penitentiary, and he maximized the use of his privileges which I benefited greatly from. On this day we played lots of basketball with the guys over in the Titanic. Even though my feet were swollen, and I only had a pair of sandals to wear, I made do. The sun was hot, I was playing hard, and before I knew it the competition grew fierce. I started playing like it was the seventh game of the NBA finals. The Penitentiary was littered with some pretty good players. There was a big six-foot three lefty named Alonzo who was really tough. Zo had previously played some pro ball in the Dominican Republic. I was checking him early on in the game and he was punishing me physically. This ignited a fire in me. I started competing and playing out of my mind. As the game progressed all the guys grew fatigued. That's when I began to catch fire. The game was tight and was fought tooth and nail as the end of our recreational time in the yard approached. The trash talk was at a fever pitch. A kid named Isiah was defending me in close quarters, when he caught me with his fingernail square in my right eye. He got me clean. It caused a corneal abrasion but in the moment I thought it was just a bad poke in the eye. After a few moments I gathered myself and continued playing with one eye. The sweat seeping into my right eye produced a stinging pain. I was so pissed. I didn't want to quit playing. I was about to throw in the towel when the guards called for everybody to clear the yard. I went back to my cell, smarting from this poke in the eye, certain I would be fine.

I woke up past midnight with my eye on fire. It's difficult to even begin trying to explain the pain I was feeling. Only people who have experienced a corneal abrasion would understand. I was in the cell screaming and cursing bloody murder. It felt like I had been shot in the eye. It felt like a knife was lodged in my eye socket. One by one inmates awoke out of their sleep and asked what was wrong with me. I was in so much pain I didn't or couldn't hear a thing. After about thirty minutes of intense pain, my eye started to settle down just enough to where I could sit composed. I had no idea what had just happened. All I could think of was the eye poke I suffered that day playing ball. The next night the same thing happened. Again, I was up cursing and hollering like an animal. This just added to my misery.

For the first three and a half weeks of prison it was a nonstop brutal experience mentally and physically. After Darline's visit, and the change in the stance of how the prison guards treated me, I was hoping things would only get better. But my swollen feet still concerned me and now I was dealing with my eye pain which, as far as I knew, was nothing more than a badly poked eye that was untreated. I relayed the information back to the States via Tim. Swollen feet and a bad eye. It was a real fucking suffer fest.

Because of some petitioning back home, and an American doctor named John May, I was permitted to get mandatory thirty-minute exercise outside of my cell every morning. Couple this with the times I spent with Jha over in the Titanic and I felt that I was getting as much blood flow as I possibly could, given my circumstance. I was really growing anxious because my feet remained swollen well past the fourth week of my incarceration. I kept thinking that these motherfuckers were going to cost me my feet. I started to grow angrier by the day. The prison nurse provided me with some basic eye drop fluid for my eye in the meantime. My feet and my eye would dog me for the remainder of my prison stay.

One particular day my path in the prison was crossed by a couple of men who were arrested in high profile cases much like mine. In the morning a light-skinned man named William Baptiste a.k.a Ti Blan because of his light skin, entered our cell with a Bible in hand. He walked right over to me and extended his hand. Ti Blan was chief of gang in the Simon Pele neighborhood of Cite Soleil. He was a wanted man and a high profile arrest. He had escaped from the penitentiary after the earthquake and since being apprehended again in a place called Dame Marie in the Grand Anse region, Ti Blan gave his life to Jesus. He was now spending his days evangelizing and spreading God's word to other inmates. We connected like a pair of long, lost brothers. I had a really-good intimate conversation with him. That made me feel a sense of normalcy which is hard to find and experience in a place like the Haitian Penitentiary.

Later that day I was in the shower room of the infirmary. In the back of that room was a window with bars wide enough that things like cigarettes, soap, weed, etc., could be passed through them. I happened to look outside of the window and saw a man who went by the name Killa Boss. He was a member of the popular rap Creole group RockFam. We were both kind of startled to see one another. We talked and it gave me a good chance to see someone I could relate to. Although he didn't get into intimate details about his own arrest, his case was high profile and well scrutinized. Both of our cases received a lot of national attention in the Haitian media. Again, this was one of the few occasions while in prison that I felt normal. Little things, like conversations with Ti Blan and Killa Boss, helped to ease my mind, heart, and soul.

On the night of June 21 Steve and I had a chance to watch the Miami

Heat led by Lebron James win a championship over the OKC Thunder. Lebron is a kid from Akron only ten or fifteen minutes from where I grew up in Barberton. This made me feel good. The stress and pressure of being in such a dark, lonely, and violent place can make one lose his mind. They say if the Haitian Penitentiary doesn't kill you physically, it will definitely kill you mentally by driving you mad.

The next morning, I ran into Patrick for the last time out in the yard. I thought that I had seen the last of him. I walked by and we talked about the game and I said Lebron grew up just minutes from me. I said I should have been home watching that game with my two sons.

Patrick responded, "What are you doing here man? Why did you ever come to Haiti of all places? You're an American with kids back home, you should have never come here," he said while shaking his head. I said, "You'd never understand." That was the last time I ever saw him. Whether Patrick acted alone or whether he was sent by his superiors to cause us anguish, we will never know. But man did he go out of his way to make things difficult and uncomfortable for me and Steve.

During one of my last times in the Titanic with Jha I sat in a small enclosed area where many of the inmates were rolling dice and talking. I started up a dialogue with a few of the men and before I realized it, the place was teeming with black faces listening to what was being said. I went on a rant about all the social ills of Haiti, and how I thought Haitian men had been "Uncle Tom'd down." Inmates began asking questions to which I gave passionate responses.

One inmate, a deportee said to me, "You speak like President Kennedy, the dude that got shot. You better be careful. If they hear you talking like this in here, they will kill you. Inside these walls, when prisoners talk too much, they go missing. Be careful Blan."

The hours and days continued to drag on while trapped inside this fortress. Steve always seemed to remain positive and upbeat for the most part. He never wavered in his belief that we would be released. I kept telling him they may let him go, but they would never let me walk out of this place. I would be lying if I said I ever really believed I would see freedom again. Every so often we would see a body on a stretcher on the prison floor waiting to be removed and sent to the morgue. It was a daily occurrence to see blood strewn on the floor somewhere throughout the prison grounds. The physical confrontations and fights were never ending. The wear and tear of Haitian prison was taking its toll.

During the long days Steve and I played cards and took turns reading a Bible that was given to us. We both wrote daily letters to our girlfriends. They would write us every day, so we returned the gesture and wrote them back. The letters were soothing to the inner senses and helped to keep us sane. Darline and Nanoune never missed a day. They brought us food and beverages every morning. They brought us clean clothes while taking the dirty clothes home to wash them. I remember the night before we were arrested, the conversation was about how we were both going to break up with these gals. How quickly one's fate can change.

The secret phone calls I was able to make with Tim changed daily. We were always left thinking that this guy named John Shattuck was going to ride in like the Lone Ranger to get us the hell out of there. One-time Tim suggested that I may get released and put into custody at a medical facility, but Steve would remain in the Penitentiary. I told him that wouldn't work for me. I wouldn't leave Steve behind. On another occasion Tim said that Steve may be released, but I wouldn't be because I was the one they wanted in the first place. Steve would then say, "Tell them if you're not getting released with me, then I'm staying with you." I told Steve that if he was afforded the chance to leave, to take it and run. "You shouldn't have been here anyway," I'd say. Steve was later told by people close to him that the Commissioner of Haiti's government Jean Renel Senatus was quoted as saying, "Steve will at the very least do two months in the Penitentiary just for being friends with Zeke. For this he is guilty." Senatus hated me, and wanted to make me pay a heavy price. He chose to make anyone close to me pay a price too.

The night of Sunday July 1 nearly ended my stay at this concrete jungle in downtown Port-au-Prince.

Late that night I slipped into unconsciousness. I went into insulin shock. I don't remember much of it other than what Steve has recounted to

390

me. He said it was late but he needed me for something. At first glance he thought I was just sleeping. He called me, then nudged me, then shook me with no response. He quickly realized something was wrong. Neither one of us ever went into a deep sleep while in prison. At the slightest whisper we were moving.

After calling at me loudly in my ear and shaking me violently with no response, he started to call other inmates over to assist him. He directed some of the guys to start calling for help so that one of the prison guards would hear and respond. It was a big problem getting the attention of guards at night. They never responded to calls for help when the sun was down, ever! They didn't care, it was that simple.

My old Haitian friend gave me the analogy of Haitians being like flies. When one dies nobody seems to notice or give a damn. In the Penitentiary this was very true.

As I laid unconscious, scores of prisoners banged on the cell bars calling out for help. After about twenty minutes of the banging and cries for assistance, some night guards finally showed up to see what the raucous was all about. When the guards opened the cell door, Chandler, the big guy with the swollen testicles, the one I told we couldn't be friends, picked up my limp body, and carried me into the room where medical treatment of inmates was handled. Chandler tried sitting me up in a chair. As he was doing that Steve smacked me in the face four different times as hard as he could to jar me awake. That didn't work. I was placed on a gurney and administered an IV which brought me back to consciousness about thirty minutes later. I was lucky to escape that situation still intact. This was life number eight used up.

Two days later, on Tuesday July 3, Steve and I were finally summoned to the paquet (tribunal). As we got ready to leave our cell that morning, we didn't know if we were being released, but we didn't want to leave any of our belongings behind. So we took everything with us. When we arrived at the courthouse, they stuck us in a room that had no air circulating and was probably ninety degrees. Out of the blue the Godfather appeared. He peeked his head in the room to see if we were in there. I asked him if we were getting out. He just sort of nodded as to say yes. He was leaving and I said, "You will come back, correct? We will see you again today, right?" He assured us that we would see him again this day.

We spent what seemed like forever in that ninety-degree furnace and sweat soaked our clothes. Late in the day a special police unit in blue camouflage called APENA rushed into the room to whisk us back to the Penitentiary.

We were again placed in the back of these armored police transport vehicles that had no air and no visibility. I was cursing at the top of my lungs the entire ride back to the prison. Just hours earlier Steve and I were on the brink of ecstasy thinking we might be released. But just like that we were headed back to the Penitentiary.

I told Steve that night, "They're not letting me out, that's not happening. You need to get the hell out of here. If your plan is to wait for me, you're going to be waiting here the next three years."

Steve answered, "Then fuck it, I'm not going anywhere. You go I go, you stay I stay. If we are gonna be here the next three years, I'm going to start running this bitch." He said he would have his daughter send money every month and he would run the joint. Steve proclaimed this with great authority. He knew in prison that money talked. Mentally we were both getting prepared for the worst.

The next morning, Wednesday July 4, we were in an area just outside of the infirmary as a sweep of the cell was done for contraband like cell phones and drugs. Agents came in and tore the place up, leaving it a mess for the inmates to clean. As we sat there watching this, we both grew enraged and had a breaking point. We figured that we were not getting out anytime soon, and we were fucking pissed. Some of the inmates were on our last nerve at this point. In this revolving door of a prison, where new inmates were coming and old ones going, we grew fatigued of the constant staring, mean mugging, asking, begging, and stealing. For the first time Steve really grew agitated and got loud, letting his emotions spill over. Every other word from his mouth was a vulgar one. Some of the inmates gestured to him and told him to shut the fuck up.

That's when I became deranged. I stood up and went off. "This is for all you dirty motherfucking animals, don't you think for one fucking second that just because me and Steve have stayed predominantly quiet and docile reading our Bible during our time here in prison, don't let that deceive you into giving you a false bravado. The two of us would fight every last one of you fucks to the death right here, right now. You fucking-filthy animals."

I walked up and around to every prisoner in my vicinity crying out these same sentiments. Steve stood with a cigarette in his mouth flicking them all off with his middle fingers just like Cool Hand Luke. Truly we were the modern-day Butch Cassidy and Sundance Kid. We put on our own Fourth of July fireworks display in the National Haitian Penitentiary.

Later that day both of us were called from our cells. We were led up front and into a room where none other than the Godfather himself was standing front and center. Bad timing for him. He was met with a ferocity derived from our current unhappiness over what happened on Tuesday. He was accompanied by the same Haitian man who was with him the last time he visited us in the prison. He immediately apologized about what happened the day before, but before he could say another word, I looked at the man next to him and said, "You translate this for him" and pointed to the Godfather. I spoke using Haitian Creole, damn well aware that the Godfather could understand everything I was saying. I said, "You tell him that if he can't get us the fuck outta here to quit wasting our time."

By this point, both the Godfather and this man named John Shattuck (who only existed in our minds) were dead to us. As we left the room I thought Steve may be ready to chastise me for speaking that way to the Godfather, but much to my surprise he didn't. All Steve said was "Fuck him!" For me personally, I didn't care about the Godfather's incredible resume, or who his lofty friends and contacts were. He was in my house, and I thought it was a privilege for him to be able to come to our aid. "Who wouldn't want that shine, who wouldn't want that smoke," I barked to Steve. "Nothing I can't stand more than false bravado." I didn't tolerate that at all.

We had basically just told the Godfather to fuck off!

The next day we had started to settle into the reality that our new lives would be the next three years in this pig pen. Although Steve and I had no real plans of ever doing three years. We were already talking escape. Two guys like us were not going out lying down.

Friday morning came and we were notified early that we were going back to court. We were both pretty annoyed by now. To change our fortune

I said to Steve, "Let's make our own luck. Let's give away most of our things to some of the inmates we're closest to." We walked throughout the cell handing pieces of clothing, our sandals, and miscellaneous items to inmates we were fond of. Worst case scenario: If we were sent back again, we would just get more of the same shit we gave away from our girlfriends. I had a really nice dry fit black shirt that I gifted to Wilio, the brother of the late Evens a.k.a. Ti Kouto, gang leader of the Boston zone in Cite Soleil. Wilio had the biggest smile on his face. I was never friends with his brother Evens. We never talked, we never hung out. But I always shared a common bond with all the guys from Cite Soleil.

Out of respect to me Wilio handed me the only picture he had left of Evens. Evens had died in this same prison just like my friend Zaro did. Wilio and I embraced. Roody told me as I was getting ready to leave that he had a sister back in the states. He handed me her number and asked me to call her for him. We embraced. Steve and I walked out of the infirmary and told them we'd see "all you sons-of-bitches in another life, God willing."

As we walked away I could hear some of the prisoners saying, "Zeke, Zeke, you're leaving us, you're going home." I didn't dare look back, afraid I would turn into a pillar of salt. (Genesis 19:26)

When we arrived at the courthouse, we were met by our Haitian lawyer much to our dismay. He had been useless to us the few times he had come to see us in the prison. His extortion attempts were blasphemous. From the first day we landed in prison we always seemed to have everything going against us, even our own lawyer. All seemed lost.

Then, on that Friday, July 6, John Shattuck showed up like the Lone Ranger we had hoped for. Steve and I were placed in a room for a good while to await our fate. Out of thin air a white man with red hair looked into the room. He said, "Hey guys, I'm John. I'll see you guys outside." Moments later we were taken to Judge Bredy Fabien's office.

Steve went in first as I was placed into another room to wait. I worried for a brief moment that this was where they were probably trying to get us to answer the same questions differently, so they could keep us in prison. After a short while Steve emerged from Fabien's office and I was called in. I had no idea what they just asked Steve. I was very concerned about saying something contradictory to what Steve told them. In my mind and heart, I believed that Steve was going home on this day either way. I also believed that I was going to be sent back to the Penitentiary, alone this time around. The Haitians didn't look at me as being a white man. They viewed me as a Haitian, just like themselves, and that was the biggest thing I had going against my chances of actually being released. That didn't bode well for me. Haiti remained a land where one Haitian despised seeing another one of his own kind fair well. It is a peyi trayi san, a country where blood betrays its own blood.

As I sat across from Fabien, I glanced over into the corner where my lawyer Jean Philippe helplessly sat. He didn't look too thrilled. Fabien had a smirk on his face as he began to speak. He said, "I've heard lots about you." I remembered seeing him late Tuesday afternoon as we left the courthouse to be transported back to the Penitentiary. I caught him staring at me as I was led away in cuffs. He said, "I don't think you need a translator like the man who was just in here. I see you are Haitian, and you know the lay of this land." Fabien said Sergeant Larose Aubain spoke highly of me when he met with him a few days ago. Larose was the first to get released.

He then said, "I'm curious, what do you have to say for yourself as far as these charges against you?"

I responded in the most-humble tone I could. "Judge Fabien, all I am guilty of is loving Haiti. She's been the only true love of my life. I've embraced all of her regardless of class, creed, color, religion, or political affiliation. If one can be found guilty of loving and consuming all things Haiti, then lock me away, I'm guilty! I am not just some random white guy arrested on a Haitian flag day march. Speaking vehemently on the radio against the illegal U.N. occupation of Haiti is why I am here, Your Honor!"

Judge Fabien smiled. He apologized on behalf of the Haitian people for my fifty days of suffering while incarcerated. He commenced in signing paperwork in front of him on his desk. My heart began to beat faster. I was starting to allow myself to smell freedom. He extended his hand to me and said, "You're free to go."

In that moment I saw all of the faces of Haiti both good and bad that I had ever encountered flash before my eyes. Emotions welled up. I fought to keep my composure. I did not believe that they were actually letting me go. They had me. They had me dead to rights, and they let me get away.

As I walked out of the room Steve was being brought over to me. We stared at each other in a final moment of disbelief. Two APENA officers approached and uncuffed us simultaneously. Our lawyer Jean Philippe came out of the judge's chambers with one of his compatriot lawyer-partners and walked next to us as we made our way to the front of the building. Before we could exit the building, the press was already filming. One familiar face was AP photographer Chery Dieu-Nalio. I had run into Dieu-Nalio on several occasions while out working with foreign journalists during violent demonstrations. Chery is as tough as they come. He is fearless.

Outside waiting was John Shattuck, and our girlfriends Darline and Nanoune. I walked over to Darline and gave her a kiss while Chery's camera clicked away. A photo he took of us kissing appeared the next day on publications around the world including the *Akron Beacon Journal*. I asked her to marry me. She said yes.

I told Associated Press reporter Trenton Daniel that it was such a beautiful thing to be free. I could not believe it. I also provided Daniel with a false last name for Darline, so that Haitian government officials would leave her alone. I just dodged the biggest bullet of my lifetime. They had me, and they made the mistake of letting me go. Unknown to them my influence among Haitians would now become even greater. In *Star Wars* Ben Kanobi becomes more powerful after he is killed. So it would be in my exodus from Haiti. I was now seen as one who physically stood up as a revolutionary, and whose words should be taken seriously. This mattered to me greatly.

We walked through the courtyard arm in arm with our ladies as free men and the press followed and snapped one photo after another. I was wearing my father's old Community 2 softball coach's shirt. My dad wore that number 2 shirt long before all-time greats like Deion Sanders and Derrick Jeter. I strongly felt his presence with me. We got in an SUV that Shattuck had rented. To our surprise the compatriot friend of Jean Philippe's invited himself along and forced his way into the vehicle. He was sent to follow along with us to see where we were staying. Jean Philippe and his cronies still wanted more money. They had done nothing on our behalf. Our people in the states had already paid him a few grand.

As we drove out of the courthouse yard, Shattuck kept telling the man that he was not permitted to go where we were going. He said, "You need to get out of the vehicle." After about five minutes of arguing back and forth with this individual Jean Philippe had sent with us, the man finally got out. Moments earlier I said to the guy, "Just give me your number. I'll call you." I knew that Shattuck just telling him to get lost would not suffice. I lied to him. I assured him that I wasn't leaving Haiti anytime soon. I said I'm going to need your help to get my car, phone, and license back anyway. That was enough to assure him that he would soon see me again. In dealing with Haitians often times you are required to outwit them. Haitians are great at telling lies and breaking promises.

So in this case I went Haitian on the Haitian.

We arrived at our destination, the Caribbean Lodge Hotel in Tabarre not too far from the airport. We had dinner that evening together, and John let me use his phone to call my brother Ben. Shattuck put us in a nice room with two big beds. Steve and Nanoune in one, Darline and I in the other. We went to bed early but were awakened by a knock at the door. It was Seanna McLeod, who currently was working at the hotel, and John with a computer in hand. The Associated Press had posted the story about our release, stating that it was a conditional release, and that Steve and I could be summoned back at any time for more questioning by Judge Fabien. John refuted this and said it was non-conditional. This is when John opened up about who, in fact, the Godfather really was, and what his influence meant in helping to get us released.

The Godfather had evidently helped a lot of Haitians throughout the years. There were people in the prison system, and in the justice system, whose lives, at one time or another, he influenced. Knowing this Shattuck reached out to him early on about helping us.

After visiting us for the first time in the Penitentiary, the Godfather called Shattuck and said, "Are you sure you really want to help this guy named Zeke?" Shattuck said yes. The Godfather then requested a letter by one of my family members vouching for me. Enter my brother Ben who wrote a heartfelt letter and sent it to the Godfather. This letter written by Ben was critical in my eventual release. So many things went on behind the scenes that Steve and I found out about months and years later.

397

Before we went back to sleep, John informed me that both he and Steve were booked on the first flight out of the country in the morning. I would not be able to join them, however, because my passport had been stolen by another John. The John that was closest to me, the one I raised. And because we were released on a Friday, I wouldn't be able to get an emergency passport made until Monday. Early the next morning Shattuck came to the room to get Steve. The three of us took a photo together. The shirt I was wearing for the photo had the words FADED GLORY printed on the tag. John handed me some cash and advised me to stay in the room until I departed for the U.S. Embassy on Monday morning. He said, "You'll be booked on every American Airlines flight out of Haiti on Monday." He handed me a camouflaged Navy Seal hat he was wearing and told me it was a gift. Ironically, I had always wanted to be a Navy Seal since I was a kid.

Steve and I embraced, and I felt like this might be the last time I'd ever see him. I told him I loved him. He said, "I love you too fuck head" in his Boston accent. Steve then whispered to me that Judge Bredy Fabien told him if he ever needed us that he would indeed call on us. He told me to be careful. Even then Steve was showing great concern for me. He didn't want to leave me behind. Steven Parker Shaw proved the Bible right to me. Truly there is a friend closer than a brother. Steve was the truth. He never whined, moaned, complained, or blamed. He's as hardcore a warrior soul that you'll ever meet. I wouldn't have wanted anyone else next to me during that dark stretch. Thank you, Steve.

That night Darline and I finally had some time alone together. We had animal sex in the shower. It was eight weeks since I had an orgasm. It made me feel normal again. The next morning, I sent Darline back to Carrefour to retrieve a few of my belongings. I was only planning on traveling with a carry on. There would be no chances with checked luggage. I was leaving most of my things behind with Darline in Haiti. I really had no choice.

That Sunday was a long day of doing nothing. I was closed-up on the inside of the hotel room and couldn't step outside the door should anyone see me. I had arrived there on Friday evening as the sun was going down.

398

It was now Sunday evening, and nobody knew I was at the hotel other than John Shattuck and Seanna McLeod. It was as though I was still in prison, but I wasn't complaining. Darline and I had one last night of love making. We made plans. I'd return to the States and get paperwork started to bring her to the States via a fiancé visa.

Monday morning I was on heightened alert. I put on a long sleeved white thermal shirt and jeans. I wore the Navy Seal hat that Shattuck gifted me. So all my tattoos were covered. I jumped on the back of a motorcycle. Darline got on the back of another motorcycle and accompanied me to the U.S. Embassy in Tabarre. I needed an emergency passport made ASAP. Darline braided my hair the night before so I looked totally different in my appearance. I was hearing through back channels that Commissioner Jean Renel Senatus was not aware I had been released on Friday. Upon finding out over the weekend he was not happy about it. I was on edge. I kept thinking the worst. I thought at some point I would be arrested again and taken back to prison before I could ever board a plane.

When I walked into the embassy all eyes were on me and a few of the embassy employees' eyes lit up when they saw me walk by. I think they were shocked that I actually got out of prison. I went right up to one of the consular windows and handed a card that Shattuck had given me with a few names and numbers on it to a lady that was on duty. Her eyes got big like saucers as she scanned the card. She said, "How do you know Shattuck?"

"I don't," I said, "but he knows me, and he instructed me to give that card to you. You can feel free to call him." She grabbed her phone and started to dial. She found Shattuck on the other end and he informed her that I was booked on every flight out of the country that day by a State Department contact.

The lady came back to the window and said, "Wow, you really do know John Shattuck." I reiterated that I didn't know him, but that God had delivered me through him. As I continued to wait while they processed my situation, I thought about how I would avoid being apprehended before I got to the airport. My disguise was being covered from head to toe with my hair braided and wearing a hat.

When I got all my paperwork situated and did everything required to receive my emergency passport, I began my walk out of the building. All the consular officers behind the windows watched me walk out. A couple of them gestured towards me with some goodbye waves, including a woman who had come to see me at the Canapé Vert jail back on May 20. She was one of the people that I chastised Obama to. She was of Haitian origin. I liked her a lot. Needless to say, I'm sure that the Obama White House would have been most pleased to see me rot in that hole I was in.

Darline and I had a chance to talk and share one final intimate moment together underneath a tree. We hugged and kissed. I told her that once we arrive at the airport, I was heading straight in. There would be no time for saying goodbyes. My final words to Darline were "I love you, and I'll send for you soon. You jump I jump." Together we hopped on the back of one motorcycle this time. I paid the driver in advance. I said, "You drop me at the airport and then don't look back. Take her directly home to Lamentin 54 in Carrefour." I slipped him some extra money to make sure she got home safe.

I arrived at the airport very paranoid. I walked through and it seemed everything was in slow motion. I could see and hear people pointing and whispering as I went by. I was thinking at any moment that government agents would rush in and take me away. After a couple of long miserably slow hours I finally boarded an American Airlines flight to Miami. As the plane barreled down the runway, I was having flashbacks of the last twenty-one years of my life. I asked the individual next to me the date. He said July 9. I thought wow, my ex-wife Aslyne's birthday. Oh the ironies of life. I never felt at ease until I landed in Miami and was all the way through customs.

After getting in and out of customs, I could at long last breathe.

This moment of respite wouldn't last long, however. My last conversation with Tim from behind prison walls went like this:

Tim said, "Even if you do get out of prison, coming back to the States will be like coming back to another sort of prison altogether. Between me and you, nobody in your family is really looking forward to you coming back home." I responded that I knew this was the case. I felt it. Part of me was thinking about taking my chances and staying in Haiti. But that choice would have been suicide ultimately. I was up against it either way.

BACK IN OHIO

When I returned to Barberton late on the ninth I stayed up most of that night on my mom's computer. I was reading and researching my case in Haiti. A article online from the Beacon Journal had a comments section for readers. It provided people access to give their opinions. A lot of hateful and nasty comments were directed my way. One individual said if I loved the people of Haiti so much, I could rot in prison with those "niggers." I just sat there reading and re-reading one nasty negative comment after another. It was very sobering. The biggest impression made on me this night however was a message left on social media by Haitian author, radio host, and political analyst Jafrikayiti (Jean Elissaint Saint-Vil). His message was re-posted by human rights lawyer, political analyst, and social commentator Ezili Dantò. I came across it on her Facebook page. It was written in Haitian Creole. Here it is translated into English:

> Is this Zeke Petrie a good white man? He asked for men to quit playing games. When a white arrives in Haiti and says a few words that flatters our egos, many Haitians are prepared to give said white credit that he does not deserve. Do you not know that the CIA has been operating in Haiti for the last two centuries. Do you think if they send agents that they will do so without disguising them? Their technique of infiltration is something that is very developed. In the 1960s that's how they infiltrated the Civil Rights Movement in the United States. They even went as far as having whites support the Black Panthers, Malcolm X, and many others. Do you believe it's true? In any event, Petrie's contacts are very suspect. This guy is in Cite Soleil, he's friends with Charles Baker, he's hanging out with Jean-Claude Duvalier, he's involved in Haitian Hip Hop, and after all this they find him in the middle of the remobilized soldiers of

401

the old Haitian military. What kind of passport does he have? And the other older white man that was with the soldiers, what do we know of him? Do you remember Zeke saying that he was with Billy and Tupac during moments when Cite Soleil was very hot with political tension. How do these white guys come and go out of Cite Soleil, have connections with gang leaders, bullets are flying here and there, they are very visible, but they are never victims. All their Haitian friends however die at the end of the movie. What mission was Zeke really on truthfully?

After reading this I grew angry and went after Ezili on social media. The more I thought about it though the more I realized it was the greatest compliment that I ever received even though it was meant to discredit me. In fact, the words of Jafrikayiti just cemented my legacy in Haiti once and for all. I was always present and always supporting all Haitians regardless of their circumstances. I embraced them, all of them. Inclusion and unity, that is what I was about in Haiti for twenty-one years. The powers that be did not like this.

In the coming days I would be notified by several credible sources in Haiti that I was tagged as Persona Non Grata "Not Wanted" and banished from the country. My entire adult life Haiti was all I knew. My life would never be the same again.

Memo to Jafrikayiti: The CIA wasn't created until September 18, 1947.

The next morning my brother Ben told me the Channel 5 Cleveland ABC News affiliate wanted to interview me. Without hesitation I told Ben that I had no desire to do any interviews whatsoever. I did not want to be bothered. Ben pleaded with me and quickly reminded me that it was these folks at WEWS in Cleveland who had given my case some attention and that it was the least I could do. I reluctantly agreed.

Channel 5's Bob Jones came to my mother's house on Lloyd Street in Barberton to interview me. I knew that I would have to answer his questions guardedly, because I was doing my best to protect Darline in Haiti so the Haitian authorities wouldn't bother her. Darline and I were both concerned about reprisals against her on account of me. I tried to give an honest recount of what I had just lived through. In my interview with Jones, I forgot to mention going into insulin shock the Sunday before my eventual release due to the fact that I didn't have any recollection of it at all. I also forgot to mention the eye injury I suffered. After my interview with Channel 5, I interviewed with the *Akron Beacon Journal*. Future events would soon have me dancing with Channel 5 and the Beacon Journal once again.

A few nights later I woke up out of a deep sleep with my right eye on fire again. My eye was really aggravated this time, so I went to the emergency room at Barberton Citizens Hospital. While in the emergency room I was seen by an African American doctor that was on duty. I told him about my eye and how much I was suffering. I told him I injured it about a month before in prison in Haiti.

"Wow, you're one tough guy, man," he said. He told me there was nothing he could do and I had to see an eye specialist. "I don't know how you managed this long without getting that taken care of," he said. I told him I had no choice in the matter. I was very fortunate that I got out of prison and the country of Haiti when I did.

I set up an appointment to be seen by an ophthalmologist named Dr. Anita Dash-Modi. I had been seen by her in years past for my eyes due to my being diabetic. After looking into my eye she diagnosed me with a corneal abrasion. She instructed me on what to do and how to care for my eye going forward. My mom was gracious enough to help me pay for this visit to Dash-Modi's office, because I had not a dime to my name. The corneal abrasion would dog me in the months and years to come. Often times I'd aggravate it at night. This forced me into wearing a plastic ventilated eye shield when I slept.

"Extraordinary afflictions are not always the punishment of extraordinary sins, but sometimes the trial of extraordinary graces."

Described so fittingly by Matthew Henry, this would not be the last of what seemed to be nonstop afflictions coming my way.

Photo by MarathonFoto

PART FIVE

REDEMPTION

HOMECOMING

My coming home party was short-lived. On the morning of August 1 my mom informed me that I could no longer stay at her house. I could sense this coming a few days earlier. She said I needed to find somewhere else to go. She didn't want me there anymore. She was trying to avoid being in the middle of any verbal altercations I might have with my ex-wife. Aslyne was much closer to my mom than I was. She called her Mom.

Aslyne had lost her mom in Haiti when she was nine years old. My mom essentially became her mom over the course of the last eleven years. She had a new baby girl with Kevin, and my mom was a part of their family. She often babysat Moses, Spartacus, and Aslyne's new daughter, who was a toddler.

Knowing that Aslyne looked on me with lots of spite, and for good reason, my mom thought it best that I not-be there any longer than I had to. I understood, I really did, but it didn't make me feel very good.

Help would come in the form of two of my oldest companions while growing up, Jay Belkey and Mike Koncz. The night of August 1 I went to stay with Jay Belkey. I was basically homeless, and Jay took me in. On that particular night his son, Jayson, had a friend sleeping over. A half hour after I arrived Jayson's friend left abruptly. When Jay asked Jayson why his friend left, Jayson said he had heard that Zeke was wanted for attempted murder. A few days earlier he had overheard some parents in Norton talking about a previous article in the Beacon Journal concerning my case in Haiti. That night was the lowest point for me. I was homeless, with no money, no job, a bad eye, bad feet, bad health, separated from my kids, and the country that I loved. This was the very beginning of a very long and dark road to perdition for me. I was lost. I had no idea where I was going, or what I was going to do. I had no plan B of any sorts. I was covered in tattoos. I had no desire to fit back into what society deemed normal. I was devastated. And frankly, I thought I was too good and too great to be in such a position. Being homeless and taking handouts from people? I was now mad at everyone.

Several days after arriving in Barberton, Mike called and said he wanted to take me out to get some things. I was a little embarrassed. I assumed he saw the interview that I gave Channel 5, when I mentioned that I lost everything. I said, "Thanks Mike, I really appreciate it. I'll get back to you." I never called him back. I had no intention of calling him back, at least not for any handouts. I had way too much pride for that.

A few weeks later he called again. This time he was a little angry with me for never calling him back. He said, "I'm coming to get you right now. Where you at? I'm coming, be ready!"

He picked me up and took me shopping for some new clothes but didn't stop there. He got me a job driving people with mental and physical disabilities for his uncle Don. I was scheduled to start work on August 20. This was huge because at this point, I wanted no part of going out and about to put job applications in. I feared being rejected by employers because of all the recent Beacon Journal news articles about my imprisonment in Haiti and because of all my many tattoos.

But before commencing my new job, I would have best man duties for my cousin Greg Petrie's upcoming wedding with Julie Tompkins scheduled for August 18. Julie and Greg had me penciled in to be the best man in their wedding about a year earlier. They were starting to get worried that I may not be back in time to see it through after my arrest and imprisonment. God willing, I made it, and a beautiful wedding it was.

On Monday August 20 I started the new job. In the beginning I didn't really like it at all. I felt that it was beneath me, but again, I had no choice. My work days were split in half. I drove in the morning and had the midday off. Then I drove again in the afternoon. During my midday breaks I'd run six to eight miles. I started to feel like my body was beginning to quit on me. I was going through a dark, lonely, depression-filled state, which was not beneficial to my health at all. The exercise was life-saving during that stretch in my life.

While driving during the day I listened to La Mega 87.7 FM out of Cleveland. It was the closest thing I could find to make me feel like I was back in Haiti. While in Haiti I often listened to Latin hits from the Dominican. La Mega introduced me to guys like Nikki Jam, Tony Dize, Tito El Bambino, and the Mambo Kings. Listening to this genre of music every day started to slowly but surely bring my swagger back. It helped me to remind myself who I was. I can't state this enough. This was huge for my mental well-being.

I was officially introduced to Andre "Dre" Travis in early September.

Lisa Somers was the individual in charge of the Dayhab that many of the people I transported went to everyday and she introduced us. She led me over to this young-looking, baby-faced black man with cerebral palsy who was confined to a wheelchair. He had no use of his distorted looking arms and legs. She said, "Zeke, you and Dre both love sports, I think you would really be good for him."

Dre was looking at me, smiling and thinking to himself, "Who is this tattooed freak?"

I was thinking, "What the fuck is this guy smiling at me like this for? He can't be this happy to see me."

Lisa then asked me if I was at all interested in making extra money by taking Dre out to appointments, the grocery store, the mall, sporting events, or anywhere that he needed to go. I responded yes, but only because I needed the money. I had no intentions of trying to get close with Dre in any way whatsoever.

How hard could this be? I pick him up, take him out, and bring him back home. It sounded easy enough. I'd get paid, so I didn't give a damn.

The first couple of times I took Dre out was real uncomfortable for me. I was starting to think I bit off more than I wanted to chew. I was way out of my league on this one for sure. Every other Saturday I was supposed to pick Dre up, and spend approximately six to eight hours with him. He was totally dependent on me for everything. Although I was required to change him of the Depends he wore, I never did. Dre and I had a man code that we upheld from the start. This was one of the lines I drew early on. If he soiled himself, he either sucked it up and sat in it, or I took him all the way back to the group home he was staying in so they could change him.

We went to Summit Mall in Fairlawn, Ohio, a couple of times to hang out. As we walked the mall people stared, pointed and whispered about this odd-looking pair. I was now responsible for feeding him, and I didn't care for that at all. While sitting in the food court feeding Dre people were walking by trying to act as if they weren't noticing us. I just hated it, and soon wanted no part of taking him out in public on these terms. I was on the brink of throwing in the towel when something came to mind. One afternoon I suggested that instead of going to the mall, we go to a track and he could run with me. I said I'd push him in his chair. This was going to be done on my terms going forward. I selfishly manipulated the situation into what amounted to me getting paid to work out. And that's exactly what I did. I previously said publicly that I started running with Dre to get in shape and take care of my health post-prison. That was only half truth. It was my own insecurities that led me to taking this action ultimately.

The first time Dre and I headed over to the old running track in Norton, Ohio, that sat off of Cleveland Massillon Road. I had started running there with my dad many years ago and had since resumed running there in August when I moved in with Jay Belkey. I could easily walk to the track from Jay's place. It was a sunny but chilly October day when Dre and I ran our first three and a half miles together. I could feel Dre's energy palpitating in his chair. He loved it. Two weeks later we went and ran again.

As we ran Dre said to me, "I love when we do this. It makes me feel like I'm flying. It makes me feel close to God." In that very instant something washed over me. Tears welled up in my eyes. I cried for the duration of that run while trying to hide my emotions so Dre would not see. I felt human again for the first time in a very long time.

After we finished that second run we were sitting off to the side of the track. I was lamenting to him about all my problems. I looked over and noticed him intently listening to what I was saying. I appreciated him for that. He seemed to genuinely feel my hurt and my pain. I blurted out, "We should go run a marathon. Yeah, let's do it, let's go run a marathon together like Dick and Rick Hoyt."

Dre got a big smile on his face and said, "Yeah, let's do it."

Although Dre had no clue who the Hoyts were, the very idea of us

410

doing our best Dick and Rick Hoyt imitation was birthed on that October day in 2012. We never looked back. We started our training right then and there. We were very flamboyant about it too, at least I was. Dre was much more humble.

We informed everyone around us that we were going to run a marathon together. Usually people would look at us with kind of a dumb smile on their faces as if to say, "What are these fools talking about?" We didn't mind, however. It was us against the world. That's how we preferred it to be.

I had been living in the states now for the last three months trying to find a way to fit back into society. I had already started paperwork to bring Darline to the states via a fiancé visa. That fall and into the winter months there was a lot of down time, a lot of idle, lonely time. In these idle moments during my midday breaks or during the long evening hours I fell back into the same vices and addictions of an individual who was very lost. I was once again on local chat line numbers. I was also chatting with and meeting women via social media. I was treating these women like pigs. I had a predetermined disrespectful attitude towards all of them. I could have cared less.

I even started chatting with a few Haitian women that were steeped into the Vodou religion. Each one of them desired to be in a personal relationship with me. I used this as a platform to start asking more in-depth questions about Vodou. This led to me not only becoming more knowledgeable about the black magic these women were mired in, but it also morphed into kind of a sexual perversion. Talking and texting with these ladies had me headed down a road that was starting to get really dark. It became a spiritual darkness that I finally had to cut ties with and run from.

In the meantime my ex-wife Aslyne had great spite towards me, and I was not getting along with her at all. My mom had put me out of her house, so I was pissed at her. And I didn't get along with my sister Jennie whatsoever. I held her in the highest of contempt. Women across the board ranked the lowest of my priorities, and how I treated them coincided with that. By the end of January 2013 Darline joined me in the states from Haiti. She came on a ninety-day fiancé visa. We were on the clock. We had to get married within those ninety days or she could no longer stay legally in the United States. Surely this would change my luck going forward. She would somehow magically fill a great void in my life, so I thought.

Because we were now in the winter months, and it wasn't feasible for me and Dre to run outside, we began training at the JAR Arena on the University of Akron's campus. There is an indoor track that sits above the basketball court where we ran ten to twelve miles every other Saturday. This is when our relationship really started to blossom. It was always my intention that Dre be looked at and viewed as my equal. I treated him like my equal. This was of prime importance to my psyche. Had Dre been mentally handicapped, I would have never attempted to enter into the deep waters I was about to enter with him.

In March of 2013 we started running on the outside track at the University of Akron. We trained in the cold, we trained in the rain, we would train in the hot sun too. I treated Andre like just any other athlete. I treated him like a man, like a warrior. I pushed him to places he'd never previously seen or visited physically or mentally. I wanted to see what fabric he was really made of. I needed to know if he was really worthy of this. I wasn't just some nice guy good deed doer, showing up for some publicity stunt photo op, pushing a guy in a wheelchair.

One afternoon as I was getting ready to take Dre home from his work place, I noticed him smiling. I asked, "What's so funny? Why are you always smiling? You can't be that fucking happy. You're in a fucking wheelchair, there can't be anything fun about that." I was reminded of the movie *Born on the Fourth of July*, when Tom Cruise's character was trying with all his being to make love to a woman after being paralyzed in Vietnam. That scene crushed me. I felt the emotions of Cruise's character well up in me and I said to Dre, "Why don't you try wiping that smile off from your goddamn face, and give me a Kobe Bryant scowl instead?"

Dre didn't like the way I was speaking to him. He asked me why was I always so angry. I said, "You don't want to know that." He said, "Yes I do."

I told him that a year ago I was living my life in Haiti, the way I wanted to and on my terms. I kept company with presidents and generals, and now I was stuck here "driving you in this fucking shit van."

Dre struggled to position himself upward in his chair as though to

412

project himself forward into my direction. He said, "You motherfucker, if I could get out of this chair, I would kick your motherfucking ass you son of a bitch."

I said, "Now you're talking! You ain't getting out of that chair though, are you? Doesn't feel very good does it? That's the person I need to see. That's the scowl I want to see on your face."

"Why do you have to be such an asshole?" he said. I said one day soon he would thank me for being such an asshole. "Come race day you better bring that scowl. You better show the fuck up."

We rode home in total silence that afternoon. Not another word was spoken. Far too often for my liking, I watched Dre treated like a baby by his friends and caretakers. I detested that profusely. If I was going to push him 26.2, then he was going to take some abuse just like everyone else. And take it he did, and boy did he give it back too. Dre would later say we were like Tupac and Eminem going at each other all the time. We were an odd couple to say the least. But we would be heard from, that was already written! Our mark left on the great state of Ohio's history was coming.

Darline and I were quietly married in a courthouse wedding on April 18, 2013.

Throughout the winter months and into the spring we tried to get some help finding a race chair that I could push Dre in. We had no luck. At every turn nobody could help us. We didn't let this discourage us, however. Up to this point we had trained using his regular wheelchair, so we didn't know any different. If that's all we had to use, then that's what we were going to roll with.

Lisa Somers reached out to Dre's case manager Jennings Cross. Jennings reached out to the Team Hoyt people who directed him to a lady named Georgeann Haviland in the Columbus, Ohio region. Georgeann was running My Team Triumph's Columbus, Ohio chapter. They are a non-profit organization that finds volunteers to push children and young adults with disabilities in running events. Jennings relayed this info to Lisa, and she sent it on to me. The rest of it would fall squarely on my shoulders. I started an open dialogue with Georgeann via emails and phone calls. We had two pretty-lengthy conversations by phone where I tried to best explain to her my story and what Dre and I were trying to accomplish.

413

Georgeann agreed to lend us one of her race chairs but she would first need to get approval from her board of directors at My Team Triumph. She also added that if the board approved she would go as far as to bring the chair all the way up from Columbus a couple of times so we could practice training with it.

Towards the end of May, I reached out to Akron Marathon race officials with a request that they let me and Dre run their race. I never imagined that it was a big deal. Certainly, they wouldn't refuse us. Operations Director Laura McElrath sent me an email explaining that in situations where requests were made that fell outside of their standard rules and regulations, they needed to receive board approval. I was asked to send a letter to the marathon board explaining our intentions on how we wished to participate in this year's Akron Marathon. Then they would vote on it. In its prior ten-year history, nobody had ever run the race pushing a wheelchair.

I came away a little dismayed after my first communications with the Akron Marathon bureau. They weren't in any way, shape, or form jumping at the prospect of me and Dre running their race. They wanted to know a lot more about us. In retrospect I understand why. But back in 2013, I was pissed that they didn't immediately embrace us. They said, "So you've never run a marathon before, and you're just going to show up pushing a wheelchair for your first time?"

I said yes, that's the plan.

It would have been very interesting to see the look on Akron Marathon President Anne Bitong's face as I made those remarks over the phone during our initial conversation. I walked away from that first convo feeling as though they may not agree to let us run their race. Besides, I went from speaking to the President of the Marathon to now being relegated to emailing with the operations director. This couldn't bode well for us, I thought.

So, I did three things. I wrote and submitted a letter on June 12. Then, I asked Georgeann to please intervene on our behalf by sending an email endorsing me and Dre to Akron Marathon officials. And finally, I looked into an insurance policy. I reached out to an old friend at the *Akron Beacon Journal*, Katie Byard. If Akron Marathon officials were refusing us the opportunity to compete in their race, I'd have Katie all over the story. Katie was the author of a couple of featured write ups that the Beacon had done about me in previous years from the earthquake in Haiti to my time incarcerated there. I knew that I could count on her to come to our aid. I also had one of Dre's aides compose a letter as he dictated to her just in case the board of directors' vote didn't go in our favor. A letter that I never had to use. A letter that to this day I still have. Brian Polen is the only other person to ever see it.

On July 1 I received an email from Anne Bitong thanking us for our interest in their race and explaining how existing rules and regulations were designed for the safety of all participants. She elaborated on safety concerns that they had to take into consideration. She then posed to me a list of about eight questions they wanted me to answer in better assisting them in their decision-making process.

If that wasn't discouraging enough, now some people in Dre's camp including his doctor wanted tests done to make sure that his body could withstand the physical pounding of rolling along for 26.2 miles as I pushed him. At every turn we faced different obstacles adding to my stress level. We both knew how much we had invested in this journey. We were not going to be denied.

It was July 17 when I received an email from Georgeann stating that her My Team Triumph board approved me and Dre using one of their chairs for the race.

The next day, July 18, I received an email from Anne Bitong letting me know that they had agreed to permit me and Dre to run in their race on Saturday, September 28, 2013, but only upon our agreement to conditions. My initial excitement was tempered immediately. She gave a list of things that we must agree on. At that point I was going to agree with just about any damn thing they asked or required of us. Except for one thing. They were requiring Dre to wear a helmet. I said sure thing no problem although I had no intention of complying with that condition. I kept that info all to myself. Dre was an athlete, not some goddamn special needs charity case.

Wearing a helmet reeked of special needs, it reeked of disability, it reeked of "I'm scared," it reeked of "I can't." This was going to be Dre's day to show the world that he was able. We would show up on race day without a helmet and I was damned if I would take no from them.

All the pressure would be on them to comply with us by then. Staying disruptive was all I knew.

On Saturday, August 10, Georgeann came up from Columbus with the race chair. She met us at my mom's house with both Katie Byard and Michael Chritton of the *Akron Beacon Journal*. Dre and I went on a run just short of ten miles over in the neighborhood where I grew up. It's a hilly route to train on. On this particular day I struggled pushing Dre in the heat on those hills.

A few days later Georgeann called me. In a roundabout way she suggested that I run the marathon with Dre using another teammate to help me push him the 26.2 miles. She explained that it was all about Dre finishing at the end of the day. She went on to elaborate about how they did things at My Team Triumph. She said all of their volunteers that push people with disabilities work together in teams of two or three at the very least. The more she talked the madder I got. I wasn't trying to hear any of this nonsense. It really pissed me off even though I gave her no inclination of that while on the phone with her. I remained cordial but was fuming on the inside. This was a special journey that Dre and I undertook together. I wasn't going to let anyone dictate the narrative of what we were trying to do under any circumstances. Damn her, damn the Akron Marathon race officials, and damn everyone else who didn't really think Dre and I could pull this off.

A few weeks before the race in early September Georgeann made one last trip up to Barberton with the race chair. She was leaving the chair in my possession now. She only had a few minutes to hang out and do a final rundown of the chair. I thanked her for advocating on our behalf so the folks at the Akron Marathon could agree to let us compete in their race.

Right before she departed, I said, "So, have you ever run a marathon before?" She grinned. Well, gee, golly, shucks, "yes I did once. I ran the Cleveland Marathon in 1987." I asked her time and she said, "Well, I actually won the race."

I was dumbfounded. She told me she won the women's race with a time of 2:55.23. She added, "I don't really ever talk about it."

I said, "Are you kidding me? If I had been the winner of a marathon, I'd

416

remind people on a daily basis. I'm kind of glad you never mentioned it to me before today. I would have looked at you much different and possibly been somewhat intimidated."

I never looked at Georgeann the same way again. My respect for her went through the roof. She is a true legend.

Dre and I went on one more training run three weeks before the race. We ran 15.6 miles on my hilly Morgan Street home route. I got us well prepared. On Monday, September 23, we appeared on the front page of the *Akron Beacon Journal*. We had Northeast Ohio abuzz over our friendship and our attempt to become the first push-chair team to ever compete in the Akron Marathon. Bigger still, we were attempting to be the first push chair team in Ohio to ever run 26.2 miles. Another individual in a wheelchair had before been pushed 26.2 miles, but he was pushed by four men. I was the only one who would be pushing Dre.

The phone at Total to Care Dayhab (where Dre spent his time during the week) was ringing off the hook. Folks from all over wanted to somehow be a part of this history. Eric Bailey and Ashley McComb from Summit DD's communication department wanted to interview, take photos, and film us for a featured documentary. Although I wasn't very thrilled about it at first, I agreed to go along with it because Dre really wanted to do it. I was beginning to feel pressure mounting on my shoulders.

The day before the race I was getting ready to head out to get Dre for the Marathon Expo, and received a call from Bob Jones of WEWS Channel 5 in Cleveland.

"Is this the same Zeke that I interviewed fourteen months ago when you came home from prison in Haiti?" he said. When I said yes, he said, "Wow, that's pretty extraordinary."

He quickly inquired about my availability in meeting up with him that morning. I told him that I was leaving to get Dre and head over to the JAR Arena. The Zips were having their first team practice of the season. Coach Dambrot had invited Dre over to watch. In previous years Dambrot coached Dre's cousin Romeo Travis. From there we were going directly to the Marathon Expo.

To be honest, I was a little annoyed just because I didn't want to be bothered at all. I was focused. But because it was Bob, I agreed to provide him that access. We interviewed with Bob on the track at the JAR where we had trained all winter while the Zips practiced. After that we went down on the floor where Dre addressed the Zips basketball team. Former player Jeremiah Wood was present, and Dre really enjoyed the opportunity to speak with him. Coach Dambrot gave us some shirts, wished us luck, and we were off to the Expo.

At the Marathon Expo we were interviewed by Dave Hunter. Dave always handled interviewing the elite runners competing in the race each year. We told Dave that we wanted to finish in under five hours. After that we had a more intimate interview with the Summit DD communications people who were working on the documentary. After that it was time to go. Later that evening I received a phone call from first-year race director of the Akron Marathon Brian Polen. He called to check in on me and see how I was doing. That was one of those gestures that you never forget. After a nice chat with Brian, my childhood friend Tim Widner called. Tim always had a way of finding time for a phone call when the stakes were the highest. Earthquake, prison, or marathons, Tim was always there. All he said was this: "You better fucking finish this race," and he hung up. That's all I needed to hear. That was great motivation for me.

That night sleeping was tough, so I turned to my dad for some inspiration. I opened up my iPad and went straight to YouTube to watch Secretariat win the 1973 Belmont Stakes to fire me up. The three of them — Dre, Secretariat, and my late father — were more than enough to have me jacked up and the juices flowing. It had been a very long time since I felt butterflies in my stomach like this. It was show time.

Downtown Akron was alive that morning. Dre and I pulled into VIP parking where we were afforded all the luxuries of the elite runners. Warming up with African runners like Joseph Mutinda from Kenya was a real thrill for us. The Africans probably thought I looked out of place because I was wearing forty-four long hoop shorts to run in. I was a ballplayer, not a distance runner, so I dressed like it. I was decked out in the Haitian flag colors of blue and red. Dre wore all red from head to toe. I kept thinking that I wished my dad were here to see this. He would be so proud.

My breakfast that morning was a banana, and a bag of Skittles. At the

418

start line we both took in the moment. Andre was beaming with pride during his first national anthem as an athlete. He let out a roar after the anthem ended. I was feeling the pressure and embracing it at the same time. We were already local celebrities from the newspaper and TV stories about us, yet we still had not one full marathon distance on our resume. Too many people were watching and counting on us. We had to finish this race.

Our personal goal time for our first marathon was a sub five-hour time. As the clock struck 6:59 a.m. we were off. Race director Brian Polen let us out of the gate a minute earlier than the other athletes. He did that so we could get out in front and over to the far right to avoid the stampede that was soon to come from behind us. We started out all alone to the cheers of the multitudes that lined the road on both sides. The lights of cameras and smart phones were flashing and popping one after another. The crowd was incredible. It was electric.

A police motorcade followed us, then broke out ahead of us as the elite runners approached from behind sounding like three hundred heavy horses. At least that's what they sounded like to me. My heart was pounding. Goosebumps were raised on the skin of my entire frame. We covered the first mile in seven minutes and sixteen seconds. I was gassed. I remember briefly thinking to myself, "How in the blue hell am I gonna be able to do what I just did in that first mile twenty-five more times?"

As we continued on the route, one runner after another passed by me and Dre congratulating, thanking, and encouraging us. Dre responded to and addressed every last one of them. For me personally, I didn't want to be bothered. It annoyed me, especially because nothing had yet been fulfilled. My old JV basketball coach at Barberton, Duane Daily, yelled out, "Petrie," just as he had done twenty-five years ago when I was in his gym class the day I found out that I was diabetic. More goosebumps ensued. Georgeann had instructed me to drink fluids by mile marker three, which I did. I absorbed all of her counsel after discovering that she had big time credentials. I labored, grinding hard through the first six or seven miles before I could find a comfortable rhythm. By mile eight I began to feel we were moving like a well-oiled machine. The enthusiasm from the large crowds brought us great energy. The musical marching bands that aligned

419

the course added more spirit to my legs each time.

Georgeann had told us prior to the race that she would see us at the mile ten marker but we never saw her. As a matter of fact, we were already at mile twelve when she arrived at mile ten. Georgeann was very surprised. She was in communication with Katie Byard of the Beacon via cell phone when Dre and I had stopped for some fluids at mile twelve. Members of Dre's family were waiting for us at the bottom of the North Howard Street hill and E. Lods. Georgeann remembered our first training run we did with the race chair back in August. On that run we completed just under ten miles, and it took us over two hours to do that. On this day we reached the 13.1 mile marker on the towpath in under two hours. Georgeann never anticipated that we were capable of going that fast, and even suggested to Katie that she hoped I was trying to run a smart and tactful race so that we would see the finish line. She worried at this pace we might not finish.

Close to exiting the towpath there was a small bridge that we had to cross. While crossing this bridge I suffered a real scare. Both of my calves started to tighten up. It felt as though with each step that they were going to pop. It really frightened me. I immediately slowed our pace. We came off the towpath in Merriman Valley and began running on pavement once again. My calves were still causing me lots of grief. I had to stop, stretch, and collect myself. Although we had already traversed sixteen miles, the race was just getting started. The farthest Dre and I had ever run together was 15.6 miles on our hilly course back home. We were now in uncharted waters with ten miles to go. As I tried to start up again my calves were still at the point of explosion. I continued on slowly and methodically, pushing Dre as we began to climb the hills in Merriman Valley. I was in so much pain.

This is when Georgeann and her husband finally made an appearance. I told them I was hurting pretty-bad. Georgeann advised me to just take it easy and walk it out for the time being. Of course I was trying to not hear that. If we were going to be out on that course competing, we were going to run as hard as we could.

After taking in some more fluids and listening to all the wise counsel from Team Haviland, we set off uphill. The short break seemed to help. When we got to going again, I was able to grind forward and upward without as much pain. The tightness in the calves subsided a little bit. Then there was Dre quarterbacking from the front of the chair. He was talking me through it all. He kept encouraging me to fight, yelling out, "No pain no gain. Let's go, we got this." His inspiration and leadership from the front was a life-giving force.

Early on in the race, part of me dared to believe that we had a chance to run a 4:15 marathon. But that old Akron Marathon race-course didn't really start until mile sixteen, and on the backside those hills were unforgiving. There was a three-mile stretch of nothing but going uphill. It was a real dogfight for us.

At mile 22.5 we hit the Akron Marathon's version of Heartbreak Hill. This is when a male runner came over to us asking me if I needed help. I didn't respond as my head was down, and my legs were churning. The man then reached over to place his hand on Dre's chair. Before he could touch the chair, I slapped his hand away and said get the fuck off. Although he was well intentioned, he had no idea of what we had invested in this. He then sprinted ahead of us, stopped, pulled his smart phone out, and took a selfie with us in the background coming up behind him. That's when I finally realized what we were doing was kind of special. As we turned left from Portage Path onto Market Street to head downtown, we were somewhere around two miles or so to go from the finish line. This is when my friend and co-worker, the late Mike Radovic, appeared out of nowhere and ran over to embrace me and Dre. Mike thought the world of what we were doing and was really proud of us. He was moved to tears.

On Market Street we were greeted by long lines of cars honking, people screaming and cheering, and police officers saluting us. My leg muscles were burning to the bone, but I just closed my eyes and could hear the 1973 Belmont Stakes playing in my head. Secretariat is grinding now, he is moving like a tremendous machine. Secretariat by 12, Secretariat by 14 lengths on the turn. Thinking of Secretariat, 1973, on my dad's lap, after everything I had lived through, especially in the last two and a half years, my eyes welled up.

As we barreled down Market Street and onto Main Street I looked over to our right and witnessed Georgeann running on the sidewalk alongside of us. She had appeared from out of nowhere. She ran all the way to the

421

stadium entrance with us. As we approached the entrance to the stadium, scores of police officers were saluting and cheering our effort. Hundreds of people lined both sides of Main Street calling out to Dre.

It was the most euphoric feeling I had ever experienced in my lifetime. I can't overstate enough just how big and spirited the crowds were in Akron on that day.

We turned down the ramp that leads into the stadium, and I was trying to take deliberate steps to not slip and fall on a surface that felt slick to me underneath my feet. When we got to the bottom of the ramp I stopped. Dre was trying to look back at me to see what I was doing. I reached down into a bottom basket on the race chair, pulled out my Haitian flag, and draped it over my shoulders. I had no idea of what time it was, or what our race time was. I was wearing a brand new watch for this race because I thought it would make me look like a real runner. But I had forgotten to set it.

As we entered the stadium the sun was shining bright on us. The crowd inside of this field of dreams had been following our story as they played our pre-race interview and gave updates on our progress through announcements over the loud-speaker and while watching on the Jumbo Tron. We ran the last fifty meters of the blue line carpet to the roar of the crowd. We stopped again several feet from the finish line.

I came around from behind the chair, bent over, and gave Dre a kiss. I said, "I'm proud of you Dre, I love you!" We walked to the finish line.

Members of the media were lined up and snapping pictures that captured this historic event. Dre and I were given a stand-still Michael Jeffrey Jordan moment in time that most human beings never sniff. There was one photographer from behind our chair that caught a shot of us crossing the tape and looking up at the clock, which read 4:53.53.

The earthquake in Haiti happened on Tuesday, January 12, 2010, at 4:53 p.m. I was draped in the Haitian flag. You could have not made this up if you tried.

Everyone in that stadium was on their feet. Dre was overwhelmed with emotions. We had accomplished what we had set out to do eleven months earlier. It was us against the world, and we delivered a show that will not soon be forgotten. The performance given on this day would in the near

422

future open up doors for other wheelchair athletes at the Akron Marathon.

We became the first push chair team of two that ever went 26.2 miles in the history of the state of Ohio. In doing so we succeeded in bringing a multitude of people together. On this day the Akron Marathon did record numbers. I like to think me and Dre had a lot to do with that. We forced people to once again believe in the triumph of the human spirit. We made thousands that day stop in their tracks, and witness something they had never seen before. We made everyone feel some type of way. We wanted all the smoke and we got it.

Dave Hunter quickly pulled us off to the side and interviewed us right there on the spot. The crowd watched on the Jumbo Tron as medals were placed around our necks. I was so ignorant as to how things worked, I thought that the medals were reserved for me and Dre only. I had no clue that every participant was awarded a medal.

During the interview in front of a jubilant crowd, I thanked Dick and Rick Hoyt. I said they were the Michael Jordans of this type of event. We were just trying to do our best Kobe Bryant imitation. I thanked my late father. I thanked the late Larry Soyars. Finally, I thanked the people of the country of Haiti. My sons Moses and Spartacus made their way down to the stadium floor with my wife, Darline. It was such a special moment. If time could have only stood still forever at that moment I would have been content.

This was my Secretariat at the Belmont Stakes moment. It was my Michael Jordan walk off buzzer beater moment. It was my Ted Williams rounding third base spitting up at the press box moment. It was the ultimate thumbing of my nose to everyone that ever doubted me.

I left Canal Park stadium with my wife that afternoon and had to walk Dre's race chair all the way back up to where we had started the marathon that morning. That's where my van was left parked. We briefly met up with Georgeann a short distance away from the downtown area to return the race chair to her.

As I started driving back to where we were living in Akron, I got a little disoriented. I pulled off to the side of the road right as I was getting ready to go on the expressway. I looked at my wife and told her I had no idea where we were. Unbeknownst to me, and fortunately for me, Georgeann and her husband Bryan had followed us closely. They pulled up behind the van. I told them that we were lost. I suspect from the brief convo I had with Georgeann while transferring the chair she must have felt something wasn't right. I was a little embarrassed. I gave them the address to where we were staying. Bryan then drove my van as Georgeann followed us there.

My sugar dropping was a huge factor in this event. It was a precursor of health issues to come.

WHAT COMES NEXT?

On Tuesday, September 24, a day after the *Beacon Journal* had run the front page story about me and Dre, my ex-wife Aslyne re-tweeted Jeanne Bryant's tweet about relationship withdrawal. The reason why breakups are so hard is because our brains go through withdrawals. Just like drug addiction, we are addicted to love. Since I was the only past relationship she ever had in her life before being with her current boyfriend Kevin, I took it as her way of acknowledging me, and paying tribute to what I had meant to her. After all, I was the one that buried her mother. I was the one that brought her to the United States. I was the father of her first two children.

Coming off the article about us that received so much attention in Northeast Ohio, I felt as though I was vindicated. For my ex-wife, for my mom, for my sister, for my aunts, for my work associates, and for any and all of my haters in Haiti and my hometown of Barberton, this was a defiant act with my finger pointed at all of them. It was my way of reminding them that I was Zeke of Haiti, and that I was still to be reckoned with. Greatness was still at my fingertips. Let history record it as such.

On Sunday, September 29, Pastor Jean M. Hansen of Faith Lutheran Church in Akron gave a sermon entitled, "Fighting the Good Fight of Faith," where he used me and Dre as an example. Hansen said, "I do not know if Zeke Petrie considers himself to be a Christian, but his actions made a difference and speak to us."

Speaking of me and Dre and our effort to run the Akron Marathon, he said, "What I see is righteousness, godliness, faith, love, endurance, and gentleness, along with mutual support. That makes a difference not only in one or two lives, but it seeps into the air and changes the atmosphere in which we dwell."

Going through pain had nourished both me and Dre's courage. Julius Caesar once said, "It's easier to find men who will volunteer to die, than to find those who are willing to endure pain with patience." Being willing to embrace pain is really what in the end defined how we were able to inspire thousands of people.

One day not long after the Akron Marathon I was sitting in my work van talking with Dre. "Everyone is now asking what's next?" he said.

I said, "What do you mean what's next? I'm done. That was my walk off home run. No mas like Roberto Duran. Besides, I can't run any longer just to run. I would need a new challenge. That's just me, it's who I am. I always push the limits. Unless you want to try a triathlon or something, I'm out."

I was hoping and expecting him to say no thanks to get me off the hook. Of course, he said "Let's do it."

I thought, oh fuck man, *that's just what I didn't want to hear.* Dre and I were on top of the world. We could only go down from here, I thought.

On October 21 Dre and I were invited to speak at the All Agency Inservice of the Summit DD Board at the John S. Knight Center in downtown Akron. I suggested we wear pink for Breast Cancer Awareness month. I invited Anne Bitong and Brian Polen of the Akron Marathon to be present. I thanked them for the opportunity to participate in their race. A ten-minute documentary video that the Summit DD Communications Department put together was unveiled to a crowd of about six hundred. After the video was played Dre and I took to the stage. We were awarded some really nice plaques made by the folks at Summit DD. The plaques were really impressive. My mom, my wife, and my friend Donny Pavlik were along with me on this day. I told the three of them that I was just going to speak from the heart and be totally honest. I can never go wrong with the truth.

Certain parts of my speech concerning my training protocol with Dre, my verbal interactions with him, and my initial negative attitude towards those with disabilities, upset some people in the audience. I eluded to us training in the rain where I told Dre we would drown out here if need be.

It very well could rain on race day. We needed to be prepared for that. We ran and trained on warm days in the hot sun. We were prepared for anything. I was very arrogant and wanted Dre to prove he was worthy of this. I spoke of breaching certain subjects like politics and religion just to see how Dre would respond. All of this was disconcerting to many in the audience.

I wasn't made aware of this until about four or five days later. Lisa Somers brought it to my attention. She said, "You've been issued a disciplinary write up from those at the top for some of the things you said during your speech with Dre." After reviewing the paperwork I said to Lisa, "You tell them this for me: they were all very fortunate that I even decided to show up. I did them a great favor. If they are now choosing to be this ungrateful that's on them." Am I not generous?

During this sequence I was also made aware of what was going on behind the scenes since the day of our speech. Dre had been interviewed about me. During that interview Dre stated that I often talk about Haiti, and sometimes that irritated him. Dre went on to say that he felt as though we both had different goals for participating in the Akron Marathon. This revelation pissed me off. When I saw Dre again, I said to him, "You are only where you are on this day because of Haiti and the Haitian people. Don't ever forget that. You're welcome!" Then I walked away.

On the day of our speech at the John S. Knight Center it was revealed that five Billboards featuring Dre and me that read "Supporting Greatness" were going up all over Summit County. They were left up for about four months. One was placed on Wooster Road in Barberton, one on Arlington Road in Akron, one on Cuyahoga Falls Avenue in Akron, one on Route 8 in Akron, and one on Thornton Street in Akron.

With Lebron no longer in town, it was Dre and I who were now carrying the city on our backs. We both received a letter from the Ohio House of Representatives. The letter sent to me referred to me as one of Ohio's finest citizens for my exploits shown on September 28, 2013. It was signed by members of the 130th General Assembly of Ohio: Representative Zack Milkovich, Representative Vernon Sykes, and the Speaker of the Ohio House William G. Batchelder.

426

PART FIVE - REDEMPTION

The letter credited me for my talent, spirit, and leadership. It read:

> You are a remarkable individual, with combined talent and competitive spirit, with the highest ideals of good sportsmanship to establish yourself as a truly incredible athlete. An unwavering commitment to excellence has earned you the respect and esteem of many and deserving of high praise. Your accomplishments and leadership both in and out of competition is a great source of pride and outstanding reflection of you.

I was commended on my personal successes and saluted as one of Ohio's finest citizens. Just fifteen months earlier I was sitting in one of the world's worst prisons.

The great Jerry Izenberg of the New Jersey *Star-Ledger* once said, "You can't anticipate greatness. You can't really define it. It's something that God, every once in a while, sticks in somebody. And because it comes from God, the gift can't be ignored, and it can't be defeated."

This was on full display in my fortieth year on this planet. Beaten up and downtrodden for over a quarter of a century in a diabetic frame, I rose up like Shammah in a Lentil field carving out history. I was now feeling pretty good about myself. I had arisen from the abyss. I was dead, but alive again. You don't give somebody like me a second chance. You don't do it. When I was in prison in Haiti, I begged God for a new life and another chance. I would mutter to myself, "Y'all better not let me out of here." I sincerely never believed they were going to let me out of prison anyway. But they did, and I was here making shit happen with a vengeance. In earlier years I used to ride the Metro bus to get around. Friends were now texting me pictures of my image on the rear of these same buses. Images of me and Dre were now on billboards, buses, calendars, and catalogs. We were even on a commercial that got a lot of run on local cable television. I was on top of the world.

In November I got a YMCA membership. This is not something that I would have normally done. I needed to teach myself how to swim all over

427

again, but this time do it the right way, and to be good enough to pull Dre in a raft behind me. I looked at a lot of YouTube videos. I humbled myself to ask questions of a ninety-year old woman named Betty who swam quite often at the YMCA's facility in Barberton. Betty was an outstanding swimmer and always gracious in answering my questions.

I got in touch with an old high school classmate of my brother Ben named Jeff Chalmers. Ben had recently run into Jeff's dad, Bob, at a golf course where they chatted for a bit. Bob was the one who had called me on the phone when I was going into my high school years about coming out for the soccer team. He mentioned to Ben that his son, Jeff, competed in triathlons. I was currently trying to steal any useful knowledge that I could concerning these three disciplines, but especially the swimming. So I reached out to Jeff via Facebook to ask him a couple of questions.

When Ben brought Jeff's name up, my first reaction to him was, "You mean little Jeff Chalmers?" I hadn't seen him since 1991. I remembered him being little and scrawny. Jeff was an inferior athlete to me in those days. He grew and matured in college, however, to a strapping six foot two, 170 pounds. He ran the 2001 Detroit Marathon where he averaged a five minute and thirty-one-second mile for the entire 26.2, finishing with a time of 2:24.58. That led to being an invited runner at the Boston Marathon. By this feat alone he had my attention and respect. This was important to me.

Ironically, I once viewed endurance athletes with great contempt. I would say to myself, "Don't these people have anything better to do with their time? Do they not play real sports?"

Jeff became sort of a middle-man for me. I knew he had played different sports growing up. Through him my view of these endurance athletes softened. I inundated him with questions. One question turned into two questions, then three, then four. It was to the point where I was pestering Jeff quite frequently without shame. I was hungry for the wealth of wisdom he could share with me. He basically became my best friend by default. I was not his best friend by any means, but he was mine. I wanted to know everything. My training for an Iron Man 70.3 race with Dre was under way.

In the meantime, Darline and I moved once again. When she first arrived from Haiti, we were staying at Jay Belkey's place. From there we stayed for a while in Akron at the residence of Tyarlo Geffrard, uncle of Houston Texans linebacker Whitney Mercilus. We then moved back to my mother's place, the house I grew up in on Lloyd. Fifteen months after she put me out, she took me back in. I didn't have a lot of money. My wife wasn't able to work as of yet. Having the public's adoration after what I accomplished with Dre helped in how my mom viewed me. Staying at her place would give me a chance to finally save some money. When I returned from prison in Haiti, I had nothing. Medical bills for continued treatment of my corneal abrasion mounted. I invested all the money I had in bringing Darline to the states from Haiti. I was paying child support for my two sons. I was still in the poor house. But I was optimistic. We were heading into 2014 and it was looking to be a good year for me. I was starting to feel somewhat normal again. It was a rebirth of sorts. Only time would tell.

2014-2015
LIFE IN MARATHONS

That entire winter of 2014 I trained at the YMCA to compete with Dre in an Iron Man 70.3 event. I swam nearly every day. After swimming I would get on the bike. I was doing heavy mileage. Actually, to say I was overdoing it is an understatement.

I was happy to see the spring months roll in. Training indoors is nice, but it can wear on you over time. I was so thirsty just to get outside. As part of our Iron Man training, we would be running the Cleveland Marathon on May 18, which was the two-year anniversary of my arrest and imprisonment in Haiti. The year prior I spent this anniversary in Boston, interviewing with Haitian Jonas and Tele Boston. On this special day I'd be pushing Dre 26.2 miles. We were soon going to find out if we could duplicate what we had done just eight months earlier. In April I had suffered an injury to my rib wrestling around with my wife. This put me on the shelf for the entire month and set me way back with my conditioning. I only had two and a half weeks to prepare for Cleveland.

Freelance Cinematographer PJ Mozingo would join up with us on this journey. He came to Cleveland to film the race, and subsequently began to make a documentary about our Iron Man quest, with an ultimate goal of reaching Kona in Hawaii.

By mile fifteen in Cleveland, my legs had left me, and it became a real suffer fest. I continued on in a lot of pain and we finished in a time of 5:21. This was nearly a half hour slower than our Akron time, and on a much easier course. It proved to be a great test for us, however. I was not in any sort of elite shape whatsoever, but we were able to show some character by finishing regardless. We took some positives away from that race and learned to never take anything for granted. Every race was different. The training block was different, the time of year, the weather, how we felt physically. We were learning along the way and trying our best to trust the process.

By the end of May, Dre was starting to sing a different tune about participating in an Iron Man triathlon, even though we were already registered for Iron Man 70.3 in Muncie, Indiana, slated for July 12. One morning he said that he didn't know whether he was still going to be able to do the Iron Man race. When I asked him why, he threw every excuse in the book at me. As I questioned him further, he said that his health aides told him that he shouldn't go through with the race. They evidently had told him that it was too risky.

Later that day while sitting in the van together I blurted out, "Cut the shit man. What the fuck? You wanted to do this. You were saying everyone wanted to know what was next. I've been spending money every month training for this race, man. I've been going to the YMCA all winter long getting half naked to go swimming, training to pull you in a raft. We are two months out from this race and now you decide you want to quit? Don't bullshit me bro. You're scared of the water, you're fucking scared of the water, aren't you?"

Dre gave me a blank stare with no response. His eyes welled with tears. I said, "You want to quit? Then fucking quit!"

By this time, we'd had several speaking engagements with elementary, middle school, and high school students. Dre's mom had given him up to the foster care system when he was only eight years old and his dad was in prison. Being confined to a wheelchair wasn't the only thing he had going

430

against him. During those motivational speeches Dre pointed out these hardships and would tell the students to never quit, and never give up.

I used this against him and called him a quitting ass coward. I said, "You go talk all this shit to all these kids and you don't live that life. If you ain't about that life, quit lying to these kids, goddammit."

I tore into him like nobody had ever done in his entire existence. I treated Dre no different than I did any able-bodied son-of-a-bitch. I dealt with him as my equal and gave it to him just like I would have anybody else. I immediately called Wanda. She was responsible for taking care of Dre. I said, "We, need to go to the YMCA this weekend and get Dre comfortable around the water. We can't wait any longer. Dre needs to get in the water and get over his fear of it." I told her not to worry, that I would get into the water with him, I just needed her present.

We went to the Y that weekend, and Dre ended up having the time of his life. He was timid at first. He saw me in the water firing him up and talking trash. When his fragile frame was finally submerged in that warm water of the YMCA's therapy pool, he was good to go. He had a life jacket on, and with it the confidence to keep his head above water while floating on his back. It was a huge victory for him to overcome that fear. Nobody even knew he was afraid of the water because he kept it to himself. I brought it out of him and remedied it this way. I told him I was afraid, too. I then challenged him, and he met the challenge. We were now one step closer.

On a Saturday in June we headed to Portage Lakes State Park for a training run for all three disciplines, the swim, the bike, and the run. We were graced by the presence of a legend when Georgeann Haviland showed up. She was gracious enough to lend us a raft for me to pull Dre in during the water portion of the race. She also brought along something called a Wike for me to pull Dre in during the bike portion of the race. Dre had a new race chair which Wanda bought for him. So, we were all set. I can't overstate enough how much Georgeann Haviland's role in our journey really gave us the chance we needed to compete. Without her assistance none of this stuff would have happened. The time and material she invested in us was a very selfless act that she didn't have to do. She owed us nothing and gave to us everything.

The second week of July we traveled to Muncie, Indiana. On Friday, July 11, the day before our race we shared the front page of the *Akron Beacon Journal* with Lebron James, whom Dre adored so much. We fought proudly through the 1.2 mile swim.

The fifty-six-mile bike portion did us in.

I was given advice by Jeff to acquire some clip pedals, and clip pedal shoes for the bike, which I never did. Not only did I not adhere to that sound advice, I had the audacity to show up to the race with a mountain bike for me to pull Dre with.

I thought, how hard could it really be? *I'm just pulling Dre on a bike, no big deal.*

There's a reason for athletes to use road bikes and clip pedal shoes in distances of fifty-six and 112 miles. Mountain bikes plus no clip pedal shoes, especially pulling someone from behind, was a disaster waiting to happen. On this day it was windy. It was like pulling a parachute against the wind. Total torture. By the time we finished the fifty-six miles on the bike we were ten minutes past the cut off time. We would have continued on, but my legs totally shut down on me. They cramped up and I couldn't move. I couldn't walk, let alone run at that point. I started vomiting profusely. It was a devastating blow to both me and Dre.

When the *Akron Beacon Journal* ran a story about our Iron Man quest, failing was not an option. Failing never entered into the equation. We only had a plan A. That was to get through the swim, and we'd be good. The swim was physical. We took a beating in the water, getting hit and kicked on several occasions. At one point during the swim, a male swimmer got caught between me and Dre. He got tangled in the cord of my harness. He nearly overturned the raft which would have sent Dre into the water. I was cursing him as I choked down some water that smelled and tasted like gasoline. After getting through the swim and coming out of the water, we were already celebrating victory.

But on this day, just like many times before in my life, failure would be achieved because of my blatant disregard for doing things the right way. I tried to console Dre about our disappointing finish. He wouldn't look at me. All he wanted was his medal. He refused to leave until they gave him one. Competitive greatness was revealed in him on this day, and I couldn't have been more proud of him.

A couple of days later the *Akron Beacon Journal* again ran a story about us. Although this time it was concerning our failure at Iron Man Muncie. I was quick to blame our failure on faulty and inferior equipment. I didn't have the luxury of a customized race chair to push and pull Dre in.

In fact, my total disregard of wise counsel and my plain arrogance is what cost us the finish. Probably didn't help any that I was having sex with my wife in the hotel just eight hours before the race. Women make the legs weak.

That failure was a bitter pill to swallow. I apologized to PJ Mozingo and his crew for having them come all the way out to Muncie, Indiana, just to film us failing. Mozingo said, "Are you kidding me Zeke, that was some of the best stuff I've ever shot. The emotion, the passion, the struggle, the fight, the defeat, that is what makes great movies, my friend." PJ gave me a new perspective on that day. Although it didn't make me feel any better, I was glad he wasn't angry with me. Because I was very angry with me.

A few weeks past, and I was now growing antsy. I needed to prove a point to myself that I could finish an Iron Man race without Dre. I hastily signed up for Iron Man Louisville 140.6, which was scheduled for Sunday, August 24. This time around I would be ready, or so I thought. Jeff sent me some clip pedals for the bike, and money to buy a pair of clip pedal shoes. With that said I still made two grave mistakes. I rented a road bike from Century Cycles in Peninsula, Ohio, and I only wore the clip pedal shoes once for a couple of minutes the day before the race. I had zero experience training with them. On Saturday, August 23, I had entertained the idea of having the tires on the bike checked and cleaned out, but decided against paying the sixty dollars to have it done.

It rained hard in Louisville the two nights leading up to the race. The Ohio River was nice and swollen. The first part of the 2.4-mile swim was upstream against the current. At the very start of the race, I felt that I made a nice jump into the river, trying to steer clear of other swimmers. It was only a moment later I got hit hard in the head by another athlete, and now I was sucking down water. I was coughing and choking with snot bubbles popping from my nose. For a brief moment I contemplated quitting right there, and I wasn't even fifty meters into the 2.4 mile swim.

As I was about to tap out, I thought of all the guys I was in prison with. I thought about my late father. I thought about my two sons. I thought about Dre. I couldn't quit. That's when I decided I'd prefer drowning to giving up.

The day before leaving for Louisville I had called my friend, Margie Kinsinger, to bring me something to take for a bad summer cold. It was like having the flu in the summer. My sugars were running high. I felt like shit. I was miserable. She brought me a few things she thought would help, including some salt tablets. The race day temp forecast was calling for 95 degrees. Surely the salt tablets would come in handy.

I grinded that swim out in a time of two hours and two minutes showing a lot of heart and toughness. Once again, I thought OK, worst part is over. I'm good. I mounted the rental road bike and set off for the very challenging 112-mile hilly trek through the scenic Louisville countryside.

I wasn't three miles out of the gate and already suffered a flat tire. Because of my lack of experience with the clip pedals, I couldn't get myself unhitched from the bike and I went down like a ton of bricks. My left knee was now a bloody mess. By the time I got my flat fixed a good amount of time off the clock had passed. I wasn't in last place, but I was way behind the majority of the other athletes at this point. I was finally on my way again, discouraged but not defeated.

At this point a guy named Andrew McBeath Wright, an avid cyclist from Kentucky came riding up alongside of me. Although he was not an actual participant in the race, I enjoyed his company thoroughly.

About an hour and a half or so later I went down hard again, suffering another flat tire. This fall was even worse because I had been traveling downhill at a high rate of speed when the tire ruptured. I had gravel lodged in my back, my arm, and in my knee. I was bleeding through my shirt. The gash on my knee was now opened and gushing. I felt the stinging sensation throughout my body as the sweat invaded all these open wounds. Andrew fixed the flat for me. I lost a lot more time off the clock after this fall before I got up and moved forward again. This is where Andrew and I separated. I was very demoralized.

At one point a female athlete was riding next to me as we climbed up a hill together. She had come up from behind me and was evidently

434

observing just what kind of mess my tri suit had become. I was bathed and covered in mud and blood. She loudly proclaimed, "What a badass!" as she passed by me. I didn't feel like much of a badass.

I was now at mile fifty-six. I had been asking Andrew and some of the volunteers working the event what time it was throughout the day because I didn't have a watch on, and my bike was not outfitted with a time device. I was informed that I was required by race rules to be at the sixty-mile marker in less than fifteen minutes, or I was going to be removed from the course because of not making the cut-off time. I knew that I wasn't going to make it. It was 95 degrees. I was fighting a bad summer cold with high blood sugar. My body was on fire, and I was in tremendous pain from absorbing the shock of two very hard falls on the bike. I said to myself, "I'll be damned if they are going to remove me from this shitty course. I'll walk off this bitch before I give them that pleasure."

And walk off I did, at mile fifty-seven. I had now been in two Iron Man races in a month and a half, and I failed both of them. I was defeated.

I headed back home to Ohio and had every intention of quitting and letting Dre know I was done. Whatever racing it was, marathons or triathlons, I was fucking done. When I arrived in Ohio, I didn't talk to anyone other than Darline and my mom. I had to look at both of them, and somehow try to explain and justify how I managed to pull off another expensive failure. Triathlon is not a sport for poor people like me. I was investing money in this stuff that I really didn't have. And for what? I was so pissed.

Before I could call to tell Dre that I was never doing another race, I received a phone call from him. He said, "Hey Zeke, can we do the Akron Marathon again?"

I could hear the excitement in his voice. I sensed him anticipating a yes. I closed my eyes as I prepared to tell him no. Before I could even get the no out, he started to talk about all the people that he wanted to run for.

Fuck me, man.

"Yeah for sure bro, let's do it."

Dre said, "Let's go defend our title. Akron is where it all began a year ago. This is home, let's do it." I couldn't tell him no. Truly I was a glutton for punishment.

About two weeks before the Akron Marathon, I received a phone call from a lady named Hope Carr. Hope worked for a nonprofit organization called The Arc of Ohio. She had set up a speaking engagement for me and Dre at Stow Kimpton Middle School. Hope ran a program educating young people about different disabilities such as blindness and cerebral palsy. She had a deep understanding of what cerebral palsy was all about, because both of her children were afflicted with it. This endeared me to her greatly. I always felt a pull in the direction of people who knew and understood what it was like to really suffer great hardship. On September 18, a little over a week before the race, we spoke to four hundred eighth graders at Kimpton. One of the students, a boy named Alexander, was greatly moved by our presentation. So much in fact that he showed up with his mother Karen on the morning of the Akron Marathon to greet and have a picture with us. We ran that race much faster than our first marathon. We bettered our time by about fourteen minutes.

On October 13 Dre and I were invited guests on WAKR 1590AM radio. We did an hour question and answer spot with James Carney. A lady that worked at the station approached me afterwards and said, "Have you ever done radio before? You have a great voice. You seem to be a natural at it."

I responded, "Well, I once spoke to two million Haitians on the radio. Does that count?"

FM 94.9 WQMX radio host Lynn Kelly was very gracious to us on this day. Lynn embraced us with lots of love and encouragement. We took a selfie with her and then went on our way.

On October 16, three days before the Columbus Marathon, we were guest speakers at St. Vincent St.-Mary ("St. V") High School, Home of Lebron James. While there, we spoke to the Athletes in Action for Christ student group.

Before going to St. V to give a presentation, I was told of a story about an eleven-year-old girl named Rachel who had pushed a disabled twelve-year-old boy named Ethan in a triathlon. Ethan suffered from autism and cerebral palsy. A lady named Lisa Sheppard Chaplin who had been our bike attendant at the Akron Marathon told me about the pair. I asked Lisa to reach out to the parents of Rachel and Ethan on my behalf. She knew both families and obliged me. I invited them along to speak at St.

V with us. It was such a proud moment for all involved. Just like my time in Haiti spent encouraging inclusion, so here it rang true again. Trying to make everyone feel important, feel like equals, regardless of their personal situations, is the precedent I always tried to set. I had a big heart for the underdogs in life – the disenfranchised, and now the disabled. It was for people like this that my heart bled.

I thought about the Hoyt tree, and how from them branched off other push chair teams. Rachel had been in the stadium a year earlier when Dre and I came running into the finish line. She was so inspired by what she witnessed that she went forward and took action. Such an admirable thing to do for a young girl her age. The maturity Rachel exuded was off-the-charts impressive to me.

During the Expo for the 2014 Akron Marathon we had been introduced to another push chair team. Adam Bracken and his father Steve. Steve, suffering from ALS, was pushed by his son and a group of other runners representing Team Trample ALS. Adam pulled me aside and expressed some heart-felt sentiments. He said, "Me and my dad are both here running today because of you and Dre. What you guys did at last year's Akron Marathon inspired us to come out and run this year."

As Adam was finishing his thoughts a group of people walked by pointing at me saying that's the guy from the Program. The 2014 Akron Marathon Official Program and Events Guide dawned a blown up picture of me and Dre on page four with the full schedule of events for that Friday and Saturday.

I thought for a brief moment of how selfish I had been. Had I told Dre I quit just weeks earlier, none of this would be happening. I had to keep reminding myself, "It's not about you."

For who is greater, he who sits at the table, or he who serves?

Going back in time to November of 2013, Dre and I had gone to Columbus to run in a 5K for veterans. Race day forecast called for wind and temps in the 30s. We were invited by Georgeann Haviland. After all she had done for us, we couldn't turn her down.

On the morning of this race, a lady approached us and said, "I'm here today because of you guys. I saw your story and was moved to action. I'm changing my life and getting in shape."

It's not easy to explain what words like that make you feel inside. Dre and I had a platform, and we needed to take full advantage of it. In this life windows and doors open and close quickly.

We turned right back around and made another trip to Columbus shortly thereafter for the years end celebration of My Team Triumphs Columbus Ohio Chapter in 2013. While there Dre and I had more of an intimate opportunity to meet other people just like us. Those suffering from disabilities, and those that pushed them in race chairs. I presented the plaque given to me at the John S. Knight Center back in October of that year by the Summit DD people to Georgeann. To this very day it's still hanging in her office. I gave my shirt that I wore the day of the 2013 Akron Marathon to Georgeann. On the back of it read, "Happiness cannot be achieved by a reasoned plan of existence, but must be earned through suffering." On the front of it read, "Jesse Ventura for President 2016."

Andre presented to her the red socks he wore the day of that life-changing event. This is where in a private moment together with Georgeann at her family home, she admitted to me that she had her doubts about us being able to finish our first Akron Marathon. She said at one point she didn't think I was going to be able to make it the entire 26.2 miles pushing Dre. She never had anyone in her organization ever push someone that far on their own.

I said, "That's OK, I understand. My mom's sisters – all three of my aunts – from Virginia didn't think I was going to be able to do it either."

For me it was always a great pleasure to remind people, "I told you I could do it! I told you I would do it! I told you so!"

———————

Next up for us was the 2014 Columbus Marathon, which is run in October, usually about three weeks after the Akron Marathon. I had been told the marathon course takes you through "The Horseshoe" at mile seventeen. That's where the Ohio State Buckeyes play football. Dre was a big Buckeye football fan. Neither one of us had ever been to "The Shoe" before.

I went online to see about getting us registered for the race, only to find it was already sold out. I didn't accept this as a final answer, however. I stayed disruptive.

I reached out to both Brian Polen and Georgeann Haviland about seeing if they could use their pull to get me and Dre a chance to run in that race venue. Brian had nothing but good things to say about Columbus Marathon Race Director Darris Blackford. He encouraged me to get in touch with him. Georgeann went a step further, and actually gave me Blackford's personal cell phone number. I didn't hesitate to call him. When he answered the phone, I told him who I was, and before I could say anything else, he said, "I'm well aware of who you and Dre are. I was at the Akron Marathon and saw the both of you at the starting line." I told him of our dilemma. I expressed to him my desire to see Dre live out one of his dreams to go inside "The Horseshoe."

Blackford said, "Sure no problem." He said that if I paid my entrance fee that Dre could run for free. I said that's a deal.

I then got greedy and asked if we could start up front just like we do at the Akron Marathon. He asked for my best marathon time. I said 4:39. He said "You guys will be starting in the third corral then. You need a 4:15 time to start up front."

I responded, "But Darris, it would be so much easier to be up front and afforded the opportunity to get out of the way of all the other runners as quickly and efficiently as possible, just as we had done twice before in Akron and once in Cleveland."

He repeated that we need a time of four hours and fifteen minutes to start up front."

I stepped out of line a little bit and said to him, "We will run your race in 4:15." Upon hearing this he laughed out loud.

I said, "Thank you so much Mr. Blackford, we will see you at the finish line."

The morning of the race it was very chilly. My right ankle was stiff, and had been bothering me the day before, and in the early morning hours leading up to race time at seven a.m. It was this same ankle that had plagued me with pain for years on end.

We lined up in the third corral. Starting out we ended up behind what seemed like thousands of feet which proved to be very difficult. As we ran through the start line the song *Blow* by Kesha was blasting. I'll never forget that moment. My eyes never left the ground for the first two miles of the race. I had to make such a concentrated effort on making sure that I didn't hit anyone. Dre's chair was sort of like a weapon. If I didn't control it just right, while running behind all these feet, I could have easily ended someone's race by causing them an ankle, foot, Achilles, or calf muscle injury. It was an arduous task, and we ran painstakingly slow behind hundreds of other runners. I was growing frustrated because we wanted to run a fast time. To make things worse, by mile two I already had to pee. On the mornings of races, I would give no insulin to avoid any low blood sugars that could ruin a race before it ever got started. I would always error on the side of my sugars running high which would cause me to pee a lot more than I would have liked.

I parked Dre outside the porta-potty, and after taking a long piss that had cost us at least two minutes of clock time, I came out pissed off and cursing loudly. This was not the start we wanted or expected to have. I said, "Let's go reel all these motherfuckers in Dre." I stayed running angry the rest of the course.

At mile seventeen we entered the legendary "Horseshoe." We ran down into the players tunnel that led onto the field as *Script Ohio* was playing on stadium loudspeakers. *Our Honor Defend* was written on the tunnel wall.

I immediately flashed back to my father marching around the dining room table with me as a young child with *Script Ohio* playing before we'd sit and watch an Ohio State football game. Tears welled up in my eyes. Goosebumps ran along my spine. Dre peered up in total awe of what he was seeing for the very first time. I thought, "Is this heaven?"

I strongly felt my dad's presence come over me. When Dre and I got onto the stadium floor we were just like two little kids coming down the stairs on Christmas morning. We just stopped to soak it all in. We stared up into the stands. Dre was gazing at the end zone and couldn't look away from it. It was a magical moment.

We were in such a great rhythm upon arriving at the stadium, that stopping wasn't in our best interest. But this was the major reason that we

440

came to Columbus in the first place, especially for Dre. I had no choice. We had to stop.

Heading out of "The Horseshoe" after about five minutes I started to hurt approximately four hundred meters down the road. My legs started cramping. I cursed myself for stopping. When you're running distance and you get in a good rhythm, the last thing you want to do is stop. Nevertheless, we continued to grind. We ran all out to get to that finish line as fast as we could. We finished with a time of 4:11.43. I immediately started looking for Race Director Blackford. I wanted badly to enjoy the pleasure in telling Darris that I told him so. He was nowhere to be found. Had we not stopped in the stadium our time would have certainly been right at about a four-hour marathon. Before we stopped, I felt strong.

After stopping and getting a little cold I was no longer feeling that strength and power. The last 9.2 miles were very painful. But I had called our shot like Babe Ruth and smashed our goal time of a 4:15 marathon. Those two full marathons in the fall of 2014, three weeks apart, gave me new life and new perspective.

Dre and I now set our eyes on redemption in a new Iron Man 70.3 race going forward into the new year. Iron Man Steel Head in Benton Harbor, Michigan, set for the month of August was our new goal and my personal obsession.

In January of 2015 I started to feel something wasn't right with me. After workouts at the YMCA, I'd come home and was forced to lay down because my head was spinning. I was still working split shifts, driving in the morning and again in the afternoons. My three-hour midday break is where I continued to do the majority of my training. It usually consisted of me swimming a mile and a half, and then running six miles behind that. I did this type of work at least five or six times a week. I chalked up the dizziness to working out too hard.

It didn't ever go away, however. As the days, weeks, and months passed, it grew worse. I was so obsessed with doing this Iron Man race, that I kept pushing and grinding, ignoring what it was doing to me physically.

On April 26 Dre and I ran in the Pro Football Hall of Fame Marathon in Canton, Ohio. *Canton Repository* writer Tim Botos mentioned in a pre-race article how Dre and I had developed a sort of cult following, which continued to gain traction as we ran in support of a young girl named Melanie from Stow, Ohio. Melanie suffered from severe epilepsy. She was enduring eighty to one hundred seizures a night. She was required to have a series of brain surgeries and had to have her head shaved.

Inspired by Melanie's courage we ran a 4:25.10 time on a very challenging course. After the race I presented my medal to her. Dre and I were both really proud of Melanie. It was days like this that made all the pain we went through worth it.

Three weeks later on May 17 we set out to run the Cleveland Marathon for a second time. Days before the race I went to see my family doctor. I continued to suffer from dizziness and was struggling with my balance. During this particular doctor visit I was diagnosed with severe contracture of the tendons in my hands. I could barely make closed fists and was dealing with quite a bit of pain. The middle finger on my right hand was bent in half. My left index finger was the same way. I have suffered from some nerve damage in my hands due to the diabetes, and after nearly three years of pushing and pulling Dre it got pretty uncomfortable. The only remedy for this newest ailment was surgery. I said thanks but no thanks.

On this day I competed on the same track with John Squires. The same John Squires who had ended my football career back in the eighth grade. I hadn't seen him since October of 1986. Squires, paralyzed from the waist down, was in the wheelchair division. He would start fifteen minutes before us.

Jeff Chalmers was also competing that day and attempting to break the Guinness World Record for fastest time running a marathon while dribbling a basketball. All of us took a pre-race photo together as the rain began to fall. Temperatures on this day were in the 70s with the humidity at 91 percent.

Later in the race Dre and I encountered Squires out on the course. John had already hit the turnaround between mile seventeen and eighteen and was headed back towards town. We were still on our way out to that turnaround. I was hurting badly at this point. The humid air had stolen my legs from underneath me. My hands were aching. As I continued to labor on pushing Dre I could see Squires coming straight for us on the other side of the road. John was laying on his back cranking and grinding using his upper body. Our paths crossed at about mile fifteen for us, and closing in on about mile twenty for him, without speaking a word we both simultaneously reached toward one another to give a fist bump. He reached up and I reached down.

What happened next is unexplainable. As our fists came together I was expecting to feel some pain but instead a jolt of electricity went through my entire frame sending chills throughout my body. Immediately I felt a new energy and a new will to surge ahead. This is significant because nearly twenty-nine years earlier this same guy took my will and made me quit. This day he gave me the will to fight on. I was moved to tears while my body remained on fire. It felt extraordinary.

Dre hollered from the front of the chair, "We in the land nigga, let's go." It was one of the more exhilarating moments in my entire existence on this planet. We fought on and ran hard to the finish line coming in at a time of 4:25.50. Anytime we were able to run sub 4:30 going 26.2 was a great race for us. This was now the third time we had accomplished that.

By the end of June I could no longer stand it. Not only did I feel dizzy every day, I was also suffering from a high pitch ringing in my left ear that never went away. That constant ringing and not having balance from dizziness was torture.

I need to back up here to add that I was always addicted to soda. When I was a young diabetic my mom used to buy me diet soda pop. She did that for me because I was not supposed to eat and drink what the other kids were consuming. Although my mom was well intentioned, it led to my addiction of carbonated beverages. Throughout my entire adult life this addiction continued. On several occasions over the years parents of kids with diabetes would ask me to speak to their youngsters about the disease. Every time I did, and every time I'd say do as I say, not as I do.

Here I was training for marathons and Iron Man triathlons while drinking soda and eating McDonald's food. Not ideal for any athlete let alone a diabetic. This took its toll on my body and overall health.

I needed to find out what was wrong with me.

Enter Karen Gonidakis. She was the mother of the eighth grade student

443

Alexander Gonidakis who had taken interest in us after our presentation at Stow Kimpton back in September of 2014. Both Karen and Alexander developed a blossoming friendship with Dre. They had become pretty close with him and visited the group home where he was now living in Barberton as often as they could. Karen started a fundraiser and ran a Team Dre Facebook page on our behalf. Overall, she became a real driving force in affording us a realistic opportunity at another Iron Man race.

After sharing a little bit about my health situation with Karen, she suggested I pay a visit to Dr. Matthew Lutz in Stow, Ohio. I had nothing to lose. I followed her advice and made an appointment to see him.

I met Dr. Lutz on July 24, 2015. He said to me with a smile, "I know who you are. You and Dre passed me at the Akron Marathon." I liked him from the jump.

After some testing on my ears, he ordered a brain MRI. During the tests I was barely able to hear anything in my left ear.

A few days later the examination of my brain revealed that I had a tumor. Weeks before the diagnosis I expressed to my mom that I was very fearful of having a tumor in my head. I was spot on. I just knew my own body better than anyone else. I wasn't surprised at this diagnosis. I was suffering from Acoustic Neuroma. The best news, there was no cancer, it was a benign tumor.

Lutz gave me all my options. Radiation or surgery were both out of the equation for me, I told him. I then asked him his age. He told me that he was forty years old. This was the first time in my life that I had ever been seen by a doctor of any kind who was younger than me.

I said Doc, "I'm forty-two years old, and I've seen it all man. Nobody is cutting on my head, no way, no how! I know that I would never be the same again and you know I'm right."

Just hearing him mention the recovery time as being a three to six-month process laying around in bed most of the time made me say thanks, but no thanks! My decision was to do nothing.

Lutz suggested I return every six months for a new brain MRI, so we could monitor the growth of the tumor. I replied OK. I never returned, and I haven't been back since. That was well over four years ago.

It was now August and time for our Iron Man Steelhead race in Benton

Harbor, Michigan. The tumor in my head was still causing me a lot of grief. I did my best to conceal what I was going through from my employer. At that time, I probably shouldn't have been driving during the weekdays, let alone doing an Iron Man triathlon, but I was obsessed. Nobody was going to tell me no. My wife and I and Karen traveled to Michigan on Friday, August 7. Dre came behind us with his people and arrived the following morning. We spent Saturday at the race expo getting mentally prepared. Sunday, the morning of the race, I gave no insulin and went out of my way to eat a bunch of candy before it started. I didn't want to be pulling Dre in a raft in Lake Michigan and suffer a low blood sugar episode. So, I overcompensated.

The swim cut-off time was one hour and ten minutes. We finished the swim in one hour and eight minutes. It was a struggle. I needed to be better than that. Going into the bike leg of the race I could already feel my sugars running high. Early in the bike portion the chain popped, and we wrecked. I never trained for these races while actually pulling Dre behind the bike. All my training was done on a stationary bike at the YMCA. So pulling Dre behind a road bike with clip pedal shoes that I never used felt really awkward. I managed to bloody up the same knee that I did the year before in Louisville. Dre was OK. We got up and pressed on.

Throughout the fifty-six-mile course I had to dismount the bike four different times to pee. That cost us several minutes each time. Getting off and on the bike repeatedly was a laborious task. Struggling with my balance was a real issue. I kept reminding myself that no matter what happened, we were finishing this race. The defeat from a year before was my motivating force. I didn't want to feel that ever again. We took one downhill at 30 mph. I was so concentrated and so focused. One slip up pulling Dre behind me at that rate of speed was very dangerous, especially considering the dizziness I was experiencing from my tumor.

When we finally finished the bike, we were now tasting it. I still felt pretty strong. Not long into the 13.1-mile run, however, I began to lose all of my steam. That ended up being an excruciating half marathon pushing Dre. We finished with a time of eight hours and fifty-two minutes and fourteen seconds. We were considered a DNF "Did Not Finish" due to the strict Iron Man rules concerning finishing within a certain time frame.

In a full distance Iron Man doing 140.6 miles the time limit is seventeen hours. In a half Iron Man 70.3-mile race, that's chopped down to eight hours and thirty minutes. For me and Dre going into the race our goal was 8:29:59. We missed our target time by about 23 minutes. I needed to be much faster in the water. But where we hurt time-wise was in our slow transition times, our wreck early on during the bike, and most of all having to stop to pee on multiple occasions. That killed us. We should have more than bested our goal time, but once again, I failed.

I have to emphasize that I failed because Dre was a warrior. He deserved much better than I gave to him. In the bigger picture the ultimate goal was finishing, and we did that, period!

Failing better each time out became our battle cry. Both Dre and I were constantly fighting and battling health issues. Nothing was ever pretty. Nothing was ever easy. It was an ugly hungry nasty grind. We were cut from a different cloth, so we didn't mind.

After the race while back at the hotel with my wife and Karen I started vomiting profusely. I laid in front of the toilet throwing up my guts with my head spinning. Once again, I chalked it up to pulling and pushing Dre 70.3 miles. This is just what happens when you're diabetic with a tumor in your head exerting yourself like this. So, no big deal.

A little over a month later on September 19, Dre and I decided to take a crack at NC24, an Ultra Marathon up at Edgewater Park in Cleveland right off of Lake Erie. In this twenty-four-hour endurance race we would try and accomplish a goal of a hundred-mile run. I believed with all my heart we could do it. In eight hours and fifty-six minutes we had covered forty and a half miles. We ranked pretty high on the leader board, which for us was big considering we were the only push-chair team competing in this race. I hadn't eaten anything all day. By mile 42 when I tried to start eating, I couldn't keep anything down. This is when the wheels began to fall off. I started vomiting. It got real ugly.

By hour thirteen of the race in the dark of night I came undone. It felt like I was dying a slow agonizing death. By this time I was vomiting uncontrollably. My body had grown cold as the evening temperatures dipped. I was shivering and convulsing on the ground. Even though I did everything in my power to stay moving on the course, by mile fifty-five I could not continue. It was Karen who finally stepped in to have me removed. She feared for my life, while I was fearing not reaching a hundred miles.

Karen rushed me to nearby Lutheran Hospital, which is affiliated with the Cleveland Clinic. Doctors there diagnosed me with Rhabdomyolysis. Rhabdo is the destruction or degeneration of muscle tissue (from traumatic injury, excessive exertion, or stroke) accompanied by the release of breakdown products into the bloodstream and sometimes leading to acute renal failure. Signs and symptoms are muscle pain in the shoulders, thighs, or lower back; muscle weakness or trouble moving arms and legs, and dark red or brown urine or decreased urination. In severe cases it can result in multi-system organ failure because of the stress put on the kidneys. The kidney failure means dangerous levels of toxins in the blood are free to pass to the liver.

They gave me an IV that filled my body with three liters of liquids while in the emergency room. Other than providing them with one small urine sample, I didn't pee all night. In the early morning hours on September 20 they wanted to admit me, but I declined. They made me sign paperwork stating that I refused to be admitted after being advised that they wanted to have me stay, and that I was leaving on my own account, even though they desired to treat me further. I was thinking about how we just failed, how big the medical bill was going to be, and would I be able to run the Akron Marathon the following week? I said fuck it, I'm outta here. Surely, this was the last of my nine lives used up. I had never felt so close to death than I did on that night.

The morning of the NC24 ultra-marathon race we had to break down Dre's race chair to transport it to Cleveland. When Karen put it back together before start time of the race the alignment was never the same. Every few feet I was forced to pull the chair back to the left as it continuously pulled right. After nine hours of doing that my upper body was shot. That's when Akron Marathon race director Brian Polen, who had generously given me a brand-new pair of Hoka running shoes for this race and was present on this afternoon, pointed out that he thought the

447

alignment was off. It had never crossed my mind, not once. Brian adjusted it and I battled, scratched, and clawed through the next four hours until I no longer could continue. It wasn't just the Rhabdo that caused us not to obtain the hundred-mile goal.

I had been suffering from Rhabdo for several months by then. I was suffering from Rhabdo during the Iron Man race in Michigan, I just didn't know it. Ultimately the combination of my diabetes, the tumor in my head, and now Rhabdo proved too much for me to overcome.

Going into the ultra-marathon, the longest I had previously run in preparation was a month earlier at the Iron Man race in Michigan where I pushed Dre a half marathon. Suffering from Rhabdo, even though unknown to me at the time, really kept me from running long distances during my training. The more time I spent running the more time I spent vomiting.

Looking back now I think of how absurdly obsessed I was, and how far I could have gone if I was just running on my own and not pushing Dre.

By Monday morning I was already game planning to run the Akron Marathon. It was now just six days away. When my wife and Karen found out about my plans, they were both very upset with me. They were in the emergency room when a doctor at Lutheran Hospital told me to shut it down for a few months and rest. Being that the two of them were the only real support system I had, I gave into their wishes and decided not to run.

Enter my friend Jeff Chalmers. I told Dre that I was not going to be able to push him at Akron on Saturday, but that it was next man up. "The show must go on," I said to him with great passion. I asked Jeff to run in my stead and he agreed. He was at one time an elite marathoner. He had just come off of completing a full Iron Man 140.6 distance, and after coming up short in his attempt at the Guinness World Record for fastest marathon time dribbling a basketball back in May, I knew that he was extra motivated and would look forward to the challenge of pushing Dre 26.2 miles. I mentioned to Dre that he was now for the first time going to see what it was really like to run fast.

That Saturday at Akron Dre and Jeff ran a 3:28.56 marathon. Other than Dick Hoyt, I didn't know of any other runner that's ever pushed someone in a wheelchair 26.2 miles in a sub 3:30 time. Jeff was incredible on that day. It was very humbling because I knew how much it took out of me to run a sub 4:30 time, let alone a sub 3:30 time.

I proved to Dre over that period that it wasn't about me, and that I was a team player. The show must go on no matter what.

A few days after the Akron Marathon I was feeling kind of empty once again, maybe a little bit depressed even. After all I had been through, I still could never seem to find true happiness of any kind. I was never content. Nothing was ever good enough.

On this particular occasion I happened to be online when I came across an advertisement for the Escape from Alcatraz Triathlon. It was one of the most iconic triathlon races in the world. I watched it with my dad years before when it was broadcast on NBC Sports. I decided to enter my name into the lottery for a chance to compete in this historic venue. I never thought or believed that I would actually win a chance to get in. But I longed for the opportunity to prove to myself that I could do a race of this caliber and do it without Dre. The chip on my shoulder since I was a kid was still sitting up there. I always had something to prove in my mind. I didn't want people viewing me as a one trick pony. I didn't want people thinking that all I could do was push a chair in marathons. And although Dre and I finished our Iron Man 70.3 Race in Michigan I still wasn't satisfied. I needed to show that my game could travel and travel alone.

2015/2016 - MY ALCATRAZ LEGACY

Anytime I had ever raced with Dre it was a big deal. We received VIP treatment wherever we went. In this venue at Alcatraz I'd be just one of possibly a couple thousand athletes. And make no mistake about it, if my name was drawn in the lottery, I wasn't going to travel all the way across the country to ride a bike and run on some trails. If I was lucky enough to have the opportunity to go, it was for the iconic swim alone that I would make that trek.

It was the end of September when I entered my name in the lottery. It wasn't until early December that I found out I was chosen to compete in the race. I didn't believe it was real. I was so excited. I thought this was my destiny playing out. Even though it was a very expensive endeavor I still was dead set on doing it. I was already the first Ohioan to ever push a wheelchair 26.2 miles in the state of Ohio. Now I wanted to be the first Barbertonian to ever swim the Rock at Alcatraz. This mattered to me greatly. Showing the people of my hometown that I was one of the all-time great athletes to ever come out of the Magic City was important to me and my legacy.

I called my good friend, world renowned photojournalist and humanitarian Lisa Kristine, who lives a mere fifteen minutes from Alcatraz. I told her that I was coming to San Francisco in June with my two sons, Moses, Spartacus, and a friend of Moses, Eli. She invited us to stay at her place during our time there. I was honored and humbled. Although I didn't feel worthy, I wasn't going to turn down an offer like that from a living legend like Lisa. She informed me that she may be out of the country during our stay, but that we could use her home in Mill Valley.

I worked my ass off during that winter preparing for the Alcatraz race. I did all my training at the local Barberton YMCA. I never trained a minute outside. I swam in the pool, biked on a stationary bike, and ran on the treadmill. This was going to be my legacy race.

In April of 2016, just two months before I was to go to San Francisco I decided to give in to my wife's desire to have a baby. On April 17, the eve of our third wedding anniversary I got her pregnant.

Back in the fall of 2014 we had started the process of bringing her daughter Daina from Haiti to live with us. After my divorce from Aslyne in March of 2010, I wanted no more children. None. For this reason, when I originally brought Darline to the United States in January of 2013, I left her daughter behind in Haiti. At that point I was not negotiating the having-more-kids deal. After spending about a year and a half seeing her sad and missing her daughter, I finally gave in and we started the paperwork to bring Daina from Haiti to live with us. Now I had given in yet again by agreeing to give her this new baby. Although I wasn't very happy about it, I felt as though I owed it to her. Daina was still months away from joining us stateside, and Darline, in the early stages of pregnancy, was the last thing on my mind. The only thing on my radar was Alcatraz.

PART FIVE - REDEMPTION

On May 7 Lisa Kristine invited me, Moses, Spartacus, and Eli to visit the National Underground Railroad Freedom Center in Cincinnati, Ohio, for her Enslaved Exhibit. On display was an incredible visual story of modern day slavery. Lisa spoke that morning in the Harriet Tubman Theatre. She insisted that me and the boys sit front and center. A representative from the Obama White House was in attendance.

At the end of May, after one of my final workouts in preparation for the big race, I ran into my childhood hero Mr. Leon Ricks at the Barberton YMCA. I told him that I was going to swim Alcatraz. He immediately grabbed my arm and told me not to do it. Mr. Ricks being an old Navy man was well aware of how treacherous the waters at Alcatraz could be. He said, "You have two young boys to think about. Please don't do it. Promise me right here and now that you will not do it." He hadn't yet released his grip while looking right through me and said, "Promise me."

I said, "OK Mr. Ricks, I promise you."

My mind raced back to those early years on 5th Street when I used to promise Mr. Ricks that I would ask my mom first before eating the candy he gave me. Some thirty-eight years later and I was still lying to him.

It was June 9 and the time had come for me to go cross-country with the boys and see once and for all if my game could travel. I had failed in Muncie, failed in Louisville, didn't finish how I wanted to finish in Michigan, and didn't finish how I wanted to finish in the NC24 Ultra. It's one thing to race in your hometown or the vicinity in which you live. But when you are required to travel to other cities and states, when you're living out of hotel rooms and food you're unaccustomed to, it can be very difficult, especially for a diabetic.

We left on a Thursday morning out of Cleveland. The race wasn't until Sunday. The first time we traveled across the Golden Gate Bridge was breathtaking. Seeing the Rock sitting out there in the San Francisco Bay gave me goosebumps. It was a glorious sight for my sore eyes. Only four years removed from my own prison experience I felt all the emotions running through me.

The morning of the race on Sunday, June 12, I was really starting to feel some stress. I was talking to myself by this time, saying, "Well, you have spent a lot of money that you really didn't have to spend. You've come all the way across the country with your kids, you better fucking finish this swim."

I briefly spoke to Jeff Chalmers on the phone, and all he said to me was, "Motherfucker do not come back to Ohio if you don't finish the swim."

I needed to hear this from him in that moment. On the bus ride from Marina Green to Pier 3 where we boarded the boat to go to Alcatraz I ate a banana, and a bag of Skittles just as I had done before the 2013 Akron Marathon. While in San Francisco I didn't have much of an appetite. I mostly ate McDonald's and snack foods. Lisa ended up being in town and made an incredible spaghetti dinner for me the night before the race.

I traveled with my wetsuit but rented a road bike from a local bike shop. This time around I made sure that it was equipped with puncture resistant tires.

On the ferry boat ride out to the Rock I never once looked outside of the vessel. As the National Anthem played before the start of this iconic race I pissed in my wetsuit. As the bombs were bursting in air, a stream of yellow urine was running down onto my white feet. Many of the athletes had their ears and feet covered with protective gear to help keep them warm in the freezing water. I didn't want or require that luxury. I needed and wanted to feel and experience all the hurt.

As the horn went off to begin the race, I started to make my way down from the second level of the boat. The anticipation of jumping into those legendary waters had my nerves running high, but I remained calm, steely focused, and determined. The experience I gained from swimming the Ohio River and Lake Michigan had prepared me for this moment. I was ready for this monumental challenge.

I approached the opening of the doorway to make my leap off the Hornblower and my entire life flashed in front of me. I pulled out my photo engraved dog tag chain of my boys that I was wearing underneath my wetsuit, gave it a kiss, then glanced over to my right and saw the Rock. Two days earlier staring down at it from atop the Golden Gate was awe inspiring. This ground level perspective out in the ocean was much different, however, and much more intimidating.

I closed my eyes, heard an individual yelling out, "No hesitation," said to myself, "All of my love," and I jumped into the Pacific Ocean waters of San Francisco Bay.

452

When your adrenaline is running high, and you hit ice cold water, with the knowledge that there is big marine life lurking in the murky waters directly beneath you, this can easily disrupt your breathing. Swimming is all about breathing. This is where, mentally, you must be at another level.

I jumped, went under, came up to the surface, and I was in an instant dogfight. Bodies were leaping from the boat and splashing into the water one after another right behind me. On this particular day in the bay the chop was incredibly difficult to deal with. For perspective, Andy Potts, 2007 Ironman 70.3 World Champion and six-time Alcatraz winner, would be quoted post-race as saying the 2016 Escape from Alcatraz triathlon swim was top five toughest of his career.

My biggest concern going into the swim was that the waves would be coming in from my right, which they were. I only breathed to the right side. With my worst-case scenario already realized, I had to quickly learn how to time and roll with the chop. I was getting smacked in the teeth pretty good to start off, swallowing some ocean water. Thirty minutes into the swim I looked over my right shoulder and I could still see the prison. It didn't appear to me that I had advanced very far. This was very discouraging. I looked back up and saw nobody. I lost visual contact on all the other athletes. I couldn't see any kayaks or rescue boats. It was just me, all alone, in waters that were once believed not swimmable.

Before the race, athletes were told they'd have a better chance getting bumped into by a four-hundred-pound seal than an encounter with a shark. In the fall of 2015, the first ever great white shark attack of a seal in the bay was caught on film. This was now eight months later, but it was still in the back of my mind.

Forty minutes into the swim I felt a burning sensation on the back of my neck and I had doubts on whether I could make it to the shoreline. Not having much experience swimming in a wetsuit, I totally forgot about using lube. The constant spotting in rough ocean water is a great strain on one's neck. The wetsuit was digging into the back of my neck, causing a gash in my skin. I wouldn't know until after the race just how gruesome the wound looked.

I peered back at the prison, then gazed up at the Golden Gate Bridge, and I said to myself, "Who gets to do this? Let me embrace this moment and enjoy the sheer thrill of being alive and having an opportunity to experience it. If they are forced to pull me from the water than so be it. But until then I'm going to keep grinding."

I put my head down and started to recite, "All my love, all my blood, all my guts, for my pops, for my kids, for Haiti."

Fifteen minutes later I looked up and saw that I was surprisingly just off the coastline. I made the L cut where I turned right and was now swimming with the current. About ten minutes later my feet touched down on the sand. It was one of the most euphoric experiences of my lifetime. It was better than sex. You can do an Iron Man race and people will forget. You swim Alcatraz, and you are forever a legend, it's that simple. Other than Kona, which is the Super Bowl of all triathlons, Alcatraz is the greatest and most iconic triathlon venue on the planet, and it's not even close.

I went on to finish the race in four hours and six minutes, and forty-five seconds. I placed 1,144 out of about two thousand athletes. My goal was to place 999. But on this day more important than anything else I crossed the finish line in front of Moses, Spartacus, Eli, and Lisa. Who gets to do stuff like this? What diabetes? What brain tumor? I was defying the odds just like I had always done, but now it was more visible. I'd given the majority of my race medals away. The Escape from Alcatraz triathlon race medal is the one I cherish the most. San Francisco proved to be one of the most incredible places I had ever seen.

Upon returning back to Barberton with my two sons and Eli, my sister Jennie told me that two days before the Alcatraz race, my mom and Darline were in a car accident. The collision completely took off the front section on the passenger's side of my mom's car where Darline was seated. My wife was two months pregnant. They both were tended to at the hospital. My mom was the driver at fault. I was very upset when I found this out, which was why they kept me in the dark about it until I got back home. It kind of jarred me back into reality. I had a baby on the way. And Darline's daughter Daina was now about four months away from joining us in the states. My life was going to be changing yet again real soon.

PART FIVE - REDEMPTION

2017 - GOOD-BYE TO RACING

In September Dre and I took to the Blue Line in the Akron Marathon one last time. At around mile 8 or so former Ohio State Buckeyes head football coach Jim Tressel hollered at us and waved. That was really cool. Dre was on cloud nine. For about the next 400 meters we debated on whether to go all the way back to visit with the legendary coach. While we were going back and forth about it, I lost my concentration on the road and rolled my right ankle in a manhole. That same right ankle caused me more grief. From about mile nine to mile 26.2 I ran with a mild sprain. It hurt like hell. At one point later in the race, Dre and our bike attendant, Lisa, were chatting about something. They wanted my attention. I shamelessly barked at both of them to leave me the fuck alone. I was in pain and I didn't want to be bothered. Dre and Lisa were two of the nicest and kindest human beings on planet earth. They didn't deserve that type of treatment.

I knew right then and there that my race days were officially over.

When we hobbled across the finish line I dropped to my knees and vomited on the grounds of Canal Park Stadium. I was done. Alcatraz was my legacy race. I was done!

On October 25, 2016, John Shattuck, the man who had delivered me from the Haitian Penitentiary, brought my wife's daughter Daina home from Haiti for us. On January 9, 2017, our daughter Zippora Sahala entered into this God-forsaken world. I didn't want to bring another innocent soul into this place. I didn't. I swear I didn't. But she was here, and so was Daina, and there was nothing I could do about it but try and let them teach me about life. And that they began to do. I used to only ever want boys. I never wanted a daughter. I didn't want my wife's daughter. I didn't want Zippora. It was not until Daina and Zippora showed up, however, that I began to look at women as human beings and not just as sexual objects. They have been so loving, so affectionate, so tender, so caring, and so tolerant of me. I looked to the Heavens and said, "You truly do know what You're doing Almighty God!" Every trial and tribulation I went through, I came out the other side better. Through the fire and the pain came a new spirit, a new hope, a new belief.

Please God don't let this life of mine be in vain. Please let there be something greater than this in the life hereafter. I beg of You, please!

In February of 2017 an old classmate named Dean Jones who I had graduated with in 1991 called me. He asked me if I'd run on a marathon relay team in the 2017 Pro Football Hall of Fame Marathon set for April 30 with him and another guy we graduated with named Brian Bidlingmyer. It was Brian's plan originally. I didn't have any sort of relationship with Brian, so I didn't really have any desire to do it. Besides, Bidlingmyer was one of those old high school basketball teammates of mine who I still looked upon with great contempt. And I was no relay guy to boot. When I said that I was done running I meant it. I really did.

It was around this same time that I had asked Jeff Chalmers to once again push Dre for me at Akron in September. Jeff said he would love to but that he wouldn't be available. He was going to be racing in Iron Man Tennessee the day after the Akron Marathon. Knowing this and knowing that Dre needed to be present at Akron in September made me give the relay thing more thought.

After thinking about it a little longer I said to Dean, "OK, I'll do it, on one condition. You get me Lieutenant Duane Milford of the Barberton Fire Department to run with us. If he agrees to run, I'll run."

That same day Dean called me back and said it was a done deal. They went on to add a fifth member named Alan Bittinger. Milford and Bittinger were both '91 Barberton graduates. Truth be told the real reason I agreed to do it was because of Brian Bidlingmyer's mother. Affectionately called Mrs. Bid around Barberton, she had provided me with free needles, alcohol swabs, and insulin when I returned home from prison in Haiti. That gesture from his mom gave Brian credit in his account with me. Since then, the five of us have continued on providing the arms and legs for Dre's legacy to march forward. Besides, my biggest responsibility to Dre was to make sure that the show went on with or without me. His mission must outlive me. It must. It has to, period!

In June of 2017, however, Andre fell deathly ill with pneumonia. He

456

had some really bad bed sores and lost a lot of weight. He would go on to spend that entire summer between the hospital and a rehab facility fighting to get back to his normal self. Both of us were constantly battling something it always seemed.

On August 19, 2017, I checked myself into the Emergency Room at Barberton Citizens Hospital. I spent the previous months really struggling with my health. When I went out to run my breathing was labored. I was constantly fatigued. I just chalked it up to being a diabetic living with a brain tumor.

Hours earlier while mentioning these things to my mom she suggested that I take it seriously. She reminded me that heart problems run in the family. My dad had his first heart attack at 47. After being examined that night I did a follow-up with my family doctor, who sent me for blood work. I also took a stress test at Akron General Hospital on September 12. After finishing the test, the two individuals who were charged with my care commented that was the best stress test completed at Akron General in a very long time. Although that made me feel good, I still felt as though something was dreadfully wrong. When the blood work results finally came in, I was diagnosed with hypothyroidism and placed on a medication called Levothyroxine for the rest of my life.

A little over a month later, on October 16, 2017, Zippora was sitting in the kitchen with me. She was nine months old. I grabbed my Escape from Alcatraz medal and placed it around her neck. She held, caressed, and ran her little fingers all over it. She could not take her eyes off of this shiny object. I began to snap one picture after another to capture her interaction with the medal that I most cherished. Then, as though it was scripted, Zippora shed a single tear that ran down her cheek on the right side. I continued snapping photos on my IPhone-7 to the tune of seventy-six images in total. I knew and always felt like she was different. In that one magical moment captured in time I could feel her emotion in that lone tear drop. It was as if to say, "I know how much this meant to you Dad. While you were in San Francisco standing on the Golden Gate Bridge looking out at the Rock, I was in a car accident with mom. He saw you through your swim and He sparred our lives. Surely God's favor is upon us."

With all I have been through in this life, all the pain, a lot of it self-inflicted, I was very fortunate to never lose my sensitivity. On this day Zippora provided me with the most extraordinary experience of my life. For that I am so grateful. And to think, I never wanted a daughter. God knows best!

On September 29, 2018, Andre Travis ran his sixth consecutive Akron Marathon to tie Michael Jeffrey Jordan's six rings. I pushed Dre at the start of the race for the first 5.8 miles. We enjoyed a police escort in the first few hundred meters, just as we had during our first marathon in 2013. While crossing the Y-Bridge about a mile into the race, Jeffrey Chalmers approached us from behind. He was running the full 26.2 miles. The last time Chalmers was on this course he was pushing Dre three years earlier. He rubbed up close to me on my left side and whispered, "Get the fuck out of my way Zeke of Haiti." He continued looking back at us as if to say, "C'mon fellas, let's go." Soon he disappeared from our sight.

In that moment I felt chills, and great emotion swept through my entire being. I had to catch my breath and steady myself. I couldn't help but think that my time was now over. It was time for me to step aside and get out of the way of this new generation of young leaders. In this life, you only get a small window of opportunity. You're only afforded but a brief time to make an impact and then it's all over. Just like that in a blink of an eye it's all over. Seize the day.

So, with these final strokes of my pen I'm moving over and getting the fuck out of the way, just like Chalmers had told me to do. It takes a legend to know one – a legend can only be given such instructions and heed them if, and only if, these come from another legend. Thank you, Jeff!

THANK YOU FOR READING this for all of you who made it this far. Although at times written with a spirit of arrogance, this has been my life, and my journey in all its truth and transparency. I do not and will not apologize to anyone for sharing my experiences both good and bad. If anything, use it as a gospel of what not to do. Have you not been entertained? I've always had inside of me a sensitive heart. But make no mistake about it, that same sensitive heart is as big and as strong as Secretariat's, and as hard and savage as one of King David's Twelve Mighty Men. I've lived the life experiences of a thousand men, and I'm prepared to stand against the gates of hell. Remember Me!

Zeke of Haiti

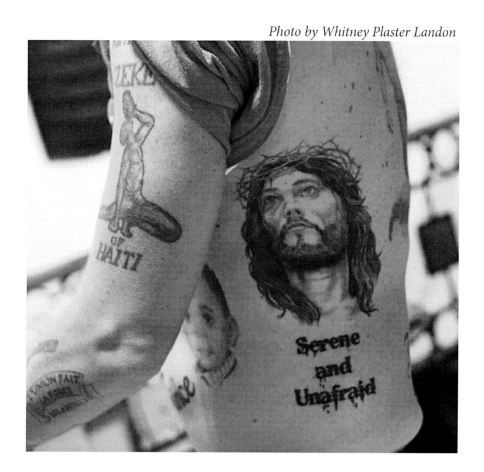

Photo by Whitney Plaster Landon

AFTERWORD

This book has been nearly ten years in the making. I flirted with undertaking this project with a really talented writer named Thais McThais back in October of 2014. After several months, we weren't able to see anything through. Thais was a single mom, working full time, and going to college. Time did not allow for her to see it to fruition. When that didn't work out, I spoke to and considered doing it with another really talented writer named Corrigan James Clay. Corrigan was living and working in Haiti, but at the time was separated from his kids and just going through a tough stretch in his life. He wasn't able to dedicate the time to it. When that didn't work I came across another talented storyteller named Lynne Warberg, a.k.a. Blond Voodoo. Lynne had been on the set of the movie *The Serpent and the Rainbow* back in the 1980s. Because of Lynne's schedule it did not appear that anything was going to work out. I was ready to throw in the towel. Writing my life story on paper seemed way too overwhelming and intimidating.

Enter the dream of a woman named Meliana Doree Reyes. On February 21, 2015, Meliana dreamed that she had started a campaign to bring me back to Haiti. She had previously been told, like everyone else, that I had been banned and exiled from the island. In her dream, she created an uproar with the Haitian government and had people demonstrating in the streets. Oddly enough it was on her birthday that this dream manifested itself. The next day she shared this dream privately with Corrigan James Clay who was a mutual friend of ours. He then shared it with me. At that time, I didn't know Meliana. Fast forward a little over two and a half years later in November of 2017, and Meliana introduced me to a friend of hers named Aslan Rentz Noakes. After getting acquainted with Aslan by texting and talking over the course of a few days, I opened up to her about some private personal information. I let her know that just a couple weeks earlier I had a conversation with God. I said "God, this is it. Either show me somebody to help me do this book, or I'm putting it to bed forever."

I said to Aslan, "I think God has sent you in my path via Meliana for a reason. Would you at all be interested in helping me write my life story?" I had read some of her blogs about Haiti. I watched her on YouTube give an address to a church about Haiti. I thought "Wow, this chick is really talented." She had a presence about her. She is married. She has a young son. She's involved in Haiti. She speaks some Haitian Creole, and she's a nurse. All of this life experience under her belt would be a big bonus to me in putting my story on paper, I thought. Almost dying after childbirth gave Aslan even a greater perspective and insight most people didn't have.

Aslan said yes. She talked to her husband Brian about it and he was excited. He was on board. She helped me shape and polish the early years of my life story up until the ninth grade. Because of her family, her job as a nurse, and her business, she wasn't able to keep the pace and continue to devote the time to the project that it demanded. Her being on west coast time made it somewhat difficult also. To Aslan's credit, beyond her helping me shape and polish my early years, more important than that even were the many hours we spent on the phone talking through the secret, intimate, and painful experiences that I was writing about and going to be covering on this journey. At that point in time she was the only one that I had ever come clean to about certain details in these life stories. I almost gave up. But I had come so far in my writings, I decided to press on all alone. Enter TriMark Press Publishing with Barry Chesler and Lorie Greenspan. They have guided me throughout. Thank you both, especially Lorie for all her work editing, and having patience, and tolerating me the entire way.

I finished writing my story on October 2, 2018. Because I chose to write drafts, then type them out after the fact, I wasn't completely done until November 18, which ironically was the date in 1803 of the last major battle in the Haitian fight for Independence at the Battle of Vertières. November 18 is widely celebrated in Haiti as the day of victory. This, too, was a day of victory for me. I had commenced this journey the second week of November 2017. It was a very long twelve months. The editing process was long and tedious and took another twelve months leading up to the end of 2019. It was a great struggle for me dealing with my diabetes, a brain tumor, and having little kids in the house once again, especially an infant daughter turned toddler overnight in Zippora.

The writing of this book has been the most difficult thing I've ever embarked on. I'm not a writer. When you write you need a clear mind. You must write inspired and passionately. Being transparent and telling the truth is paramount. I tried my best to do all of that and more. Because my first passport was lost, and my second passport stolen, it was sometimes difficult to match up exact dates and sequences. Other than minor things possibly being out of sequence or dates off by a few days here and there, everything I have penned to paper has happened. It's all true.

My own quote, "Isn't it a beautiful thing to live with great courage, and to die leaving in everlasting failing, reach and fall, reach and fall," has been my life's legacy. Nobody has failed more often, more passionately, and more ferociously than I have. What makes my head continue to stay lifted high is my own self-belief, and that I am well aware that my failures have been greater than a lot of men's successes. And I stand on that Rock of Truth.

I WOULD BE REMISS not to mention just how much I have neglected the needs of my wife Darline during this entire process of writing my book. I treated her the same as I had treated Aslyne over the years. I had been treating Darline in a neglectful and verbally abusive way for several years leading up to the start of this book. It got even worse over the course of the year I worked on it. She remained my faithful sidekick throughout. However, on October 6, 2018, a very significant date because October 6, 2000 was the day I brought Moses home from Haiti, Darline checked out on me. She left. She was gone. I never saw it coming. I was left speechless. Four days after finishing the writing of this book, I lost my wife. She didn't give a damn about the book. All she wanted was my love and respect, my energy and effort, and my time and attention. Nothing else mattered to her. I had neglected her at every turn. I was very abusive to her with my tone of speech, and never really noticed the difference. The one who abuses – even if it's just in word – easily forgets. The one receiving the verbal abuse never forgets. Many years ago Aslyne said to me, "Had it just been for your promiscuity with other girls, I would have never left you. I left you because of how you treated me, how you talked to me."

Aslyne once said to Darline, "Do you really think you know who Zeke is? Has he spit in your face yet? Oh you'll learn sweetheart." Darline responded that all women are women, but all women are not the same. Just like Aslyne before her, however, Darline had her breaking point.

On October 7 many tears were shed on both sides. I apologized to her for my neglect and blatant abuse. I came clean to her about past sins and things that I was going to bring to light in this book that she needed to be aware of. It was truly my Road to Damascus moment. On October 8, Darline's birthday, I recommitted to her all over again. On October 14, as a family, we began attending Grace Church Norton Campus led by pastor Dan Gregory. I not only gave my life back to my family, I gave it back to Jesus. It's been life transforming for us. We now pray every morning. We pray every night with the kids. On one occasion while out at Chipotle restaurant in Fairlawn, we ordered our food and sat down. I went to get us some soft drinks. When I returned to the table the food was sitting there untouched. Darline said we were waiting for you to pray. Right then and there, smack dab in the middle of the restaurant, Darline, Zippora, and I prayed to Almighty God. That was an act I would have never before committed in public.

Stepping a foot back into any church is something I was not likely to ever do again either. It's been a year since this transformation. It's not been easy. I have to continuously fight against complacency not to fall back into my old ways and bad habits.

It was John Owen who said, "Do you mortify? Do you make it your daily work? Be always at it whilst you live; cease not a day from this work; be killing sin or it will be killing you." *Romans 7:21-25.*

I used to be really critical of Eve until I heard a sermon by Pastor Dan who explained that when Eve sinned in the garden, Adam was there. He was present. He failed to be the spiritual guardian of his wife, which enabled the serpent to deceive, ultimately leading to Eve sinning and the complete fall of man. Every morning when I wake up, I must hold myself

466

accountable for the spiritual guardianship of my house. I must make a conscience effort to pray without ceasing to live every day as though it's my last. I must continually look to the word of God, especially Revelations 21:1-8 as to not get discouraged and lose heart. *So, shall it soon be for me when my time comes, Acts 13:36.*

I have requested my good friend of many years Paul Howe to officiate my funeral service with the assistance of Reverend Tim Stults. I humbly request the presence of Haitian Gospel artists Villaire Pierre from New Jersey and Ruth Francois from Port-au-Prince, Haiti on the day I leave this earth. It would be a great honor for my family if Villaire could sing his rendition of *O'Kanaan* and if Ruth could perform *Konbyen Mwen Dwe*. All Glory to God – The Father, The Son, and The Holy Spirit.

Let me declare that none are worthy, and that only through God's grace are any of us saved. Jesus is the only way to the Father in heaven, Amen! Philippians 2:8-11

IN MARCH OF 2016, Robbie Haught asked me to work JR Smith's basketball clinic in Medina, Ohio. Robbie trains professional basketball players and was put in charge of running this one-night clinic for the Cleveland Cavalier shooting guard. It was on this evening that his dad, my good friend coach Paul Haught, opened up to me about his Alzheimer's diagnosis in December of 2010. At the time of the diagnosis he was only fifty-six years of age. He has been battling this awful disease since then with support from family and close friends, daily prayer, strenuous exercise (two to six hours daily), a plant-based diet, and the daily usage of CBD oil. Thank you Coach Paul for your no-quit, never-say-die example.

A WRETCHED SOUL I AM. A failure time and time again I've been. But what I have always remained is an individual that never quits. An individual that regardless of the odds, just keeps coming. I have lived with such a tenacious ferocity that the world could not help to notice who I was. I feel as though I proved to myself that I certainly would and could accomplish anything I set my heart on doing in this life despite my health issues. I currently find myself on a personal mission to prove to myself that I will reach the great Jackie Robinson standard of fifty-three years old. There's still one passion and fire that burns within me. That is to become the first human in world history with a brain tumor and diabetes to ever complete a hundred-mile trail race. Before I pass and leave this earth, I'd like to be able to see one of my future grandchildren born. I'd like to do some prison ministry. Having the opportunity to help other depraved sinners just like myself is a goal of mine. I feel as though I've been to so many dark impasses in my life, that I could help reach hundreds and thousands of men who currently live in that dark abyss.

I WANT TO BE clear this is my true-life story. I embrace all critics. No one is more critical of me than me. Many years ago, my mom once said to me, "If only people really knew you." Well mom, I would much rather everyone hate me for who I really was, than love me for who I really wasn't. To all young men, be very careful to not become the monster that you're fighting along the way.

I'm very proud of this work. It's very honest and transparent. It's not a fancy or wordy book. Anybody can read this book from any walk of life coming from any circumstances and take something away from it. It's sure to bring about a wide range of emotions in people the world over. Catholics confess their sins to a priest inside of a booth. I always thought that was absurdity of the highest regard. Ironically, I would take that, run with it, and raise the bar even higher by confessing my many sins to the entire world.

I'D LIKE TO SAY TO THE PEOPLE OF HAITI:

What transpired in your country in 2018 and 2019 is absolutely reprehensible. I'm ashamed, embarrassed, and disgusted by what the Haitians have put on display for the world to see.

Several years ago, I spoke on Haitian radio about Haiti's social ills and her negative character traits that could lead to her complete and utter destruction. I'm now left standing here at the end of 2019 looking like a prophet of old. Lynn Garrison was proved right and then some. There's not another group of black people on planet earth that are more Uncle Tom'd down, and more-quick to display cowardice tendencies in the manner in which they conduct themselves than the Haitian people. It pains me to say that because this was not the nature of their ancestors. Remember, this is the same bloodline that drove back and smashed Napoleon's army. It's a nation that's lost its identity making it all the more disheartening and despicable.

It's a never-ending battle between house and field negro who continue selling each other out to the highest bidder. This has gone on for hundreds of years. The Haiti I read and dreamt about as a kid looked much different than it does today. With an entire generation of Haitian kids not knowing their fathers, there's no end in sight to the total annihilation of Haitian society. Men like Jean-Jacque Dessalines and Capois La Mort aren't ever walking through that door again.

In my opinion Haiti is only redeemed in one of two ways. Either she cries out to Almighty God to reveal Himself, and fast until He does. Or rid themselves of all the foreigners in Haiti, and fight it out amongst their own until the rivers run blood red cleansing the entire land of the heinous individuals currently sucking the life out of the country's poor folk.

The current Haitian government, from president Jovenel Moise, to whomever is currently sitting in the prime minister seat, to all the senators and all the deputies, are cowards, save maybe Senator Patrice Dumont, and a few others. The National Police Force is inept, corrupt, and nothing but an extension of these gutless cowards. The political oppositions leadership in Haiti is riddled with men who have their wives and children living abroad just like several current sitting politicians do, including Senator Jean Renel Senatus. These men are as greedy, untrustworthy, and dishonorable as those they are trying to unseat. They don't seem to mind paralyzing daily operations in the country with violent demonstrations. Kids going to school, businesses functioning normally, and public transportation throughout the capital and across the country are brought to a standstill, all the while their immediate families are in the comforts of developed nations. Those placed in charge of Haiti's care over the last fifteen years are thieves and have squandered billions of dollars while stealing the earthquake and Petrocaribe funds. The 1.50 tax they take for every Western Union money transfer that was supposed to be invested into free schooling for Haitian children has never been accounted for. Former President Michel Martelly should be forced to give a response in the Haitian courts about these matters.

Former Prime Minister Laurent Lamothe was recently called in to answer some questions concerning allegations of the misuse of funds. And that only means anything if the Haitian courts actually worked, which they don't. Haitian judges are as disgraceful and culpable as all these players previously mentioned here. The only thing that talks in Haiti is the U.S. dollar. Whoever has the most money wins. Haitian Senators Gracia Delva, Youri Latortue, Joseph Lambert, Carl Murat Cantave, and Herve Fourcand have suspect records and need to be dealt with immediately, preferably by sending them to the Haitian Penitentiary. These five are mentioned here only because they were the first ones to come to mind, but I could name all of them, past and present, who need to be dealt with. I didn't want to waste anymore good paper space talking about all of these vermin.

Haiti's infrastructure is nonexistent, and the hospitals are nonfunctional. When Haitian politicians and Haitian elite need medical care, they travel abroad. What kind of people can tolerate such madness? The entire system is fucking rotten to the core. The poor Haitian masses are now living their daily lives in fear of a generation of delinquents who don't know their own fathers or respect any kind of authority. These young men are armed and supported financially by corrupt politicians, like gang leader Arnel Joseph. Arnel was recently captured by Haitian police at Hospital Lumiere in Bonn Fin where I was once a patient back in 1991. Coincidently, Arnel and I were both in the Haitian Penitentiary at the same time together. (He was housed in Brick #7.)

I am not even going to address the private sector controlled by light-skinned wealthy Haitian families, many with countries of origin in the Middle East. These elite are sitting in a chair that's raining pennies. They aren't going to get up out of that chair until either it stops raining, or they are forcibly removed. They are only permitted to get away with their monopoly on everything because the majority poor black masses tolerate it. What you tolerate, you indeed encourage.

Haitian musical recording artist Jean Adler Gaston a.k.a. Top Adlerman recently gave a really powerful interview on Radio One 90.1 FM

470

in Port-au-Prince, covering problems/complexities plaguing his country. In this interview he explains how Haiti is very sick, infecting the entire population, especially the politicians. He goes on to elaborate how it will be a very long time before Haiti ever sees real change. I couldn't agree with him more.

Let me also say there are a few good white foreigners in Haiti doing some good things. In my opinion, however, Catholic and Christian missionaries have failed the Haitians in their complicit cowardice silence. Most white people in Haiti have no previous knowledge of her past or recent history, nor do they seek to know. They are all too comfortable in their ignorance, for it is bliss to them. Their home countries have done nothing but destroy Haiti's chance at really being an independent nation able to stand on her own.

For example: Haiti should be exporting rice to the United States, not importing it. Ask former President Bill Clinton, he knows! Many different NGOs misused funds raised post-earthquake and threw them away on expensive hotels, rental cars, and top-of- the-line food and entertainment in Haitian restaurants, musical concerts, etc. You never hear a peep from the whites about real serious issues concerning what's best for Haitians. Most whites are never fluent enough in Haitian Creole to be able to be independent of a translator. It speaks to their lack of effort and of being careless and lazy. This opens the door for corrupt Haitian pastors to exploit them. Subsequently, this led to the whites being the root cause of why Haitian women abandon their children to be swallowed up by arguably the biggest scam in the country, the orphanage business. White people go to Haiti to save Haitians when they are the ones that need to be saved from themselves. Whites are dependent on the need to feel wanted and important. They have made the plight of Haitians more about them than they would ever want to admit.

If you're an NGO worth your weight, you work yourself out of a job and move on. If you're a serious devout and responsible Christian, you set up churches, disciple, and leave. Haiti, only the size of the state of Maryland, has been evangelized a million times over. The whites have set up shop in Haiti making it a lifetime deal. They have no plans to leave, and why would they? Their entire identities and purpose rest on poor

471

Haitians needing and being dependent on them. They are the ones being worshipped. They left God out of the equation. Their perversion of the gospel is blasphemous. They have brought religion instead of bringing Jesus of Nazareth. Continuing to watch them solicit financial support from ignorant people abroad for these missions they have infected the country with has grown tired and pathetic. When they're living better in Haiti as a missionary than they would be living as common citizens in the states, that's a red flag. They are without shame.

The whites should voluntarily leave the country en masse immediately. They've succeeded in doing nothing but bringing confusion and betrayal to the Haitian people.

The Haitian Diaspora must be better. They need to quit bickering among themselves and work together. With so many educated, talented, and wealthy Haitians living abroad, there's no way Haiti ever gets better without their input and leadership. There are some young and courageous leaders within the diaspora community that I know personally. They want nothing more than to return to Haiti and give back. Networking with honest Haitians back home already on the ground working, like Louino Robillard with the Konbit Soley Leve Movement, is how things are going to get done. Robillard is working with a group of Haitian citizen volunteers that are currently building a library in Cite Soleil.

Even if by some miracle Haitians can improve their homeland to produce a higher quality of life for its inhabitants, you still have to worry about the ever present blan that are still there working against you. In the dark, behind closed doors, and underneath the table they continue to work to divide and conquer your ranks from within under the auspices of friendship and partnership. There was a reason why Dessalines cried out to cut off their heads and burn their homes.

Good luck to the Haitian people, I wish them all the best!

Dear Haiti:
From that day in Chicago in October of 1990, you were all I could ever think and dream about. From the moment I witnessed Draba spare the life of the Thracian Spartacus, and turn his sword against Marcus Licinius Crassus, I longed to be close to people with dark skin. Thank you for giving

to me everything I love in this life. And please forgive not only me, but all the white foreigners who have helped to create and sustain your perpetual state of misery. I am so sorry. *I'll Forever Love This 1804 Republic!*

SOME WORDS OF THANKS AND GRATITUDE AND REMEMBRANCE...

A SPECIAL THANK YOU to Jim Brown, better known to me as Jefferson. I was a big fan of *The Dirty Dozen* movie as a kid. Jefferson was one of my favorite characters in the film. I was lucky enough to meet him on an American Airlines flight from Miami to Cleveland during the mid-2000s. My dad told us all the time as kids growing up that Jim Brown was the greatest football player to ever live. Getting the chance to speak with him on the plane and to tell him what a privilege it was to be in his presence was one of the greatest thrills of my life. I followed him off the plane and continued following him through the airport. When you're in the presence of greatness, you do everything in your power to hold onto that feeling, that moment, as long as you can.

THANK YOU to Dave Macik, Dave Hoover, and Bob Pence. They were like big brothers to me in my eight and a half years working in the National City Bank building at Cascade Plaza in downtown Akron, Ohio.

THANK YOU to Elyse Senora a.k.a. Blaze One "Vètè" for your music and what it meant to me while I was in the Haitian Penitentiary. You have stood alone, with your voice, with your courage, shedding light on the oppression of the Haitian masses. Your music has truly blazed a revolutionary trail for the social conscience of this 1804 Republic. I'm thrilled to see that you have now teamed up with Jimmy Revolus a.k.a. Haitian Fresh. You and Fresh are both proud Haitians that have never conformed to the system. You both have always been your own individuals never selling out to others. You both give back to your communities. You both are the exact opposite of all those coward ass Haitian politicians back in Haiti who have run the homeland into the ground with no regard for human life. Hopefully you two can inspire and rally Haitians back to what they used to be. The proudest nation on the planet. A Fresh new Blaze, Blazing a Fresh new trail of SWAGG for the younger generations.

SPECIAL THANK YOU to Dan Donnelly, his wife Kim, son Brendan, and daughter Emme. Y'all have been like family to me for the last several years. I love you guys!

SPECIAL THANK YOU to George Krska. When during a dark time and struggle to find my way back to some sense of normalcy you were always there. You stepped in without being asked to help me in a time of need. You purchased the Brooks Ghost running shoes at Second Sole in Merriman Valley that I wore to make Ohio history with Andre on September 28, 2013, at the Akron Marathon. Then, in the spring of 2018, you purchased them a second time at an auction to raise funds for Coach Tony Gotto's Barberton football program to acquire field turf with close to a million-dollar price tag. You, your wife Melissa, and son Gavin will always be family to the Petries.

JOE ONDO, PAUL HOWE, Paul Brabson, Chad Hazard, Reverend Tim Stults, Mike Theus, Ryan Mollric, Marc Williams, Greg Tuchek, and Brian Hastings. These brothers are always there to let me vent and give me some real and honest feedback in return. I appreciate you guys.

I WANT TO THANK FORMER Haitian Senator Moise Jean Charles of the Platform Pitit Dessalines Party for being the only sitting Haitian politician to reach out to me after my release from prison in Haiti. He is the only one left in the fight to purge Haiti of all her sores and cancers that I still have some faith in. He has already turned the Haitian flag under which he operates back to its original colors of red and black. Senator Moise is the only one with the courage of his convictions. (I was always fond of Senator Don Kato but the fact that he has been seen in public rubbing shoulders with guys like Youri Latortue is very discouraging. I reached out to Kato via text letting him know by doing such things he loses credibility. Had he stood alone against all his corrupt colleagues he could have possibly been

Haiti's next president. The Haitian ghettos would have adored him. I hope he does the right thing and separates himself from all those who don't have the Haitian masses' best interest at hand.)

I'D LIKE TO THANK former Haitian Ambassador to the United States Raymond Joseph for spending some time in conversation with me on a couple of different occasions, educating me on not just all things Haiti, but also on things concerning my own country's history that I didn't previously know. In the 1960s Joseph was sentenced to death in absentia by Haitian dictator Papa Doc. A man of his caliber and life experience I desired to be in the company of. In Joseph's manuscript, *For Whom the Dogs Spy* published in 2014, he sets the stage for my book by mentioning that I had announced on Facebook I was writing about my experiences in Haiti. His wife Lola Poisson was always so good to Sperlif, and he adored her.

THANK YOU TO SPERLIF Omeus. Sperlif came into my life for a reason when I needed him most. I'm so sorry that I wasn't there to protect him when he needed me. I think about him daily.

Sperlif was killed in the La Saline slum of Port-au-Prince in 2015. I choose not to write about the intimate details of his death. So much of the information I received via one of Sperlif's friends couldn't be confirmed. I was only left to speculate about the details concerning his murder. It's been nearly five years and the silence is deafening. I tricked myself into thinking that one day I would hear from him again. It could not be true that he was really gone. As far as I know his body was never recovered.

THANK YOU TO T. Sean Herbert, Guy Jackson, Ryan Kennedy, and Craig Downing. Sperlif really enjoyed your company and how important the four of you made him feel.

MY FRIEND LUISGENS JACINTHE a.k.a. Gagòt, the artist that was featured on Sperlif's single *Nou Mele,* also died in 2015. He fell ill and deteriorated rather quickly. I can only speculate but knowing him as well as I did, I think he might have contracted the AIDS virus. Although those closest to him say his death was mired in a Vodou curse.

475

REACH AND FALL

I WANT TO SAY A special thank you to British Iraqi rapper and activist Kareem Dennis a.k.a. Lowkey. Thank you for your courage, and your uplifting of the Palestinian people. #freegaza #freepalestine

THANK YOU TO PENNIE Shaw and Chelsea Shaw for your tireless efforts petitioning on behalf of me and Steve while we were in the Haitian Penitentiary.

THANK YOU TO TOTO Magloire and Guy Azor, both hailing from Jeremie, Haiti. The both of them befriended me in my early days in Haiti. We played basketball together and also had some really meaningful and impactful conversations.

THANK YOU TO WEBERT Belizaire. Webert gifted me a live chicken while I was living in Tozya. He showed me great hospitality during my time in the mountains.

THANK YOU TO ALAN Bittinger and Margie Kinsinger for the generosity you both exude to other human beings on a daily basis. You guys walk what you talk.

THANK YOU TO MY old classmate Jinka Knight. Jinka drove me to see the entire Akron Marathon course in 2013 a few days before the race. She was a veteran of this event and re-lived it with me on a ride one afternoon. Jinka is as tough and as graceful as they come. She's a beautiful human being. Thank you Jinka!

THANK YOU TO Pastor Kenny Cheatham for your lifelong services provided to the people of Barberton.

THANK YOU TO Councilman Shaun Rocky Jaber, and Anthony Jaber for all you guys do on a daily basis to help and assist people in the community of Barberton. It doesn't go unnoticed.

THANK YOU TO KEVIN Scobie, Scotti Robbins, and Ian Bates for the

476

friendship you guys offered to me during a tough stretch in my life.

HAVE I THANKED YOU yet today Mr. John Shattuck? What I owe to you I'll never be able to repay. I hope that in your eyes I have earned what you did for me. I salute you!

THANK YOU TO JEN North, Brenda Holbert, Connie Fasnacht, Wanda Haines, Craig Megyes, Joe Samples Sr. a.k.a. Front Row Joe, Dierre Chambers, Donald Farmer, Bobby Stefanko, and Tanya Jennings. I worked with them during my tenure driving people with disabilities. I appreciate you all.

THANK YOU TO MR. Jeff Ladner and all the people at Stow Kimpton Middle School. They have embraced me and Andre as family and made us a part of their eighth grade student curriculum. We give a presentation at Kimpton the beginning of every school year.

THANK YOU TO THEOLOGY teacher Mr. Dave Dages at St. Vincent St. Mary High School in Akron. He has had Andre and me come out to speak to his classes on several occasions the last 6 years. Dre always enjoys going to St.V.

THANK YOU TO MIKE Koncz and Jay Belkey. The two of them sustained me in the year after returning home from prison. Without their influence on my life, I never meet Dre and my life would look much different today.

THANK YOU, ANDRE TRAVIS. Thank you for everything. I needed you far more than you ever needed me. If there is one thing I am most proud of, however, it was bringing that killer will Kobe Bryant scowl out of you, the competitive greatness that laid suppressed in you that you never before exuded until Zeke of Haiti showed up. I'll take credit for that. We gave them a show Dre, a show they won't soon forget. Love you bro!

THANK YOU TO ELIZABETH Schrack for all you have meant to the life of Andre Travis.

THANK YOU TO LISA Somers for your Growing Wings Adult Services, and Growing Wings Life Center where you enable the disabled and give them real hope. You were the one that introduced me to Dre, thank you!

THANK YOU TO KEITH Russell and his late daughter Alanna. Keep inspiring people the world over Keith! RIP Alanna.

THANK YOU TO THE CBD Oil industry. I've been taking CBD oil capsules to help keep my tumor at bay. That along with prayer and exercise has kept me upright after all these years. Being a diabetic, with high blood pressure, a thyroid condition, and a tumor in my head have put me on my knees. It's been while in that position face down that I have sincerely found true strength and power, and true meaning in trying to emulate the life of Jesus. It was the late Dallas Willard who said, and I agree with him a 1,000 percent: "My central claim is that we become like Christ by doing one thing, by following him in the overall style of life He chose for Himself. If we have faith in Christ, we must believe that He knew how to live. We can, through faith and grace, become like Christ by practicing the types of activities He engaged in, by arranging our whole lives around the activities He Himself practiced in order to remain constantly at home in the fellowship of the Father. I personally think it is for good reason that Matthew 7:13-14 says what it says. Truly, most human beings will not make the necessary sacrifices needed to walk like Jesus. I know it took me all my life to finally try and adhere to His example.

THANK YOU TO all the schools, conferences, and athletic/sports teams in Ohio that have had me and Andre out to speak over the last seven years. There are too many to name. On one occasion we were slated to speak at Old Trail School in Bath. Dre wasn't able to make it that day because he was sick. So I went alone. In this group of fourth graders that I spoke to was Bronny James, the son of Lebron James. It was the month of March so shamelessly I requested of the kids to sing me Happy Birthday. Then I asked them to have a group picture with me so that we could send it to Dre in real time. Dre, being a huge fan of Lebron was so excited to see the picture with Bronny.

478

AFTERWORD

Thank you to both Hope Carr and Karen Gonidakis for helping to make that happen.

THANK YOU TO Roger and Elizabeth Deal for your friendship with me and my wife.

THANK YOU TO Valerio Saint-Louis and his wife Barbara for all the work they have put into promoting all things Haiti and covering news out of the homeland.

THANK YOU TO Tim Brown Sr., Geoff Roberts, and Eric Hambel for all the gamesmanship you guys shared with me and Dre while running marathons.

THANK YOU TO Rick Cherok, the late Hal Naragon, and the late Brady Spence for the gift certificates you guys gave to me in 1988 after my diagnosis with diabetes to purchase athletic clothing, shoes, and equipment in Hal's store. RIP Hal, RIP Brady

THANK YOU TO Todd Gongwer, Ganon Baker, and Governor Mike Huckabee of Arkansas. I appreciated the opportunities I had to speak with each one of you. The conversations I was afforded with you guys I'll always remember and cherish.

A SPECIAL THANK YOU and tribute to some proud Haitian men that I would roll with anytime: Bobby "Pierre Waheed Boukman X" Charles, Frankie Hill Pluviose, Robert Francois, Kedgy Dor, Willy Gerard, Greg Ber, Junior Bataille, Jephte Charles, Louino Robillard, Fenner Pierre-Gilles, a.k.a. Black FeFe, Faine Lartigue, Ivens Bastien, Schadrac "Sam" Merizema, Cashmir Deronette, Willy Ariste, Ronaldo Chery, Abdel Gérard, Thierry Prophete, Thierry Isaac, Adhler Chancy, Christian Guerrier, Thierry Despeignes, Abdullah Clifford Qualo, Wilner Nau, John Victor Boulos, Mensky Philippe, a.k.a. Frère Renel Haiti, Soukouss Jean-Baptiste, Joassaint Lecon-te, Jefferson Moliere, Kernand Emmanuel, Peterson Baptiste, Claudel P. Theagene, Edjour Edouard, Gerard-Marc Casimir, Evens Hebreux Joseph,

479

Patrick Toussaint, Jude Juste, Edjoodelky Louis, Vlad Imbert-El, Gueldy René, and Fortilus Cedieu.

I'D LIKE TO THANK nine guys that I'm not all that close with, but they have my utmost appreciation and respect: Matt Marks, Art F. McMahon, Paul Neier, Michael Robison, John Engle, David Littlejohn, Darrin Grella, Jim Thomas, and John Kitchings.

THANK YOU TO DR. Mark Matthews, Dr. Diane Minich, Dr. Anita Dash-Modi, Dr. Stephanie Aldrich, Kim Krynicky, and Della Cooper. You all have blessed my life over the years with the work that you do. I thank you, humbly!

THANK YOU TO Rony Michel and The 1804REPUBLIC clothing line for the athletic apparel they provided for me to wear while competing in races with Andre.

A VERY SPECIAL thank you to my sister Jennie for all her assistance in dealing with computers during this journey. I'm forever grateful Jennie!

SPECIAL SALUTATIONS TO SAMENDA, Elijah Jason, Machoupet, Wadna, Katiana, Sherline, Quennie, Hermanette, and Yolette.

SPECIAL SALUTATIONS TO my guys at the Barberton Post Office: Melvin Chambers Jr. and Chad Headley.

RIP DONNA, BECKY, AND DAVID STARR
RIP KEVIN AND ADAM BERKLEY
RIP JOSHUA SAVIERS AND JASON BURKE
RIP MARITANE, TITIT, MR. BANGO, BOSS CLAUDE AZOR, FANFAN, AND THIERRY LAMOUR
RIP NANCY ORNDORFF AND JULIE WESTFALL
RIP MICHAEL BRIENZO, RIP MATTHEW VECERE
RIP BENJAMIN COLE BROWN
RIP DANI TROYER

WHEN I CAME HOME from prison Wes Gardner called me and asked for my continued assistance in the opening of an Outside the Bowl super kitchen in the vicinity of Cite Soleil, but not in Cite Soleil where I had wanted them to open it. I told him if I could ever be of any assistance to let me know. I felt like Moses not being able to have the opportunity to go over into the promised land. So I would have to watch from afar as a team of good Christian people made the mission a reality. Jae Evans, the founder of Outside the Bowl, Wes Gardner, a business owner, Noel and Lori Tugwell and family, the missionaries that would run it, opened up the super kitchen at a hospital not far from Cite Soleil called Chancerelles (Isaie Jeanty Maternity Center). The work they did at this hospital was tremendous. From there they branched out and delivered food into Cite Soleil. This pleased me greatly. After a while, however, violence in the area increased, and they were forced to move their operations to Delmas 75. The Tugwell family left Haiti for good on October 27, 2016. Outside the Bowl has remained in Haiti under Haitian leadership and continues to feed hungry children.

MY FIRST WIFE LEONNE is now remarried and living in south Florida with her husband and three children.

MY SECOND WIFE ASLYNE still resides in Barberton. She and Kevin went on to have two kids of their own and eventually got married. Kevin was the best thing that ever happened to her. He's from a good family. His mom and dad are both really good people. They have treated my two sons like their own. God works all things out for good for those that love Him.

I AM STILL IN CLOSE contact with Sabine and speak to her regularly. It is a dream of mine to be able to somehow facilitate her coming to the United States to finally be in the presence of all my family. I love her so much. I stayed in contact with Mamoune for a long time and on occasion would send money to her, but we have not spoken in almost two years. I have had no contact with Lithana at all.

CONCERNING JOHN: HE HAD called my mom's house in the days following my return home from prison. It was during this conversation I told him to return everything he stole from me. I said, "You're dead to me."

During the next several years he contacted me crying and begging for forgiveness and asking me for money. On one occasion in early 2014, I made a small token gesture and sent him $25 hoping that he would return the gesture and give back the computer he stole from me. It had all my family pictures and videos stored in it. I desired to have it back in my possession badly. It was already in a pawn shop somewhere in Port-au-Prince.

Sometime after that I was told that he had fled Haiti and was living in the Dominican Republic as an illegal alien. Recently he reached out again asking for help. He apologized not only to me but also to Darline for all his wrong-doing, all the lies he told, the stealing, and the betrayal. He told Darline in a voice note via a social media app that "Zeke did not deserve the things he (John) had said and done throughout the years past." For many years in Delmas 31 I paid rent to John's biological aunt, Madam Francois. He never told me it was his real aunt. As far as I knew she was just the owner of the place we rented. I didn't find out this truth until long after I cut all ties with him. Concealing information like this was betrayal as far as I was concerned. Madam Francois treated me nice, but for all I knew they could have been in cahoots together on the rent price.

John committed all these transgressions against me, and yet I was the one who took him from the streets and cared for him, the one who trusted him, the one who he always called Pa (Father). I have asked God to forgive John for me, and to soften my heart so that I may forgive him too. If God can forgive me, surely, I can forgive him. And I do forgive him. But trust him again? That's easier said than done. There's nothing that makes one's skin crawl more than to be in the same room with someone you can't trust.

In any event, there are many that I need to make things right with in

Haiti. I pray God grants me the opportunity in the near future to do so.

PHAUBERT AND I STILL remain in contact. JhaJha, Nasson, and I still talk. I have been in communication with Amaral Duclona since September of 2013. We have spoken on countless occasions via telephone and video call. I sent him some money in November of 2013 when he was still held on house arrest in France awaiting to hear what his fate would be in the French courts. Although extradited for the murder of French citizen Henri Paul Mourral, Amaral was actually tried, convicted, then retried for the murder of Haitian-French businessman, Claude Bernard Lauture. He was eventually acquitted of that murder charge against him in February of 2016 and is currently living in Paris.

RIP TO AMARAL'S BROTHER and my friend, Raymond Duclona. He was killed in Haiti in 2013.

TO MY FRIEND JIMMY "Barbecue" Cherizier:
In years gone by, our paths crossed a few times in Delmas 2. I always thought well of and respected you because of the adoration you received from the locals. Your name has surfaced in Haiti over accusations that you participated in the La Saline Massacre on November 13, 2018. I choose to support you as a brother, but like Joan of Arc once said, "I would rather die than do something which I know to be a sin, or to be against God's will." That resonates here, especially because you were a police officer. If you are truly innocent Jimmy, God will exonerate you. If you are guilty however, He will also hold you accountable. *Hebrews 4:13*

I HAVE SPOKEN WITH Larose Aubain since coming home from prison. He told me that he gave his life to Jesus Christ and is now born again. Larose is a leader of men. He's currently involved in social work giving back to his community. He has fused together one hundred and forty two different organizations within a federation called FEPADE'H (Federation of Professionals in Action for the Economic Development of Haiti). They are a Federation of Haitians working to change Haiti for the better. God willing, I hope to be able to contribute to their cause in the future.

483

I also spoke with David Dorme. David is still in the fight to re-establish the old Haitian military. David told me that regardless of who is running the country, he and his men would guarantee my security if I ever decided to return to Haiti after being exiled from the country. I recently reconnected with Jean Fednel Lafalaise and we have been catching up on lost time. He shares the same sentiments as Dorme.

In recent days, Lafalaise, Dorme, and Yves Jeudy were part of a press conference in Boudon proposing to those in charge to re-establish the Haitian military and to give back their rightful place and rank in the armed forces where they left off in 1995 when the military was disbanded.

MY FRIEND JOSHUA HARSH ended up meeting another friend of mine named Kristin through one of my Facebook posts about the Boston Marathon bombing right after it happened. I knew them both through my involvement in Haiti. They had a child together and named him Zeke. He is one of the most extraordinary young boys I have ever met. I expect big things from this little guy in the near future. The Hand of God is upon him.

JONAH RIES, WHO WE called Joe, was a 1993 Barberton graduate. He was attending the University of Michigan on a full ride football scholarship. In the spring of 1995, he had stopped over at my mom's house to visit with me and my brother Ben.

Joe and I sat across from each other on the living room floor tossing a basketball around while talking. I was a Notre Dame fan. The Irish were football rivals with the Wolverines. Joe said that he couldn't stand Notre Dame to which I responded, "Go Irish baby, fuck Michigan."

Without batting an eye Joe thrust the basketball into my chest, knocking the wind out of me. It happened so fast I had no time to react. Joe, all six-foot-three, two hundred and ninety pounds of him, proceeded to jump on my five-foot ten-inch, one hundred and eighty-pound frame, and maul me right there on Bonnie Petrie's living room floor.

Joe hadn't forgotten what had transpired between us back in the fall of my senior year in high school. During a game of backyard football at Highland Field on the west side, where I was hobbled and playing with an air cast on my right ankle due to the devastating injury I had suffered in August of that year, I made a dirty play on him. He had thrown an interception to my brother Ben. As Ben was running the ball back to score a touchdown all that stood between him and the endzone was Joe. Joe had been kind of taking it easy on me that day because of my injury. While he was backpedaling and getting ready to set himself to make a tackle on my brother, I rolled up on him before he could plant his feet and with his momentum taking him backwards, I busted him good. He went down like a ton of bricks. Joe wasn't used to being knocked down like that, nor was I used to knocking down guys his size. I started high stepping like Deion Sanders, and I gave him the Nature Boy Ric Flair WOOOOO! Ben went on to score and I stood from a distance mocking Joe telling him to stay his ass the fuck down.

Now, four and a half years later Joe was continuing to bear all his weight upon me reminding me of that day back in 1990. He was pinching, slapping, and punching until I cried uncle, literally. I couldn't breathe. He didn't ease up until I was in tears. He would not get off of me until I apologized. When he finally relented with this onslaught, he rose up and said don't you ever talk shit about Michigan again, WOOOOO!

Four years later in 1999 my brother Ben and I entertained the idea of going to Kigali, Rwanda. I had been so deeply moved by a book I was looking at concerning the genocide that took place in Rwanda five years earlier, I had a Rwandan child tattooed on my chest. I called on Joe to go with us. He was the type of guy I wanted on my side.

Joe responded, "Anything for you Zeke."

Although we didn't make the trip, Jonah Ries proved to me what he was all about. That's how we Barbertonians roll. We are small town kids with big chips on our shoulders.

IN MAY OF 2017 after searching for a couple months on social media I found Jason Pake in Port Moresby, Papua New Guinea. Jason was only six years old the last time I saw him in 1991. He informed me that Dr. Stuart Merriam and Kege Yasinamo had both passed away. He said Patrick Osborn and Kege's son Mack Yasinamo were still alive and doing well. I hope to make the trek to Papua New Guinea in the near future to meet

485

up with Jason, Mack, and Patrick. The impact they had on my life still reverberates today.

MY HOMETOWN OF BARBERTON has produced some legends. Olympic champion and three-time gold medalist Glenn "Jeep" Davis. Legendary Michigan head football coach Bo Schembechler, the man responsible along with Woody Hayes for the greatest rivalry in North American team sports. It is *Thee* Game, Ohio State vs. Michigan. And four-time NBA All-Star Alvin Robertson of the San Antonio Spurs. Alvin averaged more steals per game than anyone in the history of the NBA at 2.7 steals a contest. He was one of only four players in history to get a quadruple double in a game. He defended Michael Jordan better than anyone.

AS FAR AS THE Petrie legacy is concerned in the Magic City, it goes way beyond just me causing a raucous. My cousins Mick and Tim Debevec both starred for the Barberton basketball program in the mid to late 1980s. Their mother, Sue, was a Petrie. Our grandpa Petries were brothers. Tim, the younger of the two went on to win the 2017 Ohio Division 1 State Championship as the head basketball coach of the Jackson Polar Bears. My brother Ben's son Solomon, who I tagged with the nickname King several years ago, was featured on a *SportsCenter* highlight with Hannah Storm as a five-year-old golfer in February of 2009. Solomon won the U.S. Kids Golf Teen World Championship in the thirteen-year-old division in 2017 at Pinehurst. He led the Archbishop Hoban Knights to their first appearance since 1992 in the OHSAA Golf Division 1 State Championship in the fall of 2018. He led them back to the State Championship again in the fall of 2019.

Dana Shaw, one of my mother's best friends, said there's something special in the Petrie bloodline. All this stuff just didn't happen by accident.

With that said, I expect special happenings from the hands of my three offspring.

MY OLDEST SON MOSES graduated in 2019, and during his graduation ceremony at EJ Thomas Hall I could hear Harry Chapin's 1974 hit single

Cat's in the Cradle playing in my head. I got emotional. Time went by so fast. I charge of my firstborn to always look out for his younger siblings, and if called on to do so, part the Red Sea, again. He's the real Moses of Haiti.

I EXPECT MY SECOND born, Spartacus, to live up to the greatness of his name. Spart has a big heart and he's an honors student. I couldn't be prouder of both my sons.

ZIPPORA IS MY LITTLE Joan of Arc in the flesh. She's much more like me than my boys are. On July 29, 2018, Zippora split the middle of her forehead open while rough-housing with Daina. Blood gushed from a gash that wasn't quite deep enough to require stitches, so surgical glue was used to close it up. After returning home from the hospital that same day she was right back at it. She's different. I pray that God guides her steps and that He also shows mercy on the poor bastard that she ends up with.

I commit these three souls that I am responsible for bringing into this life to Jesus!

TO MY STEP-DAUGHTER Daina: When I met your mother you were only sixteen months old. I've watched you grow and mature into a beautiful young lady. I'm very proud of you and I'm excited to see what the future has in store for you. Nothing makes me happier than when you come home from school and the first thing you say is "Hi Daddy, how was your day?" You've taught me so much. I'm very thankful that you have blessed my life.

ONE DAY, WHILE RUNNING on the treadmill at the YMCA in Barberton where a photo of me competing at Alcatraz is currently hanging, I had a meeting of destiny with Erik Swanson. Erik was speed walking next to me while reading a book. I said to him, "Are you a pastor by chance?" "Yes I am," he responded.

As our conversation progressed I expressed to him that if my father was in hell, that's where I'd want to go when I die. I couldn't bare the thought of him suffering for all of eternity alone. I would choose to suffer alongside of him.

Pastor Erik said, "Your primary goal should be to want to know and be close with your Heavenly Father first and foremost." His words stopped me in my tracks. I walked away with a new perspective. I don't think it was any coincidence that I had this run in with Pastor Erik. He happens to shepherd the First Evangelical Lutheran Church in Barberton, Ohio. The very same Lutheran church that my father grew up attending.

C.S. Lewis once said that Pride was the Greatest sin. Pride leads to every other vice. "It is the complete anti-God state of mind."

This Pride I inherited from my earthly father has been a lifelong sickness that I have suffered from. It's the core reason I have never reached my full potential. Pride comes before the Fall. Reach and Fall!

THANK YOU, MOM AND DAD for having me. You were far better parents to me than I have been to my own kids. The spiritual foundation that you laid in my life at an early age was huge. I have been guilty in not returning that same favor to your grandchildren. I'm doing my damnedest to make up for lost time. My appreciation, respect, and love for you both is eternal. The sting and fear of death isn't as bad knowing when I make that transition, I'll see my pops again.

LEGENDS ARE FOREVER, JEFFREY LEE PETRIE!

488

Darline and me
Barberton, Ohio, December 2019
Photo by Daniel Sabljak

THANK YOU TO MY wife Wiseline "Darline" Petrie. Thank you for being the most important human being to ever enter into my life. Thank you for tolerating me all these years. I don't deserve you. You truly are a Wild Thing! I never saw you feeling sorry for yourself, not once.

It was D.H. Lawrence who said "a small bird will drop frozen dead from a bough without ever having felt sorry for itself." He must have been speaking of you. You were imprisoned on account of me. You suffered long and lonely nights because of my selfishness. You endured heart-wrenching physical and verbal abuse at my hands that have scarred you deeply. You have never healed from the physical trauma I caused you in June of 2011, and for that I am responsible. I pushed you away at every turn but you never quit believing and praying for me. God heard and responded to your faithful prayers throughout the years. It was your constant praying that saved me from the pits of hell. It's my prayer that Jesus continues to heal and restore our relationship. Forgive me Wiseline, I beg of you to forgive me. No matter what the future holds, I will always love you. For you I am forever grateful. You're all heart!

I Love You Madam Zeke!

REACH AND FALL

Petrie family portrait, December 2007. Moses, Spartacus, Aslyne, and me. Photo by Kiddie Kandids

Dre and me, Columbus Marathon, October 2014. Photo by MarathonFoto

Early grade school picture showing the full lips and wide nose I was teased about. Photo by Barberton City Schools

490

May 18, 2012. I was driving the lead vehicle out of the military base in Lamentin 54. Photo by Ben Depp

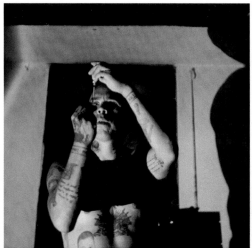

Left: Giving insulin in the dark. Mais Gate, January 2011. Photo by Les Stone

Below: Petrie Family Portrait with Lu, 1983. Photo by Olan Mills

Below left: Tammy, Lu, and me, Valentines Day 1982, Memorial School. Photo by Bonnie Petrie

Right: Andre, me, Rachel, and Ethan speak at St. Vincent-St. Mary's High School, Akron, Ohio, October, 2014. Photo by PJ Mozingo

491

Left: Aslyne and me, Delmas 31.
September 1, 2000, 11 days before the
birth of Moses.

Above right: Moments after
my arrest on May 18, 2012. Port-au-Prince,
Haiti. Photo by Haitian Media

Above: Me and Andre,
Akron Marathon Finish
Line, 2013. Photo by
MarathonFoto

Left: Right before flying
into Haiti after the
earthquake. Santo Domin-
go, Dominican Republic,
January 2010.
Photo by Matt Levitch

Right: Run4Dre Team 2017. Front row, from left: Dean Jones, Andre Travis, Chris Pinkerton Kovacevic. Back row, from left: Brian Bidlingmyer, Al Bittinger, Duane Milford, and me. Not pictured: Lisa Sheppard Chaplin. Photo by Rich Muller

Above: Petrie Family Portrait, November 2016. Moses, Spartacus, Daina, Darline, and me, awaiting the birth of Zippora. Photo by Jon Petrie

Right: Sperlif, Sabine, me, and Darline, Bwa 9, Cite Soleil, December 2011. Photo by Paolo Woods

493

Clockwise from top: JhaJha, Nasson, and me. Projects, Cite Soleil, December 2011. Photo by Lisa Kristine

Petrie Family Photo, Barberton Towpath, September 2019. Back row, from left: Spartacus, Moses, and Darline. Front row, from left: Zippora, me, and Daina. Photo by Jon Petrie

National Haitian Penitentiary, June 2012. Back row, from left: Roody, Wilio, and me. Front row, from left: Philippe and Pequeno. Photo by Dr. John May

AFTERWORD

*I'm on the brink. I'm all alone and it's quiet. I put my headphones
on, turn the volume up to its peak, and listen to Jeremy Camp's
song I Still Believe (2020 Version).*

It stirs my soul. I was Lazarus, and I was dead.

But then Jesus said, "Lazarus, Come Forth!"
And now I'm alive again.
This broken road has prepared Your Will for me Father.
God is my help!

Grand Cemetery, Port-au-Prince,
Haiti Day of the Dead
November 2010.
Photo by Dario Mitidieri

495